Text, Image, and Christians in the Graeco-Roman World

Princeton Theological Monograph Series

K. C. Hanson, Charles M. Collier, D. Christopher Spinks,
and Robin Parry, Series Editors

Recent volumes in the series:

Sammy Alfaro
Divino Compañero: Toward a Hispanic Pentecostal Christology

David L. Balch and Jason T. Lamoreaux, editors
Finding A Woman's Place: Essays in Honor of Carolyn Osiek

Paul W. Chilcote
*Making Disciples in a World Parish:
Global Perspectives on Mission & Evangelism*

Eric G. Flett
*Persons, Powers, and Pluralities:
Toward a Trinitarian Theology of Culture*

Vladimir Kharlamov
Theosis: Deification in Christian Theology, Volume Two

Mitzi J. Smith
*The Literary Construction of the Other in the Acts of the Apostles:
Charismatics, the Jews, and Women*

Jon Paul Sydnor
*Ramanuja and Schleiermacher:
Toward a Constructive Comparative Theology*

Philip D. Wingeier-Rayo
*Where Are the Poor?: A Comparison of the Ecclesial Base Communities
and Pentecostalism—A Case Study in Cuernavaca, Mexico*

Text, Image, and Christians in the Graeco-Roman World

A Festschrift in Honor of David Lee Balch

Edited by
ALIOU CISSÉ NIANG
and CAROLYN OSIEK

☙PICKWICK *Publications* · Eugene, Oregon

TEXT, IMAGE, AND CHRISTIANS IN THE GRAECO-ROMAN WORLD
A Festschrift in Honor of David Lee Balch

Princeton Theological Monograph Series 176

Copyright © 2012 Wipf and Stock Publishers. All rights reserved. Except for brief quotations in critical publications or reviews, no part of this book may be reproduced in any manner without prior written permission from the publisher. Write: Permissions, Wipf and Stock Publishers, 199 W. 8th Ave., Suite 3, Eugene, OR 97401.

Pickwick Publications
An Imprint of Wipf and Stock Publishers
199 W. 8th Ave., Suite 3
Eugene, OR 97401

www.wipfandstock.com

ISBN 13: 978-1-61097-524-7

Cataloging-in-Publication data:

Text, image, and Christians in the Graeco-Roman world : a festschrift in honor of David Lee Balch / edited by Aliou Cissé Niang and Carolyn Osiek.

xxxviii + 400 pp. ; 23 cm. — Includes bibliographical references, illustrations, and indexes.

Princeton Theological Monograph Series 176

ISBN 13: 978-1-61097-524-7

1. Balch, David L. 2. Bible—N.T.—Criticism, interpretation, etc. 3. Church history—Primitive and early church, 300–600. I. Niang, Aliou Cissé. II. Osiek, Carolyn. III. Title. IV. Series.

BS2545 S55 T30 2012

Manufactured in the U.S.A.

Scripture marked (NRSV) is taken from New Revised Standard Version Bible, copyright © 1989 National Council of the Churches of Christ in the United States of America. Used by permission. All rights reserved.

Scripture quotations marked (NIV) are taken from the Holy Bible, New International Version®, NIV®. Copyright © 1973, 1978, 1984, 2011 by Biblica, Inc.™ Used by permission of Zondervan. All rights reserved worldwide. www.zondervan.com

Scripture quotations marked (NLT) are taken from the *Holy Bible, New Living Translation*, copyright © 1996, 2004, 2007 by Tyndale House Foundation. Used by permission of Tyndale House Publishers, Inc., Carol Stream, Illinois 60188. All rights reserved.

Scripture quotations marked (REB) are taken from the Revised English Bible, copyright © Cambridge University Press and Oxford University Press 1989. All rights reserved.

Scripture quoted by permission. Quotations designated (NET) are from the NET Bible® copyright ©1996–2006 by Biblical Studies Press, L.L.C. http://bible.org All rights reserved.

Contents

Professor David Lee Balch: A Biographical Sketch / xi

Contributors / xiii

Professor David Lee Balch: A Bibliography / xv

Abbreviations / xxvi

Introduction / xxxv

PART ONE: Text and House Churches

1. The House Church as Social Environment
   —*Dennis E. Smith* / 3

2. Placing the Corinthian Common Meal
   —*Edward Adams* / 22

3. Reading 1 Corinthians 7 through the Eyes of Families—
   Margaret Y. MacDonald / 38

4. Interfacing House and Church: Converting Household Codes to Church Order—*Turid Karlsen Seim* / 53

5. Overseers as Household Managers in the Pastoral Epistles
   —*Abraham J. Malherbe* / 72

6. "Houses Made with Hands": The Triumph of the Private in New Testament Scholarship
   —*Davina C. Lopez and Todd Penner* / 89

7. The Greek Novel and Literary Ethnography: The Household in the World of the New Testament
   —*Ronald F. Hock* / 106

8. Egnatius, the Breathalyzer Kiss, and an Early Instance of Domestic Homicide at Rome—*John T. Fitzgerald* / 119

9. From Archaeology to Commentary Writing via House Churches—*Peter Oakes* / 132

viii   Contents

PART TWO: Creating Images—Verbal and Visual

Section 1: Constructions of the "Other"

10   Matthew's Others: Scholarly Identity-Construction and Absentee Gentile Great Men (Matt 20:24–27) —*Warren Carter* / 145

11   Seeing Jesus Christ Crucified in Galatians 3:1 under Watchful Imperial Eyes—*Aliou Cissé Niang* / 160

12   Rhetoric and the Art of Persuasion in the Wisdom of Solomon—*Leo G. Perdue* / 183

13   Standing Together: The Murder of Lesbians and the Martyrdom of Saints Perpetua and Felicity —*Stephen V. Sprinkle* / 199

14   Image and Religion: A Christian in the Temple of Isis at Pompeii—*Frederick Brenk* / 218

15   The Shadow of an Ass: On Reading the Alexamenos Graffito—*Oliver Larry Yarbrough* / 239

Section 2: Constructing the Visual World

16   Constructing the Spaces of Epiphany in Ancient Greek and Roman Visual Culture—*John R. Clarke* / 257

17   Melancholy, Colonialism, and Complicity: Complicating Counterimperial Readings of Aphrodisias' Sebasteion —*Hal Taussig* / 280

18   Nudity in Early Christian Art—*Robin M. Jensen* / 296

19   Bible Translation and Ancient Visual Culture: Divine Nakedness and the "Circumcision of Christ" in Colossians 2:11—*Yancy W. Smith* / 320

20   Jonah in Early Christian Art: Death, Resurrection, and Immortality—*Everett Ferguson* / 342

21   "Created in the Image of God": Greco-Roman Jewish Art-New Perspectives from Archaeology —*Richard Freund* / 354

Index of Ancient Documents / 369
Index of Ancient Sources / 379
Index of Modern Authors / 391

Professor David Lee Balch
A Biographical Sketch

PROFESSOR DR. DAVID LEE BALCH TRACES HIS CHRISTIAN ROOTS back to the Church of Christ. He says, "I was not born into a Lutheran family, but became Lutheran theologically when studying with Ernst Käsemann in Tübingen, Germany. I heard Käsemann's critique of law as a correction of my own Christian upbringing. As God justified the impious Abraham, so God counts our faith as righteousness, whatever our race, gender, class, or orientation." Balch's new perspective and orientation shaped his understanding of what it means to be a follower of Jesus Christ who died and rose with Jesus Christ to a new life to share with all people.

Professor Balch was born in West Texas in 1942 and attended Pampa High School in Pampa, Texas. His educational journey is astounding and extends from Abilene Christian University in Texas, where he received a Bachelor of Arts in Bible with a minor in Greek in 1964, and a Masters of Arts in Bible with a minor in New Testament in 1966. He moved to New York City and received a Bachelor of Divinity at Union Theological Seminary in 1969. With Fulbright grants, Balch left the United States for Tübingen, Germany (1968–70 and 1987–88) and with a Rockefeller stipend to the Ecumenical Institute (Tantur/Bethlehem/Jerusalem, 1972–73). He returned to the States and earned his PhD at Yale University in New Haven, Connecticut in 1976. After completing his PhD, Balch became Assistant Professor at Franklin & Marshall College in Lancaster, Pennsylvania (1974–1980), Associate Professor at Linfield College in McMinnville, Oregon (1980–1983), and Adjunct Professor at Lutheran Theological Seminary in Gettysburg, Pennsylvania (1979–1980). He joined the faculty of Brite Divinity School/Texas Christian University in Fort Worth, Texas, teaching there from 1983 to 2006 and since 2006, has been teaching and advising both ministry candidates and doctoral students at Pacific Lutheran Theological Seminary in California. He has been an active participant in the Society of Biblical Literature since 1975, and is also a member of the Catholic Biblical Association and the Society for New Testament Studies. Other awards he has received for study and travel include those from the National Endowment for the Humanities, the Mellon Foundation, the Association of Theological Schools, and the Lily Endowment.

Professor Balch is a passionate minister and teacher willing to share his ideas with all people. He served as Associate Pastor in Irving, Texas (1986–1987) and Interim Pastor in Abilene, Texas in 1988. He was ordained in the ELCA in 1987. He successfully organized major conferences at Perkins School of Theology (Southern Methodist University) on Matthew, which he published as *Social History of the Matthean Community* (1991); and at Brite Divinity School/TCU on *Homosexuality and the Bible* (1996); and with Carolyn Osiek on *Early Christian Families in Context* (2000). Papers of the latter conferences were also published, as *Homosexuality, Science, and the 'Plain Sense' of Scripture*; and *Early Christian Families in Context: An Interdisciplinary Dialogue* (edited together with Carolyn Osiek). Please see the comprehensive bibliography below for more details on these volumes.

Professor Balch formulated an impassioned response to the ELCA's proposed statement on "The Church and Human Sexuality: A Lutheran Perspective," published in *Currents in Theology and Mission* in 1998. More than just an unfailing minister and teacher of teachers, Professor Balch is a well-read and prolific author who made and is making profound contributions to New Testament studies, with publications on topics ranging from how early Christians lived, ate, and were affected by Graeco-Roman literature and domestic art to contemporary church issues. This is nothing short of a precious *gem* through which Professor Balch invites serious New Testament scholars to see, hear anew, and embody or reject what our ancestors in the faith saw, heard, embodied, or rejected in order to share new life with God. With our deepest gratitude, this book is our small way of honoring you for your infectious scholarship that keeps us asking more questions as we, too, seek to exercise God's new life with others.

Contributors

EDWARD ADAMS is Senior Lecturer in New Testament Studies at King's College, London.

FREDERICK E. BRENK is emeritus professor of the Pontifical Biblical Institute in Rome, where he taught Greek and Roman background of the Old and New Testament.

WARREN CARTER is Professor of New Testament at Brite Divinity School at Texas Christian University in Fort Worth, Texas.

JOHN R. CLARKE is Howard Regents Professor at the University of Texas at Austin, where he conducts research and teaches courses in ancient Roman art and culture.

EVERETT FERGUSON is Distinguished Scholar in Residence at Abilene Christian University in Abilene, Texas.

JOHN T. FITZGERALD is Professor and Chair of the Department of Religious Studies at the University of Miami, Florida; and Professor Extraordinary at North-West University in South Africa.

RICHARD A. FREUND is the Maurice Greenberg Professor of History and Director of the Maurice Greenberg Center for Judaic Studies at the University of Hartford.

RONALD F. HOCK is Professor of Religion at the University of Southern California.

ROBIN M. JENSEN is Luce Chancellor's Professor of the History of Christian Art and Worship at Vanderbilt University.

DAVINA C. LOPEZ is Assistant Professor and Chair of Religious Studies at Eckerd College in St. Petersburg, Florida, where she teaches courses in biblical, ancient, and gender studies.

MARGARET Y. MACDONALD is Professor of Religious Studies at St. Francis Xavier University in Nova Scotia.

ABRAHAM J. MALHERBE is Buckingham Professor Emeritus of New Testament Criticism and Interpretation at Yale University.

ALIOU CISSÉ NIANG is Assistant Professor of New Testament at Union Theological Seminary in New York.

PETER OAKES is Greenwood Senior Lecturer in the New Testament at the University of Manchester.

TODD PENNER is the Gould H. and Marie Cloud Associate Professor and Chair of Religious Studies at Austin College in Sherman, Texas.

LEO G. PERDUE is Professor of Hebrew Bible at Brite Divinity School at Texas Christian University in Fort Worth, Texas.

TURID KARLSEN SEIM is Director of the University of Oslo's Norwegian Institute in Rome.

DENNIS E. SMITH is LaDonna Kraemer Meinders Professor of New Testament at Phillips Theological Seminary in Tulsa, Oklahoma.

YANCY W. SMITH is a Bible translation consultant for World Bible Translation Center in Fort Worth, Texas.

STEPHEN V. SPRINKLE is Associate Professor of Practical Theology and Director of Field Education and Supervised Ministry at Brite Divinity School in Fort Worth, Texas.

HAL TAUSSIG is Visiting Professor of New Testament at Union Theological Seminary in New York, where he has taught master's-level and PhD studies in New Testament for the past twelve years.

OLIVER LARRY YARBROUGH is Tillinghast Professor of Religion at Middlebury College in Middlebury, Vermont.

Professor David Lee Balch
A Bibliography

1966
"A Comparison of the Trinitarian Theologies of Tertullian, Hippolytus and Novatian." Masters Thesis, Abilene: Abilene Christian College, 1966.

1971
Review: *The Archaeology of the New Testament*, by Edward M. Blaiklock. *ResQ* 14:1 (1971) 47–48.

1972
"Backgrounds of 1 Cor 7: Sayings of the Lord in Q: Moses as an Ascetic *theios anēr* in 2 Cor 3." *NTS* 18 (1972) 351–64.

1975
"Josephus, Against Apion II, 14—296." *SBLSP* (1975) 187–92.

1977
"Household Ethical Codes in Peripatetic, Neopythagorean and Early Christian Moralists." *SBLSP* 11 (1977) 397–404.

1980
Review: *The Cynic Epistles: A Study Edition*, by Abraham J. Malherbe. *Reflection* (Yale Divinity School) 77/3 (1980) 28.

1981
Let Wives Be Submissive: The Domestic Code in I Peter. SBLMS 26. Atlanta: Scholars, 1981.

1982

"Two Apologetic Encomia: Dionysius on Rome and Josephus on the Jews." *JSJ* 13 (1982) 102–22.

1983

"1 Cor 7:32-35 and Stoic Debates about Marriage, Anxiety and Distraction." *JBL* 102 (1983) 429–39.

1984

"Early Christian Criticism of Patriarchal Authority: I Peter 2:11-3:12." *USQR* 39 (1984) 161–73. An inaugural address at Brite Divinity School.

1985

"Acts as Hellenistic Historiography." *SBLSP* 24 (1985) 429–32.

Review: *Antioch and Rome, New Testament Cradles of Catholic Christianity*, by Raymond E. Brown and John P. Meier. *JBL* 104 (1985) 725–28.

Review: *The First Urban Christians: The Social World of the Apostle Paul*, by Wayne A. Meeks. *Zygon* 20 (1985) 452–56.

1986

"Hellenization/Acculturation in 1 Peter." In *Perspectives on First Peter*, edited by Charles H. Talbert, 79–101. NABPR Special Series 9. Macon: Mercer University Press, 1986.

With John E. Stambaugh. *The New Testament in Its Social Environment*, edited by Wayne A. Meeks. LEC 2. Philadelphia: Westminster, 1986. With British, Dutch, German, Spanish, and Portuguese editions.

Translation of Arius Didymus, "On Politics." In *Moral Exhortation: A Greco-Roman Source Book*, edited by Abraham J. Malherbe, 145–47. Philadelphia: Westminster, 1986.

1987

"Comparing Literary Patterns in Luke and Lucian." *PSTJ* 40/2 (1987) 39–42.

Review: *Jesus and Community*, by Gerhard Lohfink. *JBL* 106 (1987) 715–17.

Review: "Comparing Literary Patterns in Luke and Lucian," a review of *The Death of Jesus in Luke-Acts*, by Joseph B. Tyson. *PSTJ* 40 (1987) 39–42.

1988

"Household Codes." In *Greco-Roman Literature and the New Testament: Selected Forms and Genres,* edited by David E. Aune, 25–50. SBLSBS 21. Atlanta: Scholars, 1988.

1989

"Comments on the Genre and a Political Theme of Luke-Acts: A Preliminary Comparison of Two Hellenistic Historians." *SBLSP* 28, 343–61. Atlanta: Scholars Press, 1989.

Review: *Pseudepigraphy and Ethical Argument in the Pastoral Epistles*, by Lewis Donelson. *JR* 69:2 (1989) 235–37.

1990

Editor, with Everett Ferguson and Wayne A. Meeks. *Greeks, Romans, and Christians: Essays in Honor of Abraham J. Malherbe.* Minneapolis: Fortress, 1990.

"The Areopagus Speech: An Appeal to the Stoic Historian Posidonius against Later Stoics and the Epicureans." In *Greeks, Romans, and Christians: Essays in Honor of Abraham J. Malherbe,* edited by David L. Balch, Everett Ferguson and Wayne A. Meeks, 52–79. Minneapolis: Fortress, 1990.

Translation: Hans-Josef Klauck, "Brotherly Love in Plutarch and in 4 Maccabees." In *Greeks, Romans, and Christians: Essays in Honor of*

Abraham J. Malherbe, edited by Balch, Ferguson, and Meeks, 144–56. Minneapolis: Fortress, 1990.

"The Genre of Luke-Acts: Individual Biography, Adventure Novel or Political History?" *SJT* 33 (1990) 5–19.

1991

Editor of *Social History of the Matthean Community: Cross-Disciplinary Approaches.* Minneapolis: Fortress, 1991.

"The Greek Political Topos Περί νόμων and Matthew 5:17, 19, and 16:19." In *Social History of the Matthean Community: Cross-Disciplinary Approaches,* edited by David L. Balch, 68–84. Minneapolis: Fortress, 1991.

Review: *The Economy of the Kingdom: Social Conflict and Economic Relations in Luke's Gospel,* by Halvor Moxnes. *Int* 45 (1991) 84–86.

Review: *The Pauline Churches: A Socio-Historical Study of Institutionalization in the Pauline and Deutero-Pauline Writings,* by Margaret Y. MacDonald. *RSR* 17/2 (1991) 162.

1992

"Neopythagorean Moralists and the New Testament Household Codes." In *ANRW II, Principat* 2.26.1 (1992) 380–411.

"Household Codes." *ABD* 3:318–20.

1993

"... *you teach all the Jews ... to forsake Moses, telling them not to ... observe the customs*" (Acts 21:21; cf 6:14)." *SBLSP* 32 (1993) 369–83.

"1 Peter, Introduction and Notes." In *Harper Collins Study Bible,* 2277–85. New York: HarperCollins, 1993.

"The Canon: Adaptable and Stable, Oral and Written. Critical Questions for Kelber and Riesner." *Forum* 7:3–4 (1991 [1993]) 183–205.

1994

"The Gospel versus Greek Biological and Political Theories of Living 'According to Nature' (Rom 1:26-27; 1 Cor 6:9)." In *A Collection of Responses from ELCA Academicians and Synodical Bishops to "The Church and Human Sexuality: A Lutheran Perspective,"* edited by F. Burnford and C. Miller, 23–34. Chicago: ELCA, 1994.

1995

"Rich and Poor, Proud and Humble in Luke-Acts." In *The Social World of the First Christians: Essays in Honor of Wayne A. Meeks,* edited by Michael White and O. Larry Yarbrough, 214–33. Minneapolis: Fortress, 1995.

"Paul in Acts: . . . 'You Teach All the Jews . . . to Forsake Moses, Telling Them Not to . . . Observe the Customs' (Acts 21, 21)." In *Panchaia: Festschrift für Klaus Thraede,* edited by M. Wacht, 11–23. JAC Ergänzungsband 22. Münster: Aschendorff, 1995.

Review: *Der Verlorene Sohn und das Haus: Studien zu Lukas 15:11–32 im Horizont der antiken Lehre von Haus, Erziehung und Ackerbau,* by Wolfgang Pöhlmann. *CBQ* 57:1 (1995) 188–89.

Review: *Tradition und Theologie neutestamentlicher Haustafelethik: Ein Beitrag zur Frage einer christlichen Auseinandersetzung mit gesellschaftlichen Normen,* by Marleis Gielen. *JBL* 114 (1995) 172–74.

1996

Review: *Households and Discipleship: A Study in Matthew 19–20,* by Warren Carter. *CBQ* 58 (1996) 540–42.

Review: *Discipleship and Family Ties in Mark and Matthew,* by Stephen C. Barton. *CBQ* 58:3 (1996) 532–34.

Review: *The Pythagorean Golden Verses: with Introduction and Commentary,* edited by John C. Thom. *CRBR* 9 (1996) 134–36.

1997

With Carolyn Osiek. *Families in the New Testament World: Households and House Churches*. Family, Religion, and Culture. Louisville: Westminster John Knox, 1997.

"Political Friendship in the Historian Dionysisus of Halicarnassus, Roman Antiquities." In *Greco-Roman Perspectives on Friendship*, edited by John T. Fitzgerald, 123–44. SBLRBS 34. Atlanta: Scholars, 1997.

With Leo Perdue. "Bibel." In *Der Neue Pauly: Enzylkopädie der Antike*, edited by H. Cancik and H. Schneider (Stuttgart: Metzler, 1997) 2:618–23. Translated as "Bible," in *Brill's New Pauly: Encyclopedia of the Ancient World*. Leiden: Brill, 2003.

Translation: Hubert Cancik, "The History of Culture, Religion, and Institutions in Ancient Historiography: Philological Observations Concerning Luke's History." *JBL* 116 (1997) 681–703.

1998

"Attitudes toward Foreigners in 2 Maccabees, Eupolemas, Esther, Aristeas, and Luke-Acts." In *The Early Church in Its Context: Essays in Honor of Everett Ferguson*, edited by Abraham J. Malherbe et al., 22–47. NovTSup 90. New York: Brill, 1998.

"Rom 1:24–27, Science, and Homosexuality." *CurTM* 25 (1998) 433–40.

"Apostelgeschichte." In *Religion in Geschichte und Gegenwart*, edited by Hans Dieter Betz et al., 1:642–48. 4th ed. Tübingen: Mohr/Siebeck, 1998.

Review: "Household Conversion Narratives in Acts: Pattern and Interpretation," by David L. Matson. *CBQ* 60 (1998) 165–67.

"Evangelium." In *Der Neue Pauly: Enzylkopädie der Antike*. Epo-Gro, 4:325–28. Edited by H. Cancik and H. Schneider (Stuttgart: Metzler, 1998). Translated as "Gospels," in *Brill's New Pauly: Encyclopedia of the Ancient World*, 5:947–49. Leiden: Brill, 2004.

1999

"ἀκριβῶς ... γράψαι (Luke 1:3): To Write the *Full* History of God's Receiving All Nations." In *Jesus and the Heritage of Israel: Luke's Narrative Claim upon Israel's Legacy,* edited by David P. Moessner, 229–50. Luke the Interpreter of Israel 1. Harrisburg: Trinity, 1999.

"Response to Daryl D. Schmidt: Luke-Acts is Catechesis for Christians, Not Kerygma to Jews." In *Anti-Judaism and the Gospels,* edited by William R. Farmer, 97–110. Harrisburg: Trinity, 1999.

2000

Editor of *Homosexuality, Science, and the 'Plain Sense' of Scripture.* Grand Rapids: Eerdmans, 2000. Reprinted, Eugene, OR: Wipf & Stock, 2007.

"Concluding Observations by the Editor." In *Homosexuality, Science, and the 'Plain Sense' of Scripture,* 288. Grand Rapids: Eerdmans, 2000.

Review: "Theologie der lukanischen Schriften," by Petr Pokorny. *JR* 80 (2000) 495–97.

2002

"Family Ties: How the Early Church Became a Community." *ChrCent* 119:18 (2002) 26–29.

2003

"METABOLH POLITEIWN Jesus as Founder of the Church in Luke-Acts: Form and Function." In *Contextualing Acts: Lukan Narrative and Greco-Roman Discourse,* edited by Todd Penner and Caroline Vander Stichele, 139–88. SBLSBS 20. Atlanta: SBL, 2003.

"The Suffering of Isis/Io and Paul's Portrait of Christ Crucified (Gal 3:1): Frescoes in Pompeian and Roman Houses and in the Temple of Isis in Pompeii." *JR* 83 (2003) 24–55.

"The Cultural Origin of 'Receiving all Nations' in Luke-Acts: Alexander the Great or Roman Social Policy?" In *Early Christianity and Classical*

Culture: Comparative Studies in Honor of Abraham J. Malherbe, edited by John T. Fitzgerald, Thomas H. Olbricht, and L. Michael White, 483–500. NovTSup 110. Leiden: Brill, 2003.

"Paul, Families and Households." In *Paul in the Greco-Roman World*, edited by J. Paul Sampley, 258–92. Harrisburg, PA: Trinity, 2003.

"Commentary on Luke." In *Eerdmans Commentary on the Bible*, edited by James D. G. Dunn and John W. Rogerson, 1104–1160. Grand Rapids: Eerdmans, 2003.

"Philodemus, 'On Wealth,' and 'On Household Management': Naturally Wealthy Epicureans against Poor Cynics." In *Philodemus and the New Testament World*, edited by John T. Fitzgerald, Dirk Obbink, and Glen S. Holland, 177–96. NovTSup 111. Leiden: Brill, 2003.

With Carolyn Osiek, editors. *Early Christian Families in Context: An Interdisciplinary Dialogue*. Religion, Marriage and Family. Grand Rapids: Eerdmans, 2003.

"Paul's Portrait of Christ Crucified (Gal 3:1) in Light of Paintings and Sculptures of Suffering and Death in Pompeiian and Roman Houses." In *Early Christian Families in Context: An Interdisciplinary Dialogue*, edited by David L. Balch and Carolyn Osiek, 84–108. Grand Rapids: Eerdmans, 2003.

2004

"Rich Pompeiian *Domus*, Shops for Rent, and the Huge *Insula* in Herculaneum: A Response to Prof. Michelle George." *Annali di Storia dell'esegesi* 19:1 (2002 [actually published 2004]) 443–52.

"Rich Pompeiian Houses, Shops for Rent, and the Huge Apartment Building in Herculaneum as Typical Spaces for Pauline House Churches." *JSNT* 27 (2004) 27–46.

"Gospels (literary forms)." In *Brill's New Pauly: Encyclopaedia of the Ancient World: Antiquity*, edited by Christine F. Salazar et al., 5:947–49. Leiden: Brill, 2004.

"Everett Ferguson: Church of Christ Historian, Teacher, Elder, Theologian, Apologist." *ResQ* 46:3–4 (2004) 201–24.

"Foreword" In *In Praise of Christian Origins: Stephen and the Hellenists in Lukan Apologetic Historiography*, by Todd Penner, xi–xxi. Emory Studies in Early Christianity 10. New York: T. & T. Clark, 2004.

2005

"Zeus, Vengeful Protector of the Political and Domestic Order: Frescoes in Dining Rooms N and P of the House of the Vettii in Pompeii, Mark 13:12-13, and 1 Clement 6.2." In *Picturing the New Testament: Studies in Ancient Visual Images*, edited by Annette Weisssenrieder, Frederike Wendt, and Petra von Gemünden, 67–95. WUNT 2/193. Tübingen: Mohr/Siebeck, 2005.

2006

"Paul (Saint)." In *Sex from Plato to Paglia: A Philosophical Encyclopedia*, edited by Alan Soble, 2:748–54. Westport, CT: Greenwood, 2006.

"'A Woman Clothed with the Sun' and the 'Great Red Dragon' Seeking to 'Devour Her Child' (Rev 12:1, 4) in Roman Domestic Art." In *The New Testament and Early Christian Literature: Studies in Honor of David E. Aune*, edited by John Fotopoulos, 287–314. NovTSup 122. Leiden: Brill, 2006.

2007

Editor of *Homosexuality, Science, and the 'Plain Sense' of Scripture*. Reprinted, Eugene, OR: Wipf & Stock, 2007.

"Review of Udo Schnelle and Francis Watson on Paul." *Dialog* 46:1 (2007) 14–23.

Review: *The City in the Valley: Biblical Interpretation and Urban Theology*, by Dieter Georgi. *CBQ* 69 (2007) 145–47.

2008

Roman Domestic Art and Early House Churches. WUNT 228. Tübingen: Mohr/Siebeck, 2008.

"From Endymion in Roman Domus to Jonah in Christian Catacombs: From Houses of the Living to Houses for the Dead. Iconography and Religion in Transition." In *Commemorating the Dead: Texts and Artifacts in Context; Studies of Roman, Jewish, and Christian Burials,* edited by Laurie Brink and Deborah A. Green, 273–301. Berlin: de Gruyter, 2008.

2009

"Accepting Others: God's Boundary Crossing according to Isaiah and Luke–Acts." *CurTM* 36 (2009) 414–23.

Review: *Paul and His World: Interpreting the New Testament in its Context,* by Helmut Koester. *CBQ* 71 (2009) 180–81.

2010

"Women Prophets/Maenads Visually Represented in Two Roman Colonies: Pompeii and Corinth." In *The Interface of Orality and Writing: Speaking, Seeing, Writing in the Shaping of New Genre,* edited by Annette Weissenrieder and Robert B. Coote, 236–59. WUNT 260. Tübingen: Mohr/Siebeck, 2010.

2011

Editor, with Jason T. Lamoreaux. *Finding a Woman's Place: Essays in Honor of Carolyn Osiek.* PTMS 150. Eugene, OR: Pickwick Publications, 2011.

"Values of Roman Women Including Priests Visually Represented in Pompeii and Herculaneum." In *Finding a Woman's Place: Essays in Honor of Carolyn Osiek,* edited by David L. Balch and Jason T. Lamoreaux, 3–49. PTMS 150. Eugene, OR: Pickwick Publications, 2011.

"Cult Statues of Augustus' Temple of Apollo on the Palatine in Rome, Artemis'/Diana's Birthday in Ephesus, and Revelation 12:1–5a." In *Contested Spaces: Nature, Houses, Temples*, edited by David L. Balch and Annette Weissenrieder. WUNT. Tübingen: Mohr/Siebeck, forthcoming 2011 or 2012.

Editor, with Annette Weissenrieder. *Contested Spaces: Nature, Houses, Temples*. WUNT. Tübingen: Mohr/Siebeck, forthcoming.

Review: *Among the Gentiles: Greco-Roman Religion and Christianity*, by Luke T. Johnson. *CBQ* 73 (2011) 389–91.

Abbreviations

Ancient

Ambrose, *Off.*	*De officiis ministrorum* (Ambrose)
Ambrosiaster, *Comm. in ep. ad Rom.*	*Commentarius in epistulam ad Romanos* (Ambrosiaster)
Ampelius, *Liber Mem.*	*Liber Memorialis* (Ampelius)
Apos. Const.	*Apostolic Constitutions and Canons*
Arist. *Mag. Mor.*	*Magna Moralia* (Aristotle)
Arist., *Pol.*	*Politica* (Aristotle)
Arist., *Rhet.*	*Rhetorica* (Aristotle)
Athenaeus, *Deipn.*	*Deipnosophistae* (Athenaeus)
Aulus Gellius, *Noct. att.*	*Noctes atticae*
Basil of Caesarea, *Spir.*	*De Spiritu Sancto* (Basil of Caesaria)
Chrysostom, *Catech. illum.*	*Catecheses ad illuminandos* (Chrysostom)
Chrysostom, *1 Ep. Innoc.*	*Ad Innocentium papam epistula I* (Chrysostom)
Chrysostom, *2 Ep. Innoc.*	*Ad Innocentium papam epistula II* (Chrysostom)
Chrysostom, *Hom. Tit.*	*Homiliae in epistulam ad Titum* (Chrysostom)
Chrysostom, *Stat.*	*Ad populum Antiochenum de statuis*
Cicero, *Brut.*	*Brutus or De claris oratoribus*
Cicero, *De or.*	*De Oratore* (Cicero)
Cicero, *Resp.*	*De Republica*
Cicero, *In Verr.*	*In Verrem* (Cicero)
Cicero, *Off.*	*De officiis* (Cicero)
Cicero, *Sen.*	*De senectute* (Cicero)
Cicero, *Tusc.*	*Tusculanae disputationes* (Cicero)
Clement of Alexandria, *Paed.*	*Paedagogus* (Clement of Alexandria)
Clement of Alexandria, *Protr.*	*Protrepticus* (Clement of Alexandria)

Clement of Alexandria, *Strom.*	*Stromata*
Clement of Rome, *1 Cor.*	*The First Epistle of Clement to the Corinthians* (Clement of Rome)
Cyprian, *Ep.*	*Epistulae* (Cyprian)
Cyprian, *Fort.*	*Ad Fortinatum* (Cyprian)
Cyprian, *Hab. virg.*	*De habitu virginum* (Cyprian)
Cyprian, *Laps.*	*De lapsis* (Cyprian)
Cyril of Jerusalem, *Cat.*	*Catechesis* (Cyril of Jerusalem)
Cyril of Jerusalem, *Myst.*	*Mystagogica Catechesis* (Cyril of Jerusalem)
Dio Chrys., *Or.*	*Oration* (Dio Chysostom)
Dionysius, *Ant. rom.*	*Antiquitates romanae* (Dionysius of Halicarnassus)
Ep. *Diatr.*	*Diatribai (Dissertationes)*(Epictetus)
Ep. *Paul Sen.*	*Epistles of Paul and Seneca*
Gos. *Thom.*	*Gospel of Thomas*
Greg. of Nazianzus, *Or. Bas.*	*Oratio in laudem Basilii* (Gregory of Nazianzus)
Herm., *Vis.*	*Vision*, Shepherd of Hermas
Hippolytus, *Comm. Dan.*	*Commentarium in Danielem* (Hippolytus)
Hippolytus, *Trad. ap.*	*Traditio apostolica* (Hippolytus)
Homer, *Il.*	*Ilias*
Horace, *Carm.*	*Carmina* (Horace)
Ign. *Pol.*	*To Polycarp* (Ignatius)
Ign. *Smyrn.*	*To the Smyrnaeans* (Ignatius)
Irenaeus, *Haer.*	*Adversus haereses* (Irenaeus)
Iso., *Panath.*	*Panathanasius (Or. 12)* (Isocrates)
Iso., *De Pace*	*De Pace (Or. 8)* (Isocarates)
Jerome, *Epist.*	*Epistulae* (Jerome)
Jos., *Ant.*	*Jewish Antiquities* (Josephus)
Jos. *C. Ap.*	*Contra Apionem* (Josephus)
Jos. *JW*	*Jewish War* (Josephus)
Justin, *Dial.*	*Dialogus cum Tryphone*
Juvenal, *Sat.*	*Satirae*
Livy, *Hist.*	*Histories* (Livy)
Lucian, *Salt.*	*De Saltatione* (Lucian)
Origen, *Comm. Mt.*	*Commentarium in evangelium Matthaei*
Origen, *Hom. Jer.*	*Homiliae in Jeremiam*

Origen, *Hom. Num.*	*Homiliae in Numeros*
Origen, *Or.*	*De oratione*
Ovid, *Fast.*	*Fasti* (Ovid)
Passio Perp.	*Passion of Saints Perpetua and Felicitas*
Philo, *Agr.*	*De agricultura* (Philo)
Philo, *Congr.*	*De congressu eruditionis gratia* (Philo)
Philo, *Contempl.*	*De vita contemplativa* (Philo)
Philo, *Flacc.*	*In Flaccum* (Philo)
Philo, *Ios.*	*De Iosepho* (Philo)
Philo, *Leg.*	*Legum allegoriae* (Philo)
Philo, *Mos.*	*De vita Mosis* (Philo)
Philo, *Opif.*	*De opificio mundi* (Philo)
Philo, *Post.*	*De posteritate Caini* (Philo)
Philo, *Prelim. Studies*	*On the Preliminary Studies* (Philo)
Philo, *Prob.*	*Quod omnis probus liber sit* (Philo)
Philo, *Prov.*	*De providentia* (Philo)
Philo, *Spec.*	*De specialibus legibus* (Philo)
Philo, *Virt.*	*De virtutibus* (Philo)
Philodemus, *Oec.*	*Oeconomicus* (Philodemus)
Plato, *Epin.*	*Epinomis* (Plato)
Plato, *Gorg.*	*Gorgias* (Plato)
Plato, *Leg.*	*Leges* (Plato)
Plato, *Menex.*	*Menexenus* (Plato)
Plato, *Resp.*	*Respublica* (Plato)
Pliny the Elder, *Nat.*	*Naturalis historia* (Pliny the Elder)
Plut. *Cat. Maj.*	*Cato Major* (Plutarch)
Plut., *Comp. Arist. Cat.*	*Comparatio Aristidis et Catonis* (Plutarch)
Plut., *Comp. Lyc. Num.*	*Comparatio Lycurgi et Numae* (Plutarch)
Plut., *Cons. ux.*	*Consolatio ad uxorem* (Plutarch)
Plut., *Mor.*	*Moralia* (Plutarch)
Plut., *Praec. ger. rei publ*	*Praecepta gerendae rei publicae* (Plutarch)
Plut., *Princ. iner*	*Ad principem ineruditum* (Plutarch)
Plut., *Quaest. Rom.*	*Quaestiones romanae et graecae* (Plutarch)
Plut., *Rom.*	*Romulus* (Plutarch)
Pol., *Hist.*	*The Histories* (Polybius)
Pol. *Phil*	*To the Philippians* (Polycarp)

Ps. Dionysius, *Ecc. Hier.*	*Ecclesiastical Hierarchy* (Pseudo-Dionysius)
Quintilian, *Inst.*	*Institutio oratoria* (Quintilian)
Seneca, *Ep.*	*Epistulae Morales* (Seneca)
Stobaeus, *Ecl.*	*Eclogae* (Stobaeus)
Stobaeus, *Flor.*	*Florilegium* (Stobaeus)
Strabo, *Geogr.*	*Geographica* (Strabo)
Suetonius, *Aug.*	*Divus Augustus* (Seutonius)
Tacitus, *Ann.*	*Annales* (Tacitus)
Tertullian, *An.*	*De anima* (Tertullian)
Tertullian, *Apol.*	*Apologeticus* (Tertullian)
Tertullian, *Fug.*	*De fuga in persecutione* (Tertullian)
Tertullian, *Idol.*	*De idololatria* (Tertullian)
Tertullian, *Marc.*	*Adversus Marcionem* (Tertullian)
Tertullian, *Pud.*	*De pudicitia* (Tertullian)
Tertullian, *Res.*	*De resurrectione carnis* (Tertullian)
Tertullian, *Scorp.*	*Scorpiace* (Tertullian)
Tertullian, *Spect.*	*De spectaculis* (Tertullian)
Theo. Mop., *Hom. bapt.*	*Baptismal Homilies* (Theodore of Mopsuestia)
Virgil, *Aen.*	*Aeneid* (Virgil)
Xen, *Oec.*	*Oeconomicus* (Xenophon)
Zeno of Verona, *Inv. font.*	*Invitation to the Baptismal Font* (Zeno of Verona)

Modern

AB	Anchor Bible
AJA	American Journal of Archaeology
AJEC	Ancient Judaism and Early Christianity
AnBib	Analecta Biblica
ANF	*The Ante-Nicene Fathers: translations of the writings of the fathers down to A.D. 325*. Edited by Alexander Roberts and James Donaldson. 10 vols. Grand Rapids: Eerdmans, 1986–1989
ANRW	*Aufstieg und Niedergang der römischen Welt: Geschichte und Kultur Roms im Spiegel der neueren Forschung*. Edited by H. Temporini and W. Haase. Berlin, 1972–
ANT	*The Apocryphal New Testament: A Collection of Apocryphal Christian Literature in an English Translation based on M. R. James*. New York: Oxford University Press, 1993
APACR	American Philological Association Classical Resources
ASCS	The American School of Classical Studies at Athens
ASOR	American Schools of Oriental Research
ASR	*African Studies Review*
AUSP	*Annales Universitatis Saraviensis: Philosophie*
BCAR	Bull. Commiss. Arch. Com. Roma
BCMA	*Bulletin of the Cleveland Museum of Art*
BDAG	Walter Bauer et al., editors. *Greek-English Lexicon of the New Testament and of Other Early Christian Literature*. 3rd ed. Revised and edited by Fredrick William Danker. Chicago: University of Chicago Press, 2000
Bib Int	*Biblical Interpretation*
BRev	*Bible Review*
BZNW	Beihefte zur Zeitschrift für die neutestamentliche Wissenschaft
CBQ	*Catholic Biblical Quarterly*
CEV	Contemporary English Version (Bible)
ChrCent	*Christian Century*
CP	*Classical Philology*
CQ	*Classical Quarterly*
CRBR	*Critical Review of Books in Religion*
CUP	Cambridge University Press
CurTM	*Currents in Theology and Mission*

CW	*Classical World*
DACL	*Dictionnaire d'archéologie chrétienne et de liturgie.* Edited by F. Cabrol. 15 vols. Paris, 1907–1953
EBib	*Études bibliques*
EEC	*Encyclopedia of Early Christianity.* Edited by Everett Ferguson. 2nd ed. New York: Garland, 1990
ELCA	Evangelical Lutheran Church in America
EKKNT	Evangelisch-katholischer Kommentar zum Neuen Testament
EPRO	Etudes préliminaires aux religions orientales dans l'Empire romain
FGH	*Die Fragmente der griechischen Historiker.* Edited by F. Jacoby. Ledien: 1954–1964
FRLANT	Forschungen zur Religion und Literatur des Alten und Neuen Testaments
HDR	Harvard Dissertations in Religion
HNT	Handbuch zum Neuen Testament
HR	*History of Religions*
HSCP	*Harvard Studies in Classical Philology*
HTKNT	Herders theologischer Kommentar zum Neuen Testament
HTR	*Harvard Theological Review*
HTS	Harvard Theological Studies
ICC	International Critical Commentary
ICS	*Illinois Classical Studies*
IEJ	*Israel Exploration Journal*
Int	*Interpretation*
JAC	Jahrbuch für Antike und Christentum
JBL	*Journal of Biblical Literature*
JCA	*Journal of Conflict Archaeology*
JEA	*Journal of Egyptian Archaeology*
JECS	*Journal of Early Christian Studies*
JFSR	*Journal of Feminist Studies in Religion*
JR	*Journal of Religion*
JRA	*Journal of Roman Archaeology*
JRH	*Journal of Religious History*
JRS	*Journal of Roman Studies*
JSJ	*Journal for the Study of Judaism in the Persian, Hellenistic, and Roman Periods*

JSNT	*Journal for the Study of the New Testament*
JSNTSup	Journal for the Study of the New Testament: Supplement Series
JSOT	Journal for the Study of the Old Testament
LCL	Loeb Classical Library
LEC	Library of Early Christianity
LSJ	Henry G. Liddell, and Robert Scott. *A Greek-English Lexicon: With a Revised Supplement.* London: Clarendon, 1996
MIT	Massachusetts Institute of Technology
MTS	Marburger theologische Studien
NCB	New Century Bible
NET	New English Translation (Bible)
NIB	*The New Interpreter's Bible.* Edited by Leander E. Keck. 12 vols. Nashville: Abingdon, 1994–2004
NICNT	New International Commentary on the New Testament
NIGTC	New International Greek Testament Commentary
NIV	New International Version (Bible)
NLT	New Living Translation (Bible)
NovT	*Novum Testamentum*
NovTSup	Novum Testamentum Supplements
NRSV	New Revised Standard Version (Bible)
NTD	Das Neue Testament Deutsch
NTG	New Testament Guides
NTL	New Testament Library
ÖBS	Österreichische biblische Studien
OBT	Overtures to Biblical Theology
OCD	*Oxford Classical Dictionary.* Edited by S. Hornblower and A. Spawforth. 3rd ed. New York: Oxford University Press, 1996
OHHS	Oxford Handbook of Hellenic Studies
OLD	*Oxford Latin Dictionary.* Edited by P. G. W. Glare. Oxford: Clarendon, 1982
PAwB	Potsdamer Altertumswissenschaftliche Beiträge
PG	Patrologia graeca. Edited by J.-P. Migne. 162 vols. Paris: Migne, 1857–1886
PRS	*Perspectives in Religious Studies*
PSTJ	*Perkins School of Theology Journal*

Abbreviations xxxiii

PTMS	Princeton Theological Monograph Series
PW	Pauly, A. F. *Paulys Realencyclopädie der classischen Altertumswissenschaft*. New ed. G. Wissowa. 49 vols. Munich: Druckenmüller, 1980
RB	*Revue biblique*
REB	Revised English Bible
ResQ	*Restoration Quarterly*
Rev. Arch.	*Revue Archéologique*
RGRW	Religions in the Graeco-Roman World
RICIS	*Recueil des inscriptions concernant les cultes isiaques*
RivAC	*Rivista di archeologia cristiana*
RM	*Römische Mitteilungen*
RMSup	Römische Mitteilungen Supplement
RNT	Regensburger Neues Testament
RPP	*Revue de Psychologie des peuples*
RSR	*Recherches de science religieuse*
SAC	Studi di antichità cristiana
SBLDS	Society of Biblical Literature Dissertation Series
SBLGPBS	Society of Biblical Literature Global Perspective on Biblical Scholarship
SBLMS	Society of Biblical Literature Monograph Series
SBLRBS	Society of Biblical Literature Resources for Biblical Study
SBLSBS	Society of Biblical Literature Sources for Biblical Study
SBLSP	*Society of Biblial Literature Seminar Papers*
SBLSymS	Society of Biblical Literature Symposium Series
SBLWGRW	Society of Biblical Literature Writings from the Greco-Roman World
SC	Sources Chrétiennes
SIG	*Syllogue inscriptionum graecarum*. Edited by W. Dittenburger. 4 vols. 3rd ed. Leipzig: 1915–1924
SJLA	Studies in Judaism in Late Antiquity
SJT	Scottish Journal of Theology
SNTSMS	Society of New Testament Studies Monograph Series
SNTW	Studies of the New Testament and its World
SP	Sacra Pagina
SPPC	*Social and Personal Psychology Compass*
ST	A Social Text

STHNT	Studia ad corpus hellenisticum Novi Testamenti
SVF	*Stoicorum veterum fragmenta*. Hans Friedrich August von Arnim. 4 vols. Leipzig, 1903–1924
TDNT	*Theological Dictionary of the New Testament*. 10 vols. Edited by Gerhard Kittel and Gerhard Friedrich. Translated by Geoffrey W. Bromiley. Grand Rapids: Eerdamns, 1964–1976
Teubner	Bibliotheca scriptorum graecorum et romanorum teubneriana
TynBul	*Tyndale Bulletin*
TZ	*Theologische Zeitschrift*
USQR	*Union Seminary Quarterly Review*
VC	*Vigiliae christianae*
VChr	*Vetera Christianorum*
WA	*World Archeology*
WBC	Word Biblical Commentary
WUNT	Wissenschaftliche Untersuchungen zum Neuen Testament

Introduction

Literary documents, visual and constructed worlds are modes of inquiry and communication that ancient and modern authors, sculptors and painters employ to convey their messages—a summary thesis that *Text, Image and Christians in a Graeco-Roman World: A Festschrift in Honor of David Lee Balch* makes with twenty-one stimulating chapters. Contributors to this volume reflect on conversations initiated by the works of Professor David Lee Balch[1] and with Professor Carolyn Osiek,[2] with a view to honoring his groundbreaking contributions in the field of New Testament studies. Dr. David Lee Balch is a widely published professor from whom we learned that literary texts no longer suffice for a responsible interpretation of New Testament texts. That is evident in his bibliography. His publications reflect intriguing conversations on how academic ideas can be translated into concrete actions in the life of the church.

This volume divides into two major parts: "Text and House Churches," followed by "Creating Images, Verbal and Visual." The latter includes two subsections: "Constructing the 'Other,'" and "Constructing the Visual World." Chapters in Part One discuss features of early Christian domesticity, commensality, and spiritual formation. Dennis Smith leads off Part One by carrying the reader through ten hypotheses with which he argues that the house church can be conceived as the basic context for early Christian formation. In conversation with David L. Balch, Jerome Murphy-O'Connor, and David Horrell, Edward Adams shows how early Christians may have dined in rented, rather than domestic, spaces owned by Christian elites. With recent studies and archeological finds, Adams posits that scholars should consider "*non-domestic* possibilities" for early Christian meetings.

Margaret Y. MacDonald thinks Paul's language in 1 Corinthians 7 hints that women may have been the "main proponent" of ascetic life

---

1. Balch, *Roman Domestic Art*.
2. Osiek and Balch, *Families*; Balch and Osiek, *Early Christian Families*.

and "instigators" of conjugal "separations." Turid Karlsen Seim sees the interplay between "domestic" and "ecclesial" agenda in some of the New Testament household codes being destabilized by a movement "towards ecclesial management and sacralization of marriage." Abraham J. Malherbe explores 1 Tim 3:2–7 and Titus 1:6–9, positing that these texts follow similar self-definitions of "professional leaders, particularly of household managers" in the Graeco-Roman world. First Timothy, he avers, focuses on the leader's deportment in the church and good governance as vested in good Graeco-Roman household managers, while Titus's focus is on appointing good overseers who could teach.

Davina C. Lopez and Todd Penner insightfully highlight an intriguing tension within the text of the Acts of the Apostles between the "private" and the "public" with regard to early Christian domesticity and the worship of and presence of God. They invite scholars to revisit the house or household category prevalent in most studies of Christian origins because the house fuses the "private and the "public" horizons. Ronald F. Hock unearths from four ancient novels crucial insights on Graeco-Roman aristocratic ménage to shed light on New Testament domesticity. A close examination of the roles of the householder and the slave administrator and manager, in their respective settings, led to his conclusion that evidence drawn from the novels should supplement the work of Osiek and Balch on *Families*.

John T. Fitzgerald shows how violence against women in the Petrine community may have been inspired by earlier practices in Roman myth and religion which barred women from drinking wine. Peter Oakes argues that Balch's commentary on Luke could have included archaeological finds that would provide a powerful illustration for his study on "temple access, social reversal" and "cosmic conflict," namely the archaeological evidence from Palestine and the Graeco-Roman world.

Warren Carter's chapter spearheads Part Two by exploring "othering" in the gospel of Matthew beyond the Judean context to the Graeco-Roman sociopolitical and imperial contexts. Imperial powers, he argues, have been neglected in the interpretation of the Matthean gospel. Building on Balch's thesis that Graeco-Roman domestic art might have helped Paul share his message of the cross, Aliou C. Niang wonders whether Diola domestic art in Senegal, West Africa, would have had the same effect on how colonized Diola people saw and heard Paul's message of Jesus Christ crucified in Gal 3:1. Leo G. Perdue guides readers through the Wisdom of Solomon, describing its author as being a Hellenized Judean rhetorician who synthesizes Greek and Judean cultures to highlight the superiority of his Judean tradition. This he does in order to persuade his Judean audience to remain faithful to their ancestral tradition.

Stephen V. Sprinkle's essay explores ancient and modern cultural constructions of human sexuality by juxtaposing the martyrdom stories of Perpetua and Felicitas and the modern accounts of Julie and Lollie. While they did not die for the same reason, it is important to note that the former two died for their faith while the latter for love. Frederick E. Brenk compares the visual representations on the walls of the temple of Isis with those on early Christian churches by imagining a Christian touring the temple of Isis and realizing how Christianity adapted some visual elements of Egyptian and Roman religions. Oliver Larry Yarbrough reads the Alexamenos graffito in its Roman context, insisting that though the work elicited various responses from many authors in antiquity, its artist was simply telling of Alexamenos' devotion to his God, an ass-headed crucified God.

In "Constructing the Space of Epiphany in Ancient Greek and Roman Visual Culture," John R. Clarke offers a glimpse into how worshipers may have experienced images of divine revelation at home and during pilgrimages to sacred centers. For Clarke "architecture and rituals" enshrine a "belief system" in which the ancient worshipper's act of "looking—whether at the sacred landscape, ritual, or the image of the deity—was also an experience of being looked at." That being the case, effective sacred looking "had to be reciprocal, a kind of *darśan*." Hal Taussig's "Melancholy, Colonialism, and Complicity" engages modern readings of the Aphrodisias Sebasteion against the backdrop of imperial and Pauline constructions of the "other," namely the vanquished, with an alternative reading. The reliefs of Achillies and Penthesilea, he notes, provide the proper context for interpreting the Sebasteion in Aphrodisias which he thinks is outside Roman imperial control. In "Nudity in Early Christian Art," Robin M. Jensen shows how nudity in both ancient Roman and Christian artwork is limited to key figures. Nude figures in some Christian art emphasize redemption to new life in contrast to their Roman counterpart, which focuses on heroism and prowess.

Yancy W. Smith's "Bible Translation and Ancient Visual Culture," shows how Graeco-Roman art can help Bible translators and readers see Jesus crucified as nude on the cross—a point he insists the author of Colossians conveys. Everett Ferguson explores the "iconography of Jonah" to show how the Jonah of early Christian texts somewhat differs from the one depicted in art. In Jonah's story, he insists, early Christians saw meaning in their journey from death and resurrection to eternal bliss. Richard Freund's chapter, "Created in the Image of God," examines Jewish and rabbinic texts to see if there were some appropriate visual representations of God. Ancient Israelite and Jewish artists, he concludes, "developed a two tiered system of ancient art" from the Hebrew Bible to the Hellenistic age, "one which officially banned the worship of artistic renderings of the God of Israel but which allowed for differing images to be made and used for a variety of popular use."

Reading texts, hearing words, and exploring the visual and constructed worlds is what David Lee Balch challenges all his students and colleagues to do. He is rightly convinced that rigorous historiographical evidence that includes texts and material culture should yield a better understanding of the New Testament world and its messages. We extend our appreciation to all the authors for their invaluable contribution to the Festschrift. We are grateful for Elizabeth R. Niang who tirelessly helped to edit the manuscript. The birth of Aliou and Elizabeth's firstborn son, Micah Aliou Martin Niang, during this project was an incommensurable blessing.

PART ONE

Text and House Churches

1

The House Church as Social Environment

Dennis E. Smith

DAVID BALCH, ALONG WITH HIS COLLEAGUE CAROLYN OSIEK, HAS long been a leader in the study of the house church.[1] He has caused us to think in new ways about how the physical setting might have influenced early Christian social formation. As a contribution to that enterprise, I wish to summarize some recent scholarship on the house church and add my own proposals as to its importance. I will focus on ways in which the house church can be understood as the foundational social environment within which early Christian social identity developed and will lay out my argument in the form of ten working hypotheses.

The Graeco-Roman house was the default setting for early Christian gatherings and, therefore, for early Christian social and identity formation.

For most scholars, such a statement is a given. After all, the existence of the house church is evidenced throughout the letters of Paul.[2] My emphasis on the term *default*, however, means that no other setting

---

1. Osiek and Balch, *Families*; Balch and Osiek, *Early Christian Families*; Balch, "Paul, Families, and Households"; Balch, *Roman Domestic Art*; Osiek, MacDonald, and Tulloch, *Woman's Place*.

2. E.g., 1 Cor 16:19; Rom 16:3–5; Phlm 2; Col 4:5. See also Lampe, *From Paul to Valentinus*, who proposes up to seven different groupings of Christians indicated by the greetings in Romans 16, which is best accounted for as separate house churches (359, 374–76, 379–80).

should be assumed without specific evidence.³ It also means that the Graeco-Roman house must always be in the forefront of any reconstruction of Christian origins. This is not always the case in scholarship. Entire theories regarding early Christian social formation are built out of the literary data, and rightfully so, but such theories need also to be correlated with the physical space in which the communities evidenced by the literary data would have gathered. In what kind of house would they have gathered? Unfortunately, there is no sure answer to that question. There is not a "standard" house design. There were, however, some commonly repeated patterns, most especially in the use of a courtyard in some form of permutation, and the use of an atrium, although found in its classic form only in Italy. But there was also a great deal of variety in house design.⁴

Analysis of houses in the Graeco-Roman period has recently focused on how the house would have functioned as a context for social interaction.⁵ One issue is whether one can differentiate a distinction between public space and private space. For example, whereas the Greek house seemed to draw a sharp distinction between public and private, the Roman house often did not, or at least did not do so in the same way. Another issue is defining the function of the various rooms

---

3. A recent challenge to this thesis is the proposal by Mark Nanos that Roman Christians met in synagogues, most probably from among the numerous synagogues found in Rome at the time of the letter (*Mystery of Romans*, 13–14, 49). Whereas Acts claims Paul always preached in the synagogue first, Paul's letters do not support this idea, and Acts has been shown to be a questionable historical resource (see especially Pervo, *Mystery of Acts*).

4. In Pompeii and Herculaneum, the classic atrium house had a variety of permutations (Clarke, *Houses of Roman Italy*, 1–29) and there were other dwelling spaces in Pompeii that do not fit the atrium house model (Allison, "Domestic Spaces and Activities"). In Delos, there are three main types, "the normal house, the enlarged normal house, and the peristyle house," but in addition "there is a large variety of simple living units which cannot be classified into types or categories" (Trümper, "Material and Social Environment," 24). In Pergamon, courtyard houses are common, but there is not a standard style (Wulf-Rheidt, "Hellenistic and Roman Houses," 314–15). In Graeco-Roman Palestine, there were three primary types of courtyard houses: those with rooms arranged on one side of the courtyard ("the simple house"), those with rooms arranged around part of the courtyard ("the complex house"), and those with rooms arranged so as to completely enclose the courtyard (Hirschfeld, *Palestinian Dwelling*, 21–22, 290). Hirschfeld's examples show wide varieties in the design of these styles.

5. Examples include Nevett, *House and Society*; Clarke, *Houses of Roman Italy*; Wallace-Hadrill, *Houses and Society*; Hales, *Roman House and Social Identity*.

in the house. The easiest rooms to identify are those with permanent furnishings or clear construction patterns, such as the kitchen, the courtyard, the atrium, and the *tablinum*. Dining rooms can often be identified, especially if there are permanent couches or other built-in features to demarcate where couches would have been, such as patterns in the mosaic floor.⁶ By means of an analysis of the design of the house relative to the front door and the size and decorations of the various rooms scholars are able to propose which rooms would most likely have been bedrooms and which would have been reception rooms for receiving guests (often identified as the *triclinium* or dining room).⁷ This is an inexact science, however, and has recently been challenged by Penelope Allison, who has analyzed remains of items in the rooms of houses in Pompeii and concluded that most rooms served multiple functions.⁸

L. Michael White has traced the development from the house church to the basilica. He rejects earlier studies that posit a single line of development from house to basilica. Rather he argues that the Christian basilica was an adaptation of the imperial basilica and represented the phase in which Christianity moved from a private cult to a state religion. He also rejects studies that propose that the Christian building at Dura Europas, in which a house was renovated to create an assembly room and a baptistery, was normative for early Christianity. Rather he emphasizes that the house church within a private dwelling and centering on the dining room was the norm for most Christian groups for at least the first two centuries of Christian origins. That is to say, there was no specifically "Christian" architecture during this period. Furthermore, architectural adaptation of Christian meeting places, evidenced most specifically at Dura Europas, took place in a piecemeal fashion over time. Even the basilica did not become standard immediately upon its introduction as a Christian meeting place.⁹

---

6. Smith, *Symposium to Eucharist*, 15–17; Dunbabin, *Roman Banquet*, 36–50.

7. See, for example, the frequent occurrence of rooms identified as *triclinia* or reception rooms in Hirschfeld, *Palestinian Dwelling*.

8. Allison, *Pompeian Households*. Allison also critiques the standard practice of labeling rooms and their function in a Roman house according to literary nomenclature ("Using the Material and Written Sources"; *Pompeian Households*, 161–77; "Domestic Spaces and Activities").

9. White, *Building God's House*, 11–25.

Another important study of the house church is that of Jerome Murphy-O'Connor in *St. Paul's Corinth*.[10] He argued that a Roman villa found in Corinth, the so-called Anaploga villa, is a likely candidate for the kind of house in which the Corinthian Christians might have met. In his argument, he makes several key moves. A) He chooses a house located at Corinth and dated to the time of Paul.[11] B) He correlates his analysis with the New Testament data, most specifically the reference to the "whole church" meeting in the house of Gaius (Rom 16:23).[12] C) He tabulates the probable size of the Christian community based on the named members of the church in Corinth mentioned by Paul and in Acts and speculates on how such a group could all have been accommodated in a house of this size and room arrangement. D) He takes seriously the reference to a meal setting for the meeting. His proposal is well argued, but has been challenged in several recent studies. I will comment further on these issues below.

I propose that a differently nuanced approach to the data is needed. In this study I will not attempt to define a "typical" house. Nor will I attempt to correlate a particular house at a particular site with a particular New Testament text. What I propose instead is to define a set of "typical" features common in Graeco-Roman houses throughout the Mediterranean world. What I wish to spotlight is how the social environment of the house would have had a pivotal role in the social formation of early Christianity.

---

10. See Murphy-O'Connor, "House Churches and the Eucharist," 178–85.

11. To be sure, the dating has been challenged (see Horrell, "Domestic Space," 354), but the dating may not be absolutely critical since Murphy-O'Connor uses it as a "typical" house of this period (*St. Paul's Corinth*, 178–82). What is more pertinent is whether the category "typical house" is appropriate.

12. Murphy-O'Connor is careful in his wording: "Let us for a moment assume this was the house of Gaius, a wealthy member of the Christian community at Corinth (Rom 16:23), and try to imagine the situation when he hosted 'the whole church' (1 Cor 14:23)" (*St. Paul's Corinth*, 182). In a more recent work in which he responds to his critics, he becomes much more defensive about this assumption (*Keys to First Corinthians*, 191).

The houses often marked as "typical" in our data, from such sites as Pompeii and Ephesus, tend to be the houses of the wealthy elites. It is highly unlikely that early Christians included such elites in their numbers. The model for a house church would most likely derive from a much more modest social level.

This is one of the most important critiques of Murphy-O'Connor's work, since the Anaploga villa, like most excavated houses from the Graeco-Roman period, was of such a sumptuous size that it must have belonged to a member of the elite class.[13] He has recently responded to his critics by noting that, since Paul said *some* of the Corinthian Christians were "well off by human standards" (1 Cor 1:26; Murphy-O'Connor's paraphrase), such a status cannot be ruled out for Gaius, especially since "the whole church" was accommodated in his house (Romans).[14] Nevertheless, recent scholarship has emphasized the extent to which earliest Christianity would have been a movement among non-elites.[15] Therefore examples of more modest housing should be identified and brought into the discussion. That is what David Horrell does in an article critical of Murphy-O'Connor. As an alternative to the Anaploga villa he proposes a section of modest housing found elsewhere in Corinth as a more likely type of domestic space for the early Christian gatherings.[16]

More recently Peter Oakes has produced a detailed and compelling proposal for a non-elite Pauline house church.[17] Although his focus is on the letter to the Romans, he does not limit himself to the archeological evidence from Rome itself. Rather he proposes "reading" Romans as if it were written to a church in Pompeii, where the evidence for housing is much more extensive and where the cultural

---

13. For a review of the arguments, see especially Horrell, "Domestic Space," 356–59.

14. Murphy-O'Connor, *Keys to First Corinthians*, 191.

15. For reviews of the discussion, see Horrell, "Domestic Space," 356–59; Oakes, *Reading Romans*, 46–80; and see especially Friesen, "Poverty in Pauline Studies," and "Wrong Erastus."

16. Note, however, that more recent analysis of the site on which he focuses disputes his interpretation; see Schowalter, "Seeking Shelter," 331, 333–34.

17. Oakes, *Reading Romans in Pompeii*.

relationship to Rome is very close. His next step is to isolate a particular *insula* of houses and shops as his focus. Within that *insula* he focuses on two modest size dwellings and imaginatively populates them with the types of individuals who might have lived in Pompeii in such dwellings. He does this by identifying the shops with which the homeowners were connected. While his analysis is quite speculative (as is everyone else's) it provides a helpful model for imagining what a modest sized house for an early Christian community might have been like.[18] Furthermore, Oakes' study provides a promising new way to utilize the rich archeological data from Pompeii and Herculaneum for the study of early Christianity.

Whatever Christian gatherings consisted of, whatever form of worship or ritual was practiced, it would have been fully adapted to and integrated into the house environment.

This is a necessary corollary of my first hypothesis. In order to take seriously the house church, we cannot assume, implicitly or explicitly, that the house was a temporary location, that the community was simply waiting for the day when they could build a more appropriate meeting place that looked more like a church. After nearly 2,000 years of church architecture, it is hard for us to take seriously that the house church was fully integrated into its architectural space. But that had to have been the case. To be sure, the Letter of Pliny appears to identify two types of meetings of early Christians, one for an assembly of some kind and another for a meal.[19] Theoretically, then, there were two types of architectural space being identified, a dining room for the meal and an assembly room for the other type of gathering. The synagogue, of course, provided a contemporary architectural model for the design of an assembly hall. And it is also true that by the 3rd century, the house church in Dura Europas was remodeled to create an assembly

18. See especially Oakes, *Reading Romans in Pompeii*, chapter 3, "Model Craftworker House," 69–97.

19. Pliny, *Letters*, 10.96: "They affirmed . . . that they were in the habit of meeting on a certain fixed day before it was light, when they sang in alternate verses a hymn to Christ, as to a god, and bound themselves by a solemn oath . . . after which it was their custom to separate, and then reassemble to partake of food—but food of an ordinary and innocent kind."

room where a *triclinium* had once stood. Nevertheless, the dining room was a regular component of a house; an assembly room was not. Furthermore, everything that happened in an "assembly" was commonly found at communal dining gatherings as well.[20] While the idea that an "assembly room" could possibly have been set up in a house church is possible, it would not be a "default" use of the social space of the house, nor would it be a likely feature of a non-elite house.

The house was already established culturally as a worship/ritual space.

Drawing on Frank Brown's point that "the [public] architecture of the Romans was, from first to last, an art of shaping space around ritual,"[21] Clarke argues that the same was true of domestic space. "The Romans tended to think of each space in a house in terms of the ritual or activity that the space housed."[22] Among the "prescribed" rituals that took place in the house, Clarke notes "worship of the household gods, ceremonies of coming-of-age, marriage, birth, and death." In addition, he enumerates "secular rituals such as the visits of clients to the head of the house and the entertainment of guests at dinner parties."[23] For Clarke, the house as social environment must be considered a key factor in interpreting the rituals that took place within. "We must interpret both prescribed and habitual rituals in terms of the spaces of the houses themselves. Here factors such as size, setting, and social class provide particulars. How, for instance, did a dining room in a small city house function—as opposed to that of a grand seaside villa?"[24]

The house was the center for domestic cult activities. Its boundaries defined a zone under the protection of deities specific to the household, which were grouped under the plural term "penates." Among these deities, the most important were the "lares," frequently pictured as a pair of young men carrying drinking horns. They were sometimes

---

20. See especially the catalog of activities at the banquets of various kinds of clubs and associations in D. Smith, *Symposium to Eucharist*, 87–131; Taussig, *In the Beginning*, 67–85, 104–13.

21. Brown, *Roman Architecture*, 9, quoted in Clarke, *Houses of Roman Italy*, 1.

22. Clarke, *Houses of Roman Italy*, 1.

23. Ibid.

24. Ibid.

pictured with a representation of the *genius*, or spirit, of the *paterfamilias*. In the atria of several houses in Pompeii, shrines to the lares can be found where offerings were presented for the purpose of bringing good fortune to the house. Also present in the atrium of a house were the images of the family ancestors.[25]

Similar ritual zones were common in houses elsewhere in the Graeco-Roman world, most especially the centrality of the hearth as a sacred area in Greek tradition. One must assume, therefore, that any Graeco-Roman house in which Christians met would have shrines or other sacred spaces for honoring and invoking household deities. One should not assume that Christians would immediately begin existing in a monotheistic world in which attention would not have to be paid to the cloud of polytheistic powers and deities that encircled them.[26] Balch has reminded us of such influences with a series of studies of wall paintings of mythological scenes that are commonly found in dining rooms in Pompeii. He imagines a Christian group meeting in such a house and how the teaching of Paul might play out in a setting in which such scenes were in the background. His rich study points out the varied ways in which the polytheistic culture would have surrounded those who gathered as a house church in a variety of types of Roman houses.[27]

Jorunn Økland has recently proposed that, in 1 Corinthians, the *ekklēsia* was defined as ritually constructed space within the context of the house. Her argument is constructed out of rhetorical flourishes by Paul in which he utilizes cultic imagery (or "the discourse of sanctuary space") to characterize the worship community, but she consistently seeks to place the ritual spaces so defined within the house church and more specifically in the dining room.[28] Her work is a valuable addition to our understanding of the ritual components of the house church as social environment.[29]

---

25. Ibid., 6–10.

26. As stated, without evidence, by Dix in his influential work, *Shape of the Liturgy*: "The quaint old images of the household gods and the altar must go, of course, along with the sacred hearth and its undying fire" (23; as quoted by White, *Building God's House*, 16). In contrast, such texts as Col 2:16–21 testify to the continuing presence of polytheistic beliefs within the Christian community.

27. Balch, *Roman Domestic Art*.

28. Økland, *Women in Their Place*, 131–67, esp. 139.

29. Compare Taussig, *In the Beginning*, who emphasizes the importance of ritual studies for analyzing Christian meal gatherings (55–67).

The size of the gathering is often estimated without sufficient reference to the probable physical space in which they met. This has led to the proposal that the group would have been too large for the dining room and thus would have had to meet in the atrium. Rather we should estimate the size of the gathering based on the probable size of the default meeting space and, if the group grew larger, then we should assume that another house church would be organized to accommodate the overflow.

The most influential proposal for the size of a house church gathering has been that of Murphy-O'Connor. Based on his tabulation of the named individuals connected with the church at Corinth, and considering possible sizes of their household, he posits an assembly gathering of about 40 people. Because of this size of the group, and because of the reference to the "whole church" gathering at Gaius' house (Rom 16:23), he also proposes that such a group could not all fit in the *triclinium*, so a portion would have to move to the atrium. He suggests that this was the reason why there was a division at the Lord's supper as described by Paul, especially since those in the atrium would have to sit instead of recline (1 Cor 14:30).[30]

Balch and Osiek have also proposed that the house church met in the atrium, basing their argument especially on 1 Cor 14:23, which they translate as follows: "if therefore the whole church comes together . . . and outsiders or unbelievers enter [the house uninvited] . . ." They conclude that the setting in which uninvited individuals would enter during the community gathering would have to be an atrium, since the atrium is primarily a public space.[31]

In contrast, I would argue that the atrium is an unlikely location for the community gathering. First, atria in their classic formulation as public space, where the patron of the house met his clients, is rarely

---

30. Murphy-O'Connor, *St. Paul's Corinth*, 182–84; *Keys to First Corinthians*, 182–86.

31. Balch and Osiek, *Families in the New Testament World*, 16–17, 34. In a more recent article, Balch has revisited this proposal and enlarged his characterization of house churches to include *insulae* as well as atrium houses ("Rich Pompeiian Houses").

found, if at all, outside of Italy.[32] Yet the New Testament evidence for Murphy-O'Connor and for Osiek and Balch is based on references to the community gathering in Corinth. Second, the atrium is not a space that would normally be used for dining.[33] Third, the New Testament texts do not definitively support the proposed interpretations. The *idiōtes* ("outsider") who showed up at the Corinthian gathering in 14:23 is also referenced as a participant in 14:16. The term should be translated "outsider" in the sense that such individuals are not yet members.[34] But they would still be invited guests in order to be full participants. The reference to the "whole church" meeting at the house of Gaius is best read not as a reference to a house church gathering per se but rather as an unusual occasion when the several house churches in Corinth might come together as a group, an interpretation proposed by Murphy-O'Connor himself.[35] I would add that the reference to Gaius being "host to me [Paul] and to the whole church" (Rom 16:23) need not require that everyone named in Paul and Acts and their households were all present at the same point in time; the capacity of the house might dictate how many might be hosted on any particular occasion. The text could simply mean that a Christian was always welcome at Gaius' house. And it is not at all clear that the situation Paul addresses in 1 Cor 11:17–34 refers to the occasional church meeting at Gaius' house mentioned in Rom 16:23. Finally, it should also be noted that traditional theories about Christians meeting in a large assembly hall setting like the atrium have too often arisen out of unstated and anachronistic presuppositions that early Christian worship looked a lot like worship in a basilica.[36]

---

32. See Trümper, "Material and Social Environment," 41, who states: "Both atrium houses and atrium-peristyle houses are not only absent from Delos, Pergamon, and Ephesus, but from most cities outside Italy."

33. Based on a close study of furnishings found in atria, Allison concludes: "There is ample evidence that both household members and outsiders—those who needed to be impressed, and those more involved in domestic, Industrial or commercial activities—used the front areas of Pompeian "*atrium* houses." Notably lacking is evidence for food preparation and eating in this part of the house" ("Domestic Spaces and Activities," 273).

34. The term was used in associations to refer to nonmembers who participated in the sacrifices (BDAG, 468).

35. Murphy-O'Connor, *Keys to First Corinthians*, 192–93.

36. White, *Building God's House*, 12–17.

I would suggest that the number forty as the size of an average house church needs to be retired.[37] Murphy-O'Connor bases this number partially on names of church members that are found only in Acts, and, as noted above, Acts is not a reliable historical resource.[38] If instead we take seriously the house church as social environment, we might come up with a different number for an average house church attendance. Our starting point should be the potential capacity of the dining space. The standard *triclinium* was designed for nine diners, three couches with three spaces for diners per couch.[39] However, as indicated in vase paintings and in literary references, it was not unusual for diners to share couches and crowd in closely—they did not have the same issues with personal space that we do. So it is likely that more than nine could be accommodated in a *triclinium* if need be. Furthermore, sometimes the "*triclinium*" arrangement could be enlarged by simply elongating the three couches, as was done in the clubhouse of the builders in Ostia. In a large proportion of houses, however, there are no permanent couches or markings and one has to guess which room would have been used for dining. Dining furnishings were portable, and the furnishings could be arranged to fit the space available. Even modest sized houses have rooms that could have served for dining.[40]

In a forthcoming study of Mithraea in Ostia, Mike White has attempted to define the number of diners based on the space provided on the dining couches. In the standard *mithraeum*, the long reclining couches extend on only two sides and positions are not marked in any way. White has proposed using a measurement of five people per three

---

37. It has become a widely used round number for the average size of a house church. See, e.g., Oakes, *Reading Romans in Pompeii*, 81–83. On the other hand, Osiek and Balch, *Families*, think that 40 may be too small a number for some church meetings, based on their review of large spaces in Pompeiian houses which could have accommodated large numbers of people (203).

38. See n. 3 above.

39. See Dunbabin, *Roman Banquet*, 38–40. Note, however, that the rowdy and seemingly large banquet of Trimalchio begins with nine diners, who can be placed in the traditional *triclinium* arrangement, but then introduces five more (*Satyricon* 41–46) whose positions at the table are unclear. Also present is a host of slaves. On the dining arrangements at Trimalchio's banquet, see M. Smith, *Petronius*, 66, 98.

40. See especially the rooms identified as "reception halls" and "*triclinia*" in the catalogue of houses in Hirschfeld, *Palestinian Dwelling*.

meters, giving each person 60 cm. or roughly two Roman feet.[41] This is a promising model that can also be useful in reconstructing how many people might gather at any one time in a house church.

Access to the house church gathering would take place by means of the cultural process of hospitality; one had to be an invited guest or a member of the household.

To be sure, the house was also the owner's place of business, and in that sense it was open to the public. As Clarke notes: "The Roman house was in no way private. It was the locus of the owner's social, political, and business activities, open both to invited and uninvited visitors."[42] For the patrician *paterfamilias*, this meant receiving clients primarily in the *tablinum*.[43] The house design of these elite houses also placed a premium on "conspicuous consumption," being designed so that uninvited outsiders could freely enter and observe and marvel at the sumptuousness of the interior spaces. On the other hand, as pointed out by Vitruvius, there was a distinction between the public space of the house where business took place and the private space, including baths, bedrooms, and dining rooms, which were only for invited guests.[44] The point is that a certain degree of privacy was normal for a dining room. For the non-elite homeowners, that is, those who had no clients, the house might function both as workshop and living space.[45] For such more modest-size housing, the client system would not be operative. While a workshop attached to a house could be considered "public" space, the configurations of the house would still include private space. Nor would one expect that "conspicuous consumption" would be an issue for such houses.

On the other hand, hospitality is a standard function of the *paterfamilias* (or *materfamilias*) of a household. It defines a ritual whereby the outsider is invited and entertained as a guest of the householder. Rooms for the entertaining of guests, most commonly defined as din-

---

41. His complete argument is contained in his forthcoming article. I am grateful to Mike for letting me see an advance copy of this article.
42. Clarke, *Houses of Roman Italy*, 2.
43. Ibid., 4–6.
44. Ibid., 12–13.
45. Ibid., 25–26.

ing rooms, are standard components of the ancient house. Thus when Gaius is praised by Paul as "host" of the church, and thus as patron of the church, the term used is *xenos*, a term that derives from the semantic field of hospitality to the stranger (*xenia*).[46] This is an example of the social formation of early Christianity developing in interaction with the house as social environment.[47]

Consequently, I disagree with those who argue that uninvited outsiders could simply walk in and attend a Christian gathering in a house church.[48] Such arguments are often based on the definitions of courtyard and atrium as zones where outsiders, primarily as clients to the householder as patron, would be allowed to enter and mingle. But since such outsiders were not guests being offered hospitality by the host, they would not be expected to have access to the areas of the house where guests would be entertained.

The normal space in the house where hospitality was practiced was the dining room. This fits scholarship on the practice of hospitality and patterns in Graeco-Roman house design.

Entertaining guests in one's home invariably took place in the dining room. It was a ritualized event in which the householder/host sent out invitations, arranged guests according to rank, and took the responsibility to make sure everyone was included equally. Houses of any size so as to contain a room for entertaining guests would contain a dining room, either with couches already arranged or with a space that could easily be furnished with couches. This is a pattern found throughout the Mediterranean region in the Graeco-Roman period.[49]

---

46. Stählin, "*Xenos*"; Arterbury, *Entertaining Angels*, 53–54, 100–108; Koenig, *New Testament Hospitality*, 64–65. See also 1 Cor 16:5–12: Gal 4:13–14; Phlm 22.

47. See also Lampe, *Paul to Valentinus*, 374–76.

48. Here I disagree with Balch, "Paul, Families, and Households," 260; Taussig, *In the Beginning*, 82–85; Klinghardt, *Gemeinschaftsmahl und Mahlgemeinschaft*, 84–97.

49. D. Smith, *Symposium to Eucharist*, 22–27. See also White, *Building God's House*, 109: "The extension of hospitality through the meal setting was the central act that served to define the worshipping community, the church (*ekklēsia*) in household assembly."

The default setting of worship at table fits our New Testament data and is sufficient as the location for all that Christians did at their gatherings.

This is the working hypothesis of the Seminar on Meals in the Graeco-Roman World[50] and of Hal Taussig's important book, *In the Beginning Was the Meal*. In the letters of Paul, whenever the context of a community gathering is specified, more often than not it is described as a meal. This is true of the Antioch community (Gal 2:11-14), the Corinthian community (1 Cor 11:17—14:40), and the Roman communities (Rom 14:1—15:7).[51]

The house setting would necessitate addressing social and gender stratification.

Recent scholarship on the Graeco-Roman house has undermined the idea that it was divided into zones by gender. This idea had been based on Vitruvius' formulaic description of Greek houses, but is not clearly borne out by the design of Greek houses.[52] Scholars now give more importance to both Greek and Roman houses as interactive environments for the entire household, which includes not only male and female members of the family, but also male and female slaves, who were essential to the running of the household.[53] Already, beginning in the Hellenistic and continuing throughout the Roman period, women had begun to recline along with men at banquets.[54] Some households were led by women (*materfamilias*) who would then be expected to serve as

---

50. Seminar papers are posted at http://www.philipharland.com/meals/GrecoRomanMealsSeminar.htm/. Publication is forthcoming.

51. See further, D. Smith, *Symposium to Eucharist*, 173-217.

52. See Vitruvius 6.7.2-4. Both Jameson in regard to the Greek house ("Domestic Space," 92), and Wallace-Hadrill in regard to the Roman house (*Houses and Society*, 9) note that Vitruvius's model of gender differentiation in different portions of the house cannot be identified in the archeological design of houses, but, if present at all, perhaps in the use of the house. See also D. Smith, *From Symposium to Eucharist*, 302 n. 41.

53. See especially Osiek, MacDonald, and Tulloch, *Woman's Place*, 95-117.

54. D. Smith, *Symposium to Eucharist*, 43-44; Corley, *Private Women, Public Meals*, 24-66.

hosts of banquets in their home. Similarly, women served in a variety of roles as patrons and hosts for early Christian house churches.[55]

Since Christian *ecclesia* membership patterns emphasized household identity, and since they were meeting in homes, women, children, and slaves would have been a part of the background if not the foreground.[56] In such circumstances, one would expect issues of gender and social stratification to arise at Christian meetings. And indeed, the literature is abundant with references and even debate on these issues, with some communities, or at least Paul, advocating a policy of equality, however that was to be carried out in real life (Gal 3:27–28), and some communities reverting to another model, that of the household code (Colossians, Ephesians, the Pastorals, 1 Peter). Taussig points out how the meal setting tended to generate discussion and experimentation on such issues. This is based on the fact that banquet ideology emphasized the competing ideals of equality as well as social stratification at the table.[57] How to balance these two was a matter of continual debate, a debate that took its own form in Christian communities but one that was spurred by the context in which they met, namely, in dining rooms in private homes.

The practice of gathering a group whose membership extended beyond the household itself was most likely based on the model of the association.

The question here is how the private house could become the gathering place for a community gathering whose membership extended beyond the household itself. To be sure, a large majority of house churches may have consisted primarily or even entirely of households. But clearly their identity as a group extended beyond the household. The best ancient model for such an extended group identity is that of the voluntary association.[58]

---

55. Osiek, MacDonald, and Tulloch, *Woman's Place*, 144–93.

56. Ibid., 50–117. See also Meyers, "Problems of Gendered Space."

57. Taussig, *In the Beginning*, 145–71; see also D. Smith, *Symposium to Eucharist*, 8–12.

58. Ascough provides the evidence for translocal links among associations (*Paul's Macedonian Associations*, 91–109). See also Ascough, *What Are They Saying*, 71–94; Harland, *Associations, Synagogues, and Congregations*.

Many associations were modeled on a household model and in some cases met in homes.[59] There are examples of association "clubhouses" that are designed on the model of a house. A good example is the clubhouse of the builders in Ostia. Here there is a central courtyard with several small rooms arranged around it that open out to the courtyard. Some of these rooms contain permanent *triclinium* style couches for dining. This is not surprising, since association inscriptions emphasize the communal meal as central to association activities.[60] To be sure, associations met in a variety of locations, including temples and cemeteries, (where, incidentally, there were also facilities for dining). All associations did not look like Christian assemblies in house churches. But Christian assemblies in house churches did look like a type of association and most likely adopted that cultural model as a primary basis for their communal identity.

Conclusion

When we speak of early Christian social formation, we too often overlook or undermine the importance of the physical context for their gatherings. According to the data, early Christians met in homes, and appear to have done so for at least the first 200 years of early Christian development. Therefore the house as social environment should be taken more seriously as a social space in its own right and as a key contributor to early Christian social formation.

---

59. Harland, *Associations, Synagogues, and Congregations*, 30–33.
60. Ibid., 63–65; D. Smith, *Symposium to Eucharist*, 87–131.

Bibliography

Allison, Penelope M. "Domestic Spaces and Activities." In *The World of Pompeii*, edited by John J. Dobbins and Pedar W. Foss, 269–78. Routledge Worlds. London: Routledge, 2007.

———. *Pompeian Households: An Analysis of Material Culture*. Los Angeles: The Cotsen Institute of Archaeology, University of California, 2004.

———. "Using the Material and Written Sources: Turn of the Millennium Approaches to Roman Domestic Space." *AJA* 105 (2001) 181–208.

Arterbury, Andrew E. *Entertaining Angels: Early Christian Hospitality in its Mediterranean Setting*. New Testament Monographs 8. Sheffield: Sheffield Phoenix, 2005.

Ascough, Richard S. *What Are They Saying about the Formation of Pauline Churches?* New York: Paulist, 1998.

———. *Paul's Macedonian Associations: The Social Context of Philippians and 1 Thessalonians*. WUNT 2/161. Tübingen: Mohr/Siebeck, 2003.

Balch, David L. "Paul, Families, and Households." In *Paul in the Graeco-Roman World: A Handbook*, edited by J. Paul Sampley, 258–92. Harrisburg, PA: Trinity, 2003.

———. "Rich Pompeiian Houses, Shops for Rent, and the Huge Apartment Building in Herculaneum as Typical Spaces for Pauline House Churches." *JSNT* 27 (2004) 27–46.

———. *Roman Domestic Art and Early House Churches*. WUNT 228. Tübingen: Mohr/Siebeck, 2008.

Balch, David L., and Carolyn Osiek, editors. *Early Christian Families in Context: An Interdisciplinary Dialogue*. Religion, Marriage and Family. Grand Rapids: Eerdmans, 2003.

Brown, Frank E. *Roman Architecture*. The Great Ages of World Architecture. New York: Braziller, 1961.

Clarke, John R. *The Houses of Roman Italy, 100 BC–AD 250: Ritual, Space, and Decoration*. Berkeley: University of California Press, 1991.

Corley, Kathleen E. *Private Women, Public Meals: Social Conflict in the Synoptic Tradition*. Peabody, MA: Hendrickson, 1993.

Dix, Dom Gregory. *The Shape of the Liturgy*. London: Dacre, 1945.

Dunbabin, Katherine M. D. *The Roman Banquet: Images of Conviviality*. Cambridge: Cambridge University Press, 2003.

Friesen, Steven J. "Poverty in Pauline Studies: Beyond the So-Called New Consensus." *JSNT* 26 (2004) 323–61.

———. "The Wrong Erastus: Ideology, Archaeology, and Exegesis." In *Corinth in Context: Comparative Studies on Religion and Society*, edited by Steven J. Friesen et al., 231–58. NovTSup 134. Leiden: Brill, 2010.

Friesen, Steven et al., editors *Corinth in Context: Comparative Studies on Religion and Society*. NovTSup 134. Leiden: Brill, 2010.

Hales, Shelley. *The Roman House and Social Identity*. Cambridge: Cambridge University Press, 2003.

Harland, Philip A. *Associations, Synagogues, and Congregations: Claiming a Place in Ancient Mediterranean Society*. Minneapolis: Fortress, 2003.

Hirschfeld, Yizhar. *The Palestinian Dwelling in the Roman-Byzantine Period.* Jerusalem: Franciscan Printing Press, 1995.

Horrell, David G. "Domestic Space and Christian Meetings at Corinth: Imagining New Contexts and the Buildings East of the Theatre." *NTS* 50 (2004) 349–69.

Jameson, Michael. "Domestic Space in the Greek City-State." In *Domestic Architecture and the Use of Space: An Interdisciplinary Cross-Cultural Study*, edited by Susan Kent, 92–113. New Directions in Archaeology. Cambridge: Cambridge University Press, 1990.

Klinghardt, Matthias. *Gemeinschaftsmahl und Mahlgemeinschaft: Soziologie und Liturgie frühchristlicher Mahlfeiern.* Texte und Arbeiten zum neutestamentlichen Zeitalter 13. Tübingen: Francke, 1996.

Koenig, John. *New Testament Hospitality: Partnership with Strangers as Promise and Mission.* 1985. Reprint, Eugene, OR: Wipf & Stock, 2001.

Lampe, Peter. *From Paul to Valentinus: Christians at Rome in the First Two Centuries.* Translated by Michael Steinhauser. Edited by Marshall D. Johnson. Minneapolis: Fortress, 2003.

Meeks, Wayne A. *The First Urban Christians: The Social World of the Apostle Paul.* New Haven: Yale University Press, 1983.

Meyers, Eric M. "The Problems of Gendered Space in Syro-Palestinian Domestic Architecture: The Case of Roman-Period Galilee." In *Early Christian Families in Context: An Interdisciplinary Dialogue*, edited by David L. Balch and Carolyn Osiek, 44–69. Religion, Marriage and Family. Grand Rapids: Eerdmans, 2003.

Murphy-O'Connor, Jerome. "House Churches and the Eucharist." In *St. Paul's Corinth: Texts and Archaeology*, edited by Jerome Murphy-O'Connor, 178–85. 3rd rev. and expanded ed. Collegeville: Liturgical, 2002.

———. *Keys to First Corinthians: Revisiting the Major Issues.* Oxford: Oxford University Press, 2009.

———. *St. Paul's Corinth: Texts and Archaeology.* 3rd rev. and expanded ed. Collegeville: Liturgical, 2002.

Nanos, Mark D. *The Mystery of Romans: The Jewish Context of Paul's Letter.* Minneapolis: Fortress, 1996.

Nevett, Lisa C. *House and Society in the Ancient Greek World.* New Studies in Archaeology. Cambridge: Cambridge University Press, 1999.

Oakes, Peter. *Reading Romans in Pompeii: Paul's Letter at Ground Level.* Minneapolis: Fortress, 2009.

Økland, Jorunn. *Women in Their Place: Paul and the Corinthian Discourse of Gender and Sanctuary Space.* JSNTSup 269. London: T. & T. Clark, 2004.

Osiek, Carolyn, and David L. Balch. *Families in the New Testament World: Households and House Churches.* The Family, Religion, and Culture. Louisville: Westminster John Knox, 1997.

Osiek, Carolyn, and Margaret Y. MacDonald, with Janet H. Tulloch. *A Woman's Place: House Churches in Earliest Christianity.* Minneapolis: Fortress, 2006.

Nevett, Lisa C. *House and Society in the Ancient Greek World.* New Studies in Archaeology. Cambridge: Cambridge University Press, 1999.

Pervo, Richard I. *The Mystery of Acts: Unraveling its Story.* Santa Rosa, CA: Polebridge, 2008.

Schowalter, Daniel N. "Seeking Shelter in Roman Corinth: Archaeology and the Placement of Paul's Communities." In *Corinth in Context: Comparative Studies* on *Religion and Society*, edited by Steven J. Friesen, et al., 327–41. NovTSup 134. Leiden: Brill, 2010.

Smith, Dennis E. *From Symposium to Eucharist: The Banquet in the Early Christian World*. Minneapolis: Fortress, 2003.

Smith, Martin S., editor. *Petronius: Cena Trimalchionis*. Oxford: Clarendon, 1975.

Stählin, Gustav. "Xenos." In *TDNT* 5:1–36.

Taussig, Hal E. *In the Beginning Was the Meal: Social Experimentation & Early Christian Identity*. Minneapolis: Fortress, 2009.

Trümper, Monika. "Material and Social Environment of Graeco-Roman Households in the East: The Case of Hellenistic Delos." In *Early Christian Families in Context: An Interdisciplinary Dialogue*, edited by David L. Balch and Carolyn Osiek, 19–43. Religion, Marriage and Family. Grand Rapids: Eerdmans, 2003.

Wallace-Hadrill, Andrew. *Houses and Society in Pompeii and Herculaneum*. Princeton: Princeton University Press, 1994.

White, L. Michael. *Building God's House in the Roman World: Architectural Adaptation among Pagans, Jews, and Christians*. ASOR Library of Biblical and Near Eastern Archaeology. Baltimore: Johns Hopkins University Press, 1990.

———. "Regulating Fellowship in the Communal Meal: Early Jewish and Christian Evidence." In *Meals in a Social Context*, edited by Inge Nielsen and Hanne Sigismund Nielsen, 177–205. Aarhus Studies in Mediterranean Antiquity 1. Aarhus, Denmark: Aarhus University Press, 2001.

———. *The Social Origins of Christian Architecture*. Vol. 2, *Texts and Monuments for the Christian Domus Ecclesiae in Its Environment*. HTS 42. Valley Forge, PA: Trinity, 1997.

Wulf-Rheidt, Ulrike. "The Hellenistic and Roman Houses of Pergamon." In *Pergamon, Citadel of the Gods: Archaeological Record, Literary Description, and Religious Development*, edited by Helmut Koester, 299–330. HTS 46. Harrisburg, PA: Trinity, 1998.

2

Placing the Corinthian Communal Meal[1]

Edward Adams

It has long been accepted that the earliest Christians met in private homes. Over the past fifteen years or so, there has been increasing interest in the question of the kind of houses in which early Christian gatherings took place. Recent work of David Balch has been prominent in this development.[2] A focal point for discussion of the domestic setting of early Christian meetings has been the venue of the Corinthian communal meal, as described by Paul in 1 Cor 11:17-34. A pioneering treatment of this issue is that of Jerome Murphy-O'Connor, who pictures the Corinthians assembling in a 'sumptuous' Roman villa owned by a wealthy member of the congregation. He considers how the physical layout of the villa might have affected the social shape of the gathering. David Horrell has challenged Murphy-O'Connor's reconstruction and has proposed another kind of domestic space as a possible context of the meeting. The present essay offers a different perspective on the location of the Corinthian community meal, arguing, on exegetical grounds, that it was not the home of a church member. Drawing cautiously on the archaeology of first-century Corinth, I set out an imaginative scenario involving rented dining space.

---

1. This essay is drawn from a research project funded by the Leverhulme Trust. It was delivered as a paper to the New Testament Research Seminar, University of Cambridge, and to the Biblical Studies Research Seminar, University of Sheffield. I am grateful for the helpful feedback I received on both occasions. I am also grateful to Prof. David Horrell, of the University of Exeter, for reading and commenting on an earlier draft of this piece.

2. Osiek and Balch, *Families*, 5-35; 193-204; Balch, "Rich Pompeiian Houses" (reprinted in Balch, *Roman Domestic Art*, 42-58).

Domestic Space and the Communal Meal at Corinth: Jerome Murphy-O'Connor and David Horrell

First Corinthians 11:17–34 reflects a recurring occasion in which the Corinthian believers, who also gathered (probably more frequently) in smaller groups,[3] all came together to celebrate the Lord's Supper. In 1 Cor 14:23, Paul speaks of "the whole church" coming together for plenary worship. It seems likely, though not certain, that he is referring here to the same gathering as in 1 Cor 11:17–34, a meeting in which open worship followed the Lord's Supper. Balch and others have shown that the order fits the standard pattern of the Graeco-Roman dinner party (in which the meal was followed by learned conversation or entertainments).[4] Murphy-O'Connor's account of the material context of the community meal comes in his acclaimed book *St. Paul's Corinth*, first published in 1983, in a chapter entitled "House Churches and the Eucharist."[5] He takes as his main archaeological model the excavated Roman villa at Anaploga (in the environs of Corinth), which he dates to the time of Paul.

According to Murphy-O'Connor, the villa boasted an atrium, measuring 5 x 6 m, and a *triclinium* (dining room) with a splendid mosaic floor, measuring 5.5 x 7.5 m. He compares the house with another Corinthian villa and also with houses in Pompeii, Olynthus and Ephesus, and concludes that in design and size the Anaploga villa was "very typical."[6] He believes that the villa is representative of the sort of house required to accommodate the whole Christian community at Corinth, which he calculates at between forty and fifty persons by this time (a figure based on the number of named individuals and their likely dependents).[7] He attributes such a house to Gaius, whom, on the basis of Rom 16:23, he takes to be the host of "the whole church." whenever all the Christians in Corinth dined and worshipped together.[8] A congregation of the size estimated would have been too large

---

3. An inference drawn from 1 Cor 14:23: see, e.g., Banks, *Paul's Idea of Community*, 38, 41.

4. Osiek and Balch, *Families*, 203; Lampe, "Eucharist," 37–41; Smith, *From Symposium to Eucharist*, 188–214.

5. Murphy-O'Connor, *St. Paul's Corinth*, 178–85.

6. Ibid., 178.

7. Ibid., 182.

8. Ibid.

for the *triclinium*, which typically accommodated no more than nine diners. Gaius would thus have had to make a social distinction among his guests, inviting the better-off believers to dine in comfort in the *triclinium* while assigning the rest to the atrium, which would have been cold and over-crowded.[9]

According to Murphy-O'Connor, the projected spatial division, coupled with a distinction in the amount and quality of food served to guests, elucidates the "divisions" (*schismata*) of which Paul speaks in 1 Cor 11:18. He contends that "no other scenario has been suggested which so well explains the details of 1 Corinthians 11:17–34."[10] Murphy-O'Connor's reconstruction of the physical environment of the Corinthian communal meal has been very influential and has been appropriated by numerous interpreters. However, in an article published in 2004, Horrell expresses critical concerns, especially about Murphy-O'Connor's appeal to the Anaploga villa.[11] Horrell points outs that the mosaic floor, which Murphy-O'Connor uses to date the villa to the time of Paul, has been dated in more recent scholarship to the second or even third century CE.[12] Horrell notes that there is no clear proof that the room identified by Murphy-O'Connor as the *triclinium* actually functioned as such.[13] Furthermore, Horrell is doubtful that any of the Corinthian Christians, including the church's alleged "host," Gaius, could have owned a large, plush residence like the Anaploga villa. Persuaded to a certain extent by Justin Meggitt's critique of the "new consensus,"[14] Horrell avers that there is little firm evidence to identify any member of the Corinthian church known to us as elite or wealthy.[15]

In developing his own ideas about locating the Corinthian Eucharistic assembly, Horrell draws attention to buildings 1 and 3 on Corinth's East Theatre Street. These structures apparently served as premises for the preparation and sale of cooked meats. Horrell notes that the excavators, in the preliminary report, hypothesize the

9. Ibid., 183–84.
10. Ibid., 185.
11. Horrell, "Domestic Space."
12. Ibid., 354.
13. Ibid., 354–56.
14. Meggitt, *Paul, Poverty and Survival*.
15. Horrell, "Domestic Space," 359.

existence of upper floors, which could have been used for residential purposes.[16] Domestic space over a shop, in Horrell's view, constitutes a more realistic and socio-economically plausible setting for Christian meetings at Corinth. An upper area measuring 10 x 5 m, the dimensions given for the hypothesized upper level of building 3, could offer space for fifty or so people, though not without a considerable amount of cramming.[17] Knowing nothing about the layout of the upper level of building 3 (the number or size of rooms), it is impossible, in Horrell's view, to derive from it an architectural explanation for the divisions at the Lord's Supper, in contrast to Murphy-O'Connor's hypothesis based on the small number of guests that could dine in the *triclinium* of a Roman villa.[18] Horrell emphasizes that the East Theatre Street scenario is entirely imaginative. He advances it as "only one plausible type of setting among a range of possibilities" and urges New Testament scholars to consider the varieties of domestic space available in Corinth and other cities when conceiving of the settings of Christian meetings, rather than focusing only on elite residences.[19]

In a recent response to Horrell, Murphy-O'Connor concedes the points about dating of the Anaploga villa and the identification of one of its rooms as the *triclinium*.[20] He insists, though, that houses like the Anaploga villa must have existed in Corinth in Paul's time, and that a house of this type would have been required to host the whole Corinthian believing community.[21] He reasserts the "new consensus" view that the Corinthian church had some wealthy members, who could have owned houses like this (appealing to 1 Cor 1:26, which he takes literally).[22] As to Horrell's alternative, he finds the scenario of "50 people sitting knee to knee with their food in their laps" a socially

---

16. Ibid., 364–65; cf. Williams and Zervos, "Corinth 1985," 134, 139–42, 147–48.
17. Horrell, "Domestic Space," 367.
18. Ibid., 368.
19. Ibid., 369.
20. Murphy-O'Connor, *Keys to First Corinthians*, 190–91.
21. Ibid., 191.
22. Ibid. Murphy-O'Connor mistakenly imputes to Horrell Meggitt's thesis that Paul and the early Christians were absolutely poor. While Horrell accepts Meggitt's point that none of the Corinthian Christians can be positively identified as elite or aristocratic (as noted above in the main text), he thinks that Meggitt has underestimated levels of socio-economic differentiation among the non-elite, both in the Roman world generally and in Paul's churches (Horrell, "Domestic Space," 358).

implausible one.²³ Yet, in making this criticism, Murphy-O'Connor overlooks the fact that dining conditions would have been even more cramped in the atrium of the Anaploga villa, with up to forty people dining in 30 sq. m (reduced by one ninth because of the *impluvium*)!²⁴

Daniel Schowalter, in an essay published in 2010, reviewing scholarship on ecclesial space in Paul's Corinth, reports, in critiquing Horrell, that the conjectured upper floors of the East Theatre buildings will not figure in the final excavation report.²⁵ He tells us that the evidence originally thought to indicate upper levels has been re-interpreted by the excavators. Citing Charles Williams, Schowalter points out that the frequency and intensity of earthquakes in Corinth meant that "multi-storied constructions such as those in Rome and Ostia would not have been feasible in Corinth."²⁶ This does not, in Schowalter's view, undermine Horrell's main point that scholars should consider a spectrum of options for housing space at Corinth; it only means that second-storey domestic space should be excluded from that range.²⁷

Did the Corinthian Communal Meal Take Place in a Believer's House?

Both Murphy-O'Connor and Horrell think that the Corinthian community meal took place in domestic space, as do most other scholars. This widely held view of the setting of the "whole church" gathering at Corinth reflects the more general assumption within New Testament studies that "early Christians met almost exclusively in the homes of individual members of the congregation."²⁸ Murphy-O'Connor and others find specific exegetical evidence for the house as the setting of the Corinthian communal assembly in Rom 16:23, where Paul states that Gaius is "host to me and to the whole church" (*Gaios ho xenos mou kai holes tes ekklēsias*). Gaius here is almost certainly the

23. Murphy-O'Connor, *Keys to 1 Corinthians*, 192.

24. To be fair to Murphy-O'Connor, the house he imagines as Gaius's house is not the Anaploga villa per se but an imaginative residence based on the average floor space of the Anaploga villa and five other houses: cf. Murphy-O'Connor, *St. Paul's Corinth*, 180–82.

25. Schowalter, "Seeking Shelter," 333–34.

26. Ibid., 334 n. 20.

27. Ibid., 334.

28. Gehring, *House Church*, 1.

same Gaius mentioned in 1 Cor 1:14, as one of Paul's first converts at Corinth. His hosting of "the whole church" is understood to mean that he made available his house for gatherings of the whole church *at Corinth*. However, the majority of commentators on Romans take *kai holēs tēs ekklēsias* as implying that Gaius was renowned for extending hospitality to travelling Christians from all over.[29]

The majority view of Rom 16:23 does seem to be the more likely. There is no doubt that when Paul says that Gaius is "host to me" he means that Gaius is giving him lodging at the time of writing. It is natural, then, to infer that the words "and to the whole church" continue the same thought and indicate that Gaius has provided food and shelter for many other Christian travelers. The phrase "the whole church," on this interpretation, must thus be viewed as hyperbolic, but making hyperbolic statements is hardly alien to Paul. Earlier in the same chapter, he speaks hyperbolically of Prisca and Aquila eliciting the thanksgiving of "all the churches of the Gentiles" (Rom 16:4).[30]

James Dunn makes four objections to the majority interpretation of *kai holēs tēs ekklēsias* in Rom 16:23. First, "nowhere else in the undisputed letters does Paul use *ekklesia* of the universal church," only of churches in particular cities or regions.[31] Second, the phrase *holes tēs ekklēsias* is similar to the expression *pasa hē ekklēsia*, which occurs frequently in the LXX for actual gatherings of Israel's representatives. Third, "to speak of Gaius as host of the universal church," even in a hyperbolic way, would set his hospitality above that of others mentioned, such as Phoebe and Prisca and Aquila, "in a wholly invidious (and indeed unpauline) manner."[32] Fourth, where the universality of the gospel was under dispute, as in Rome, "to speak of the universal church would either be unrealistic or factional."[33] But none of these objections hold up. First, the claim that Paul doesn't use *ekklēsia* of the universal church is contradicted by 1 Cor 10:32 and Gal 1:13. Second, the point about *pasa hē ekklēia* is not really relevant since Paul never uses that phrase (one might argue that he deliberately avoids it because

---

29. Cf. Dunn, *Romans 9–16*, 910.

30. See also Rom 1:8, where Paul tells his Roman readers that their "faith is proclaimed throughout the whole world," by which he means that their progress in the faith is widely reported.

31. Dunn, *Romans 9–16*, 910.

32. Ibid.

33. Ibid.

of its "Israel" connotations). Third, it would be no more "invidious" to speak of the excelling hospitality of Gaius than to speak, as the apostle does, of the universal esteem in which Prisca and Aquila are held (Rom 16:4). That Paul makes mention of the special service of some does not devalue the contribution of others, nor does it undermine the Pauline principle of divine impartiality (Gal 2:6). Fourth, in a situation where the universality of the gospel is under dispute it would hardly be any more controversial to speak of the universal church than to speak of the universality of sin and redemption, which Paul does at some length in Romans.

As Robert Jewett notes, a reference to the ecumenical scope of Gaius's hospitality, extending to both Jewish and Gentile Christians, is fully consonant with the theology and ethics of the epistle.[34] It might be argued that the use of the phrase "the whole church" in 1 Cor 14:23 for the Corinthian Christian community stands in favor of the expression bearing the same meaning in Rom 16:23, but the application of a word or phrase in one context does not necessarily determine its meaning in another. As we have just noted, the broader meaning of "the whole church" fits both its immediate and wider context in Romans. If Rom 16:23 cannot be taken as proof of the thesis that a believer's home functioned as the venue of the general assembly at Corinth, then 1 Cor 11:22 and 34 seem to tell against it. In 1 Cor 11:22, Paul asks rhetorically, 'Do you not have homes (*oikias*) to eat and drink in? Or do you show contempt for the church of God?' In 11:34, he issues the instruction: "If you are hungry, eat at home (*en oikō*), so that when you come together, it will not be for your condemnation." The rhetorical questions of 11:22 and the injunction of 11:34 would have significantly less persuasive force if some of the congregants, i.e., the members of the hosting household, *were* eating in their own house. Surprisingly, few interpreters have been alert to the problem that these verses raise for the alleged domestic setting of the community meal at Corinth.

One scholar who has keenly sensed the problem is Jorunn Økland.[35] She notes that 1 Cor 11:22 seems to be "declaring that the *space of the assembly is not identical with the space of the household*."[36]

---

34. Jewett, *Romans*, 981.

35. Finney ("Conflict in Corinth," 85–87) is another scholar who sees the difficulty.

36. Økland, *Women*, 141. Similarly, Thiselton (*First Epistle to the Corinthians*, 865) thinks that Paul is contrasting domestic and ecclesial uses of the same physical space, i.e., the house.

Yet, such a declaration would contradict the assumption, which Økland shares, that the earliest Christians met in houses. Økland therefore offers another reading of the verse. Drawing on David Harvey's notions of multidimensional space, she argues that the differentiation that Paul is making here is between "alternative representations of space," i.e., household and *ekklēsia*, both of which occupy the same material space—that "of a Christian household's *villa* or *insula*."[37] However, by *oikia* in this verse (and *oikos* in 11:34) the apostle clearly means house-buildings, not the 'households' that inhabit them. Moreover, it seems unlikely that the underlying distinction between material space and represented (or symbolic) space, on which Økland's interpretation depends, could have been in Paul's mind, since it derives from modern spatial theory.[38] The natural historical inference to be drawn from 11:22 and 34,[39] if we assume that Paul is accurately mirroring the situation at Corinth, is that none of the homes of the Corinthian believers, whatever physical form these domiciles took, served as the material space of the community meal.

Envisioning Another Kind of Material Setting

If the foregoing deduction is correct, where did the Corinthian fellowship meal take place? In answering this question, illumination might be sought from the realm of Graeco-Roman associations or *collegia*. Over recent years, there has been an increasing recognition of the parallels between associations and early churches.[40] The Corinthian Christian community (as reflected in Paul's letters) in particular has been likened to a Graeco-Roman club.[41] One of the principal activities of associations was dining: club or guild members would meet regu-

---

37. Økland, *Women*, 142–43.

38. This is not to deny the great value of Økland's analysis of 1 Corinthians 11–14 in terms of modern spatial categories. She is undoubtedly correct that for Paul "the material space where the *ekklesia* gathers is rather irrelevant" (*Women*, 142). Paul is much more interested in what, from an etic perspective, can be called "ritually constructed space."

39. We might add to these texts 14:35, which also draws a distinction between *oikos* and *ekklesia*, though 14:34–35 may be an interpolation.

40. E.g., Harland, *Associations, Synagaogues*.

41. E.g., Barclay, "Thessalonica and Corinth," 71; De Vos, *Church and Community Conflicts*, 204–5; Witherington, *Conflict*, 31–32.

larly, often monthly, for the purpose of eating and drinking together. An association meal could take place in a variety of locations (including houses). In many cases, the meal was eaten in an association building or clubhouse.[42] Some clubhouses had demarcated dining spaces (usually *triclinia*), but not all association buildings had specific areas for meals.

When banquets were held, "couches could be set out in the main hall, side room, the porticoes, or the court itself."[43] Religious associations would often have their banquets in temple dining rooms.[44] A funerary club might dine at a cemetery site.[45] Small associations, especially those without premises or sites of their own, might have their communal dinners in rented dining spaces such as gardens (equipped for dining), dining halls and restaurants.[46] It does not seem likely that the Corinthian Christian community had its own clubhouse;[47] nor is it probable that the common meal was held within the precincts of a Graeco-Roman temple, though it is possible that one of the "cells" that made up the Corinthian church met in a temple dining room (1 Cor 8:10). Although it commemorated the death of Jesus, the Corinthian corporate meal was not a funerary banquet held at a tomb. Of the typical venues of association meals, therefore, some form of hired dining facility seems the most plausible option open to the believers at Corinth. A public or semipublic dining venue, such as a restaurant building, would cohere with the ability of "outsiders and unbelievers" (1 Cor 14:23) to enter into the community gathering.[48] Horrell encourages us to use "disciplined imagination," informed by local archaeology, when picturing the kind of spaces in which early Christians could have met.[49] Can the archaeology of first-century Corinth aid us in visualizing the Corinthian church meeting in hired dining space?[50]

---

42. Smith, *Symposium to Eucharist*, 102–4.

43. Dunbabin, *Roman Banquet*, 94.

44. Smith, *Symposium to Eucharist*, 102.

45. Ibid., 104.

46. Dunbabin, *Roman Banquet*, 93; cf. Ascough, "Forms of Commensality," 33–34.

47. Though this has been suggested by De Vos (*Church and Community Conflicts*, 204–5).

48. Though Roman houses (or at least elite houses) too were, to some extent, open to uninvited guests: see the discussion in Balch, *Roman Domestic Art*, 35–38.

49. Horrell, "Domestic Space," 367.

50. Schowalter's wariness of the use of Corinthian archaeology to situate, even

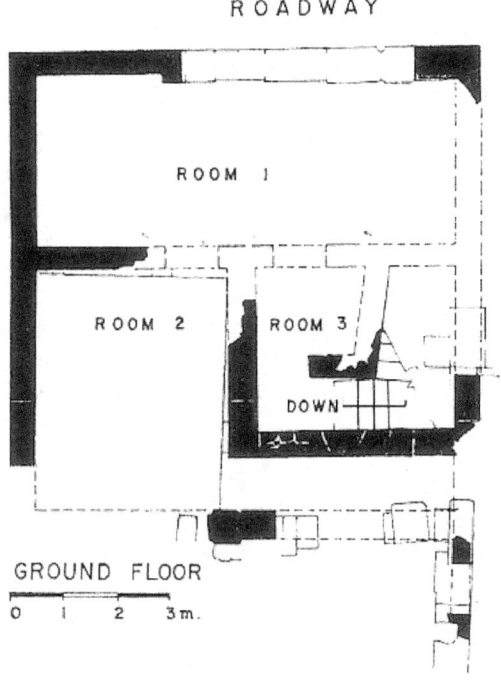

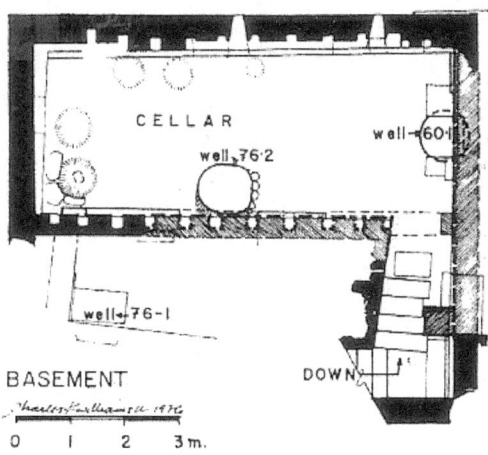

Figure 2.1: Plan of the Roman Cellar Building.

There is one structure, remains of which survive, that can perhaps give some shape to our imaginings.

The Roman Cellar Building (see Figure 2.1) lies on the southwest corner of the Roman forum. It was first discovered in 1960 and excavated in 1976.[51] The excavation uncovered the northern part of the building, revealing three ground-floor rooms and a deep cellar. The cellar measures 3.06 m x 7.82 m and runs the full width of the north side of the building.[52] A rectangular stairwell gives access to the basement, at the southeast corner. A door from the stairwell opens through the south wall of the cellar. Near the centre of the south wall is the shaft of a well. This well (Well 76-2) apparently belonged to an earlier structure dating to before 146 CE.[53] At the west end of the cellar, there lie two wide round pits. Three smaller pits run along the north wall of the cellar, and another well (Well 60-1), which seems to have been used for drainage, is located at the east wall. Although the basement is well preserved, the design of the ground floor is less easy to establish. The northernmost room, referred to as room 1, lies above the cellar. It is the largest of the three ground-floor rooms excavated. The floor of room 1 was originally supported on wooden beams that also formed the ceiling of the basement.[54] To the southwest of room 1 lies a room, identified as room 2, which is nearly square. Here a large deposit of pottery was found. Rooms 1 and 2 were probably connected by a doorway.[55] The southeastern room, room 3, contains the stairway leading down to the cellar. Room 3 was apparently entered from room 1.[56]

Deposits from the well at the east wall of the cellar (Well 60-1), the floor of room 2 and the basement and stairwell, analyzed by Kathleen Warner Slane, elucidate the history of the building.[57] According to Slane, the well fill dates to "the last decade before Christ and perhaps the first few years of the new era," which was probably the time of the

---

imaginatively, the *ekklesia* in a particular kind of space ("Seeking Shelter," 341) seems over-cautious.

51. Robinson, "Excavations at Corinth, 1960"; Williams, "Corinth 1976," 58–62.
52. Williams, "Corinth 1976," 59.
53. Ibid., 59, 61.
54. Slane, "Deposits," 274.
55. Wright, "Tiberian Deposit," 137.
56. Slane, "Deposits," 273.
57. Ibid., 317.

building's construction. The floor deposit from room 2 dates to the Tiberian period. The building appears to have suffered minor damage in an earthquake in 22/23 CE. The consequent repairs involved the raising of the floor level of room 2 (hence the floor deposit). The cellar deposit dates to the third quarter of the first century CE. The basement and stairwell were filled in as a result of damage sustained during a further earthquake in the reign of Vespasian in the 70s CE. The alteration was probably made to stabilize the building. The structure continued in use until the fourth century.

The Roman Cellar Building is not a house; its size and position indicate that it was a building open to the public.[58] The floor deposit found in room 2 consisted of the remnants of plates for eating, large serving platters, drinking cups, cooking pots and pans and other kitchenware.[59] The large quantity of material connected with the preparation and serving of food leads Slane to conclude that the Cellar Building, in its earliest phase, was "most likely to be a restaurant or a tavern."[60] If both rooms 1 and 2 were used for dining,[61] the building could accommodate around forty diners: twenty-five or so persons in room 1; twelve to fifteen persons in room 3.[62] A figure of this order has often been suggested as the size (or base size) of the Corinthian congregation.[63]

If we imagine the Corinthians holding their common meal in an environment like this, they would have been divided between two dining areas, one larger than the other. Spatial divisions among din-

58. Wright, "Tiberian Deposit," 174.

59. Ibid., 173–74.

60. Ibid., 174. Walbank ("Foundation and Planning," 123), however, thinks the building was "a formal dining-place for a *collegium*." It is possible, though, that an association might occasionally rent out its dining facilities (when they were not in use for its own banquets) to increase revenue.

61. Pompeian structures identified as inns and taverns often have a secondary dining area in addition to the main dining area: Dunbabin, *Roman Banquet*, 93. Slane, however, takes room 2 to be a pantry (Wright, "Tiberian Deposit," 174).

62. Applying the formula given by Osiek and Balch (*Families*, 201), "one half-square meter per person and an equal half square meter for furniture," to the 24 sq. m (or so) of room 1 and the 12 sq. m (or so) of room 2.

63. E.g., Dunn, *1 Corinthians*, 171; Murphy-O'Connor, as indicated above; Witherington, *Conflict*, 32. As Caragounis ("House Church," 413) points out, the phrase *he ekklesia hole* in 1 Cor 14:23 does not require the attendance of every single member of the community; "the overwhelming majority would satisfy the phrase."

ers at an association banquet were not unusual. The guildhall of the carpenters at Ostia, for example, had four distinct dining rooms, all of which were probably in operation in times of banquets.[64] It is possible that a division of the Corinthians into two dining areas would have been made on socioeconomic grounds, with the more socially distinguished members of the church dining in the smaller and perhaps nicer room. However, the Cellar Building itself offers no archaeological basis for speculation along this line. If the Corinthian believers were split between two rooms for the meal, presumably they would have tried to assemble in the larger salon for plenary worship. The room would no doubt have had to be cleared of non-fixed furnishings. Most of those assembled would have had to sit on the floor (perhaps on mats). Interestingly, as Balch point outs,[65] Paul presumes that the congregants were seated during communal worship (1 Cor 14:30). A gathering of around forty persons in a room the size of room 1 of the Cellar Building would have involved uncomfortable overcrowding, so we may have to reckon with an overspill into the second room.

It must be emphasized that there is no evidence whatever that Paul's church at Corinth ever gathered in the Roman Cellar Building. Moreover, while there is evidence to suggest that the structure may have served as a dining establishment before the earthquake of 22/23 CE, we do not know how the building was used after this date. I appeal to the Roman Cellar Building simply as a near-contemporary, local example of a type of non-domestic dining space in which the Corinthian common meal might be located. As noted above, it is unlikely that the Roman Cellar Building could have accommodated more than around forty diners (though additional dining space might have been available in the unexcavated southern part of the building), and a significantly larger number have been proposed for the church at Corinth at the time of Paul's Corinthian correspondence. Craig De Vos, for example, thinks that the community at this time would have run to around one hundred persons,[66] and Richard Hays suggests a number between 150 and 200 (though Hays recognizes that "these figures are on the high side").[67] A Christian community of such figures

64. Smith, *Symposium to Eucharist*, 103.
65. Osiek and Balch, *Families*, 203.
66. De Vos, *Church and Community Conflicts*, 204.
67. Hays, *First Corinthians*, 7. Caragounis ("House Church," 413) thinks in terms of "hundreds of members."

would have required a much large dining hall.[68] In warmer months, though, the believers could have dined outside, either in a large garden or free public space (probably outside city limits).[69] It is possible that the Corinthians, whatever the size of the congregation, varied the location of the communal meal, sometimes meeting in indoor dining space and sometimes, in good weather, dining outdoors.

Conclusion

Scholarly attempts to envision the *domestic* setting of the Corinthian community meal run aground on 1 Cor 11:22 and 34, which contrast believers' domiciles with the physical space of assembly. If, as these verses seem to indicate, the corporate meal was not held in the home of a believer, some form of rented dining establishment seems a likely venue, though the Corinthians could have dined outside when weather allowed. The Roman Cellar Building, which seems to have functioned as a public dining establishment in the early first century CE, represents a type of space in which the Corinthian Christians, if they numbered around forty persons, might have gathered together to dine and worship. Scholarship on house churches is increasingly moving away from a narrow focus on one type of house—the *domus* or atrium house—as the setting of early Christian assembly. David Balch has been among those calling for more attention to be paid to the assortment of domestic spaces in the Roman world that could have served as places for Christian gatherings.[70] One might extend this appeal and ask for greater consideration to be given to *non-domestic* possibilities for meeting.

---

68. Caragounis ("House Church," 414) suggests that the Corinthian Christians could have rented one of the (excavated) civic basilicas, a suggestion also made by Finney ("Conflict in Corinth," 85–87, 230–31).

69. An outdoor setting might help to explain Paul's prohibition of women's speech in 1 Cor 14:34–35 (if these verses are authentic).

70. Balch, "Rich Pompeiian Houses."

Bibliography

Ascough, Richard S. "Forms of Commensality in Greco-Roman Associations." *CW* 102:1 (2008) 33–45.

Balch, David L. "Rich Pompeiian Houses, Shops for Rent, and the Huge Apartment Building in Herculaneum as Typical Spaces for Pauline House Churches." *JSNT* 27.1 (2004) 27–47.

———. *Roman Domestic Art and Early House Churches*. WUNT 228. Tübingen: Mohr/Siebeck, 2008.

Banks, Robert. *Paul's Idea of Community: The Early House Churches in their Cultural Setting*. Exeter: Paternoster, 1980.

Barclay, J. M. G. "Thessalonica and Corinth: Social Contrasts in Pauline Christianity." *JSNT* 47(1992) 49–74.

Caragounis, C. C. "A House Church in Corinth: An Inquiry into the Structure of Early Corinthian Christianity." In *Saint Paul and Corinth: 1950 Years since the Writing of the Epistles to the Corinthians*, edited by C. J. Belezos 1:365–418. Athens: Psichogios, 2009.

De Vos, Craig S. *Church and Community Conflicts: The Relationships of the Thessalonian, Corinthian, and Philippian Churches with their Wider Civic Communities*. SBLDS 168. Atlanta: Scholars, 1999.

Dunbabin, K. M. D. *The Roman Banquet: Images of Conviviality*. Cambridge: Cambridge University Press, 2003.

Dunn, James D. G. *1 Corinthians*. NTG. Sheffield: Sheffield Academic, 1995.

———. *Romans 9–16*. WBC 38B. Dallas: Word, 1988.

Finney, M. "Conflict in Corinth: the Appropriateness of Honour-Shame as the Primary Social Context." PhD diss., University of St Andrews, 2004.

Gehring, R. W. *House Church and Mission: The Importance of Household Structures in Early Christianity*. Peabody, MA: Hendrickson, 2004.

Harland, Philip A. *Associations, Synagogues, and Congregations: Claiming a Place in Ancient Mediterranean Society*. Minneapolis: Fortress, 2003.

Hays, Richard B. *First Corinthians*. Interpretation. Louisville: John Knox, 1997.

Horrell, David G. "Domestic Space and Christian Meetings at Corinth: Imagining New Contexts and the Buildings East of the Theatre." *NTS* 50 (2004) 349–69.

Jewett, Robert. *Romans: A Commentary*. Hermeneia. Minneapolis: Fortress, 2007.

Lampe, Peter. "The Eucharist: Identifying with Christ on the Cross." *Interpretation* 48 (1994) 36–49.

Meggitt, Justin J. *Paul, Poverty and Survival*. Studies of the New Testament and Its World. Edinburgh: T. & T. Clark, 1998.

Murphy-O'Connor, Jerome. *Keys to First Corinthians: Revisiting the Major Issues*. Oxford: Oxford University Press, 2009.

———. *St. Paul's Corinth: Texts and Archaeology*. 3rd rev. and expanded ed. Collegeville: Liturgical, 2002.

Økland, Jorunn. *Women in Their Place: Paul and the Corinthian Discourse of Gender and Sanctuary Space*. JSNTSup 269. London: T. & T. Clark, 2004.

Osiek, Carolyn, and David L. Balch. *Families in the New Testament World: Households and House Churches*. Louisville: Westminster John Knox, 1997.

Robinson, H. S. "Excavations at Corinth, 1960." *Hisperia* 46 (1962) 111–12.

Schowalter, Daniel N. "Seeking Shelter in Roman Corinth: Archaeology and the Placement of Paul's Communities." In *Corinth in Context: Comparative Studies on Religion and Society*, edited by S. J. Friesen et al., 327–41. NovTSup 134. Leiden: Brill, 2010.

Slane, K. W. "Two Deposits from the Early Roman Cellar Building, Corinth." *Hesperia* 55 (1986) 271–318.

Smith, Dennis E. *From Symposium to Eucharist: The Banquet in the Early Christian World*. Minneapolis, MN: Fortress Press, 2003.

Thiselton, Anthony C. *The First Epistle to the Corinthians*. NIGTC. Grand Rapids: Eerdmans, 2000.

Walbank, M. E. H. "The Foundation and Planning of Early Roman Corinth." *JRA* 10 (1997) 95–130.

Williams, C. K. "Corinth 1976: Forum Southwest." *Hesperia* 46 (1977) 40–81.

Williams, C. K., and O. H. Zervos. "Corinth, 1985: East of the Theater." *Hesperia* 55 (1986) 129–75.

Witherington III, Ben. *Conflict and Community in Corinth: A Socio-Rhetorical Commentary on 1 and 2 Corinthians*. Grand Rapids: Eerdmans, 1995.

Wright, K. S. "A Tiberian Pottery Deposit from Corinth." *Hesperia* 49 (1980) 135–77.

3

Reading 1 Corinthians 7 through the Eyes of Families

Margaret Y. MacDonald

Beginning with his pioneering investigations on the household codes, his work in collaboration with Carolyn Osiek on house churches and households, and more recent studies on art in the Roman world, David L. Balch has continued to challenge scholars to consider "families" as a key category of analysis in the study of early Christianity.[1] Balch's work has caused me to rethink many of my conclusions and to expand my interpretative horizons to take account of evidence—both textual and material—that I might once have thought of as irrelevant for understanding early church interactions and identity. In this essay I propose to return to the conclusions I reached in a 1990 article, "Women Holy in Body and Spirit: The Social Setting of 1 Corinthians 7" and to reconsider them in light of our expanding knowledge of families in the Roman world.

In "Women Holy in Body and Spirit," I argued that Paul's rhetorical balancing of exhortations to men and women masked a special concern for women—the virgins (παρθένος) holy in body and spirit (1 Cor 7:34; cf. 1 Cor 7:25, 28, 36–38). I argued that this focus on women was related both to the tendency for men, in an honor-shame culture, to define their own identities (their honor) in relation to the sexual purity (the shame) of their wives and to the initiative of women them-

---

1. Balch, *Let Wives Be Submissive*; Osiek and Balch, *Families*; Balch and Osiek, *Early Christian Families*; Balch, *Roman Domestic Art*.

selves in embracing asceticism.[2] In the same year, Antoinette Clark Wire published a more complete rhetorical analysis of 1 Corinthians which placed women—especially the Corinthian women prophets—at the centre of investigation, essentially interpreting the entire epistle in light of their concerns.[3] The feminist scholarship of the 1980's and 1990's was in many ways an important influence leading to work on early Christian families.[4] In bringing the complexities of women's lives to light, feminist scholars inevitably dealt with family issues, from the implications of Jesus's teaching on divorce for women to the complex negotiations required by women's marriages to nonbelievers.[5] But in examining gender constructions more broadly, feminist scholars prepared the way for explorations of familial metaphors, with their range of possible relationships to lived-out reality, which might even include the rejection of family life altogether.[6]

I remain convinced that the feminist lens is of great use in illuminating the social setting of 1 Corinthians 7 despite some arguments in recent scholarship against a special preoccupation with ascetic women in the text.[7] However, using "families" as a category of analysis brings out aspects of the lives of women and other audience members which otherwise do not stand out as clearly; it enables us to grasp more completely the probable implications of Paul's thought for the house-church groups comprised of members of various households in the Roman world. I will begin with a brief discussion of asceticism and family life, followed by an examination of the life of couples, the issue of slaves and sexuality, the significance of the presence of children, and the relationship between household space and ritual space.

---

2. MacDonald, "Women Holy," 171–73.

3. Although published in the same year, Wire cites my work on 1 Corinthians 7. See Wire, *Corinthian Women Prophets*, 224–25.

4. This can be seen for example in the way women's lives are treated by Osiek and Balch in *Families*, 103–55.

5. See MacDonald, "Early Christian Women Married."

6. See especially Moxnes, *Constructing Early Christian Families*.

7. See a detailed, though in my opinion not completely convincing, response to the "ascetic hypothesis" (including the role of women) in May, "*The Body for the Lord*," 144–79.

Asceticism and Family Reconstruction/Disruption

In my article on 1 Corinthians 7, I argued that women, probably inspired by ideals associated with such sayings as the baptismal proclamation of Gal 3:28, sought to transcend sexual differentiation through avoidance of marriage and childrearing.[8] The notion that women were among the main proponents of asceticism gains support especially from Paul's interruption of parallelism in 1 Cor 7:33–34, to speak of women (unmarried and virgin) who strive to be holy in body and spirit and from the references to the widows (without references to male counterparts) in 1 Cor 7:39–40 in a manner that suggests that he expects to be contradicted by these seemingly independent women (I think I too have the Spirit of God!).[9] We should also consider the trajectory of ascetic women that clearly has left its mark in the literature of the first and early second centuries. The efforts on the part of the author of the Pastoral Epistles to limit the enrollment of widows to that of older women and to encourage younger widows to remarry suggests a certain (undesirable from the Pastoral Paul's perspective) gravitation of women in the direction of asceticism (1 Tim 5:3–16). Ignatius's puzzling reference to "the virgins called widows" (Ign. *Smyrn.* 13.1) and Hermas's direction to Grapte to exhort "the widows and orphans" (Herm. *Vis.* 2.4.3) also encourage us to consider seriously the possibility that later groups of ascetic and celibate women had a forerunner among the women of Corinth.

A focus on families, however, can lead us to read the efforts of ascetic women as less solitary than one might first imagine and more a matter of the reconstruction of families than the complete rejection of families, albeit there is certainly an element of family disruption reflected in 1 Corinthians 7. First of all, in a desire to remain unmarried, the widows of Corinth were demonstrating the same resolve as Roman women elsewhere, especially elite women who were increasingly publicly visible and independent in the management of their own familial affairs.[10] Women in the Roman world were household heads, as were the New Testament Mary (Acts 12:12–17), Lydia (Acts 16:14–15, 40), Nympha (Col 4:15), and probably also Phoebe (Rom 16:1–2), along

---

8. See MacDonald, "Women Holy," 161–70. I was influenced especially by MacDonald, *No Male and Female*.

9. See detailed argument in MacDonald, "Women Holy," 171–73.

10. On this topic see especially Winter, *Roman Wives*.

with other women we hear about in the writings of the Apostolic fathers such as Tavia (Ign. *Smyrn.* 13.2) and Grapte (*Herm. Vis.* 2.4.3). These early Christian women have often been understood to be widows. Although scholars continue to debate whether such a community actually existed, Philo of Alexandria's description of the *Therapeutae* celebrates the virginity/celibacy of older women in a manner that calls to mind the relationship between spiritual experience and remaining unmarried that seems to be reflected in both Paul's advice and the behavior of the Corinthians themselves (*Contempl.* 84–85).[11] The *Therapeutae* are presented by Philo as an alternative to traditional family life, but the sexual purity of these women who have spurned both the "pleasures of the body" and "desire for offspring" is described in highly conventional terms (*Contempl.* 68).

There are other possible indications of asceticism leading to family reconstruction/disruption in 1 Corinthians 7. For example, the fact that the exhortation to females is longer and precedes the corresponding instruction to males on divorce in 1 Cor 7:10–11 may suggest that women were the main instigators of the separations; while asceticism may have offered the motivation, it could easily have been combined with the desire to manage one's own household. This may sound like an anachronistic assumption, but there is compelling comparative evidence to suggest that such aspirations cannot be ruled out.[12] Similarly, the exhortations concerning mixed marriage in 1 Cor 7:12–16 offer strong indication of family disruption, and, from the point of view of the husband who expected his wife to adhere to his religious alliances, also of family disloyalty. Yet, the description of the activities of the Matron of Rome married to an immoral pagan husband by Justin Martyr points to female initiative in divorce (despite initial inclinations to follow Paul's advice to remain married and encouragement to do so from others). The Matron's resolve extends to setting her affairs in order even in the face of the possibility of a violent backlash which eventually ensues against her teacher (Justin, *Second Apology*, 2).[13]

---

11. For detailed argument see MacDonald, "Women Holy," 168–70. For recent scholarly debate concerning Philo's description see especially Taylor, *Jewish Women*.

12. On women managing households for themselves see especially Osiek and MacDonald, *Woman's Place*, 144–63.

13. See detailed discussion of this case in MacDonald, *Early Christian Women*, 205–13.

One of the clearest signs of family disruption in Corinth comes from the ambiguous passage, 1 Cor 7:36–38. Unless the "spiritual marriage" interpretation is preferred (an option which cannot be ruled out altogether [cf. 1 Cor 9:5] despite the case against in 1 Cor 7:2–5), it is most likely that the virgin is either the fiancée of the man in question in 1 Cor 7:36 or a daughter who is at risk of missing out on the opportunities for marriage.[14] As will be discussed further below, marriage was the main transition point from childhood to adulthood for women in the Roman world and to remain unmarried—for better or worse—would leave females in a liminal/transitional state, essentially as perpetual children. Here and in his teaching on mixed marriage (1 Cor 7:12–16), especially in the strange reference to the children in 1 Cor 7:14c, we find Paul in conversation with the families that populated the house church(es) of Corinth. While he was not alone in his way of life in the ancient word, Paul's celibacy set him apart from the standard social expectations of his day—both Jewish and non-Jewish. Paul's preference was not apparently inspired *primarily* by a desire for greater holiness or withdrawal from uncleanness, but was mainly a result of his conviction that the form of this world was passing away (1 Cor 7:31).[15] Yet even given Paul's belief that believers ultimately belonged to another realm (Phil 3:20) and that celibacy was a way of life he recommended for others, 1 Corinthians 7 reveals him as trying (struggling?) to sort out what his priorities mean for life organized in terms of households of couples, children, slaves and (probably) former slaves. Paul issues some challenges to the dominant social order by encouraging celibacy for the truly gifted, young and old, in the face of Augustan legislation and imperial ideology which encouraged marriage and fecundity and the remarriage of the widowed and divorced.[16] He also clearly approved of wives joining the movement without their husbands. But his cautious counsel to marry and to remain married

---

14. For a thorough discussion of the translation and grammatical issues and full consideration of the comparative evidence, see especially Winter, "Puberty or Passion?" He argues that the case refers to an engaged couple and that "full of sexual passion" (referring to the fiancé and not the fiancée) is the apposite rendering of the term, ὑπέρακμος.

15. See Wimbush, *Paul the Worldly Ascetic*; Wimbush, "Contemptus Mundi."

16. Scholars debate the extent of the impact of Augustan Legislation, especially among the non-elite classes. On the enforcement of the legislation see Pomeroy, *Goddesses*, 166.

in a variety of circumstances is sometimes less strikingly alternative than one would expect.[17] As for the Corinthians themselves, ongoing work on early Christian families should make us cautious with respect to reading the motivations of community members underlying 1 Corinthians 7 as one-dimensional. Notwithstanding the clear evidence of ascetic currents, other factors were also most certainly at play such as the fate of children if parents divorced or women remarried after widowhood (in both circumstances children remained the property of the male head of the household) or, as will be discussed further below, the implications of Paul's marriage/celibacy teaching for relations with slaves.

Marriage, Sexuality, and Slavery

In my 1990 article on the social setting of 1 Corinthians 7, I argued that the predominant point of contrast in the text was not between celibacy and marriage, but between celibacy/marriage and the dreaded disease, immorality (πορνεία). Immorality serves as unifying theme in chapters 5–7.[18] In the case of 1 Corinthians 7 it is on account of the temptation of immorality that Paul argues that marriage should take place among those who possess the gift of celibacy and that physical union must remain an integral part of the life of the couple (1 Cor 7:1–7, 9). But who are the couples of 1 Corinthians 7? New research on families in the Roman world complicates our answer to this basic question. We cannot assume that these couples were what we conceive of today as "legally married." As Osiek and I have argued it is by no means clear, even in a Romanized city like Corinth, how many members of the church would have been eligible for legally licit marriages by Roman standards and even doubtful whether this would have been of any real concern.[19] There were many forms of co-habitation (including concubinage) and a variety of parenting possibilities which did not always include parents and children living in the same houses. Inscriptional evidence demonstrates the use of marital terminology by slaves to describe their unions even when no legal capacity existed

---

17. See MacDonald and Vaage, "Unclean but Holy Children."
18. See also May, *"Body for the Lord."* In contrast to May, however, I do not view this as an argument against the "ascetic hypothesis."
19. See Osiek and MacDonald, *Woman's Place*, 23.

for marriage between slaves.[20] We cannot rule out the possibility that when Paul exhorts "married" couples he has slave couples and their children within his purview. Once we allow for this possibility, we open up various other possibilities about complex family situations among the Corinthians and we inevitably deal with questions about marriage, slavery, and sexuality.

1 Corinthians 7 has often been examined under the rubric of marriage, but rarely examined under the rubric of "parenting." In the only reference to real (not metaphorical) children in his letters (1 Cor 7:14; see further below), Paul makes it clear that children are present in the community. The limited possibility for birth control in the ancient world means that the presence of children where there are couples is inevitable, even allowing for some spiritual marriages and ascetic tendencies. Reading 1 Corinthians 7 through eyes of families reminds us that Paul could well be speaking to an audience that included slave women who brought their children to meetings and whose non-believing "husbands" were the domestic slaves of nonbelievers.[21] Once again if we allow for the slave presence to overlap with the "married" couple presence, we need to rethink the exhortations concerning mixed marriage. Behind the exhortations in 1 Cor 7:12–16 we need to envision slave parents (one believing and one non-believing) as well as free and freed parents (one believing and one non-believing). The situation becomes even more complicated when we allow for the fact that in all likelihood, the slave membership of the Corinthian congregation (see 1 Cor 7:21) would have included slaves (and slave or freed concubines?) of non-believers (cf. 1 Tim 6:1–2; 1 Pet 2:18–19). In the case of slave families, the *paterfamilias*—who could be a believer or not—was a parental figure whose authority must be kept in mind even if it is not mentioned explicitly.

The prerogatives of the husband and/or *paterfamilias* continue to shape 1 Corinthians 7, especially in 1 Cor 7:36–38, regardless of Paul's remarkably equalizing rhetoric in 1 Cor 7:2–7 with respect to sexuality.[22] The "marriage" of slave girls to other household slaves—

20. See Martin, "Slave Families."

21. For more detailed discussion see MacDonald and Vaage, "Unclean but Holy Children."

22. There has been considerable debate about how to read Paul's equalizing language. Some ancient authors did however combine hierarchical notions of marriage with emphasis on marital unity and marriage as a symbiotic relationship. See for example Plutarch, *Advice to the Bride and Groom* 142F–43A.

a situation possibly in view in 1 Cor 7:36—was not only a conventional familial expectation but also clearly a strategy of slave management.[23] Although slaves formed familial alliances among themselves and there existed a certain qualified recognition of slave families in the Roman world, the power of heads of households to separate slave families and to make use of slaves, including children, for their own sexual purposes is indisputable.[24] Given Paul's silence on the sexual use of slaves and the fact that it was such a widespread cultural expectation, we should be hesitant to conclude that such practices ceased among the first believers. However, there are a limited number of texts from the Roman world which express disapproval of the sexual use of slaves. Among the most relevant evidence is the first century BCE Philadelphian inscription from a cultic association which calls for husbands to stay true to their own wives and avoid sexual relations with other married women, slave or free (though nothing is said about *unmarried women*). Moreover, adherents are to avoid defiling or corrupting boys or virgins (μηδὲ φθερῖν μηδὲ παῖδα μηδὲ παρθένον).[25] Paul's qualified approval of the Corinthian slogan, "it is well for a man not to touch a woman," may be intended for broader purposes than the curtailing of ascetic extremism such as limiting the use of slaves (and prostitutes who were often slaves) as sexual outlets.[26]

In addition to such concrete features of familial interactions, Roman Family Studies can lead to greater appreciation of the cultural and ideological importance of married life in the Roman world. There has been great attention given to the origins of Paul's thought in 1 Corinthians 7 by New Testament scholars, especially in comparison to the philosophers of the day.[27] Yet, the interchange between Paul and the Corinthians requires that we consider also both the impact of his thought in community life and the attraction of certain ideas among the Corinthians themselves—the matters about which they wrote (1 Cor 7:1). If 1 Corinthians 7 reveals a special focus on the sexual

23. See Varro, *Agriculture* I.17.5; Columella, *Agriculture* I.8.5.

24. See Laes, "Desperately Different?"; Glancy, *Slavery*; MacDonald, "Slavery, Sexuality and House Churches."

25. For inscription see *SIG* 3:985. For detailed discussion see MacDonald, "Slavery, Sexuality and House Churches," 98–99.

26. See Ciampa, "Revisiting the Euphemism."

27. On 1 Corinthians 7 and the philosophy of the day, see especially Deming, *Paul on Marriage*.

purity of women, the male prerogatives in marriage matters and the ability of women to wield considerable power are related to the traditional function of virgins and monogamous brides to represent the shame (concern for reputation) of the house or community in ancient Mediterranean culture.[28] As is highlighted in Paul's reference to the Corinthians themselves as a chaste bride (2 Cor 11:2–3) and the author of Ephesians' use of metaphorical language to describe the identity of the *ekklēsia* as a church-bride, the sexual purity of women was a potent symbol of community identity (Eph 5:25–27). The speeches of politicians, the arguments of philosophers, and inscriptional and artistic evidence illustrate that particularly in the case of the unified married couple, presentations of family life served a variety of ideological purposes ranging from the celebration of the aspirations of particular family units in the case of funerary commemorations to political hopes for the stability of the Empire.[29] It should come as no surprise that Paul and the members of his communities construed marriage and the rejection of marriage as a means of expressing key aspects of their identity. Moreover, such marriage matters need to considered far more than they have been to date as central to the political response of Paul and his communities to the Empire and to the vision of a harmonious state modeled on a harmonious household.

The Presence of Children and Church Space

As noted above, using "families" as a key category of analysis can also cause us to rethink the shape of Paul's audience and to reassess the significance of certain references in his letters. Paul makes a fleeting and obscure reference to children in 1 Cor 7:14 which the NRSV translates as follows: "Otherwise, your children would be unclean, but as it is, they are holy." Scholarly debate has never solved the problem of the meaning of this verse despite various attempts, including an examination of Paul's theology and ethics in the hope of finding a general pattern of consistency, and explanations wrought by means of comparison with Rabbinic thought.[30] In addition, notwithstanding

---

28. See MacDonald, *Early Christian Women*, 144–54.

29. For detailed discussion see Osiek and MacDonald, *Woman's Place*, 118–43. See also Dixon, "The Sentimental Ideal," 99–113.

30. For illustration of these two approaches see Murphy-O'Connor, "Works with-

great scholarly attention, generally speaking scholars have neglected to consider why an appeal to the status of children (probably young children still living with their parents) might serve in Paul's mind as a convincing and seemingly obvious argument in favor of the preservation of mixed marriages (not to mention the celibate Paul's usual lack of interest in children as community members). Most evidently, even given their dubious and uncertain past, the holy children seem to have been part of the community but at one level their attachment to the community was in practical terms quite tentative and uncertain—how often, for example, were they able to attend church gatherings? We might also think about what would happen to these children in case of the separation of the parents. Paul presents the holiness of children as something obvious, and never states that they would become unclean in the case of divorce. But he was surely aware of different familial arrangements involving children.

Remarriage after divorce or widowhood was commonplace in the Roman world and children often lived with half-siblings and step-siblings and often mothers had children living in other houses.[31] Ties between mothers and children were especially vulnerable as children remained under the *potestas* of their father after divorce; widows often could continue to manage the affairs of their children who still lived with them, but remarriage brought with it much greater likelihood of the deceased father's family exercising authority over children.[32] The family strife associated with mixed marriage, which no doubt included the pressures for women of remaining married to hostile and suspicious husbands, also included the very real possibility of abandonment of mothers and children and the separation of mothers from their children. Paul's teaching on divorce, his recommendation that a widow is happier if she remains as she is, and his teaching on mixed marriage need to be read through the eyes of families negotiating the possibilities of ongoing contact with children.

If the obscure reference to children in 1 Cor 7:14 reminds us of the presence of children in the community, it is valuable to investigate how children and childhood impact other portions of the text.

---

out Faith," 349–61; Gillihan, "Jewish Laws," 711–44. For full discussion of the interpretative issue see MacDonald and Vaage, "Unclean but Holy Children."

31. See Bradley, *Discovering the Roman Family*, 171.

32. On the circumstances of widows, see Dixon, *Roman Mother*, 66–67.

Although in my 1990 article I highlighted the importance of the lives of virgins to the social setting of 1 Corinthians 7, using "families" as a central category of analysis leads me to examine the relationship between the lives of virgins and childhood. Studies of childhood in the Roman world have illustrated that the end of childhood was a flexible concept in this context, based on shifting stages of development rather than rigid biological-age designations.[33] The distinction between the children of 1 Cor 7:14 and the virgins of marriageable age referred to elsewhere in the chapter, is far from clear and must often have been a matter of small degree (cf. 1 Cor 7:25, 28, 34, 36–38). Girls were typically married between twelve and sixteen (to significantly older men) and for them marriage was the most visible sign of adulthood. Household rituals demarcated this transition, including the ceremony involving the bride's offering of her dolls and toys to the household gods or to Venus on the eve of her wedding celebration.[34] In a very real sense, however, marriage was merely an initiation into adulthood with much education at the hands of older females required after the wedding day (cf. 2 Tim 1:5; 3:15; Tit 2:3–5).[35]

What, then, did it mean for virgins to remain virgins in the families where one or more members were members of the Pauline churches? Was the association of female virginity with childhood a factor contributing to its potency? Paul typically attributes holiness to the whole of the believing community, and only rarely to particular groups within that community. Intriguingly, Paul attributes the designation of holiness only to two (or possibly three) groups in 1 Corinthians 7: the children (and by association? the non-believing spouses) of 1 Cor 7:14 and those who fall under the category of "unmarried woman and virgin" in 1 Cor 7:34.

Children may not have been very important to Paul (though we cannot really be certain of this given his extensive metaphorical refer-

---

33. This is in contrast to the modern connection between biological age and the rights, privileges, and responsibilities of adulthood (driving at 16, voting at 18 etc). See Rawson, *Children and Childhood*, 134–45.

34. See Rawson, *Children and Childhood*, 145, citing Varro in Nonius 863.5; Persius, *Satires* 2.70. On the age of marriage, see Dixon, *The Roman Mother*, 31.

35. Among Roman girls there was no true coming-of-age ceremony as in the case of the boys with the *toga uirilis*. Rawson (*Children and Childhood*, 142) notes the flexibility concerning the age of the boy undergoing the ceremony: "a boy might go through the ritual of attaining manhood by changing his boyhood garb (the *toga praetexta*) for the *toga uirilis*. Ages known for this ceremony range from 13–18."

ences to children), but they were almost certainly important to many members of the Corinthian congregation and Paul simply could not escape them in house churches even if he wanted to dissociate himself as much as possible from settled domestic life. By choosing the house church as a meeting place for the *ekklēsia*, Paul was entering a world (whether a large *domus* or smaller accommodations) where the presence of children was ubiquitous.[36] Some recent scholarship on Corinth has moved away from setting house-church groups in the context of the Roman villa in the direction of simple two-room dwellings.[37] If we are to envision the house church in cramped accommodation, then the presence of babies, toddlers, children of all ages would simply have been unavoidable and true freedom from familial distraction impossible.

Concentration on the nature and symbolic meaning of church space may offer insight into area of tension between Paul and certain Corinthian families or family members. Here the work of Jorunn Økland is especially suggestive. On the basis of 1 Corinthians 11–14, she argues that the Corinthian discourse of gender functions to create sanctuary space which is potentially at odds with the aspirations and faith commitments of the women of the community. Økland is mainly concerned with how Paul's discourse concerning women's ritual roles and ritual clothing leads to the gendering of the *ekklēsia* space as primarily male space.[38] She finds support in 1 Cor 11:22 and especially in 1 Cor 14:32–34 where Paul distinguishes between the space of the assembly where women should keep silent and the space of the household where women can ask their husbands questions. Within the *ekklēsia* space, "there is a particular pattern of action and a particular place for everything following a cosmic order."[39]

If Økland is correct in her interpretation of Paul's position, the family complexities as they emerge in 1 Corinthians 7 can help see the tenuousness of the Apostle's situation in terms of the real lives of the diverse Corinthian population. Order, hierarchy, silence all can easily

---

36. See Rawson, *Children and Childhood*, 214; also Osiek and MacDonald, *Woman's Place*, 93.

37. See Horrell, "Domestic Space." Horrell critiques the influential work of Murphy-O'Connor, which associates life in the house-church with the Roman villa. Murphy-O'Connor, *St. Paul's Corinth*.

38. Økland, *Women in Their Place*, 178.

39. Ibid., 151.

break down in a familial atmosphere and where a curious child can slip in unnoticed from the street, the playground of many children in the cities of the Roman Empire.[40] In the end, 1 Corinthians 7 reveals the social reality of families behind Paul's recommendations, waiting to complicate every church scenario and ascetical enterprise.

---

40. See Rawson, *Children and Childhood*, 211.

Bibliography

Balch, David L. *Let Wives Be Submissive: The Domestic Code in 1 Peter*. SBLMS 26. Chico, CA: Scholars, 1981.

Balch, David L., and Carolyn Osiek, editors. *Early Christian Families in Context: An Interdisciplinary Dialogue*. Religion, Marriage and Family. Grand Rapids: Eerdmans, 2003.

———. *Roman Domestic Art and Early House Churches*. WUNT 228. Tübingen: Mohr/Siebeck, 2008.

Bradley, Keith R. *Discovering the Roman Family: Studies in Roman Social History*. New York: Oxford University Press, 1991.

Ciampa, Roy E. "Revisiting the Euphemism in 1 Corinthians 7.1." *JSNT* (2009) 325–38.

Deming, W. *Paul on Marriage and Celibacy: The Hellenistic Background of 1 Corinthians 7*. SNTSMS 83. Cambridge: Cambridge University Press, 1995.

Dixon, Suzanne. *The Roman Mother*. London: Croom Helm, 1988.

———. "The Sentimental Ideal of the Woman Family." In *Marriage, Divorce, and Children in Ancient Rome*, edited by Beryl Rawson, 99–113. Oxford: Clarendon, 1991.

Gillihan, Yonder Moynihan. "Jewish Laws on Illicit Marriage, the Defilement of Offspring, and the Holiness of the Temple: A New Halakic Interpretation of 1 Corinthians 7:14." *JBL* 121 (2002) 711–44.

Glancy, Jennifer A. *Slavery in Early Christianity*. Oxford: Oxford University Press, 2002.

Horrell, David G. "Domestic Space and Christian Meetings at Corinth: Imagining New Contexts and the Buildings East of the Theatre." *NTS* 50 (2004) 349–69.

Laes, Christian. "Desperately Different? Delicia Children in the Roman Household." In *Early Christian Families in Context: An Interdisciplinary Dialogue*, edited by David L. Balch and Carolyn Osiek, 298–324. Religion, Marriage and Family. Grand Rapids, Eerdmans, 2003.

MacDonald, Dennis Ronald *There Is No Male and Female: The Fate of a Dominical Saying in Paul and Gnosticism*. HDR 20. Philadelphia: Fortress, 1987.

MacDonald, Margaret Y. *Early Christian Women and Pagan Opinion: The Power of the Hysterical Woman*. Cambridge: Cambridge University Press, 1996.

———. "Early Christian Women Married to Unbelievers." *Studies in Religion* 19 (1990) 221–34.

———. "Slavery, Sexuality and House Churches: A Reassessment of Col 3.18–4.1 in Light of New Research on the Roman Family." *NTS* 53 (2007) 94–113.

———. "Women Holy in Body and Spirit: The Social Setting of 1 Corinthians 7." *NTS* 36 (1990) 161–81.

MacDonald, Margaret Y., and Leif Vaage. "Unclean but Holy Children: Paul's Everyday Quandary in 1 Corinthians 7:14c." *CBQ* 73 (2011) 526–46.

Martin, Dale. "Slave Families and Slaves in Families." In *Early Christian Families in Context: An Interdisciplinary Dialogue*, edited by David L. Balch and Carolyn Osiek, 207–30. Religion, Marriage and Family. Grand Rapids: Eerdmans, 2003.

May, Alistair Scott. *"The Body for the Lord:" Sex and Identity in 1 Corinthians 5–7*. JSNTSup. 278. London: T. & T. Clark, 2004.

Moxnes, Halvor, editor. *Constructing Early Christian Families: Family as Social Reality and Metaphor*. London: Routledge, 1997.

Murphy-O'Connor, Jerome. *St. Paul's Corinth: Texts and Archaeology*. 3rd rev. and expanded ed. Collegeville: Liturgical, 2002.

———. "Works without Faith in 1 Cor., VII, 14." *RB* 84 (1977) 349–61.

Økland, Jorunn. *Women in Their Place: Paul and the Corinthian Discourse of Gender and Sanctuary Space*. JSNTSup 269. London: T. & T. Clark, 2004.

Osiek, Carolyn, and David L. Balch. *Families in the New Testament World: Households and House Churches*. Family, Religion and Culture. Louisville: Westminster John Knox, 1997.

Osiek, Carolyn, and Margaret Y. MacDonald, with Janet Tulloch. *A Woman's Place: Early Christian House Churches*. Minneapolis: Fortress, 2006.

Pomeroy, Sarah. *Goddesses, Whores, Wives, and Slaves: Women in Classical Antiquity*. New York: Shocken, 1975.

Rawson, Beryl. *Children and Childhood in Roman Italy*. Oxford: Oxford University Press, 2006.

Taylor, Joan E. *Jewish Women Philosophers of First-Century Alexandria: Philo's "Therapeutae" Reconsidered*. Oxford: Oxford University Press, 2003.

Wimbush, Vincent. *Paul the Worldly Ascetic: Response to the World and Self-Understanding according to 1 Corinthians 7*. Macon: Mercer University Press, 1987.

———. "*Contemptus Mundi*: The Social Power of an Ancient Rhetoric and Worldview." *USQR* 47 (1993) 1–13.

Winter, Bruce W. "Puberty or Passion? The Referent of ΥΠΕΡΑΚΜΟΣ in 1 Corinthians 7:36." *TynBul* 49 (1998) 71–89.

———. *Roman Wives, Roman Widows: The Appearance of New Women and the Pauline Communities*. Grand Rapids: Eerdmans, 2003.

Wire, Antoinette Clark. *The Corinthian Women Prophets: A Reconstruction through Paul's Rhetoric*. Minneapolis: Fortress, 1990.

4

Interfacing House and Church
Converting Household Codes to Church Order

Turid Karlsen Seim

UNTIL THE MID-1980S MUCH SCHOLARLY ENERGY WAS SPENT TRYING to trace the background or origins of the Christian household codes (Col 3:18—4:1; Eph 5:22—6:9; 1 Pet 2:13—3:7, and possibly also 1 Tim 2:(1)8-15; 6:1-2; Tit 2:1-10; *1 Clem.* 1:3; 21:6-9). A general consensus was established to which also David Balch made a substantial contribution. He proved it likely that the codes were derived from or akin to a moral philosophical Hellenistic tradition of expositions on household management going back to Aristotle's *Politics* I 1253b 1-14, and later represented by first-century authors such as Arius Didymus and Dio Chrysostom.[1] In this tradition, the intimate association of *oikonomia* and *politeia*, defined household management not as a private matter but as a public showcase, and traditional conventions of a patriarchal household were reinforced at a time when imperial attention was paid to family restoration.[2]

---

1. Balch, *Let Wives Be Submissive*. Later in 1988 Balch summarized the status quaestionis in "Household Codes."

2. Augustus's legislation concerning marriage (Lex Julia SD and Lex Papia 9SC) represented a restoration of what was held to be the old Roman family ideals. It was aimed at increasing legitimate reproduction of the Roman nobility. The laws were resisted and they probably were unsuccessful in achieving their aim. The officially ruling ethos was not necessarily the common one. However, the legislation implied that responsibility and supervision of this moral domain was placed with the emperor himself as *pater patriae* to whom each *paterfamilias* ideally was responsible. See Des Bouvrie, "Augustus' Legislation on Morals"; and Dixon, *Roman Family*, 19-23.

Certain recurring formal features seem to constitute a relatively fixed *topos* yet with great flexibility, and even if the περὶ οἰκονομία tradition helps situate the Christian household codes strategically, it does not explain their particular internal structure.[3] Many issues pertaining to the interpretation of the household codes therefore still remain, among them also the odd fact that they, as far as we can see from the sources known to us, occur only in a very limited range of Early Christian writings and seem to disappear after a time span of more or less a generation. In Ign. *Pol.* 4:1–3 and also Pol. *Phil* 4:2–3, as well as in the even later Pseudo-Ignatian letters formal traces of such codes are still discernible, but they are faint and would probably by themselves not have been taken to indicate a particular *topos*. Indeed, already in the Pastoral Letters the codes, although formally still distinguishable, seem to dissolve as household regulations thematically are made to blend with ecclesial concerns and church governance.[4] An explicit interaction with ecclesiology can be observed also in the Ephesian household code even if it is very different from the codes in the Pastoral Letters.

This essay does not aim at explaining historically why the household codes faded from fashion. The intention is rather to provide some further insight into how an interface between a domestic and an ecclesial agenda increasingly becomes discernible in some of the codes and the ripple effect of this both formally and in terms of content.

Symbiotic Interdependence in the Ephesian Household Code

The all-dominant theme of the letter to the Ephesians is unity or rather reconciliation and re-unification both at a cosmic level and in the human community. Alienation is brought to an end, and everything and everyone who are apart should be brought together into one. The mystery of God's will, having been made known in Christ, is a plan for the fullness of time when all things in heaven and on earth will be gathered up in him (1:9–10). The readers of the letter are called upon to manifest this unity and the unity of the Christian *ekklēsia* as a sign of the all-embracing cosmic unification. However, unity is not

---

3. Verner, *Household of God*, 84–91, observes this and it is still a valid assessment.
4. Again Verner (ibid., 91–107) was acute in his observations.

the same as harmony, and the unification discourse further requires some understanding as to how dualistic or even binary articulations might be reconciled, be it through hierarchical ordering, absorption, conversion or transformation. This should be kept in mind when reading the household code in Eph 5:21—6:9 in light of the over-arching perspective of unification.

Furthermore, the fact that in the first century the ideal of harmony, or *concordia*, was, with imperial encouragement, applied to common marriages as well as to the imperial house, glossing over the many realities of life,[5] does not necessarily entail that conformity to conventional social patterns in Christian writings in every case conveniently may be ascribed to clever tactic maneuvering aimed at pleasing or placating a non-Christian environment. It is indeed possible that the Ephesian household code did not primarily have an apologetic function, and also that it speaks to Christian and not to mixed families as the code in 1 Peter clearly does.[6]

The Ephesian code has the same structural patterns and sequence of sections as the code in Col 3:18—4:1 on which most interpreters assume that it somehow relies. However, whereas the section on wives and husbands in the Colossian code is extremely brief, it heavily outweighs the other sections in the Ephesian version.[7] Wives are, as in the other codes, told be subject to their husbands, but, as I have argued elsewhere, the emphasis in the Ephesian code is not as much on instructing the wives to be submissive to their husbands as it is on providing argumentative support for the husband's exercise of headship.[8] Since at the beginning of the Ephesian household code in 5:21, the overarching ethos is spelled out in a heading where all irrespectively are called to "be subject to one another out of reverence for Christ," any claim to or exercise of headship would have to defend itself. Hence the introductory exhortation to mutual submission is in the following vv. 22–33 further negotiated to accommodate the conventional hierarchical relation in marriage.

5. Dixon, "Sentimental Ideal."

6. Concerning this question, I have changed my mind since my article "A Superior Minority?" As I see it now, the argumentation in the code depends on both spouses being Christians.

7. The ten words directed to husbands in Colossians are outnumbered by the one hundred and forty-three words in Ephesians.

8. Cf. n. 4 above.

> ²²Wives, be subject to your husbands as you are to the Lord. ²³For the husband is the head of the wife just as Christ is the head of the church, the body of which he is the Saviour. ²⁴Just as the church is subject to Christ, so also wives ought to be, in everything, to their husbands. ²⁵Husbands, love your wives, just as Christ loved the church and gave himself up for her, ²⁶in order to make her holy by cleansing her with the washing of water by the word, ²⁷so as to present the church to himself in splendor, without a spot or wrinkle or anything of the kind—yes, so that she may be holy and without blemish. ²⁸In the same way, husbands should love their wives as they do their own bodies. He who loves his wife loves himself. ²⁹For no one ever hates his own body, but he nourishes and tenderly cares for it, just as Christ does for the church, ³⁰because we are members of his body. ³¹For this reason "a man will leave his father and mother and be joined to his wife, and the two will become one flesh." ³²This is a great mystery, and I am applying it to Christ and the church. ³³Each of you, however, should love his wife as himself, and a wife should respect her husband.

By defining the relationship between husband and wife as analogous to the relationship between Christ and the church, the husband's headship is firmly established. The analogy assumes that headship is a prerogative common to Christ and husbands, but the similarity is not spelled out in ontological terms. It is invoked by a transfer of relational terms primarily indicating attitude and behavior which also leaves the author free to make non-transferable Christological statements. The husband's headship is qualified by the requirement that it be Christ-like in that it mirrors Christ's caring love. Christ's paradigmatic love is self-giving but it is undoubtedly also a hierarchical expression and exercise of power. A conventional patriarchal construction of power is thereby maintained and restrained at the same time.

The analogy of husband-wife/Christ-church becomes operational and effective by means of a body discourse. According to 5:22–24, the wives should be subject to their husbands as they are to the Lord since the husband is the head of the wife as Christ is the head of the church, which is his body. Body language and *kefalē* (headship)-structure are thereby combined so that the organic image of the church as a multifunctional body is combined with the hierarchical idea of headship. Whereas both images or rather discourses are present in Paul, they are in the Pauline usage kept distinctly separate as they serve different purposes.⁹ In Ephesians 5 the argumentation depends on the combination of them and the potent merger of Christology and ecclesiology is made ethically effective in shaping the husband-wife relationship. Within certain limits, the analogy works interactively, the impact of which should not be underestimated.

The lengthy address to the husbands from v. 25 onwards mirrors what has been said to the wives in the preceding verses. The reciprocity is, however, formal. The perspective has moved from body to head, from downstairs to upstairs, and the language of submission in the address to the wife is replaced in the corresponding address to the husband not by explicating the executive power but by love talk. Patriarchal power is not just sweetened by love; it dresses itself in the guise of love. There is as yet no better term for this than "Liebespatriarkalismus."[10]

However, in v. 28, a shift takes place from attending to the responsibilities of the husband-head towards his dependent wife to considering how the husband as his wife's head may appropriate her body. Hence, sexual differentiation is simultaneously negated and maintained. The husband is his wife's head and she is subsumed as his body, a necessary part of the "self" that a man cannot despise but will have to love. In his commentary on Ephesians, Markus Barth insists that v. 28 be translated: "In the same manner also husbands owe it to love their wives for they are their bodies."[11] I find his argumentation persuasive, even if Barth's own overall concern is to rescue the letter's author, to him the apostle Paul, from defending his cause on the basis of men's self-love and self-interest.

Having taken on his wife as if she were his body and treating her accordingly, the husband represents an inbuilt plurality. Indeed, in Ephesians 5, marriage is presented as a transformation into the an-

---

9. In 1 Cor 11:3 the notion of a husband being the head of his wife, is part of a conventional pattern that included and defined the marital relationship within a more comprehensive cosmological hierarchy of relationships. This, however, entails that Christ in 1 Corinthians 11 is the head, not of the church as his body, but of every Christian man.

10. The term was coined by Ernst Troeltsch in *Die Soziallehren*. Gerd Theissen reactivated it effectively in his *Studien zur Soziologie*, 23–25, 104–5.

11. Barth, *Ephesians*, ad loc. Barth claims that the positioning of *kai* before *hoi andres* makes it unmistakably clear that the *houtos* at the beginning of the sentence points back to the love of Christ and not forward to what he calls an egoistic love. Only if καί was put before bodies would it affirm that husbands must love their wives as (or because) they love their own bodies.

drogynous potential of Adam reappropriating what in fact is his own flesh and bone. This duality may also help explain the sudden use of the plural in v. 30: for *we* are members of his body. The union is not primarily pneumatic; it is in body—even in flesh as it is rather harshly stated in v. 29. This choice of term may reflect that the verse deals with the wife's need for nourishment and care, which are the needs of the sarkic body. More likely and highly significant is, however that it proleptically depends on Gen 2:24, which in v. 31 is quoted in extenso: "For this reason a man will leave his father and mother and be joined with his wife, and the two will become one flesh." Husbands thus constitute a duality in that the husband's body is his wife whose head he is. Bodily boundaries are blurred, as the body of the wife is (re)appropriated by the husband. Indeed, the extraordinary postulation, in a patrilineal/patriarchal context, that a man should leave his mother and father to be with his wife, would not make sense other than in some indirect or symbolic sense.[12] In fact, the added introduction to the Genesis text "for this reason" may be taken to indicate that Gen 2:24 is itself explained through the preceding contention that the husband is the wife's head and the wife her husband's body so that they are one flesh. Beyond this, almost as an added thought, the author mentions that Gen 2:24 harbors a greater mystery—the key to which has already been partly revealed in the analogy of the relationship between husband and wife to that between Christ and the church.

The introduction of the scriptural quotation and its inherent mystery brings the analogy to change direction. So far Christ's relation to his church has been used paradigmatically to explain why the relationship between husband and wife should be defined hierarchically and also that the husband should love and care for his wife just as Christ cares for his church. Now, a biblical saying about the primordial marital union is said to hold a mystery about Christ and his church—as the saying's allegorical or typological meaning is revealed. The pronoun *touto* refers back to the Genesis text just quoted, and the emphatic *egō de legō* in 32b indicates that this typological interpretation probably is not the only one but the one held by the author.[13] In

12. For the many attempts to interpret this social anomaly, see Sampley, *Two Shall Become One Flesh*.

13. Sampley, *Two Shall Become One Flesh*, has tried to trace possible alternative interpretations of Gen 2:24 over against which the author of Ephesians profiles his particular understanding. He observes that in Jewish material, especially of rabbinic

the argumentative flow this comment represents a digression and it is not further explained. It has, however, preoccupied a host of later interpreters bending the reception of Eph 5:21–33 towards ecclesiology and the ecclesial status of marriage.

The symbiotic understanding of a union in flesh makes it possible for the husband/head also to remain embodied. He is a head like Christ is head and yet a member of Christ's body. The husband's love for his wife is therefore encouraged and defined by his love for himself. The commandment to love one's neighbor as oneself, assuming an affinity also seen elsewhere in Gen 2:24 and Lev 19:18,[14] is in fact applied in the concluding exhortation in v. 33: "Each of you, however, should love his wife as himself, but a wife should have fearful respect for her husband." As for the wife, none of the household codes requires that she should love her husband. Love is made to correlate with power.

Notwithstanding the differences, Paul's reasoning in 1 Cor 6:12–20 provides an interesting sounding board for the interpretation of the Deutero-Pauline exposition in Eph 5:21–33. In 1 Corinthians 6 Paul reflects on the body as the arena and symbolic space of domination and belonging, and the relationship between the believer and the Lord is set forth primarily in terms of body and member. The individual bodies of the believers are said to be the members of Christ; they somehow make up the body of Christ by being his members.[15] Furthermore, their belonging to the Lord is spelled out in terms of oneness. Anyone united to Christ becomes one spirit with him, that is neither flesh which is not exceptional, but nor is it body. In contrast, whoever is united with a prostitute becomes one body with her, since—presumably by sexual intercourse—the two become one flesh. In support of his point of view Paul refers to Gen 2:24, quoting the

---

times, Gen 2:24 is frequently quoted or alluded to almost exclusively in order to serve halakic purposes. It is one of the prime texts in maintaining the ordinance of marriage and by subtle exegesis it is also used to determine prohibited marital relations.

14. Cf. Sir 13:15–16:"Every creature loves its like, and every person his neighbor; all living beings associate by species, and a man clings to himself."

15. It is, however, striking that the term "body of Christ" is not explicitly used in this passage—even if most commentators seem not to pay much attention to this fact and simply introduce the term in order to support their interpretation. Martin, *Corinthian Body*, 174–79, depends on this for his argumentation. Cf. also Conzelmann, *1 Corinthians*, 111 n. 25, who explicitly assumes that "the underlying thought is that of the body of Chris," whereas Barrett, *First Epistle to the Corinthians*, 148–52, operates with greater care.

last part of the verse which refers to the two becoming one flesh. Also Paul sees it as referring to a symbiotic union, but its function in 1 Cor 6:12–20 is negative rather than positive. It is not used to support marital union but rather to deter believers from fornication or perhaps preferably from any sexual bodily union. It violates their spiritual union with the Lord, to whom their bodies belong.[16] The union with Christ is pneumatic and therefore different, indeed incompatible with any somatic union in sarkic terms.[17] Their bodies have been converted to temples of the holy spirit, devoted to glorify God.

In my reading 1 Cor 6:12–20 is an ascetic passage, which also explains why the question to be entertained next (1 Cor 7:1) is whether it is good for a man not to touch a woman. In the Ephesian household code, however, asceticism is certainly not an ideal and Gen 2:24 is taken mysteriously to reveal that the symbiotic relationship between husband and wife is not just analogous to the relationship between Christ and the church, it somehow mirrors it and vice versa.

The early reception of this part of the Ephesian household code is fragmentary and sometimes difficult to distinguish since the influence of Gen 2:24 and similar sayings may depend also on other sources. However, the Ephesian reference is obvious when Ignatius in his *Letter to Polycarp* 5:1b–2, writes as follows:

> Speak to my sisters that they love the Lord, and stay content with their husbands (*symbioi*) in flesh and spirit. In the same way enjoin on my brothers in the name of Jesus Christ "to love their wives as the Lord loved the Church." If any man can remain in continence to the honor of the flesh of the Lord let him do so without boasting. If he boasts he is lost, and if it is made known except to the bishop, he is finished. For it is

---

16. The cases of immorality mentioned in 1 Corinthians 5–6 all concern male offenses and no charges are brought against the women involved. Thus Paul has so far spoken of men and to men only. In 1 Corinthians 7 Paul's fraternal persuasion continues; his speech is directed to a male audience (7:29, 32, 35) and women are spoken of in the third person and are at best eavesdroppers to this intra-male conversation.

17. However, when in 1 Cor 7:11–13 he warns the Christian partner in a mixed marriage against seeking a divorce, his advice limits a wide-ranging application of his previous advice against fornication in 6:15–18. In a mixed marriage the Christian partner sanctifies the non-Christian rather than him/herself being polluted. Deming, *Paul on Marriage*, 129–43, finds that Paul refutes the belief represented among the Christians in Corinth, that Christian partners were polluted by non-Christian spouses. He also finds that the rhetoric of the Corinthian situation is quite close to what we find among the Stoics, including Philo and Ben Sira.

right for men and women who marry to be united with the consent of the bishop, that the marriage be according to the Lord and not according to lust. Let all things happen to the honor of God.

The passage appears as part of a series of exhortations directed to various groups such as widows, slaves, wives and husbands named as "those who live together." It may thus be taken to represent a vague reminder of a household code most clearly in what is being said to the husband. Marriage is recommended as a union in flesh and spirit but needs the consent of the bishop to be according to the Lord and not a matter of lust. In this there may be an echo also of 1 Cor 6:12–20, and the ecclesial office is introduced for the union not to be fornication. However, marriage is not compulsory in that the passage makes space for an ascetic lifestyle. Male ascetics are not condemned as long as their continence does not give cause to boasting. It is in that case positively qualified as being "to the honor of the flesh (*sarks*) of the Lord"—perhaps referring to the fact that according to the gospel traditions the incarnate Lord had been himself a celibate. This is supported by Tertullian, *De Monogamia* V who also alludes to Eph 5:22–33:

> the last Adam (that is, Christ) was entirely unwedded, as was even the first Adam before his exile. But, presenting to your weakness the gift of the example of His own flesh, the more perfect Adam—that is, Christ, more perfect on this account as well (as on others), that He was more entirely pure, stands before you, if you are willing (to copy Him), as a voluntary celibate in the flesh. If, however, you are unequal (to that perfection), He stands before you a monogamist in spirit, having one Church as His spouse, according to the figure of Adam and of Eve, which (figure) the apostle interprets of that great sacrament of Christ and the Church, (teaching that), through the spiritual, it was analogous to the carnal monogamy. You see, therefore, after what manner, renewing your origin even in Christ, you cannot trace down that (origin) without the profession of monogamy; unless, (that is), you be in flesh what He is in spirit; albeit withal, what He was in flesh, you equally ought to have been.

Tertullian's reception of the Ephesian code is here limited to the Genesis-based analogy which allows for marriage for those who are unequal to the perfection of Christ, who, when he was in the flesh, was a voluntary celibate. However, the Ephesian analogy legitimizes in the flesh what Christ is in the spirit, namely monogamous.

The Codes in the Pastoral Letters: A Household of God in the Making

The Pastoral Letters allege that the Apostle Paul is the author and they are addressed not to a community but to two community leaders, Timothy and Titus. The two are greeted as Paul's beloved and loyal children having been his trusted companions. Titus is said to have been left behind to put things in order on Paul's behalf among the Christians in Crete, whereas Timothy was placed in Ephesus to call to order certain people who might desire to be teachers but had deviated from the divine plan known by faith. This setting of the epistolary scenes means that all instruction in the letters takes on a two-level or two-stage perspective. Only Timothy and Titus are addressed directly while the community and its members are spoken to only indirectly as Timothy and Titus are told how to instruct them. Thereby a chain of authorization as well as a notion of faithful traditioning is introduced. This represents a move towards institutionalized authoritative teaching and the pattern also has consequences for the formal structure of the exhortations in the letters and probably contributes to the disintegration of the household codes as they deal as much with ecclesial matters as with household relationships.

Generally, it is characteristic for the household codes that they are prescriptive and not descriptive, and accordingly they are characterized by imperatives.[18] However, the code in Tit 2:1ff. is not formulated as a sequence of imperatives as is usually the case. Rather, the imperatives are directed to Titus as the recipient of the letter, who is told what he should proclaim to groups of members in the community. The first-line instructions to Titus are therefore characterized by imperatives such as "proclaim," whereas Titus's own second line instructions are rendered as a series of adjectives with the verb "to be"

---

18. Osiek, MacDonald, and Tulloch, *Woman's Place*, 19. However, they mention this in order to underline that the household codes should not be taken as information about the life that actually took place in Christian households but as ideological promulgation of an ideal which some saw the need to reinforce.

subordinate to what he himself is under obligation to proclaim.[19] The infinitive "to be" does not have the force of an imperative, and even if rules are established in terms of content, formally the rules appear rather like a catalogue of duties. In 1 Timothy 2 and 6, however, the admonitions vary in form, including the imperative when women are instructed to remain silent.

The household code in 1 Timothy 2 is normally taken to begin in v. 8. Yet the previous part, vv. 1–7, urging that supplications, prayers, intercessions, and thanksgivings be made for all in high offices may seem to provide the same kind of introduction as in 1 Pet 2:(11)13–17. Here the whole group of beloved, later addressed diversified into three groups as slaves, wives, and husbands, are told for the Lord's sake to accept and honor every human institution, not least emperor and governors. This is a formal feature which is integral to the *topos*, and it defines the following specification of requirements as a further pursuit of what acceptance of imperial governance entails if they wish "to lead a quiet and peaceable life in all godliness and dignity" (1 Tim 2:1). It is, however, singular in the household codes when in 1 Timothy 2 the introductory reference in 2:1 to supplications, prayers, intercessions, and thanksgiving acceptable in the sight of God, spills over into the further regulations in v. 8. Differently from the other household codes in the New Testament, a context of worship is thereby established and what may seem like a household code serves in fact as a church order which details how men should pray and women behave in a situation of prayer. This further triggers general regulations about women's appearance and conduct, including their good deeds and submission to men's authority. Since a prayer and/or assembly context and not a household context appears to be the setting, the wives' submission should be expressed by silence while the men pray and teach.[20] The passage is a close parallel to the disputed Pauline passage in 1 Cor 14:34–35, which regulates women's presence in the assembly by ordaining silence and referring wives to be taught by their husbands at home—with the further claim that this is common practice in all

---

19. Dibelius and Conzelmann, *Pastoral Epistles*, 139. See also Verner, *Household of God*, 92–94.

20. As do many others, Dibelius and Conzelmann, *Pastoral Letters*, 44–45, assume that women also pray, but this is at best implicit in the passage and to my mind it would have been explicit if such were the case.

the churches of the saints.[21] There is in 1 Cor 14:34–35 a possible interface with the household codes, but one might equally well regard the similarity as a shared reference to a wide-spread practice or even church order regulating married women's appearance and role in the assembly.

First Timothy continues in 3:1–13 by listing qualifications for ecclesial offices (bishop and deacon).[22] There is hardly any mention of the functions of these offices, only personal requirements, heavily charged with household respectability. To be suited for an ecclesial office, a man must have proven himself able in governing his own household: "If someone does not know how to manage his own household, how can he take care of God's *ekklēsia*?" (1 Tim 3:5). Household management and ecclesial management are thus intimately interrelated, not only in the sense that both require managerial skills but rather because the ideal of social control and transparency was shaped by a patriarchal, hierarchical order for which household management was emblematic.

Especially from the end of the first century AD onwards, one should not exclude the possibility that Christians assembled in workshops or in rented accommodation.[23] But to the degree that Christians congregated and worship took place in relatively small-scale private houses, a spatial overlap may have furthered an ideological cross-over from household code to church order—even if a house-church setting is not necessary for the connection to work. Carolyn Osiek and Margaret MacDonald have together explored whether entering a house church "was to step into a women's world."[24] They emphasize

---

21. Wire, *Corinthian Women Prophets*, 230–33, summarizes the various interpolation theories, but since they differ so much among themselves, she in the end accepts the passage as Pauline. I find the inconsistency as it now stands even more difficult and belong to those who think that 1 Cor 11:34–35 is somehow an early insertion made by the same Pauline tradition evident in the Pastoral Letters. In a textual tradition where these letters were accepted as having been written by Paul, there would be no reason not to accept an insertion in 1 Corinthians as Pauline. It remains, however, a complex and open case.

22. Whereas only male householders can serve as bishops, both men and women may become deacons—although the qualifications are not identical and the implications of the virtues mentioned might be gender-specific, cf. Kartzow, *Gossip and Gender*, 135.

23. The archeological evidence is later—as it in fact is also for house churches. See an article in Norwegian by the archaeologist Siri Sande, "Huskirker og tituluskirker."

24. Osiek and MacDonald, *Woman's Place*, 144–63 (quotation on 163).

the significance of women who were patrons and of widows who had autonomy and managed their own households. Furthermore, there is no doubt that in addition to slaves, women did most of the work in the household and that the spatial overlap may have encouraged their participation when the Christians came together in the house.

However, in many passages which deal with household management and church order, there is an intriguing ambiguity at work. On the one hand the ideal patriarchal system of hierarchical ordering is put in place in the church as in the household. On the other side an important distinction is introduced between household and *ekklēsia*. Women are told to possess themselves in silence during worship in the *ekklēsia*, but this does not necessarily apply "at home" or "in the household" where they are allowed to speak but should beware of gossip and "old women's tales."

Paul's intervention in a dispute over practices at the common meal in Corinth (1 Cor 11:17–33) deals with a situation where the difference between house as home and house as *ekklēsia* had become confused or was non-existent. In order to solve the conflicts, Paul outlines the necessity of keeping apart the social sphere/space of the house, including the social, communal life of the *ekklēsia* which probably took place there, and the ritual sphere/space of the ecclesial gatherings.[25] The Corinthians do not sufficiently mark the difference between their own regular household meals and the meal of the Lord, *kyriakon deipnon*, at which they become manifest as the body of Christ. The difference between these meals and the particular significance of the *kyriakon deipnon* is established as the narrative of Jesus's last meal with his commandments for the future meals of his disciples, is recited or recollected. This moment of transmission represents the ritual demarcation of a different discursive space in a location that, outside of this ritually defined occasion, may house ordinary household functions. In other words, the Corinthians' celebration of the Lord's Supper is disgraceful because they act as if they were at home without awareness of *ekklēsia* as a different space where a certain social interaction is required. The relation between their *ekklēsia* and the body of Christ and the meal's significance in establishing and maintaining this relation,

---

25. This may indeed apply to the whole chapter 1 Corinthians 11, including the requirements in the first part about men's and women's hairdresses and conduct during worship. For this and the following, see Økland, *Women in Their Place*, 133–67. She draws on Jonathan Z. Smith's ritual theory.

appear to be of no consequence to them. Paul's fiery rebuke is therefore aimed at changing their messy practices by making undoubtedly clear to them the distinction between domestic space and ecclesial space.

Unless a special space might be set aside for the *ekklēsia* within the private house or in a different, separate place, the presence of two kinds of space in the same location would not, of course, presuppose a constant simultaneous existence but an occasional suspension of one for the other. It is, however, not unlikely, that the Corinthians' difficulty in keeping household and *ekklēsia* detached, was not uncommon and that a process of conflation increasingly took place. Whereas Paul stays clear of blurring the boundaries and never speaks of *ekklēsia* as the household of God, later writings do, such as 1 Tim 3:15 and also 1 Pet 4:17. It may be that, as the later household codes show, ecclesial concerns become explicit as they increasingly buy into a household discourse. With respect to public exposure and official credibility, the *ekklēsia* was vulnerable and in need of establishing or earning a social standing whereas a properly functioning *oikos* was not.[26]

The other household code in the Pastoral Letters, Tit 2:1–10, addresses slaves in a traditional manner but when it comes to men and women who are not slaves, the focus is almost exclusively on gender-divided age groups. It is worth noticing that Titus may address the older and the younger men directly but the young women only by way of the older women. The older women are given directions as to how they should encourage the younger, married women to love their children and their husbands to whom they also should be submissive. More generally, they should be self-controlled, chaste and kind, as well as good managers of the household. When the old women rather than being gossipers and slaves to drink, teach the younger women such proper conduct, they behave reverent and are *kalodidaskoloi*, teaching others to do well. Both this code and the one in 1 Timothy 2 pay attention to women's speech. Taken together, the pattern appears to be that women should remain silent in *ekklēsia*, but are at free to speak at home, i.e., in the household, as long as they do not meander from house to house gossiping. The silence imposed on women in an assembly where men and women are together (1 Tim 2:11) is therefore

---

26. Cf. The many attempts at defining an organizational model which the *ekklēsia* might fit or appropriate—funeral society, voluntary association, philosophical or rhetorical school or circle—and household. See Meeks, *First Urban Christians*, 74–110.

suspended in an all-female group if the teaching is *kalos*, that is instruction about the proper *habitus* for a housewife—including being a good manager in the household.[27]

Again a distinction between household and *ekklēsia* is decisively important. At the same time, however, the Pastorals speak of *ekklēsia* as the household of God, managed by a householder who has proved himself able and trustworthy by the way he has governed his own house. The principal concern in the Pastoral Letters is to encourage an ecclesial consolidation internally and externally by a transfer to the church of the hierarchic structure of the ideal household. The purpose is recognition of the *ekklēsia* as a recognizable social institution, accountable, honorable, and respectable, as well as open and transparent to the public eye.[28] However, for this to work it becomes even more important to uphold the household virtues for the sake of the *ekklēsia*. The Pastorals' immediate concern is therefore not so much the contents of the adverse teachings as their disruptive social effects (2 Tim 3:1–7) and the disintegration of households and families in the community (Tit 1:10–16). Leaving an eschatological worldview behind, the Pastoral Letters situate the Christians in a common world of human existence. Using a slightly different discourse, one might say that they develop the notion of good Christian citizenship marked by piety, dignity and prudence. This process should be understood in the context of a transformed self-understanding of the church.[29]

The Pastoral vision of this world makes best sense if the addressees are seen to be a group of relatively wealthy Christians, representing well-established family households where patron status, social reputation and political recognition were all the more important and part of their social frame of reference.[30] It is, however, important to note that this interpretation moves beyond a construal which understands the ethos of the household codes as a public relations strategy whereby the Christians protected themselves against suspicions or accusations of

---

27. Kartzow, *Gossip and Gender*, 148–49, who further comments that "an all-female community is ideal and commendable when the old ones spend their time teaching the young ones proper family values, but destructive if the young women learn to be idlers, gossipers, and busybodies as they wander about in the houses."

28. For this and the following, see Fatum, "Christ Domesticated," 179, 187.

29. Dibelius and Conzelmann, *Pastoral Letters*, 39–40, 141.

30. Fatum, "Christ Domesticated," 192; Dibelius and Conzelmann, *Pastoral Letters*, 40.

subversive attitudes and activities—nurturing the assumption that it was more or less forced upon them.

Concluding Remarks

MacDonald asks whether a postcolonial analysis may help find new ways of approaching the question of the function of the household codes.[31] Applying Homi Bhabha's theory of mimicry as a framework, she suggests that the codes might offer insight into a borderline experience which is the margin of hybridity, where cultural differences contingently and conflictually touch. She locates Ephesians and Colossians as being on this borderline or margin whereas elements of resistance are far less revealing in the household code material in the Pastoral Letters. Here the border has been crossed.

This corresponds strikingly with my observations in this essay. In the Ephesian household code the ecclesial reference is part of an analogical reasoning that further develops the Pauline language of the church as the body of Christ. It reinforces a symbiotic yet hierarchical understanding of the relationship between husband and wife and endows it with a sacred/sacramental dimension—encouraging later ecclesial reception of the text to connect this to a particular ecclesial structure and ecclesiological positioning. In the Pastoral Letters, the body language is absent and the church is molded on and depends on well managed Christian households for its credibility both corporatively and with regard to its leadership. Ecclesiology buys into household ideology, in a manner that has had a long-lasting impact that would have been even more massive if the same letters had not left some small loopholes open for women and probably even more importantly, lost the battle against Christian asceticism.[32]

Finally, are we closer to an answer to the introductory question about the discontinuity of the household codes? In the case of the Ephesian code, the analogy introducing Christ and the church as well as the digression about the mystery in the interpretation of Gen 2:24 destabilize the rest of the code and already in the early reception one

---

31. MacDonald, "Beyond Identification," made available to me as manuscript and forthcoming in *NTS*.

32. Interesting in this perspective is the revitalization and reinstatement of the Household Codes in the Lutheran reformation.

can perceive the beginning of a process towards ecclesial management and sacralization of marriage. In the Pastoral Letters the ecclesiological influx in the service of which the household ethos is enrolled, radically changes the frame of reference for the household codes. The result is confusion and partial collapse of the Pauline distinction between *ekklēsia* and *oikos* and indeed of the literary and ethical pattern of the *topos* itself.

Bibliography

Balch, David L. "Household Codes." In *Greco-Roman Literature and the New Testament: Selected Forms and Genres*, edited by David E. Aune, 25–50. SBLSBS 21. Atlanta: Scholars, 1988.

———. *Let Wives Be Submissive: The Domestic Code in 1 Peter*. SBLMS 26. Chico, CA: Scholars, 1981.

Barrett, C. K. *A Commentary on the First Epistle to the Corinthians*. 2nd ed. Black's New Testament Commentaries. London: Black, 1971.

Barth, Markus. *Ephesians*. 2 vols. AB 34–34A. Garden City, NY: Doubleday, 1974.

Conzelmann, Hans. *1 Corinthians*. Translated by James W. Leitch. Hermeneia. Philadelphia: Fortress, 1975.

Des Bouvrie, Synnøve. "Augustus' Legislation on Morals—Which Morals and What Aims?" *Symbolae Osloensis* 70 (1984) 93–113.

Deming, Will. *Paul on Marriage and Celibacy: The Hellenistic Background of 1 Corinthians 7*. SNTSMS 83. Grand Rapids: Eerdmanns, 2004.

Dibelius, Martin, and Hans Conzelmann. *The Pastoral Epistles*. Translated by Philip Buttolph and Adela Yarbro. Hermeneia. Philadelphia: Fortress, 1972.

Dixon, Suzanne. *The Roman Family*. Ancient Society and History. Baltimore: John Hopkins University Press, 1992.

———. "The Sentimental Ideal of the Roman Family." In *Marriage, Divorce, and Children in Ancient Rome*, edited by Beryl Rawson, 99–113. Canberra, Australia: Humanities Research Centre, 1996.

Fatum, Lone. "Christ Domesticated: The Household Theology of the Pastorals as Political Strategy." In *The Formation of the Early Church*, edited by Jostein Ådna, 175–207. WUNT 139. Tübingen: Mohr/Siebeck, 2005.

Kartzow, Marianne Bjelland. *Gossip and Gender: Othering of Speech in the Pastoral Epistles*. BZNW 164. Berlin: de Gruyter, 2009.

MacDonald, Margaret Y. "Beyond Identification of the *Topos* of Household Management: Reading the Household Codes in Light of Recent Methodologies and Theoretical Perspectives in the Study of the New Testament." *NTS* forthcoming.

Martin, Dale B. *The Corinthian Body*. New Haven: Yale University Press, 1995.

Meeks, Wayne A. *The First Urban Christians: The Social World of the Apostle Paul*. New Haven: Yale University Press, 1983.

Økland, Jorunn. *Women in Their Place: Paul and the Corinthian Discourse of Gender and Sanctuary Space*. JSNTSup 269. London: T. & T. Clark, 2004.

Osiek, Carolyn, and Margaret Y. MacDonald, with Janet H. Tulloch. *A Woman's Place: House Churches in Earliest Christianity*. Minneapolis: Fortress, 2006.

Sampley, J. Paul. *"And the Two Shall Become One Flesh": A Study of Traditions in Ephesians 5:21–33*. SNTSMS 16. Cambridge: Cambridge University Press, 1971.

Sande, Siri, "Huskirker og tituluskirker—salmer i heimen eller på badet?" *Kirke og Kultur* 104 (1999) 5–16.

Seim, Turid Karlsen. "A Superior Minority? The Problem of Men's Headship in Ephesians 5." In *Mighty Minorities?: Minorities in Early Christianity, Positions and Strategies: Essays in Honour of Jacob Jervell*, edited by David Hellholm et al., 167–81. Oslo: Scandinavian University Press, 1995.

Theissen, Gerd. *Studien zur Soziologie des Urchristentums*. WUNT 19. Tübingen: Mohr/Siebeck, 1979.

Troeltsch, Ernst. *Die Soziallehren der christlichen Kirchen und Gruppen: Gesammelte Schriften I*. Tübingen: Mohr/Siebeck, 1912.

Verner, David C. *The Household of God: The Social World of the Pastoral Epistles*. SBLDS 71. Chico, CA: Scholars, 1983.

Wire, Antionette Clark. *The Corinthian Women Prophets: A Reconstruction through Paul's Rhetoric*. 1990. Reprinted, Eugene, OR: Wipf & Stock, 2003.

5

Overseers as Household Managers in the Pastoral Epistles

ABRAHAM J. MALHERBE

FORTY YEARS AGO, DAVID BALCH, ALWAYS THE THOROUGH researcher, examined ancient philosophical discussions of household management in his study of the domestic code in 1 Peter.[1] He recently returned to that literature in a study on wealth.[2] Jens Herzer, seeking to describe the ecclesiology of the Pastoral Epistles, has lately appealed to the same material.[3] It is timely, then, that I offer David some brief remarks on two texts from the Pastoral Epistles (1 Tim 3:2-7; Titus 1:6-9) that betray traces of the same literary tradition.

Martin Dibelius found the origin of the listing of virtues in the two passages in lists of virtues of ancient professionals (e.g., a military tactician, a physician, a dancer) that had no explicit relationship to their actions. The virtues were attached to the professionals, he thought, in a manner that suggests that a fixed schema or pattern existed. Despite

---

1. Balch, *Let Wives Be Submissive*, 21-62. See also, independently, Lührmann, "Wo man nicht mehr Sklave," 53-83; Lührmann, "Neutestamentliche Haustafeln," 83-97. Karen Lehmeier, a student of Lührmann, treated this material extensively in her learned dissertation, *Oikos und Oikonomia*, which does not treat the Pastoral Epistles. I only became aware of this book while this article was in editorial process and could therefore not benefit from it.

2. Balch, "Philodemus, 'On Wealth,'" 177-96. Cf. Malherbe, "Godliness, Self-Sufficiency," 1:376-405, 2.73-96, where attention is drawn to attitudes about the acquisition, preservation, disposition and use of wealth in discussions of estate management.

3. Herzer, "A Bishop . . . must manage"; cf. Herzer, "Rearranging the 'House of God,'" 547-66.

the sketchiness of Dibelius's proposal, he has been followed, with some modifications, by commentators.⁴

My offering to David in these few pages is more modest: I neither construct a schema nor describe an ecclesiology. I merely wish to illustrate briefly that 1 Tim 3:2–7 and Titus 1:6–9 share much with widespread ancient descriptions of professional leaders, particularly of household managers. In this I share the conviction of Luke Johnson that, "[t]he concept of 'good management of a household' provides the best access to the particular virtues of the supervisor."⁵

1 Timothy 3:2–7

Before proceeding to this text, a couple of matters should be remarked upon.

The Language Used

The qualities of an overseer are introduced in 1 Tim 3:2 with a stock phrase, δεῖ οὖν ἐπίσκοπον ἀνεπίλημπτον εἶναι. The generic singular with δεῖ is also used, for example, in specifying the qualities of a ruler (δεῖ τὸν ἄρχοντα),⁶ and of a dancer, whose qualifications are stated in an inclusive manner (ἀνεπίλημπτον), as the overseer's are here. In general, "the dancer should be perfect in every point (δεῖ πανταχόθεν ἐπηκριβῶσθαι), so as to be wholly rhythmical (τὸ πᾶν εὔρυθμον), graceful, symmetrical, consistent, unexceptionable, impeccable, not wanting in any way (ἀνεπίλημπτον, μηδαμῶς ἐλλιπές), blent of the highest qualities, keen in his ideas, profound in his culture, and above all, human in his sentiments" (Lucian, *Salt.* 81; trans. A. M. Harmon, LCL).

The grammatical construction, δεῖ plus accusative generic singular, and a list of seemingly general virtues is similar to 1 Tim 3:2–3 and Titus 1:7. The article being generic, the singular noun should not be

---

4. See Dibelius and Conzelmann, *Pastoral Epistles*, 50–51; cf. Schwarz, *Bürgerliches Christentum*, 95–98; Roloff, *Erste Brief an Timotheus*, 15–151; Oberlinner, *Pastoralbriefe*, 111; Towner, *Letters to Timothy and Titus*, 240.

5. Johnson, *First and Second Letters to Timothy*, 223.

6. See Plut. *Princ. iner.* 781CD; cf. δεῖ in *Praec. ger. rei publ.* 800A.

taken to refer to a single bishop.⁷ The construction is used extensively in descriptions of what a Stoic sage should be.⁸ For example, Epictetus's description of the ideal Cynic in *Diatr.* 3.22 is given in response to a question (1) about what sort of man the Cynic ought to be (ποῖόν τινα εἶναι δεῖ τόν κυνίζοντα), and the proper qualities are then stipulated with δεῖ throughout the rest of the diatribe (e.g., 13, 14, 19, 26, 62, 90, 100).

A serious philosophic seeker, Epictetus warns, does not casually, without carefully examining the task and his own capacities to undertake it, say to himself (3), "I must be a manager of this house (ἐμὲ δεῖ οἰκονόμον εἶναι)." Epictetus has in mind the Stoic view of the universe as a household and of the ideal philosopher in his universal mission.⁹ The philosopher, here described as the ideal Cynic, but Stoic in conception, unhindered by family or other local entanglements, goes forth as the messenger (ἄγγελος), scout (κατάσκοπος) and herald (κῆρυξ) of the gods (69–70). His duty is to oversee (ἐπισκοπεῖν) all mankind (72, 78). The oversight (ἐπισκοπή) of their affairs is his proper concern (97).¹⁰ Despite superficial similarities, there are considerable conceptual differences between the Cynic or Stoic wise man and the Christian overseer. Among these differences is that, in contrast to the philosopher, the Christian overseer's activity is local, his attention directed towards those in his household.

The description of the philosopher as overseer has to do with his function rather than an office. In the Pastoral Epistles too the concern is with function, and it is best to avoid the translation of ἐπίσκοπος as "bishop" in favor of "overseer" or "supervisor," as commentators increasingly do.¹¹ This lessens the danger of anachronism, reading later ecclesiastical use into the 1 Tim 3:1–2.¹²

---

7. The exegetical decisions reflected in this chapter will receive extended treatment in my Hermeneia commentary on the Pastoral Epistles.

8. E.g., in Stobaeus, *Ecl.* 2.67, 21–22 Wachsmuth (*SVF* 3.604); 2.114, 16 (*SVF* 3.605); 2.114, 4 (*SVF* 3.601).

9. See Billerbeck, *Epiktet: Vom Kynismus*, 48–50.

10. For the philosopher as scout (κατάσκοπος), see Epictetus, *Diatr.* 24–25; cf. 1.24.3–10; 3.24.3–10; Diogenes Laertius, 6.43; cf. ἐπίσκοπος, ἐπισκοπεῖν, 97; Maximus of Tyre, 15.9c–d. See Norden, "Beiträge zur Geschichte," 373–475.

11. E.g., Collins, *I & II Timothy and Titus*, 79; Towner, *Letters to Timothy and Titus*, 239; Oberlinner, *Pastoralbriefe*, 1.110.

12. BDAG, s.v. ἐπίσκοπος; Towner, *Letters to Timothy and Titus*, 244.

The Epistolary Situation Envisaged

According to 1 Tim 1:2, Timothy was left in Ephesus to oppose heterodox teachers. Much of the letter does that and also exhorts readers to the moral life.[13] The author does not write to introduce a new hierarchy in the community, and there is no indication in the text that the qualities listed in vv. 3–7 qualify men who have yet to assume the office of bishop.[14] Verse 1 should not be interpreted in light of vv. 10 and 13 and Titus 1:5. The function of oversight (ἐπισκοπή) is already being carried out by men who strongly desire (ὀρέγεται, ἐπιθυμεῖ; cf. 1 Pet 5:2) to do so. The virtues enumerated describe the qualities of character and conduct of those who are exercising oversight rather than qualify them for an office yet to be filled.

The qualities of overseers and deacons conclude the first major section of 1 Timothy which ends in 3:14–15. The purpose of the letter up to this point (ταῦτα) is stated as being to inform Timothy about the proper conduct "in God's house (ἐν οἴκῳ θεοῦ ἀναστρέφεσθαι), which is the church of the living God." The ταῦτα refers to everything antecedent, beginning with 1:3–4, where the proper concern of orthodox teaching is said to be God's household management in faith (οἰκονομίαν θεοῦ τὴν ἐν πίστει) in contrast to heterodox teaching and endless speculation and controversy. The qualities listed in 3:2–7, then, are to be seen from the perspective of a household management, which is concerned with the cultivation of moral conduct and adherence to correct doctrine.[15] It is the household of God, ordered and conducting itself accordingly, that is the pillar and support of the truth (3:15).

---

13. Thurén, "Struktur der Schlussparënese," 241–53, argued that the entire letter is directed against false teachers and their sins and commends true doctrine.

14. Herzer, "Rearranging the 'House of God,'" 558–59.

15. Οἰκονομία is used extensively with this meaning in the literature on household management (e.g., in Xenophon, *Oec.* 1.1–2; Arist., *Pol.* 1.2.1 (=1253b); Philodemus, *Oec.* 1.6–10 [References to Philodemus's work is to Jensen, Πηιλοδεμι Περὶ Οἰκονομίας.] For three different interpretations, among others, of the meaning here, see Marshall, *Pastoral Epistles*, 367; Johnson, *First and Second Letters to Timothy*, 164; Towner, *Letters to Timothy and Titus*, 113–14. For ταῦτα as referring to everything in the letter up to 3:15–16, see Marshall, *Pastoral Epistles*, 497–98.

Qualities of the Overseer

These qualities, listed in a series of adjectives, specify what is meant by the requirement that the overseer be above reproach (ἀνεπίλημπτος), which, if taken by itself would be striking for its absoluteness, as in the description of Lucian's dancer, and a similar one of a teacher in Ps.-Plutarch, *Educ.* 4B.[16] The list is bracketed by explicitly domestic requirements which form an *inclusio*, beginning with the requirement that the overseer had been married only once (v. 2: μιᾶς γυναικὸς ἄνδρα),[17] and ending with the requirement that he care well for his household (vv. 4–5), which contains the clearest traces in this passage of the *topos* on household management. A more general requirement, that he not be a neophyte, is tacked on (v. 6) before the qualities are concluded by requiring that the overseer have a good reputation with outsiders (v. 7), which echoes the call that he be blameless.

The ten qualities listed between the two explicit domestic requirements are general in nature, but closer examination shows that they fit well with descriptions of domestic virtues, particularly but not exclusively of old men. So, νηφάλιος and σωφρών, with which the list begins (v. 2), and σεμνότης, with which it ends (v. 4), describe the old men in Titus 2:2.[18] Orderly (κόσμιος) belongs with

---

16. See also 1 Tim 5:7, where the purpose of teaching moral qualities to widows is to make them ἀνεπίλημπτοι; the purpose clause is then followed by more domestic virtues (vv. 5–10).

17. On the different interpretations of the phrase, see Towner, *Letters to Timothy and Titus*, 250–251. The analogous phrase, used of a widow who remained single after her husband's death, may suggest that the reference here is to a widower. See Malherbe, "How to Treat Old Women and Old Men," 296. This might reflect a commitment by a surviving husband to remain unmarried, his dead wife remaining his wife forever, a *coniunx perpetua*, on which see Treggiari, *Roman Marriage*, 246. But see also Cokayne, *Experiencing Old Age*," 208 n. 106, for the difficulties Augustan law and the expectations of society would have caused (131).

18. See Chrysostom, *Hom. Tit.*, Hom. 4 (PG 62.681-82), who thinks that these qualities are mentioned to counteract the view (commonly held) that old men are slow, timid, forgetful, insensible and irritable. For σωφροσύνη of old men, see Arist., *Rhet.* 2.1389a13-14; *moderatio* in Cicero, *Sen.* 1, 33; for "old men of self-control (*moderati*), who are neither churlish (*difficiles*) nor ungracious (*inhumani*)," see Cicero, *Sen.* 7, "a slightly ponderous but effective equivalent for κόσμιοι καὶ εὔκολοι," Plato, *Resp.* 329D, which he follows here (Powell, *Cicero Cato Maior de Senectute*, 11–118). For σεμνότης (*gravitas*), see Cicero, *Sen.* 10, "dignity tempered with courtesy (*comitate condita gravitas*)," on which see Powell, ibid., 122; Cokayne, *Experiencing Old Age*, 21: "The majority of the old men in Roman portraiture appear solemn, which was indicative of the *gravitas* of old age, the dignity to be emulated by the young."

σωφροσύνη in 2:9, describing the adornment of the domestically responsible wife;[19] the notion of orderliness, here of the overseer, is also a quality associated with household management.[20] Hospitableness is overtly domestic, and is required in 5:10 of widows more than sixty years of age who are to receive financial aid from the church. Aptness to teach (διδακτικός) is expected of heads of households (see below, on Titus 1:9), and in 1 Tim 5:17 is a function of the old men who exercise care well (οἱ καλῶς προεστῶτες πρεσβύτεροι), especially those who labor in speaking and teaching (οἱ κοπιῶντες ἐν λόγῳ καὶ διδασκαλίᾳ).[21]

Criticism of the elderly shimmers through in v. 3 (πάροινος, πλήκτης), and in the antitheses to ἐπιεικής, ἄμαχος, ἀφιλάργυ-ρος: "... the critics say, old men are morose (*morosi*), troubled (*anxii*), irascible (*iracundi*), churlish (*difficiles*); if we inquire, we'll find that some of them are misers too." (Cicero, *Sen.* 65).[22] But even when old age is not criticized in this manner, the commended behavior of Appius Claudius in ruling his household is striking for its assertiveness: "Appius, though he was both blind and old, managed four sturdy sons, five daughters, and a great household, and many dependents; for he did not languidly succumb to old age, but kept his mind ever taut, like a well-strung bow. He maintained not mere authority, but absolute command over his household; his slaves feared him, his children revered him, all loved him, and the customs and discipline of his forefathers flourished beneath his roof. For old age is honoured only on condition that it defends itself, maintains its rights, is subservient to no one, and to the last breath rules over its own domain" (Cicero, *Sen.* 37–38; trans. W. A. Falconer, LCL).

Such an insistence on his prerogatives as *paterfamilias* could easily lead to domestic violence, probably alluded to by πλήκτης and

---

19. See Malherbe, "*virtus feminarum* in 1 Timothy 2:9–15," 56–57, 60–64.

20. Hierocles, *ap.* Stobaeus, *Flor.* 4.505, 5–19; cf. the requirement that the οἰκονόμος be skilled in the proper arrangement (κοσμητικός) of possessions in the household (Philod., *Oec.* A 3; 10.33, 39; 11.1 [διακόσμησις]; Ps.-Arist., *Oec.* 1.6.1344b26–27. See Plut., *Cons. ux.* 609E, for Plutarch's grieving wife maintaining order in the household (κατεκόσμησας τὸν οἶκον).

21. See La Fosse, "Age Matters."

22. For such criticism and further references, see Malherbe, "How to Treat Old Women and Old Men," 272.

ἄμαχος (4).²³ In contrast to such belligerence, the overseer should be gentle, irenic and generous (ἐπιεικής, ἄμαχος, ἀφιλάργυρος) in caring for his own household. These gentle qualities follow immediately the requirement that he be διδακτικός, a connection also made when speaking of Timothy's responsibility to teach all people (2 Tim 2:23–25).

Managing the Household Well

Vices or virtues like the ones just enumerated were thought to determine whether someone would be a bad or good steward.²⁴ The virtues in 3:2-3, are qualities of the overseer who manages his own household well (v. 4, τοῦ ἰδίου οἴκου καλῶς προϊστάμενον). The change from adjectives to this participial clause draws attention to the major quality of the overseer, his domestic governance. The description of the overseer's domestic responsibility that follows consists of two parts: (1) the requirement that the overseer care for his own household (τοῦ ἰδίου οἴκου προστῆναι οἶδε), specified as having obedient children, and (2) the consequent ability to take care of God's church (ἐκκλησίας θεοῦ ἐπιμελήσεται) (3:4-5).

Traditional discussions of household management held that the function of a good manager was to manage his own household or estate well (εὖ οἰκεῖν τὸν ἑαυτοῦ οἶκον),²⁵ and to teach others how to manage theirs.²⁶ In 1 Tim 3:4-5, the administrative dimension is in view, in Titus 1:9, the didactic. The two word groups used in 1 Timothy (προΐστημι and ἐπιμελέομαι) were used extensively in discussions of household management.

It is not possible to distinguish sharply between the two groups of words. For the most part, they were used interchangeably.²⁷ In both,

---

23. On domestic violence in general, see Fitzgerald, "Early Christian Missionary Practice," 24–44.

24. Cf. Philodemus, *Oec.* 23.40—24.47, and see Tsouna, *Ethics of Philodemus*, 164, 184–87.

25. Xen., *Oec.* 1.2; see 1.5 for a distinction between οἶκος and οἰκία, on which see Pomeroy, *Xenophon Oeconomicus*, 213–14. Philodemus, *Oec.* 1.16–17 offers a critique of Xenophon; see Tsouna, *Ethics of Philodemus*, 169–70.

26. Philodemus, *Oec.* 3a.6–16.

27. See, e.g., Plato, *Gorg.* 520A; Philodemus, *Oec.* 20.20, 39; Philo, *Prob.* 45; *Post.* 181; *Virt.* 58, 63.

there is the notion of managing or caring, with a shading toward a more general caring in προίστημι and a more specific taking care of something or someone in ἐπιμελέομαι, yet some differences are notable. According to some Stoics, only the wise man could be a head of a household (προστάτης), for only he knows how to raise funds and expend them properly, as in the management (ἐπιμέλεια) of property and the people who work in his fields.[28]

The administrative nature of the activity was also touted by the more latitudinarian Stoic, Hierocles, who held that husband and wife both "take thought for the management (προστασίαν) that is incumbent on them of their household and their servants, and the rearing and care (κηδεμονίαν) of their children, and a concern (ἐπιμέλειαν) for the necessities of life that is neither strained nor slack, but is balanced and attuned."[29] The phrase προιστάναι τοῦ οἴκου appears in 1 Sam 13:17; Prov 23:5; Amos 6:10, and Paul uses προίστημι of compassionate caring (Rom 12:8, coupled with exhortation, generosity, mercy, love; cf. Rom 16:1-2), and of one particular means of psychagogy (1 Thess 5:12).[30] The meaning in 1 Tim 3:4-5, where it is used of domestic responsibility and in conjunction with ἐπιμελέομαι approximates discussions of household management like that of Hierocles.

In such discussions the person who manages (ὁ οἰκονόμος or ὁ προεστώς) is ultimately responsible for providing proper care (ἐπιμέλεια) for the household or estate,[31] which included the care of parents, wife and children,[32] and, frequently mentioned by the

---

28. Stobaeus, *Ecl.* 2.7a.11d (2.95, 9-33 Wachsmuth); see Natali, "*Oikonomia* in Hellenistic," 115. For administration, see Spicq, *épîtres pastorales*, 1.443n3. For financial administration, cf. Luke 12:42; 16:1, 8. Wolter, *Lukasevangelium*, holds that in 12:42 a slave is in charge (464), in 16:1, 8 an appointed freedman (545).

29. Hierocles, *ap.* Stobaeus, *Flor.* 4.22a24 (4.505, 15-20 Hense). Konstan, in Ramelli, *Hierocles the Stoic*, 77. See 4.504, 19, for the wife who takes over her husband's part in his absence so that the house is not left without a manager (ἀπροστάτητος οἶκος). For Hierocles's more egalitarian attitude, see 5.697,11-700, 20, and Ramelli's notes on pp. 128-33 on other moral philosophers on the same subject.

30. See Malherbe, *Letters to the Thessalonians*, 312-14.

31. Philod., *Oec.* 14.9-15; 21.37-44; Philo, *Prob.* 57; cf. Plut., *Comp. Arist. Cat.* 3.2, οἴκου προστάτης ἢ πόλεως.

32. Dio Chrys., *Or.* 69.2; Xen, *Oec.* 7.5; Philo, *Post.* 181; cf. Jos., *Ant.* 2.236 for the πολλὴ ἐπιμέλεια, which the young Moses received, and see further, Spicq, *Lexique théologique*, 560.

Epicurean Philodemus, wealth,[33] and farm management.[34] The manager could, however, teach slaves with the proper aptitude new skills.[35] So Joseph the steward (ἐπίτροπος) had charge of Pharaoh's entire household (συμπάσης τῆς οἰκίας ἡ ἐπιμέλεια).[36] That effective household management prepared one for a similar role in a larger arena was a common conviction, and is frequently documented in commentaries.[37] For Philo, Joseph's appointment as steward prepared him for command of cities, a nation and a large country. "For the future statesman needed first to be trained and practised in household management (οἰκονομίαν); for a house is a city compressed into small dimensions, and household management may be called a kind of state management, just as a city too is a great house and statesmanship the household management of the general public. All this shews clearly that the household manager is identical with the statesman, however much what is under purview of the two may differ in number and size" (Philo, *Ios.* 38–39; trans. Colson, LCL).

This understanding, that personal qualities demonstrated in the management of a household are required for management in a larger arena, is represented in the rhetorical question in 3:5. The question justifies the requirement in 3:4 that the overseer manage his household well, with dignity, thereby emphasizing why that requirement is important.

Why the Qualities Are Listed

The qualities of the overseer in vv. 2–7 are enumerated to inform Timothy about proper behavior in the household of God, which is the church of the living God (πῶς δεῖ ἐν οἴκῳ θεοῦ ἀναστρέφεσθαι, ἥτις ἐστὶν ἐκκλησία θεοῦ ζῶντος, 3:15). The overseer's manner

---

33. Philodemus, *Oec.* 19.34, 47; cf. 18.23; 20.20; 24.38; A 22–25. See Balch, "Philodemus, 'On Wealth' and 'On Household Management'" (n. 2 above).

34. Xen., *Oec* 7.41; cf. Philo, *Virt.* 58; *Agr.* 64, for farming; and *Spec.* 1.16, for the sun having the ἐπιμέλεια καὶ προστασία over nature. For political supervision, see Spicq, *épîtres pastorales*, 1.445–47; Spicq, *Lexique théologique*, 562.

35. Ps.-Arist., *Oec.* 1.5.1344a27–29; Xen., *Oec.* 12.4.

36. Philo, *Ios.* 37.

37. See, e.g., Dibelius and Conzelmann, *Pastoral Epistles*, 53; Spicq, *épîtres pastorales*, 1:436. See also Lips, *Glaube, Gemeinde, Amt*, 127; Malherbe, "*Paulus Senex*," 207 n. 44; Herzer, "A Bishop . . . must manage," 6 n. 16.

of management, exemplifying his personal virtues, commend those virtues to the people in his charge. These are virtues one would expect from any moral individual, with the possible exception that he not be a novice, and would meet with the approval of outsiders (v. 7). Elsewhere, Philo shows interest in the psychagogic manner in which Joseph the manager goes about his task, in the style of a responsible teacher or philosopher varying his speech, warning, admonishing or correcting, as is appropriate to the individual circumstance.[38] No such interest, however, is shown in 3:4–5.[39] Nor is there a stress on teaching, as there is in Titus 2:9. The delineation of the overseer's character and actions is adequate for its paraenetic purpose; the modeling of the behavior suffices.[40] "For the frequent seeing, the frequent hearing of (good men) little by little sinks into the heart and acquires the force of precepts" (Seneca, *Ep.* 94.40; trans. R. M. Gummere, LCL). Our author shows interest elsewhere in this feature of paraenesis (1 Tim 4:12; Titus 2:7; cf. 1 Tim 1:16).

One wishes for greater detail about the overseer's management, since that is where the emphasis lies. Johnson points out that only two of the qualities mentioned point to activities, that the bishop be hospitable and apt to teach.[41] Viewed thus, very little can be said about the management in view. The letter does, however, show an interest in administering the church's life: behavior in the home and the church assembly (2:8–15), Timothy's responsibilities as minister (4:11–16), and, especially characteristic of the duties of the οἰκονόμος, the use of financial resources (5:1–16, 17–23; 6:1–2, 3–20).[42] It is the Apostle who directs attention to these matters in his letter, but he writes with a view to his absence, when conduct in the household of God will be

---

38. For psychagogic practice, see Malherbe, *Paul and the Thessalonians*," 81–94; Malherbe, *Letters to the Thessalonians*, index, s.v. psychagogy; Glad, *Paul and Philodemus*.

39. For the Pastorals' reticence toward this tradition, see Malherbe, "'In Season and Out of Season,'" 235–43 (repr. in *Paul and the Popular Philosophers*, 137–45).

40. See Seneca, *Epistles* 6.5–6; 52.8; Pliny, *Epistles* 7.1.7; cf. 2.6.6. For this feature of paraenesis, see Malherbe, *Letters to the Thessalonians*, 83. Commentators increasingly recognize the paraenetic function of the list of virtues: e.g., Roloff, *Erste Brief an Timotheus*, 148; Oberlinner, *Pastoralbriefe*, 1.110; Towner, *Letters to Timothy and Titus*, 148.

41. Johnson, *First and Second Letters to Timothy*, 223.

42. See nn. 25, 30, and Malherbe, "Godliness, Self-Sufficiency," n. 2.

the charge of the overseer (3:15, cf. 5). All these administrative functions are local, and the personal qualities enumerated are congruent with the values of society, which thus secure a good reputation from outsiders.[43]

Summary

The language of 1 Tim 3:1–7 as to form and content is similar to that of philosophical discussions of household management, which are largely concerned with function rather than office or position. Verses 4 and 5, in the larger context of 1:4 and 3:15, belong to those discussions. The listed qualities of the Christian overseer are widely accepted virtues and also frequently appear in domestic contexts, as they do in 1 Timothy. Those qualities exemplify the manner in which the overseer cares for his household and the church. In the process of doing so, he serves as a model for those in his care. The focus in 3:4–5, the culmination of the qualities, is on administration, and the overseer's qualities characterize him as he administers the details of the Christian community's life and worship.

Titus 1:5–9

The epistolary situation presumed in Titus differs from that in 1 Timothy. Paul, somewhere on his way to Nicopolis, writes to Titus, who is in Crete, to join him in Nicopolis. Titus is to be replaced by Artemas and Tychicus (3:12). In the meantime, Zenas and Apollos are on their way to Crete and beyond (3:13). Paul had left Titus in Crete, commanding him to set right what remained to be done in the churches by appointing elders, also referred to as overseers, in every city. The emphatic way in which Titus is reminded of his appointment to his task draws attention to the importance of the appointees.[44] In the midst of

---

43. Viewed as local by von Lips, *Glaube-Gemeinde-Amt*, 95–96; Roloff, *Erste Brief an Timotheus*, 159. Oberlinner, *Pastoralbriefe*, 124–26, thinks the perspective is *gesamtkirchlich*, extending beyond the local church to include all churches.

44. Note the emphatic elements: 1. the prominent position of τούτου χάριν, "this is the reason why," 2. ἀπολείπω was used of the installation of government officials (see Wolter, *Pastoralbriefe als Paulustradition*, 3. the emphatic ἐγώ σοι διεταξάμην. Zahn (*Introduction to the New Testament*, 2:45–47) thought Paul was so emphatic because Titus had informed him, perhaps in a letter, that he found it difficult to carry out his charge.

the mobility of Paul and his associates, stability in the churches is to be achieved by the elders continuing the teaching and exhorting that Titus in the meantime is to engage in.[45]

Qualifications of the Elders/Overseers

What are qualities of character or demeanor exemplified in the process of overseeing the affairs of a church in 1 Tim 3:2–7, here become qualifications for appointment to the role of overseer. The overseer is explicitly called God's household manager (θεοῦ οἰκονόμος, v. 7) and as such must have virtues that qualify him to perform his proper household functions. The virtues listed (Titus 1:6–9a) are similar to the ones in 1 Timothy 3, but differ in primarily two respects: the structure of the list of qualifications, and the emphasis on teaching. Both features are due to the primary functions of the overseers/elders specified in this context, namely to exhort with sound teaching (παρακαλεῖν ἐν τῇ διδασκαλίᾳ τῇ ὑγιαινούσῃ) their hearers, and to reprove (ἐλέγχειν) those who contradict them (1:9b). The heretics are to be shut up, for they are unruly, idle talkers and deceivers (ἀνυπότακτοι, ματαιολόγοι καὶ φρεναπάται) who subvert entire households with the erroneous doctrine they peddle for the sake of personal gain.[46]

The List of Qualifications

In the face of the danger to domestic stability, the list stresses the domestic nature of the elders'/overseers' qualifications. This is evident in the way the list is structured. The qualifications begin, as in 1 Tim 3:2 (ἀνεπίλημπτος), with the requirement that the elders/overseers be blameless (Titus 1:6, ἀνέγκλητος), which is further specified as having one wife and whose children are not morally dissolute or unruly (ἀνυπότακτα). In contrast to the heretics who are unruly

---

45. Titus: ἔλεγχε (1:13); λάλει ἃ πρέπει τῇ ὑγιαινούσῃ διδασκαλίᾳ (2:1); παρακάλει (2:6); παρακάλει καὶ ἔλεγχε (2:15). The elders: παρακαλεῖν ἐν τῇ διδασκαλίᾳ τῇ ὑγιαινούσῃ καὶ τοὺς ἀντιλέγοντας ἐλέγχειν (1:9).

46. An analogous situation is envisaged in 2 Tim 3:1–7, where Timothy is warned against heretics who are characterized by a list of nineteen (!) vices, who sneak into houses to capture silly little women with intellectual pretensions (cf. 1 Tim 5:13). But whereas Timothy is told to avoid them (v. 5), the elders are to reprove them and shut them up in Titus 1:9, 11).

(ἀνυπότακτα) and destabilize households,⁴⁷ the elders/overseers are to have a stable family life. The reason (δεῖ γάρ) for this qualification is then given (v. 7): the overseer must be blameless as God's household manager (τὸν ἐπίσκοπον ἀνέγκλητον εἶναι ὡς θεοῦ οἰκονόμον), which is further specified in a series of antitheses with five vices and five virtues. These virtues are similar to those in 1 Tim 3:2–4, and function as they do in being paraenetic, a function enhanced here by the antithetic style.⁴⁸ Unlike those virtues, these are explicitly related to the domestic role of the overseer as οἰκονόμος.

In addition to these differences is the way the list ends. Like 1 Tim 3:4, there is a change from adjectives to a participial clause that describes the major function of the qualifications. In 1 Timothy, it is προϊστάμενος, which leads to further discussion of church management (προστῆναι . . . οἶδεν). Domestic virtues underlie proper care of the church.

In Titus 1:9, the list begins with a series of adjectives and culminates in a participial clause which has to do with teaching rather than administration: ἀντεχόμενον τοῦ κατὰ τὴν διδαχὴν τοῦ πιστοῦ λόγου ("holding fast to the trustworthy message that conforms to the teaching"). In 1 Tim 3:2, διδακτός describes the capacity to teach in managing a household and is one in a list of such qualities. Here, teaching stands in the culmination of the qualifications of God's manager, and is expanded in two directions. Looking backward, it is the standard (κατά) by which the trustworthy message, to which the manager is devoted, is measured. Looking forward, the purpose (ἵνα) of holding to this teaching is that the household manager have a twofold ability, to exhort with sound teaching (παρακαλεῖν ἐν τῇ διδασκαλίᾳ τῇ ὑγιαινούσῃ) those under his care, and to reprove (ἐλέγχειν) those who oppose him.⁴⁹

That the οἰκονόμος should engage in teaching should not surprise, for philosophers expected the manager to teach members of his

---

47. Cf. 1 Tim 4:3, κωλυόντων γαμεῖν.

48. For antithesis and lists of virtues and vices in paraenesis, see Malherbe, "Paraenesis in the Epistle to Titus," 303–5.

49. Cf. 1 Tim 5:17, οἱ καλῶς προεστῶτες πρεσβύτεροι . . . οἱ κοπιῶντες ἐν λόγῳ καὶ διδασκαλίᾳ, where the πρεσβύτεροι, however, are old men rather than the occupiers of an office (thus, Malherbe, "How to Treat Old Women and Old Men," 282; La Fosse, "Age Matters"). For the different ways in which the orthodox and the heretics are to be treated, see Malherbe, *Paul and the Popular Philosopher*, 125.

household as well as others. Husbands were responsible for teaching their wives about household management,[50] and slaves too received instruction in how to manage a farm.[51] Furthermore, the good manager's concern stretched beyond the administration of his own household, for he taught others how to better manage their own households.[52] Marcus Cato, for one, was judged as no less proficient in the conduct of his own household than of the city. "He not only increased his own substance, but became a recognized teacher of domestic economy (διδάσκαλος οἰκονομίας) and agriculture for others, and compiled many useful precepts on these subjects" (Plutarch, *Comp. Arist. Cato* 3.2; trans. B. Perrin, LCL). The overseer whom Titus is to appoint also engages in teaching, but evidently only of those under his care; his sphere of responsibility is local.

Summary

Titus was directed to appoint elders/overseers in churches without permanent leaders. The qualifications the appointees are to have stress their domestic virtues. As God's household managers, these virtues would make them able to exhort their churches and shut up those who harm the churches by destabilizing entire households. Consequently, the list of qualifications is structured to give prominence to teaching as a qualification of an overseer and an activity in which he is to engage.

Conclusion

The language, including grammatical structure, used to describe the overseer in 1 Timothy 3 and Titus 1 is derived from ancient descriptions of ideal figures, particularly that of the manager of a household. The description in 1 Tim 3 appears in a context in which behavior in the church, the household of the living God, is the subject. The list of virtues characterizing the manager/overseer are qualities he demonstrates as he performs his domestic duties. His main activity, as indicated by the structure of the list, is his administration of the

---

50. See Antipater, *ap.* Stobaeus, *Flor.* (4.510, 3–5 Hense); Xenophon, *Oec.* 2.4–12; 9; cf. Pomeroy, *Xenophon Oeconomicus*, 267–74.

51. Xenophon, *Oec.* 12.4.

52. E.g., Philodemus, *Oec.* 3, 6.

affairs of the church. In the process of taking care of the church, he demonstrates the moral life he wishes to inculcate.

The description of the elder/overseer in Titus 1 is derived from the same philosophical traditions, but is put to a different use. Here, the virtues are qualifications to be met by candidates for appointment to overseership. The form of the list shows that here the major qualification is faithfulness to traditional teaching, which enables the overseer to exhort with it and confute opponents who undermine the church by upsetting entire households.

An awareness of how the author appropriates the discussions of household management shows that he has done more than unthinkingly purloin lists from some tradition to attach them to his Christian functionaries. He rather shapes the two lists to the epistolary situations he reflects in the two letters. In 1Timothy, his interest is in behavior in the church and he concentrates on good administration, one of the two major functions the ancients assigned to a good household manager. In Titus, his interest is in the appointment of overseers who would be able to exhort the faithful and confute gainsayers, so he emphasizes the other major function assigned to a good manager, namely teaching.

Bibliography

Balch, David L. *Let Wives Be Submissive: The Domestic Code in 1 Peter.* SBLMS 26. Chico, CA: Scholars, 1981.

———. "Philodemus, 'On Wealth' and 'On Household Management': Naturally Wealthy Epicureans against Poor Cynics." In *Philodemus and the New Testament,* edited by John T. Fitzgerald et al., 177–96. NovTSup 111. Leiden: Brill, 2004.

Billerbeck, Margarethe. *Epiktet: Vom Kynismus.* Philosophia Antiqua 34. Leiden: Brill, 1978.

Cokayne, Karen. *Experiencing Old Age in Ancient Rome.* London: Routledge, 2003.

Collins, Raymond F. *I and II Timothy and Titus.* NTL. Louisville: John Knox, 2002.

Dibelius, Martin, and Hans Conzelmann. *The Pastoral Epistles.* Translated by Philip Buttolph and Adela Yarbro. Hermeneia. Philadelphia: Fortress, 1972.

Fitzgerald, J. T. "Early Christian Missionary Practice and Pagan Reaction: 1 Peter and Domestic Violence." In *Renewing Tradition: Studies in Texts and Contexts in Honor of James. W. Thompson,* edited by Mark H. Hamilton et al., 24–44. PTMS 65. Eugene, OR: Pickwick, 2007.

Glad, C. E. *Paul and Philodemus: Adaptability in Epicurean and Early Christian Psychagogy.* NovTSup 81. Leiden: Brill: 1995.

Herzer, J. "'A Bishop ... must manage his household well' 1 Tim 3:4." Paper presented to the annual meeting of the Society of Biblical Literature, Boston, December 2008.

———. "Rearranging the 'House of God': A New Perspective on the Pastoral Epistles." In *Empsychoi Logoi, Religious Innovations in Antiquity: Studies in Honour of Pieter Willem van der Horst,* edited by A. Houtman et al., 547–66. AJEC 73. Leiden: Brill, 2008.

Jensen, C. Πηιλοδεμι Περὶ Οἰκονομίας *qui dicitur libellus.* Leipzig: Teubner, 1906.

Johnson, Luke Timothy. *The First and Second Letters to Timothy.* AB 35A. New York: Doubleday, 2001.

La Fosse, Mona Tokarek. "Age Matters: Age, Aging and Intergenerational Relationships in Early Christian Communities, with a Focus on 1 Timothy 5." PhD diss., University of Toronto, 2010.

Lehmeier, K. *Oikos und Oikonomia: Antike Konzepte der Haushaltsführung und der Bau der Gemeinde bei Paulus.* Marburger theologische Studien 92. Marburg: Elwert, 2006.

Lips, H. von. *Glaube, Gemeinde, Amt: Zum Verständnis der Ordination in den Pastoralbriefen.* FRLANT 122. Göttingen: Vandenhoeck & Ruprecht, 1979.

Lührmann, Dieter. "Neutestamentliche Haustafeln und Antike Ökonomie." *NTS* 27 (1980) 83–97.

———. "Wo man nicht mehr Sklave oder Freier ist. Überlegungen zur Struktur frühchristlicher Gemeinden." *Wort und Dienst* 13 (1975) 53–83.

Malherbe, Abraham J. "Godliness, Self-Sufficiency, Greed and the Proper Use of Wealth: 1 Timothy 6:3–19, I." *NovT* 52 (2010) 376–405.

———. "Godliness, Self-Sufficiency, Greed and the Proper Use of Wealth: 1 Timothy 6:3–19, II." *NovT* 53 (2011) 73–96.

———. "How to Treat Old Women and Old Men: The Use of Philosophic Traditions and Scripture in 1 Timothy 5." In *Scripture and Traditions: Essays on Early*

Judaism and Christianity in Honor of Carl R. Holladay, edited by P. Gray and Gail R. O'Day, 263–90. NovTSup 129. Leiden: Brill, 2008.

———. *The Letters to the Thessalonians*. AB 32B. New York: Doubleday, 2000.

———. "'In Season and Out of Season': 2 Timothy 4:2." *JBL* 103 (1984) 235–43.

———. "Paraenesis in the Epistle to Titus." In *Early Paraenesis in Context*, edited by J. Starr and T. Engberg-Pedersen, 297–317. BZNW 125. Berlin: de Gruyter, 2004.

———. *Paul and the Popular Philosophers*. Minneapolis: Fortress, 1989.

———. *Paul and the Thessalonians: The Philosophical Tradition of Pastoral Care*. Philadelphia: Fortress, 1987.

———. "*Paulus Senex*." *ResQ* 36 (1994) 297–307.

———. "The *virtus feminarum* in 1 Timothy 2:9–15." In *Renewing Tradition: Studies in Texts and Contexts in Honor of James W. Thompson*, edited by M. H. Hamilton et al., 44–65. PTMS 65. Eugene, OR: Pickwick, 2007.

Marshall, I. Howard. *The Pastoral Epistles*. ICC. Edinburgh: T. & T. Clark, 1999.

Natali, C. "*Oikonomia* in Hellenistic Political Thought." In *Justice and Generosity in Hellenistic Social and Political Philosophy: Proceedings of the Sixth Symposium*, edited by A. Laks and M. Schofield, 95–128. Cambridge: Cambridge University Press, 1995.

Norden, Eduard. "Beiträge zur Geschichte der griechischen Philosophie." *Jahrbücher für classische Philologie*, Suppl. 19 (1893) 373–475.

Oberlinner, Lorenz. *Die Pastoralbriefe: Erste Folge: Kommentar zum Timotheusbrief*. HTKNT 11 2/1. Freiburg: Herder, 1994.

Pomeroy, Sarah B., translator. *Xenophon Oeconomicus: A Social and Historical Commentary*. Oxford: Clarendon, 1996.

Powell, J. G. F. *Cicero Cato Maior de Senectute*. Cambridge Classical Texts and Commentaries 28. Cambridge: Cambridge University Press, 1988.

Ramelli, Ilaria. *Hierocles the Stoic: Elements of Ethics, Fragments and Excerpts*. Translated by David Konstan. SBLWGRW 28. Atlanta: Society of Biblical Literature, 2009.

Roloff, Jürgen. *Der Ertse Brief an Timotheus*. EKKNT 15. Zürich: Benziger 1988.

Schwarz, Roland. *Bürgerliches Christentum im Neuen Testamentum? Eine Studie zu Ehtik, Amt und Recht in den Pastoralbriefen*. OBS 4. Klosterneuburg: Österreichisches Katholisches Bibelwerk, 1983.

Spicq, Ceslas. *Les épîtres pastorales*. 2 vols. EBib. Paris: Gabalda, 1969.

———. *Lexique théologique du Nouveau Testaament*. Fribourg: Éditions universitaires de Fribourg, 1991.

Thurén, Jukka. "Die Struktur der Schlussparënese, 1 Tim 6,3–21." *TZ* 26 (1970) 241–53.

Towner, Philip H. *The Letters to Timothy and Titus*. NICNT. Grand Rapids: Eerdmans, 2006.

Treggiari, Susan. *Roman Marriage: Iusti Coniuges from the Time of Cicero to the Time of Ulpian*. Oxford: Clarendon, 1991.

Tsouna, V. *The Ethics of Philodemus*. Oxford: Oxford University Press, 2007.

Wolter, Michael. *Das Lukasevangelium*. HNT 5. Tübingen: Mohr/Siebeck, 2008.

———. *Die Pastoralbriefe als Paulustradition*. FRLANT 146. Göttingen: Vandenhoeck & Ruprecht, 1987.

Zahn, Theodor. *Introduction to the New Testament*. 1909. Grand Rapids: Kregel, 1953.

6

"Houses Made with Hands"

The Triumph of the Private in New Testament Scholarship[1]

DAVINA C. LOPEZ AND TODD PENNER

"It is not enough to demythologize texts with Bultmann. Before doing such, the world and human beings need to be demythologized, in, say, their self-mastery, their ideology, and the religious superstition to which they have surrendered."

—Ernst Käsemann[2]

---

1. We appreciate Aliou Niang's graciousness in extending an invitation to participate in this *Festschrift*, and we thank Carolyn Osiek for her patience and expertise in the editing process. We respectfully and gratefully offer this essay as tribute to the scholarship and friendship of David Balch. David has been most welcoming, collegial, and inclusive of us as junior scholars—at times boldly so—not unlike the idealized picture of the early Christian community in Acts. While he has not always seen eye-to-eye with us regarding our scholarly conclusions or methods, David has never stopped engaging and supporting the two of us. Having recently revisited his *Let Wives Be Submissive* for this essay, we were challenged to rethink the already well-entrenched analytical categories he employed in his work on the house(hold). We are indebted to the detailed argumentation and stimulating insight that David contributes. Even more, we value his steadfast commitment to making connections between the New Testament (especially in ancient cultural contexts) and the contemporary world (especially the church). While we may disagree with some of David's assumptions and methods, we remain adamantly in solidarity with him on the latter score: scholarly investigation of early Christian literature and social history has meaning only insofar as it engages what it means to be human in our world. It is a great honor to pay homage, even in this small way, to an exemplary human being such as David.

2. Käsemann, *On Being a Disciple*, xiii.

One of the more famous passages in Acts depicts Stephen, the soon to be "first martyr of the church," standing before his Jewish opponents, proclaiming that the God of Israel does not live in "houses made with hands" (7:48). This climactic punctuation of his narrative retelling and prophetic critique of the history of the "stubborn" people of Israel seemingly agitates the situation, bringing about his death at the hands of those same opponents. Although the narrative is not entirely clear, the final lines of Stephen's speech appear to represent a denunciation of Jewish tradition, including the worship of God in the Jerusalem Temple. Throughout Acts, it is made evident that the "Most High" does not dwell in temples, buildings, or any kind of human construction. Paul proclaims the same message to the Greeks in Acts 17:24: God does not exist inside temples, just as God cannot be worshipped in and through objects constructed with "human hands."

Yet for all the claims that God does not dwell in "houses made with hands," it is surprising that the Acts narrative pays so much attention to exactly those houses. From the first moments of the "Pentecost event" in Jerusalem in Acts 2, to the culmination of the narrative in Acts 28, where Paul is under "house arrest" in Rome, everywhere early Christians are inside—in private spaces, homes, houses—seemingly peacefully sequestered off from the public sphere, which is largely represented as hostile towards the early Christian movement. Jewish, Greek, and Roman authorities continually oppose Christians in open spaces. Trials and accusations exist in public—but in private we see the miracles of God, the preaching of Paul, the communion and worship of those first believers, the "safe" place to hide when Peter is in prison, the space in which whole households are brought to knowledge of the "Most High." Saul, in his role as persecutor of the early Messianic community, goes "house to house" (8:3), dragging out "believers" to imprison them; in some way his actions provide a counter point to the early Christians, who also go "house to house" to proclaim and teach (5:42; 20:20). Of course, after being blinded by the light, it is to a "house" that Paul first goes—that of Ananias in Damascus. One might wonder how, if all the early Christians had sold their property as narrated in Acts 4, there were any dwellings left to inhabit. Still, Acts makes it clear that Christians from Jerusalem to Rome lived in houses—which were the primary locus of their spiritual, communal, experiential, and perhaps also political activities. This perception is continually reinforced in the narrative as the apostles and other leaders and heroes move in and out of such spaces, creating the impression that these "private" realms are "set apart."

It is rather predictable, then, that modern New Testament scholarship has been so consumed, for nearly a century, with categories like "house church." Aside from various social and communal terminology in canonical epistolary literature—which from an earlier era of form-critical scholarship demanded some kind of *Sitz im Leben*—the Acts narrative parades the house before the readers' very eyes, in some sense creating deep and penetrating desire for the private space of Christian life and communion. It is somewhat ironic that houses in Acts are thought to be "private" at all, since everywhere its writer appears intent on exposing houses and "goings on" inside. Scholars such as Jerome Neyrey have attempted to negotiate this rather startling feature by suggesting there are three types of spaces in Acts: "public" (political); "private" (non-household association); and "private" (household).[3] Despite an effort to draw on numerous ancient literary examples to create a socio-typological framework for ancient spaces, Neyrey's formulation reveals a palpable problem: private space is displayed everywhere—it is not hidden and not "inside" or beyond the "public eye." There is no "hidden transcript" in Acts—the transcript is available for all to see as readers are invited to gaze openly into the *domus* of early Christian existence. It might be that the "Most High does not dwell in houses made with hands," but it is not the case that God and the gospel are absent in such houses throughout Acts. Indeed, we might consider Acts as a "triumph" of the "houses made with hands" over the public spaces of the Jews, Greeks, and Romans.

Given the predominance of house terminology in Acts, it is no wonder that New Testament scholarship has focused on the "house church" as a site for the formation of early Christian social and theological identity. Some seventy years ago, Floyd Filson proposed the following:

> The house church was a vital factor in the church's development during the first century, and even in later generations. It provided the setting in which the primitive Christians achieved a mental separation from Judaism before the actual open break occurred. It gave added importance to the effort to

---

3. Neyrey, "'Teaching You in Public.'"

> Christianize family relationships. It explains in part the proneness of the apostolic church to divide. It helps us gain a true understanding of the influent[i]al place of families of means in what has sometimes been regarded as a church of the dispossessed. It points us to the situation in which were developed leaders to succeed apostolic workers. Obviously the apostolic church can never be properly understood without constantly bearing in mind the contribution of the house churches.[4]

We see in this distinction a basic paradigm for what would follow in subsequent studies of house churches. One might now consider it an assumed datum of historical inquiry that early Christians met in private spaces, whether those were specifically homes of wealthy patrons or alternative private meeting spaces. Commitment to the *private* nature of the early Christian social and "religious" experience has become foundational. We note that Filson also describes a commitment to "separation from Judaism." Acts might indicate such a configuration, as Paul first goes to the synagogue and then to the "house." Certainly, as an ideological space for modern scholarly imagination and desire, the house as a social space in the ancient world provides a conceptual framework that stabilizes and sustains a *pure* Christian identity over against Jewishness or Graeco-Romanness. Without the category of "house" and "private space," it would be difficult to envision "Christianness" as a category. It is the defining and delimiting nature of this space, its function of separation, that allows scholars to conceptualize a structure that contains and shapes the identity that early Christian theology, as derived from the literature, seems to sustain, idealize, and extol.

Thus, "house" represents a critical category for modern classification of early Christian social structures as privately oriented. By the time Wayne Meeks completed his landmark work *The First Urban Christians*,[5] the Filson trajectory had won the day. In fact, while Meeks might be credited with changing the landscape of modern perceptions of early Christian social realities, his basic premises effectively represent an extended meditation on the above-mentioned summary of Filson. In particular, upwardly mobile Christian communities needed elite spaces in which to meet and locate their being. Meeks produced

---

4. Filson, "Significance," 112.
5. Meeks, *First Urban Christians*.

a large corpus of data utilized to imagine and reconstruct the urban environment that became the *habitus* for early Christian identity. Such evidence was critical, as this "social" identity functions as a signifier for "theological" identity—even more so than "religious" identity. In other words, it is not enough to analyze Pauline theology. One requires a context in which theology can be placed and make sense; ultimately, such a context must be stabilized and made coherent. At the same time, this form of contextualization solidifies the boundaries that could contain "Christianness," formulating a broad structure delineating the identity of these "first urban Christians." Such social realities both reflect an emergent Christian theology and, at the same time, exert a formative influence on that theology.

Herein our main contention is that the assumptions and categories that have been employed for analysis of early Christian social and theological realities are in need of revisitation and reimagination. At stake in much of this discourse on early Christianity are claims on specific formulations of modern political and economic identities, now grafted onto the past in a way that legitimizes and universalizes these contemporary filiations. As part of a larger ethical interpretive project, we submit that sustained critical engagement with scholarly historical paradigms provides one way to interrogate the identities and masked social realities we inhabit and promote, often unbeknownst to ourselves and yet with persistent social effects.

Demythologizing the Private

Whatever scholars might think about describing Christian origins through a reconstruction of "house" as space and metaphor where origins occurs, and whatever stories about social relations the results of such quests might engender for ancient and modern contexts, we suggest that the basic dichotomy between "public" and "private" must be located as revealing not of an ancient historical orientation, but of contemporary liberal theories of social organization that arose in 18th and nineteenth-century European contexts.[6] Connecting the "public" sphere with official workings of government and other insti-

---

6. For an historical orientation to the "public sphere" as that which is opposed to "private," see Habermas, *Structural Transformation*. For a critical appraisal of Habermas's contributions to articulations of public and private spheres, see Crossley and Roberts, *After Habermas*.

tutions, naming it as a place (for free males) to speak and "get business done" with one another and on behalf of a democratic citizenship, is a modern construal. Likewise, designating non-citizen duties such as personal family and household organization as non-public (and "effeminate") is constructed and reified as natural within this same historical context. In this schema, the public realm denotes an interaction with authority, while self-determination and expression belongs to the private sphere where such authority cannot prevail. In fact, Martin Heidegger famously argued that the private sphere, and specifically the privacy of inner consciousness, is where people retreat to become their most authentic selves.[7] We find significant resonance here, as quests for Christian origins can be methodologically positioned as quests for the legitimation of early Christian consciousness, experiences, and selves. Thus, "private" is a useful category for situating the originality and authenticity of early Christianity, particularly as represented in New Testament literature. Conversely, "public" becomes the space where the Christian mission formulated in "private" is catalyzed.

While New Testament scholars find designations of public and private as useful—perhaps the most useful—categories for social description of early Christian phenomena, methodologically we cannot afford to downplay the ideological contours of such categories as construed in the present, even if we state that our primary concern is the distant past. As categories, "public" and "private" describe types of activity as well as discursive and physical spaces. In particular, "private" denotes the house in conjunction with the immediate context of the property on which it sits, and "public" is linked to all outside the house as such. The spaces are thought to be reflective of their functions in a material way—for example, domestic visual decoration is positioned as an expression of personal taste and self-consciousness and only marginally linked to wider cultural norms, whilst the same decoration in a non-home space might be labeled as political propaganda or another form of "public art." Similarly, certain types of literary representation are designated as privately oriented, such as familial and household management discourses, while oratory and historical narrative are the responsibility of the public. The point is not so much whether available data happens to fit with modern conceptions of "public" and "private"—one might say that data will always fit the categories we make if

---

7. See Heidegger, *Being and Time*.

we work hard enough. Rather, the methodological point is that these naturalized structural oppositions are taken to be "ancient" when it is more accurate to say that they are mapped onto the ancient world as a means to create and maintain modern structures of meaning.

Modern boundaries between public and private as separate spheres of human interaction, influence, and meaning-making have not been without criticism. Feminist and Marxist interpreters such as Nancy Fraser have articulated that such constructions replicate concerns of the upper class, reinscribing hierarchies that perpetuate the marginalization of the underclass and hiding the "subaltern counterpublics" that the marginalized create.[8] Michel Foucault argued for a redescription of such post-enlightenment-based oppositions in light of emergent biopower and biopolitics.[9] Building on Foucault's work, Michael Hardt and Antonio Negri have proposed a wholesale reconsideration of the distinctions between public and private, stating that these differentiations are predicated upon a capitalist framework where disparities between economic interests inheres. Hardt and Negri posit that a productive way to negotiate our analytical categories in a late-capitalist environment—to use their language, in the midst of "empire"—might be to reconfigure such spheres away from private possession toward sharing resources and goods.[10] Such interventions and complications assist in understanding that the categories held to be natural, universal, and divinely ordained are in fact named and located in time and space, and profoundly human in construction, appropriation, and deployment. According to a historical-materialist framework, "public" and "private," as categories, are thoroughly unstable and "made with hands"—even as we might faithfully accept them to be otherwise.

As students of the New Testament inclined to front materialist methodological questions, concerns, and concepts in the present as critical for any engagement of the past, we concur with Hardt and Negri that our late-capitalist context demands an ethics that reimagines "public" and "private" toward a common future where all might flourish. We further contend that there is not now, nor has there ever been, an *a priori* set of distinctions between these categories and the

8. Fraser, "Rethinking the Public Sphere."
9. See Foucault, "Different Spaces."
10. Hardt and Negri, *Commonwealth*.

spheres to which they are applied. In other words, calling a set of practices and spaces "public" or "private" does not merely describe or reflect reality. Rather, naming is the process by which we construct the reality that we accept as divisible into public and private spheres. When we deploy "public" and "private" in various modes of scholarly labor, whether biblical exegesis, theological reconstruction, or social-scientific interpretation, it is worth considering the ways in which we participate in the ritual of naming in the present through our projections into the past.

Despite ideological machinery that reifies sentiments to the contrary, social relationships and hierarchical arrangements are arbitrary and anything but coherent. It is rhetoric, and not reality, that creates and secures public and private spheres in relationship to one another. Furthermore, we must remember that the ancient literary and visual representation available to us is paltry, rhetorically charged, and as data indicates slipperiness and instability between public and private spheres of influence. To illustrate this point, we turn to New Testament studies prioritizing "house," "household," and "house church" as basic organizing units for socio-historical descriptions of Christian origins. "House," as physical and metaphorical locus for the development of early Christianity, is posited as "private" with attendant functions. If we take seriously that the distinctions between public and private are always contestable and tenuous, we might see "house," Christian origins, and our own circumstances differently. To that end, we offer below a sampling of methodological challenges in several significant areas of interest related to "house" as a category of analysis and signifier in the field.

"From House to House"

New Testament scholarship configures "house" as space and structuring principle, using the categories "household" and "house church" as a means to negotiate various theological and social issues in early Christian life. "House" signifies such negotiations because it is considered to be private and separate from public life in the spaces in which the "first urban Christians" lived. As urban private space, "house" designates a space free of influence from "outside" venues such as the synagogue, a public place that shapes Jewish (religious) identities, as well as the agora or forum, places that shape Graeco-Roman (political) identities. Neither completely religious nor completely political, "house" signifies the place and community where early Christian self-definition occurs according to modern assumptions about the private sphere. And as private space for self-definition protected from public interference of either religion (Judaism) or politics (Greekness and Romanness), it could be said that "house" is the place where a new orientation, Christian theology, is born. In scholarly discourse, "house" provides the context for the "newness" of Christian theology and ethics experimented with and developed in isolation from Jewishness, Greekness, and Romanness.

Such premises find support through material culture, where archaeological remains of ancient houses are construed as expressions of wealth and elite status and a robust private family-oriented life—which the early Christians then adopted and manipulated by virtue of their "going private" into homes for ritual activities. House decorations—wall paintings, mosaics, statuary, furniture—are interpreted as reflecting tastes of inhabitants and their desires to express status to visitors and, mostly, to themselves. Similarly, it is thought that the very walls of the house had family hierarchies "built in"—in the orientation of rooms, their visual programs, and their supposed functions. The spatial organization and visual language of "house," then, provide important legitimating factors for social descriptions of early Christianity as private and house-bound.

It is precisely when we start to acknowledge the shifting landscapes hidden by articulations of stark differences between public and private that we are able to see that the data do not necessarily support such neat cleavages. For instance, while archaeological discoveries suggest that houses might look a certain way, we only have somewhat intact remains of larger houses in well-preserved places like Pompeii to help us. Cities like Rome have been continuously inhabited, making it nearly impossible to locate the "ancient world" among the topography; highly managed public space projects like the Roman Forum render it otherwise, even as they are modern fabrications that "looks like ruins." House remains elsewhere are rare and, in the provinces, almost unreadable as domiciles. Additionally, the places where the majority of (impoverished) people may have lived in the ancient world have vanished from the material record.[11] It is therefore predictable that New Testament scholars should create an ancient domestic world that happens to consist of large elite homes,[12] where early Christian communities such as those thought to be described in Acts and Paul's letters might have met and constructed their modes of accommodation and resistance to public authorities and influences.

We have also assumed that we can successfully associate the various spaces of private homes with various activities corresponding to "roles" the various members of the household may have played when they were not out in public. Decorative elements such as wall paintings are seen as that which can assist us in this regard, as they are thought to reflect the personal proclivities and identities of homeowners. However, as Peter Stewart notes, it is quite possible that ornamental programs excavated from homes such as those in Pompeii and Herculaneum were not determined by the client, but by artists who, as workshop laborers, had stock visual themes readily applicable to houses when owners came calling.[13] And Shelley Hales has questioned naturalized assertions about relationships between the *domus* and ancient social identities as belonging to an individual's desire for self-determination, proposing that the arrangement of domestic space is as rhetorically oriented and ideologically charged as literary representations about ancient houses and social relationships. Contents of wall paintings, then, are not solely determined by a house-holder's personal beliefs, but rather might construct house-holders as fully part of a larger Roman social hierarchical system. The conduct of business in the house, including client reception and political maneuvering that "spilled out" into the so-called public arena, further suggests that a house is anything but a retreat from the world. Simply put, there

---

11. Beryl Rawson contests the idea that the majority of Romans lived in the *atrium* house: "I envisage the great majority of the population . . . living in small, cramped apartments which had little space for more than the conjugal family and a small number of slaves . . . this line of investigation may well prove profitable for early Christian families" ("'Roman Family,'" 124).

12. See, for example, Clarke, *Houses of Roman Italy*; and Wallace-Hadrill, *Houses and Society*. The so-called house church building at Dura Europos, including a "baptistery," "chapel," and "Christian" frescoes, supports theories that early Christians met and worshipped in homes such as those at Pompeii earlier on, and then moved to hybrid house-church structures by the second and third centuries CE. For a bibliography and discussion, see Pagulatos, *Tracing the Bridegroom*.

13. Stewart, *Social History*, 10–38.

is little about the structure or decoration of an ancient dwelling that proves a certain set of social relationships and hierarchies or supports a division between public and private spheres.[14] While it may be the case that the house belonged to a *paterfamilias* and household, we must entertain the notion that constructions of space can be seen as public gestures toward belonging not to private selves, but to an ideological orientation embedded in public social order and, to be sure, on display. If the house proves anything, it is its inhabitants' participation in social order. We must ask, then, to what extent early Christian deployment of "house" as locus of activity suggests not a removal from the world, but a strategic embeddedness in and an ideological negotiation of that world, the historical reality of which is completely beside the point.

Further complicating "house" as a spatial environment, structuring principle, and metaphor for that which is private and removed from public spheres of interaction are accounts of Roman displays of the private in public processions. Literary representation suggests that rituals such as births, deaths, and marriages—what we might label as "family" affairs—were announced through processions from house to house (marriage and death) and decorations of entryways (birth).[15] In this sense, machinations of the "public" affect and manage affairs of the "private," significantly troubling such distinctions. Perhaps most arresting, though, is the connection of the house to imperial ideology through that (in)famous Roman ritual of conquest: the triumphal procession. According to literary representation, the triumph parades conquered peoples and conquering Romans through public urban space, announcing victory over foreigners.[16] Not only representative peoples and personifications of nations, though, were hauled through city streets—wagons displaying weapons, coins, precious metals and jewels, paintings, and statues from conquered lands are narrated as occupying large portions of parades. Roman literature often divides war spoils displayed in triumphal processions into categories, and foreign household items figure fairly prominently.[17] In an account of

14. Hales, *Roman House*.

15. Ibid., 2, 11–39.

16. For a recent discussion of the complexities of the triumph as ritual, narration, and that which has captured the imagination of classical scholars, see Beard, *Roman Triumph*.

17. For a discussion of these representations as critical to imperial ideology, see Östenberg, *Staging the World*.

Manlius Vulso's triumph over the Asiatic Galatians, for example, "foreign luxuries" occupied a prized placement: bronze couches, exotic tapestries, and pedestal tables were taken from homes and brought to Rome (Livy, *Hist.* 39.6–7). Similarly, the famous Arch of Titus in Rome is often interpreted as visually portraying the triumph over Jerusalem through narrative reliefs.

Figure 6.1: Arch of Titus, Rome. Interior narrative relief depicting a parade, possibly of Judean captives, carrying Jerusalem temple objects through a triumphal arch. Photo by Davina C. Lopez.

The ritual celebrating the Roman seizure of these oversized objects from the "house" of the God of Israel occupies prime placement on this public monument.

Of further interest for the present study is what happens to triumphal spoils and other foreign household items once the parade is over. Katherine Welch has suggested that war spoils were not simply dumped in a public repository following the triumph, nor was everything taken to museums or temples for safe-keeping. Rather, material and literary evidence suggests that, beginning in the Republican period, victorious Romans may have enhanced their houses with spoils. From affixing weapons of the conquered to walls and entryways, to adorning gardens and rooms with foreign statues, furniture, and tapestries, Roman houses became visual theater spaces of sorts through which memories of victory and affirmations of empire were rehearsed and preserved.[18] In this way, "house" becomes a setting where public meets private, where family meets military, where conquered others meet imperial selves. Through the triumph, "house" becomes a highly contestable space that fundamentally challenges its location as removed from public view. Moreover, "house" becomes the place that represents the public, however idealized, and perhaps even participates in its creation.

In sum, we observe a significant disjunction between how we, and the ancients, conceptualize ancient private spaces—at least, as far as we can know according to literary and visual representations. Evidence suggests that the ways in which we have delineated early Christian conceptions of "public" and "private" does not cohere with ancient categories. There certainly appears to be fluidity between "public" and "private" that modern classifications cannot justify, rendering these categories devoid of meaning. It might well be that we need to stop deploying such conceptions for the socio-historical analysis of early Christian communities. Indeed, in light of the preceding observations, we would argue that the term "community" is itself a futile category for classification, as it as depends on spaces in which it can be located for definition and presupposes stable identities and boundaries.

A Not-So-Private Conclusion

The critical formulations we invent to categorize our perceptions of the social realities and identities of early Christian communities are inherently inconsistent and somewhat misleading. In the case of "house," we have inadvertently placed a set of categories on the past that are shaped by more recent political and social developments. We have conscripted the past, even if unwittingly, as a means of naturalizing and universalizing these categories of modern existence, especially those that might serve the interest of the modern nation-state and the global market economy. It is intriguing, for instance, that it is during the rise of the middle class in the modern economy that scholars began to think about the elite Christians of antiquity. "Dispossessed" mem-

18. Welch, *"Domi Militiaeque."*

bers of those communities slowly faded from view. Our constructions of Christian origins in this sense reflect something fundamental about our own class and social standings, and, in light of twentieth-century political realities, a turn away from Marxist interpretations of early Christianity. "Cold War" ideologies have in fact shaped the way we do scholarship!

We maintain that early Christian social realities and identities were much more complicated and contestable than our scholarly proposals are wont to suggest. Despite containment efforts, it appears as difficult to reconstruct broad social delineations in early Christianity as it is theological constructions. Ultimately, we know a lot less than we realize, which few New Testament scholars are willing to acknowledge. Quite the opposite: the triumph of scholarship is to parade an early Christian private sphere from "house to house" until one day Christianity itself emerges victorious in the form of the basilica or emerges as the new (public!) ruling elite. The developmental nature of this enterprise is especially alarming, as it suggests that scholarly desire for Christian triumph lies at the heart of such work, even among those who suggest they adamantly eschew and oppose any investment in victory. Moreover, our own social, economic, and political investments lie just beneath the surface. Claims to so-called liberal agendas aside, there is a core desire for the triumph of current configurations of power and authority that best suit our own houses and households.[19] Such is reminiscent of the *Ars Amatoria*, where Ovid offers a reflection on how to woo a lover whilst watching the chaos of a triumphal procession:

> Then if some fair one shall ask of you the name of this or that defeated monarch, what all these emblems mean, what country this, what mountain that, or what that river yonder represents, answer at once . . . what you don't know, tell her as if you did. "Here's the Euphrates, with his sedgy crown; and that old fellow there, with sky-blue hair, why, he's the Tigris; and those? . . . hum! . . . well, they're Armenians. That woman yonder? She is Persia, where the son of Danaë was born. That town till lately rose up amid the vales of Achæmenes. That prisoner there, or that other one yonder? Oh, they are captured generals." And if you know them, give their names. If you don't, invent them. (Ovid, *Ars Amatoria* 1.220–25; our translation)

---

19. See further, Penner and Lopez, "'Homelessness as a Way Home.'"

We suggest that scholarly desires echoed in conjuring the past operate little different. We are, in effect, creating real or imagined historical worlds in service of present desires to stabilize our own social realities and identities. If we know them, we give names, and if not, we are quite capable of invention. We aim to reveal this process, hidden from view by the scholarly imaginary, as that to which we have surrendered—and which must therefore be demythologized. "House churches" and "households"—and "associations" as well—are merely, in the end, "houses made with hands," strategic concepts that construct and reify our ideological commitments, serving to absolutize and naturalize our "truth" claims. As such, we would do well to remember that, if Stephen is correct, the "most high" does not, (un)fortunately, dwell in such "houses."

Bibliography

Balch, David. *Let Wives Be Submissive: The Domestic Code in I Peter*. SBLMS 26. Atlanta: Scholars, 1981.

Beard, Mary. *The Roman Triumph*. Cambridge: Belknap, 2007.

Clarke, John R. *The Houses of Roman Italy, 100 BC—AD 250: Ritual, Space, and Decoration*. Berkeley: University of California Press, 1991.

Crossley, Nick, and John Michael Roberts, editors. *After Habermas: New Perspectives on the Public Sphere*. Sociological Review Monographs. Oxford: Blackwell, 2004.

Filson, Floyd V. "The Significance of the Early House Churches." *JBL* 58 (1939) 105–12.

Foucault, Michel. "Different Spaces." In *The Essential Works of Foucault, 1954–1984*. Vol. 2: *Aesthetics, Method, and Epistemology*, edited by J. D. Faubion, 175–86. 3 vols. Translated by Robert Hurley et al. New York: New Press, 1998.

Fraser, Nancy. "Rethinking the Public Sphere: A Contribution to the Critique of Actually Existing Democracy." *ST* 25/26 (1990) 56–80.

Habermas, Jürgen. *The Structural Transformation of the Public Sphere: An Inquiry into a Category of Bourgeois Society*. Translated by Thomas Burger, with the assistance of Frederick Lawrence. Studies in Contemporary German Social Thought. Cambridge, MA: MIT Press, 1989.

Hales, Shelley. *The Roman House and Social Identity*. New York: Cambridge University Press, 2009.

Hardt, Michael, and Antonio Negri. *Commonwealth*. Cambridge, MA: Belknap, 2009.

Heidegger, Martin. *Being and Time*. Translated by Joan Stambaugh. SUNY Series in Contemporary Continental Philosophy. Albany: State University of New York Press, 1996.

Käsemann, Ernst. *On Being a Disciple of the Crucified Nazarene: Unpublished Lectures and Sermons*, edited by Rudolf Landau, in cooperation with Wolfgang Kraus. Translated by Roy A. Harrisville. Grand Rapids: Eerdmans, 2010.

Meeks, Wayne A.. *The First Urban Christians: The Social World of the Apostle Paul*. 2nd ed. New Haven: Yale University Press, 2003.

Neyrey, Jerome H. "'Teaching You in Public and from House to House' (Acts 20:20): Unpacking a Cultural Stereotype." *JSNT* 26 (2003) 69–102.

Östenberg, Ida. *Staging the World: Spoils, Captives, and Representations in the Roman Triumphal Procession*. Oxford Studies in Ancient Culture and Representation. New York: Oxford University Press, 2009.

Pagulatos, Gerasimos. *Tracing the Bridegroom in Dura: The Bridal Initiation Service of the Dura-Europos Christian Baptistery as Early Evidence of the Use of Images in Christian and Byzantine Worship*. Piscataway, NJ: Tigris, 2009.

Penner, Todd, and Davina C. Lopez. "'Homelessness as a Way Home': A Methodological Reflection and Proposal." In *Holy Land as Homeland? Models for Constructing the Historic Landscapes of Jesus*, edited by Keith Whitelam et al. Sheffield: Sheffield Phoenix, forthcoming.

Rawson, Beryl. "'The Roman Family' in Recent Research: State of the Question." *Bib Int* 11 (2003) 119–38.

Stewart, Peter. *The Social History of Roman Art*. Key Themes in Ancient History. Cambridge: Cambridge University Press, 2008.

Wallace-Hadrill, Andrew. *Houses and Society in Pompeii and Herculaneum*. Princeton: Princeton University Press, 1996.

Welch, Katherine. "*Domi Militiaeque*: Roman Domestic Aesthetics and War Booty in the Republic." In *Representations of War in Ancient Rome*, edited by Sheila Dillon and Katherine E. Welch, 91–161. New York: Cambridge University Press, 2006.

7

The Greek Novel and Literary Ethnography
The Household in the World of the New Testament

Ronald F. Hock

Introduction

ONE OF DAVID BALCH'S LIFELONG INTERESTS IS THE GRAECO-ROMAN household. This interest began with his influential dissertation, *Let Wives Be Submissive*, published in 1981,[1] and has been evident ever since, especially in 1997, with the publication of *Families in the New Testament World*, which he co-authored with Carolyn Osiek.[2] The latter volume is a superb contribution—comprehensive in coverage, sophisticated in method, and fully documented. There is in many ways little to add to their study, but I would like to honor David by highlighting some data that were overlooked in *Families*. These data come from the roughly contemporary Greek novels. The Greek novels I am thinking of include those by Chariton (mid-first century), Xenophon of Ephesus (early second century), Achilles Tatius (early second century), and Longus (late second century).[3]

---

1. Balch, *Let Wives Be Submissive*.
2. Osiek and Balch, *Families*.
3. For the latest critical texts of these novels, see Reardon, *Callirhoe narrationes amatoriae*; O'Sullivan, *Xenophon Ephesius*; Garnaud, *Achille Tatius d'Alexandrie*; and Reeve, *Longus, Daphnis*. In addition, all four novels are now readily available in the Loeb Classical Library (LCL). The novel by Achilles Tatius has long been available in the LCL. Chariton's was added in 1995, those by Longus and Xenophon of Ephesus in 2009. English translations of all the novels and fragmentary ones are conveniently available in Reardon, *Collected Ancient Greek Novels*. All translations here, however,

While basically stories of love and marriage, the novels also provide lengthy, detailed, and coherent accounts of many of the institutions and social roles in the world of the New Testament. Given the centrality of the aristocratic household to this world, it should not surprise that the novels contain valuable data on a variety of households. The purpose of this study is to indicate some of the ways that these novels can help us to reconstruct the Graeco-Roman household and to clarify the typically briefer accounts of households in the New Testament.

More specifically, this study will begin with some brief, general remarks about the aristocratic and lesser households that appear in the novels (I), and then focus on three individuals that shed special light on the conventions of behavior that governed the management of the household—the οἰκοδεσπότης, or householder II), the διοικητής, or slave administrator III), and the οἰκονόμος, or the slave manager of the householder's rural properties IV).

General Remarks

Speaking generally, the four novels mentioned above include considerable data on nine aristocratic households, and a smattering of data on eight others. But it's not just the number of households that is significant, but the fact that these households are viewed in action, caught up in the day to day activities and crisis situations that allow us to see how these households operated. In other words, when taken as a whole, the novels present us with the opportunity to do a virtual ethnographic, or at least a literary ethnographic, study of the various people, venues, and activities of functioning aristocratic households.

Let's run through the major components of a household—the householder, his properties in the *polis* and *chora*, and the people that make up such a complex organization. Householders are the authoritative figures in an aristocratic household, and to achieve that authority they are typically described as good (using either ἀγαθός or χρηστός), as can be seen in the case of Dionysophanes, a leading aristocratic householder in Mytilene on Lesbos, where this quality has the emphatic last place in Longus's introductory description of him.

---

are my own. On the Greek novel in general, see Schmeling, *Novel in the Ancient World*. The journal *Ancient Narrative*, which began in 2001, publishes research on the novels.

He is, Longus says, "middle-aged, but tall, handsome, and still able to compete with those much younger; moreover, he was wealthy as only a few were and good (χρηστός) as no one else was" (Longus 4.13.2).[4]

Aristocratic households included a house in the *polis*,[5] or urban center, that, to use that of Dionysius, was "large and magnificent" and situated on one of the harbors of Miletus (Chariton 1.13.1; 3.2.11); in the *chora*, or agriculturally productive area surrounding the *polis*, Dionysius had many properties, including one beside the sea (2.1.2) that had a country home (ἔπαυλις), complete with a second floor (2.11.1; 3.1.2), a bath (2.2.2), and rooms enough for his entourage from the *polis* to stay (2.3.10). Near this country home was a temple of Aphrodite, apparently the product of Dionysius's devotion to the goddess (2.2.7). Dionysophanes's properties in the *chora* are more fully described: they comprised "mountains that produced wild game, plains that grew wheat, hills that were covered with vineyards, and pastures on which sheep grazed" (Longus 1.1.2), along with a country house (ἔπαυλις) where Dionysophanes and his wife Cleariste would stay when in the *chora* (4.15.4) and a walled-in garden (παράδεισος) that grew all kinds of flowers and trees and had an altar, temple, statue, and paintings of familiar stories about Dionysos (4.2.1–3). Either on or near his properties were the households of peasants, such as those of Dionysophanes's slave goatherd Lamon and his family (1.3.1), and several others, enough households to make up a village (1.11.2). Even the most marginal of households are included in the novels, such as that of the very poor fisherman Aegialeus on the shore near Syracuse (Xenophon of Ephesus 5.1.1).

The numbers and variety of roles of the people in an aristocratic household point to a complex social organization. In the urban house are not only the householder's immediate family, such as Dionysophanes; his wife, Cleariste; and their son Astylos (Longus 4.13.1; 24.1), but other relatives or guests who might live there for short or extended pe-

---

4. For more examples of householders in the novels who are described as "good" and the applicability of this description for interpreting the parable of the laborers in the vineyard (Matt 20:1–16) whose householder (οἰκοδεσπότης) defends his hiring practices by saying that he was "good" (ἀγαθός) (v 15), see Hock, "Romancing the Parables," 11–37, esp. 31–37.

5. One feature of Balch's and Osiek's book that is especially welcome and valuable is the careful use of archaeological data to reconstruct the physical characteristics of ancient households (see *Families*, 5–35).

riods of time. Thus in Achilles Tatius's novel the householder Hippias of Tyre welcomes his brother's wife and daughter who are fleeing from war (Achilles Tatius 1.3.6), in Xenophon's novel Perilaus of Tarsus admits a shipwrecked victim from Ephesus (Xenophon of Ephesus 3.4.3), whereas in Longus's novel Dionysophanes allows the parasite Gnathon to stay permanently in his house (Longus 4.10.1; cf. 4.16.3) and he invites Chloe to stay until her biological parents can be found (4.33.4). And there are the assorted friends and freedmen associated to some degree with these households (Chariton 2.3.3; 5.1; 4.2.8; Achilles Tatius 6.2.2; 8.14.5).

Most roles in the urban household, however, were filled by slaves. The novels, taken together, identify the following slave roles: household manager (διοικητής) (Chariton 1.12.7; X 2.10.4), σύντροφος (Xenophon of Ephesus 2.3.3), nurse (Chariton 1.14.1), παιδαγωγός (Xenophon of Ephesus 1.14.4), as well as female slaves (Chariton 1.1.15) and male waiters (Longus 4.34.3), doormen (Achilles Tatius 2.26.1), guards (Xenophon of Ephesus 2.7.1; Achilles Tatius 5.25.1), grooms and muleteers (Chariton 2.3.3), and messengers and letter carriers (Longus 4.1.1; Chariton 4.5.1). Out in the *chora* are more slaves in the roles of οἰκονόμοι (Chariton 2.1.1), διοικηταί (Achilles Tatius 7.7.3), ἐπίτροποι (Achilles Tatius 6.9.6); cowherds, shepherds, and goatherds (Chariton 2.3.2; Xenophon of Ephesus 2.9.2); slaves in chains digging (Chariton 4.2.5); and guards and executioners (4.2.5, 7).

The activities of a household are likewise numerous and varied. We see householders giving orders for a symposium (Longus 4.32.2), visiting rural properties (Chariton 2.3.1–4), taking on public duties (Xenophon of Ephesus 2.3.1–4), arranging marriages (Achilles Tatius 1.18.3), and punishing and praising slaves (Longus 4.13.4 and Xenophon of Ephesus 5.5.4). We see wives of householders attending religious festivals (Chariton 1.1.5), being sent to the safety of other households in time of war (Achilles Tatius 1.4.1), arranging for the marriage of a son (Chariton 8.4.6), and being honored with funeral processions and magnificent burial (1.6.2–5). We see sons of householders leaving home to spend their days in the gymnasium (Xenophon of Ephesus 1.5.1), hunting in the countryside (Longus 2.12.2), and participating in religious processions (Xenophon of Ephesus 1.2.2–3). We see their sisters playing instruments and singing (Achilles Tatius

2.1.1–3), walking in gardens adjacent to the house (1.15.1), making seductive overtures to newly-purchased slaves (Xenophon of Ephesus 2.3–5), and being told whom they would marry (Chariton 1.1.14). We see slaves in charge of managing households (Chariton 1.12.8), delivering letters (Achilles Tatius 1.3.5–6), purchasing slaves (6.3.3), letting in adulterers (1.4.9), receiving their freedom (Longus 4.33.2), suffering abuse and excruciating punishment (Xenophon of Ephesus 2.6.2–5), and running away and joining a brigand gang (2.12.2; 14.2–5). And in the countryside we see tenant and slave peasants herding sheep and goats (Longus 1.2.1; 4.1), picking grapes and making the new wine (2.1–3), caring for the householder's garden (4.4.1–2), winnowing grain (3.29.1), turning brigand when opportunities arise (Xenophon 3.12.2), and dedicating the tools of their trade toward the end of their lives (Longus 1.4.3; 4.26.2).

Given the complexity, the urban/rural components, and the number of social roles and activities associated with an aristocratic household, we might well ask: Who's in charge? How is this complex institution managed so that it increases—αὐξάνειν, to use Xenophon's word[6]—in wealth by producing a surplus (περιουσία)[7] and indeed enduring for generations?

At one level such success depends on the various skills of those in the household. Dionysophanes, for example, depends on the skills of those who work his land. Note the skills of one of his slave-peasants, Daphnis: Not only can he herd goats, his principal responsibility, but he can also plough a field, harvest and winnow grain, plant and prune vines, and pick grapes, press them, and pour the new wine into large vessels (Longus 2.1.3; 3.29.2). Still, skilled people need to be managed to work productively, and that management is provided, ultimately, by the householder but more typically by his managers, both in the *polis* and in the *chora*. Details on such management are again provided by the novels. In what follows I will attempt a literary ethnography of household management around three roles—first, a householder, namely, Longus's Dionysophanes; then, a διοικητής, or slave administrator of his master's household, namely, Chariton's Leonas; and fi-

---

6. See, e.g., Xenophon, *Oec.* 2.1; 3.15; 5.1; 6.4; 7.8; and 11.12.

7. Another favorite, whether as a noun, as here, or as a verb: Xenophon, *Oec.* 1.2; 2.10; 7.36; 20.1; 20.21; and 21.9.

nally, an οἰκονόμος, or manager of the property in the *chora*, namely, Chariton's Phocas.

Dionysophanes as οἰκοδεσπότης

Although we may tend to think of household managers as slaves, Xenophon calls Ischomachus himself an οἰκονόμος[8], reminding us of the administrative responsibilities of the householder. These responsibilities are never clearer than when he initiates and eventually participates in a central event for assuring the economic success of his household. This event is the periodic visit of the householder to inspect and oversee the production of his properties in the *chora*. These visits are typical in traditional or agrarian societies. They are, more fully, carefully orchestrated events in which the social distance between peasants and householder is emphasized as well as bridged by having various intermediary messengers of increasing status announce and precede the householder's visit. These visits are important, both for peasants who want to be praised rather than punished for their work and for the householder who wants his properties to produce at a high level.[9]

The novels provide numerous examples of such visits.[10] One in particular, however, is especially well described, the visit by Dionysophanes of Mytilene at the end of Longus's novel.[11] Dionysophanes's properties had suffered undetermined damage from the marauding forces of Methymna (2.19–20). Dionysophanes, therefore, decided to visit these properties in order to assess the damage. Word of this upcoming visit first reaches Lamon, one of Dionysophanes's slave goat herders, in late summer (3.31.4). Lamon does not act on this information, but with the arrival of autumn there comes another slave from Mytilene, a ὁμόδουλος, that is, one of equally low status to Lamon's. This slave announces that their master (δεσπότης) Dionysophanes would visit later, shortly before the vintage (4.1.1). Lamon immediately gets busy

---

8. See Xenophon, *Oec.* 1.2.

9. See Feder, "Latifundia and Agriculture," 83–97, esp. 85–89.

10. See, e.g., Chariton, 2.3.1–5; 3.8.2–9; Xenophon, 2.1.2; 11.1; and Achilles Tatius, 5.17.2–10.

11. For a fuller description of Dionysophanes's visit than is possible here, see Hock, "Social Experience," 311–26, esp. 314–19.

"preparing the countryhouse (where Dionysophanes will stay) . . . , cleaning the fountains . . . , carrying out the manure from the farmyards . . . , and lavishing attention on the garden" (4.1.2–3). Lamon orders his son Daphnis to fatten his goats as much as possible. Accordingly, Daphnis shows his goats every attention by taking them out very early in the morning and not bringing them back until supper time. In addition, he leads them to drink twice a day, seeks out the best pasture, makes many new milk pails and larger cheese baskets, and oils the goats' horns (4.4.2–4).

While these preparations are underway a second messenger comes from the city with orders to harvest the grapes as quickly as possible. He says that he will stay until the new wine has been made and then will go back to Mytilene in order to return with his master (4.5.1). This messenger, aptly named Eudromos, is clearly of higher status than the ὁμόδουλος, for Longus identifies Eudromos as "one who had shared milk" (ὁμογάλακτος) with the householder's son Astylos (4.9.3). In other words, he is Astylos's σύντροφος, a privileged slave in the household whose status derived from being raised with the aristocratic child and having a long and close relationship with him. A σύντροφος would doubtlessly become Astylos's διοικητής whenever he would succeed his father as householder.

In any case, Lamon and Dryas give Eudromos a warm welcome and then begin to pick the grapes, carry them to the wine presses, and pour the sweet new wine into large containers (4.5.2).[12] Eudromos then leaves but returns shortly to say that Dionysophanes would arrive in three days and that his son would do so on the very next day (4.9.2). Astylos does arrive next day, representing an even higher status in the individuals who precede the householder. And with the authority of a son Astylos resolves a problem, the earlier vandalism of the garden by a jealous peasant that had put Lamon and Daphnis in a precarious situation (cf. 4.7.2–4) and could have meant severe punishment for Lamon and Daphnis (4.10.1–3). But Astylos takes the blame for the

---

12. That Eudromos stays and presumably oversees the vintage is another indication of his future role as διοικητής. For a fuller account of the activities involved in a vintage and the obvious need for oversight, see Longus 2.1.1–3. This detailed account is also relevant for what the οἰκοδεσπότης in the parable of the laborers in the vineyard expected those he hired to do (see further Hock, "Romancing the Parables," 32–34).

destruction by blaming his horses and then amuses himself by hunting rabbits (4.11.1).

Two days later, with everything prepared, Dionysophanes arrives from the *polis* with his wife, other men and women, slaves and animals (4.13.1–2). On the first day of his visit Dionysophanes sacrifices to the deities of the *chora*—Demeter, Dionysos, Pan, and the Nymphs (4.13.3). On the following days, however, he inspects (ἐπεσκόπει) the ploughed fields, the trimmed vines, and the beautiful garden (4.13.3–4). Longus's story line does not require a detailed description of all these inspections, but he does pause to describe in greater detail Dionysophanes's inspection of the pastures and Daphnis's goats. Lamon speaks on his son's behalf: "Master, Daphnis is the herder of your goats. You gave me fifty she-goats to pasture and two males, and Daphnis has produced one hundred she-goats and ten males. Do you see how sleek they are, how shaggy their coats are, and how strong their horns are? And he has made them musical as well. In any case, they do everything to the sound of the pan-pipes" (4.14.2–3). As a result of these inspections Dionysophanes was exceedingly pleased (ἥδετο περιττῶς), praised (ἐπῄνει) Lamon, and promised to give him his freedom (4.13.4).

Assured now that his properties in the *chora* were producing a surplus (περιουσία), Dionysophanes can end the visit to his property and return to Mitylene (4.33.2). This visit not only accomplished its economic objective, but has also involved the entire household—householder, his family, urban slaves, and rural peasants. The social distances between groups have been preserved by the sequence of messengers, but once the social distance has been bridged by them there are also moments of general interaction and celebration, the latter highlighted by a display of Daphnis's musical talents (4.15.1–3) and by Dionysophanes's hosting of a rural symposia for everyone (4.25.2).

Leonas as διοικητής

While a householder is involved in such periodic inspections of his rural properties, he can usually delegate the day-to-day management to a slave administrator, or διοικητής. Again, the novels provide data on this slave role,[13] and an exceptionally well drawn example is Leonas

---

13. For others in the role of διοικητής, see Xenophon of Ephesus 2.10.4, and Achilles Tatius 5.7.3–10; 6.3.3; and 7.7.3.

from Chariton's novel. He is the slave administrator of the household of Dionysius of Miletus. In fact, he is introduced as the διοικητής τῶν ὅλων (1.12.8), that is, he is in charge of Dionysius's household as a whole.

As a διοικητής Leonas occupies a privileged and powerful slave role in Dionysius's household that entailed many responsibilities. His privileges are evident in his having living quarters that are like those of a free man (1.13.2) and in his being in the small party that accompanies Dionysius to his property in the *chora* while the rest of the entourage had gone on before (2.3.4).

The power that Leonas wields is especially plain when he wants to purchase a slave-nurse for Dionysius's infant daughter whose mother had recently died. A slave is preferable, he thinks, because, should Dionysius remarry, a step-mother would mean a loss of power for him (1.12.9). Accordingly, he assumes the responsibility of not simply attending to his master's needs (1.13.1), but takes the initiative to purchase a slave when the opportunity arises (1.12.8). He has access to Dionysius's money, in the amount of a talent, and goes ahead and purchases a slave woman Callirhoe (1.3.7; 14.5). Having purchased the slave, he orders Phocas, the rural manager (οἰκονόμος), to take care of her (2.1.1) and then seeks out information on Sybarites living in Miletus in order to learn more about the alleged origin of the newly purchased slave (2.1.9). He goes to the marketplace to get registration papers for this slave (2.1.6). Leonas also suggests that his master should visit his rural properties to check on the herds and fields at harvest time (2.3.1), but his real purpose is to manipulate the grieving Dionysius to see the newly purchased and beautiful slave (2.3.1).

But Leonas's privileges and exercise of power are built on something more than just his role as διοικητής. Several details suggest a closer relationship between Leonas and his master: Leonas had sung the wedding song at Dionysius's first marriage (2.1.2); he knows the poets, specifically Homer (2.1.5; 3.7); he has the care of Dionysius's infant daughter since her mother had died (1.12.8); he is sensitive to Dionysius's grief at the loss of his wife and seeks to comfort him (1.12.9); he feels free to reprimand his master when he mistakes Callirhoe for the goddess Aphrodite (2.3.6); he is privy to Dionysius's feelings for Callirhoe once he had seen her (2.6.1).

These details suggest a closeness that can be explained by Leonas's having been Dionysius's σύντροφος.[14] In other words, having been raised with Dionysius, Leonas has had a relationship with his master that is long-term and close, such that Dionysius can assume Leonas's good will (εὔνοια) and loyalty (πίστις) and indeed can say to him: "I keep nothing secret from you" (2.4.6). As a former σύντροφος, Leonas makes the ideal διοικητής.

Phocas as οἰκονόμος

We turn finally to the role of οἰκονόμος in the *chora*. And again we turn to Chariton's novel, where Dionysius's οἰκονόμος of his properties by the sea is Phocas (2.1.1; 3.7.1). He is, as we have seen, subordinate to Leonas, the διοικητής, in that Leonas commands Phocas to care for Callirhoe, the newly purchased slave (2.1.1). But otherwise he is in charge. When, for example, Dionysius and Callirhoe visit the property after the birth of their son, Phocas prepares a magnificent feast (3.8.3). Also, when Dionysius finds something amiss on the estate during a visit, he holds Phocas responsible and rebukes him (2.6.2).

But Phocas's responsibility goes beyond that for the rural properties to the welfare of the household as a whole, as shown in the following incident. Towards the beginning of the novel Callirhoe, the wife of Chaereas, has been kidnapped by the pirate Theron, taken to the *chora* of Miletus, and sold as a slave to Leonas, as we have seen. Callirhoe was kept on Dionysius's property by the sea, and when he visited that property he saw Callirhoe and fell in love with her. They marry, though only because of Callirhoe's desire that the baby she is carrying from her husband Chaereas (unknown to Dionysius at the time) be raised in freedom (3.1.4–2.5).

Some time later Chaereas, as part of the embassy to ransom his wife, drops anchor at Dionysius's property and, along with his friend Polycharmus, visits the local temple of Aphrodite (3.6.2–5). Now Phocas enters the picture. Having seen the ship on which the embassy had arrived and anchored, he questions some of those on it, learns what the embassy was for, and realized that the ship represented a terrible threat to Dionysius since the loss of Callirhoe would give

14. On Leonas as Dionysius's σύντροφος, see above regarding Eudromos and Astylos and further, Hock, "Educational Curriculum," 15–36, esp. 21.

Dionysius no reason to live. Being φιλοδέσποτος, or devoted to his master (3.7.2), and wishing to head off this threat, Phocas persuades the local garrison to attack the ship, which left the ship in flames and those on it either killed or captured (3.7.1–3).

Callirhoe soon learns of the visit of the young men to the temple and tells Dionysius about it, confident that he would investigate further and learn the visitors's identity. Her confidence is not misplaced. Dionysius, suspecting a plot on his marriage, summons Phocas and asks who the visitors were and why they were there. Phocas, fearing that Callirhoe who would destroy him and his wife Plangon if he told the truth, prevaricates. Dionysius then gets even more suspicious and orders Phocas to be tortured to find out the truth. Phocas then tells the whole story about the visit, the subsequent attack, and the (presumed) death of Chaereas (3.9.4–11).

On hearing Phocas's story, Dionysius hugs Phocas and says: "You are my benefactor (εὐεργέτης), you are my genuine and most faithful protector . . . Because of you I still have (ἔχω) my wife and son. Now, I would not have ordered you to kill Chaereas, but since you have already done the deed, I do not blame (μέμφομαι) you because your unjust act (τὸ ἀδίκημα) was that of a slave devoted to his master (φιλοδέσποτος)" (3.9.12). Phocas is then instructed to tell the others what had happened, save for the detail about the survival of some of those on board the ship (3.10.1). This incident not only shows the devotion of an οἰκονόμος to his master, but also his moral horizon, not to mention that of his master, in that an unprovoked attack on a ship as well as the capture or murder of those on board are considered unjust, to be sure, but also trumped by the higher concern for the welfare of the household.[15]

Conclusion

What the Greek novels, and Chariton's and Longus's in particular, have permitted us to do here is to produce what I have called a literary ethnography of the day to day and crisis operations of the Graeco-

---

15. This scene between Phocas and Dionysius is especially helpful in interpreting the parable of the unjust steward (Luke 16:1–8), more so, I think, than Mary Ann Beavis's use of Aesop's slaves who outwit their masters, an interpretation endorsed by Osiek and Balch (see *Families*, 187; cf. Beavis, "Ancient Slavery," 37–54).

Roman household. Three roles that are especially responsible for these operations have been highlighted: the authoritative social role of the householder (οἰκοδεσπότης) when he visits his properties in the *chora*, the executive administrative role of the urban manager (διοικητής) in carrying out all kinds of tasks in meeting day to day and crisis situations, and the trusted role of the rural manager (οἰκονόμος) in insuring that the household remains productive and secure. Generalizations from anthropological models and scattered references in various literary sources are indeed helpful, as Osiek and Balch have so ably shown over a wide variety of aspects of the Graeco-Roman household, but generalizations and references only go so far. They still fall short of the novels in providing virtual ethnographic accounts of these households that are unparalleled in detail, continuity, and coherence. For example, the behavior, character, and relations of Dionysius, Leonas, and Phocas in Chariton's novel are carefully drawn and nuanced so that these important household roles come to life. And the same could be said of other household roles. But enough has been said to conclude that the value of these novels for supplementing the contribution of Osiek and Balch on the Graeco-Roman household should now be obvious.

Bibliography

Balch, David L. *Let Wives Be Submissive: The Domestic Code in 1 Peter*. SBLMS 26. Chico: Scholars, 1981.

Beavis, Mary Ann. "Ancient Slavery as an Interpretive Context for the New Testament Servant Parables with Special Reference to the Unjust Steward (Luke 16:1–8)." *JBL* 111 (1992) 37–54.

Feder, Ernst. "Latifundia and Agriculture in Latin America." In *Peasants and Peasant Societies*, edited by Teodor Shanin, 83–97. New York: Penguin, 1971.

Garnaud, J.-P., editor. *Achille Tatius d'Alexandrie, Le roman de Leucippé et Clitophon*. Paris: Les Belles Lettres, 1991.

Hock, Ronald F. "The Educational Curriculum in Chariton's *Callirhoe*." In *Ancient Fiction: The Matrix of Early Christian and Jewish Narrative*, edited by Jo-Ann Brant et al., 15–36. SBLSymS 32. Atlanta: Society of Biblical Literature, 2005.

―――. "Romancing the Parables of Jesus." *PRSt* 29 (2002) 11–37.

―――. "Social Experience and the Beginning of the Gospel of Mark." In *Reimagining Christian Origins: A Colloquium Honoring Burton L. Mack*, edited by Elizabeth Castelli and Hal Taussig, 311–26. Valley Forge, PA: Trinity, 1996.

Osiek, Carolyn, and David L. Balch. *Families in the New Testament World: Households and House Churches*. The Family, Religion, and Culture. Louisville: John Knox, 1997.

O'Sullivan, James N., editor. *Xenophon Ephesius de Anthiae et Habrocome Ephesiacorum Libri V*. Teubner. Munich: Saur, 2005.

Reardon, Bryan P., editor. *Collected Ancient Greek Novels*. Berkeley: University of California Press, 1989.

―――, editor. *De Callirhoe narrationis amatoriae Chariton Aphrodisiensis*. Teubner. Munich: Saur, 2004.

Reeve, Michael D., editor. *Longus, Daphnis et Chloe*. 2nd ed. Teubner. Leipzig: Teubner, 1986.

Schmeling, Gareth, editor. *The Novel in the Ancient World*. Mnemosyne: Bibliotheca Classica Batava. Supplementum 159 Leiden: Brill, 1996.

8

Egnatius, the Breathalyzer Kiss, and an Early Instance of Domestic Homicide at Rome

JOHN T. FITZGERALD

ALTHOUGH THE TERM "DOMESTIC VIOLENCE" IS A MODERN ONE, THE reality it describes is a widespread ancient phenomenon. Instances of it appear in numerous pagan, Jewish, and Christian sources,[1] and I have argued elsewhere that the *Haustafel* in 1 Peter addresses a situation of household violence directed at Christian wives and Christian slaves.[2] As is well known, the pseudonymous author of 1 Peter depicts himself as writing from Rome, which he calls Babylon (1 Pet 5:13),[3] and in this brief essay I wish to focus on a much earlier instance of violence that four ancient authors allege happened in Rome in its earliest days. The essay comprises three parts, with the first part devoted to the social practice that provides the context for the incident; the second part deals with the potential repercussions when a woman violated a key component of the cultural code of conduct expected of her; and the third part examines the case of one abusive husband, who is called Egnatius Maetennus in one source, Metennius in a second source, Mecennius in a third source, and Egnatius Mecennius in a fourth source. The name of his wife, the victim in this story, is not given in any source.

---

1. For an orientation and pertinent bibliography, see Fitzgerald, "Domestic Violence," 101–21.

2. Fitzgerald, "Early Christian Missionary Practice," 24–44.

3. Balch, *Let Wives Be Submissive*, remains unsurpassed as the most important foundational study of 1 Peter and the *Haustafel*.

The Social Context and Practice

Plutarch of Chaeronea (ca. 45—ca. 120 CE) had a strong interest in Rome,[4] visited Italy on several occasions,[5] knew Latin well enough to do research in Roman sources,[6] and devoted one of his antiquarian works, the *Quaestiones Romanae* (*Roman Questions*), to various queries about the Romans and their customs. As its Greek title (Αἴτια Ῥωμαϊκά) suggests, that work, written after ca. 105 CE,[7] was explicitly etiological and constituted Plutarch's attempt to give the reason or reasons for some of Rome's more unusual customs, many of which were believed to derive from the time of Romulus.

Of the 113 practices discussed by Plutarch in this treatise, it is the sixth that merits our attention in this essay: "Why do the women kiss their kinsmen (συγγενεῖς) on the lips?" (*Quaest. rom.* 265b).[8] It was an old question, especially among the Greeks, having already been addressed by Aristotle (frg. 609 Rose) and Alcimus of Sicily (*FGH* 560 F 2) more than four centuries earlier.[9] As is often the case, Plutarch provides several different answers for the origin of this peculiar custom, and the answers make clear that "kinsmen" here includes the woman's husband as well as other male relatives. Some authorities saw the "kinsmen's kiss" as originating prior to the inception of limited kinship marriage among the Romans and as originally symbolic of the friendly affection (φιλοφροσύνη) that should exist among members of the same kinship group (συγγένεια). Because marriage and sexual relations were not yet possible among more distant blood relatives, a kiss on the lips was the extent of affection that was deemed socially permissible (*Quaest. rom.* 265d).

---

4. Jones, *Plutarch and Rome*.

5. For the thesis that Plutarch had two sojourns in Rome—one in the 70s and a second in the 90s—see Gianakaris, *Plutarch*, 17–18.

6. Plutarch's facility with Latin was much greater than his modest statement in *Dem.* 2 suggests. Among other authorities, he cites Livy, Varro, and Verrius Flaccus.

7. Jones, "Towards a Chronology," 61–74, esp. 73.

8. In general, all translations (sometimes slightly modified) are either those of the LCL or my own.

9. For the fourth century BCE as the date of the Sicilian Alcimus, see Cesare Cassio, "Studies on Epicharmus," 37–51, esp. 44 n. 23. The text is preserved by Athenaeus, *Deipn.* 10.441a–b.

Other authorities attributed the origin of the custom to the women themselves, who began kissing the men out of fear (φοβηθεῖσαι) and as an effective means of extinguishing male wrath (ὀργῇ) and of achieving reconciliation (διαλλαγέντων) with the men (265c).[10] Still other authorities, however, thought the practice originated with the men, who in an honor-shame culture viewed the kiss as a means of bestowing honor (τιμὴν) and power (δύναμιν) on the women (265d).

But in that case why was the kiss given "on the mouth" (στόματι) rather than on the cheek or on the forehead, or, for that matter, on the hand? The "honor-power" explanation provided no clear answer to that query, and for that reason was not the explanation most frequently given for the practice. The most popular answer (οἱ πλεῖστοι) was one that focused on the mouth as the place of the kiss, and the answer was that it was an ancient "breathalyzer test" administered to detect the unauthorized consumption of wine. "Is it, as most authorities believe, that the drinking of wine was forbidden to women, and therefore, so that women who had drunk wine should not escape detection, but should be detected when they chanced to meet men of their household, the custom of kissing was established?" (265b).

Roman tradition traced this prohibition of the consumption of wine by women back to the early days of Rome itself, to either Romulus, Rome's legendary founder, or Pompilius Numa, the legendary second king of Rome. Numa was revered by later Romans as a lawgiver (Cicero, *Resp.* 2.26; Plutarch, *Comp. Lyc. Num.* 3.7) who, while seeking to preserve Romulus' desire that wives be treated with total honor and good will (Plutarch, *Rom.* 19.6: μετ' εὐνοίας τιμὴν ἅπασαν), sought simultaneously to inculcate certain traits that he regarded as appropriate for women. These included modesty (αἰδώς),[11] a lack of meddlesomeness (πολυπραγμοσύνην), silence (σιωπᾶν) when their husbands were not present, and sobriety (νή φειν). The latter entailed total abstention from wine: οἴνου μὲν ἀπεχομένας τὸ πάμπαν ("wine they were to abstain from entirely") (*Comp. Lyc. Num.* 3.5).

---

10. On the ancient understanding of reconciliation, see Fitzgerald, "Paul and Paradigm Shifts," 241–62, 316–25; and Fitzgerald, "Riconciliazone (NT)," 1158–62. On the common link between anger and reconciliation, see Fitzgerald, "Anger, Reconciliation, and Friendship," 359–70, 462–73.

11. On αἰδώς see esp. Cairns, *Aidos*.

Corroborating evidence is offered by both Cato the Censor (234–149 BCE) and Aulus Gellius. According to Pliny the Elder, "Cato says that the reason why women are kissed by their male relations is to know whether they smell of 'tipple' [*temetum*]—that was then the word denoting wine, and also the word 'tipsy' [*temulentia*] comes from it" (*Nat.* 14.89) In a similar way, Aulus Gellius, writing ca. 180 CE, comments on the lifestyle commonly attributed to Roman women who lived "in olden days." It focuses on their abstention from intoxicants: "Those who have written about the life and civilization of the Roman people say that the women of Rome and Latium "lived an abstemious life"; that is, they abstained altogether from wine (*vino*), which in the early language was called *temetum*; that it was an established custom for them to kiss their kinsfolk for the purpose of detection, so that, if they had been drinking, the odor might betray them" (*Noct. att.* 10.23.1).[12]

Polybius (ca. 200—ca. 118 BCE) provides additional testimony for this custom. "Among the Romans," he says, "women are forbidden to drink wine . . . A woman cannot go undetected when she drinks wine; this is because, first of all, women are unable to hold their wine, and on top of that they are required to kiss their own relatives and their husband's relatives as far extended as first cousins once removed, and to do so every day, whenever they first see them" (*Hist.* 6.11a.4).[13] Similarly, Tertullian says that the women of archaic Rome "were compelled to offer to kiss their relatives—that they might be judged by their breath" (*Apol.* 6.5).

Cicero equates the Greek word αἰδώς with the Latin term *verecundia*, "a sense of shame," depicts abstention from alcoholic beverages as "instruction in the sense of shame" (*disciplina verecundiae*), and claims that the effect of this training was that "all women

---

12. As the inclusion of Latium suggests, the practice was often seen as extending beyond the city of Rome itself. Alcimus of Sicily in his *History of Italy* extends it to Italy: "all the women in Italy do not drink wine" (*FGH* 560 F 2).

13. It should be noted that this passage, which is part of the so-called *archaeologia* of Polybius (6.11a.1–10), is not contained in the original LCL edition of W. R. Paton, though it will undoubtedly be included in the revised LCL edition of Polybius being done by F. W. Walbank and C. Habicht. The passage is preserved by Athenaeus, *Deipn.* 10.440e–f, and I have used, with one modification, the new LCL translation of Athenaeus by S. D. Olson.

abstain from alcohol" (*temeto*) (*Resp.* 4.6).¹⁴ A similar claim is made by Pliny the Elder (23/24–79 CE), who says, "At Rome women were not allowed to drink wine" (*Nat.* 14.89). Additional evidence is provided by Valerius Maximus, who wrote during the reign of Tiberius (14–37 CE): "At one time the use of wine was unknown to Roman women, no doubt for fear they might slip into some dishonor, for that after Father Liber the next step in intemperance is apt to be illicit love-making" (*Mem.* 2.1.5b).

As this evidence suggests, there was a widespread belief at the time of the Roman Republic and Roman Empire that the women of archaic Rome were prohibited from drinking wine, and that the chief means of ensuring their compliance with this stipulation was the breathalyzer kiss, which was administered by the woman's husband and the male relatives of both the woman and her husband. This prohibition was grounded in the belief that the wife's consumption of wine would lead to sexual misconduct. Consequently, in order to prevent the latter, the former was prohibited.¹⁵ The concern was thus to eliminate a perceived potential threat to the social order by controlling the conduct of women.¹⁶ It is striking that the supposed scarcity of wine in the days of Romulus and Numa (Pliny, *Nat.* 14.87–88, 91) was never related to this prohibition, which was justified morally rather than economically or in terms of limited availability.

At the same time, the prohibition apparently was not regarded as absolute but focused on the kind of wine (*temetum*) most likely to lead to intoxication and adultery. Polybius, for example, claims that archaic Roman women drank syrupy "raisin wine" (*passum vinum* = πάσσος οἶνος) instead of regular wine.¹⁷ As the name suggests, raisin wine (Plato, *Leg.* 8.845b) "is made from raisins, and when you drink it,

---

14. Cicero's equation of αἰδώς with *verecundia* is particularly evident in *Resp.* 5.6, where Scipio makes the Stoic argument that Nature has endowed humans with *verecundia* so that they will seek to avoid the shame of justified censure. For the Stoic definition of αἰδώς as "avoidance of justified criticism," see *SVF* 3.105.40 (§432). I owe the latter reference to Zetzel, *Cicero*, 89 n. 4.

15. The connection between the consumption of wine and illicit sexual activity remained a typical fixture in Roman thinking. When Augustus, for instance, exiled his daughter Julia on account of her adulteries, he not only denied her male companionship but also prohibited her from consuming wine (Suetonius, *Aug.* 65).

16. Eckstein, *Moral Vision*, 156.

17. See also Eustathius, *Comm. Il.* 19.160, p. 1243, citing Polybius.

it resembles Aegosthenic[18] or Cretan[19] grape-must; this is why people consume it when they are desperately thirsty" (Polybius 6.11a.4).[20] As might also be expected, certain sacred occasions were an exception to this rule.[21]

In view of this wealth of literary evidence in support of a fairly strict prohibition of female consumption of wine in archaic Rome and the surrounding area, it is important to register a caveat regarding the historicity of this depiction. There is some literary and archaeological evidence that gives a different picture of archaic Central Italy. Livy, for instance, depicts the royal daughters-in-law "wasting time in conviviality with their peers" (*in convivio luxusque cum aequalibus*) while their husbands drank wine with one another in an army camp (*Hist.* 1.57.9). There is no hint by Livy that the wives were punished for doing so. Furthermore, archaeological excavations in Latium suggest that Livy's depiction of the partying princesses was typical of aristocratic society during the archaic period. As Brigette Ford Russell has noted,

> The archaeological record . . . indicates that women in Rome and other Latin towns did in fact take part in the aristocratic culture of feasting and wine-drinking . . . Elite male burials of the eighth century [in Latium] are distinguished by arms and armour which testify to aristocratic warrior status. In the seventh century, arms give way to articles of convivial display. Significantly, female burials also contain the paraphernalia of feasting and drinking: mixing bowls on folding bronze stands, and Punic amphorae containing imported Sardinian wine. Thus the Latin matron of the seventh century emerges as a

---

18. Aegosthena was located in the bay of Porto Germano, on the easternmost point on the Corinthian Gulf, in the territory of Megara.

19. For Cretan *passum* see Juvenal, *Sat.* 14.269–270 and Martial, *Epigr.* 13.106, who calls it the drink of the poor (*pauperis*).

20. The point is that one can consume great quantities of *passum* to counteract thirst and without risking inebriation. In addition to raisin wine, Aulus Gellius (*Noct. att.* 10.23.2) says that archaic Roman women drank "after-wine" (*loream*, i.e., wine of the second press), "spiced wine" (*murrinam*, i.e., wine spiced with myrrh), and similar sweet-tasting drinks. Of these other drinks, spiced wines were regarded quite highly. "The finest wines in early days were those spiced with a scent of myrrh" (Pliny, *Nat.* 15.92; for wine flavored with myrrh see also Mark 15:23).

21. Servius, *Comm. Aen.* 1.737. For the consumption of wine by an old woman and girls during a sacred rite, see Ovid, *Fast.* 570–80, where the old woman becomes drunk; on the Ovid passage, see the brief discussion by Keegan, "Seen, not Heard," 129–53, esp. 142–43.

hostess who presides over the mixing and serving of wine at the banquets which were such an integral part of aristocratic culture in Central Italy during the seventh century.[22]

In short, the evidence for consumption of wine by females during the archaic period of Rome and Latium is mixed. What is important for the purposes of this article, however, is that all of the authors who discuss the prohibition of wine fully accepted the myth of the *mos maiorum* of archaic Rome, and they reported instances when that ancient moral code was breached.

The Potential Punishments for Females' Consumption of Wine

According to Dionysius of Halicarnassus, the Greeks viewed a wife drinking wine "as the least of all faults" (*Ant. rom.* 2.25.6). Romulus's attitude was completely different. He believed that there was a strong correlation between a wife's consumption of wine and the act of adultery, and he viewed the former as the occasion of the latter. Consequently, he permitted the woman's relatives and husband to judge cases involving both acts and "allowed them to punish both these offences with death, as the worst crimes women could commit, considering adultery as the beginning of madness and drunkenness of adultery" (Dionysius, *Ant. rom.* 2.25.6). In a similar way, "Marcus Cato states that women were not only censured but also punished by a judge no less severely if they had drunk wine than if they had committed a heinous act like adultery" (Aulus Gellius, *Noct. att.* 10.23.3).[23]

In addition to the case that we shall examine in the third part of this essay, there was at least one alleged case of capital punishment for the consumption of wine. According to Fabius Pictor in his *Annals*, "a matron was starved to death by her relatives for having broken open the casket containing the keys of the wine-cellar" (*apud* Pliny, *Nat.* 14.89). Tertullian knows this same story: "when a matron once unlocked the wine cellar, her family made her starve to death" (*Apol.* 6.4).

---

22. Russell, "Wine, Women," 77–84, esp. 80. Russell (83–84) also discusses the Livy passage.

23. All translations of Dionysius of Halicarnassus and Cato are those of Dillon and Garland, *Ancient Rome*, 350, 354.

Capital punishment, however, was not the only option. The alternative was to fine the woman who had consumed wine. That would seem to have been the usual and preferred option if adultery was not involved. Marcus Cato (the Censor) not only refers to fines for wine-drinking in one of his speeches[24] but also in his speech *On the Dowry* (*De doto*) makes an important distinction between punishing a wife who has drunk wine and one who has committed adultery: "When a man divorces his wife, he judges the woman as a censor does, and has full powers if she has committed any wrong or disgraceful act; she is punished if she has drunk wine; if she has done wrong with another man, she is condemned to death" (*ORF4 221* = Aulus Gellius, *Noct. att.* 10.23.4).[25] Furthermore, Pliny says that "Gnaeus Domitius once gave a verdict that a certain woman appeared to have drunk more wine than was required for the sake of her health, and he fined her the amount of her dowry" (*Nat.* 14.91).

Finally, Romans viewed these severe penalties for wine-drinking and adultery as vital to the success of marriage, for they prompted women to conduct themselves with moderation and proper decorum (Dionysius, *Ant. rom.* 2.24.1), thereby removing a potential reason for divorce. Consequently, "both these [crimes] continued for a long time to be met by the Romans with implacable wrath" (Dionysius, *Ant. rom.* 2.25.7). The result was that divorce was ostensibly unknown among the ancient Romans for more than 500 years (Dionysius, *Ant. rom.* 2.25.7; see also Tertullian, *Apol.* 6.6: "in the six hundred years following the foundation of Rome, no house registered a divorce").

Egnatius and His Wife

The most infamous instance of domestic violence in archaic Rome involved Egnatius and his wife. We have four accounts of this incident:[26]

24. See Walbank, *Historical Commentary on Polybius*, 1: 671.

25. See also *ORF4* 222 (= Aulus Gellius, *Noct. att.* 10.23.5), where Cato infamously enunciates a double standard for husbands and wives in regard to adultery: "If you should get your wife in adultery, you may with impunity put her to death without a trial; but, if *you* should commit adultery or indecent acts, she should not dare to lay a finger on you, nor is it lawful."

26. Münzer, "Egnatius (28)," derives all four accounts from the Roman writer Varro (116–27 BCE), whom he views as probably having derived it from an old jurist and as having cited the anecdote as proof of the strength of the ancient moral code of the Romans. See also his *Beiträge zur Quellenkritik*, 189–91.

Among various instances we find that the wife of Egnatius Maetennus was clubbed to death (*interfectam fusti*) by her husband for drinking wine from the vat (*dolio*), and that Romulus acquitted him on the charge of murder (Pliny, *Nat.* 14.89). Publicia, who had poisoned her husband, the consul Postumius Albinus (cos. 154), and Licinia, who had done the same to her husband Claudius Asellus, were strangled by the decree of their relatives: for those men of severity did not think that in so obvious a crime they should wait for a lengthy public enquiry. And so they made haste to punish the guilty, whom they would have defended had they been innocent. Their severity was aroused to exact punishment by a great crime, that of Egnatius Mecennius, for a far slighter reason. He beat his wife to death with a cudgel (*fusti*) because she had drunk some wine, and his action found no one to prosecute or even criticize it, for all the best men considered that the penalty she had paid to injured sobriety was a good precedent. For assuredly any woman who desires to drink wine without moderation closes the door to all virtues and opens it to all vices. (Valerius Maximus, *Mem.* 6.3.9)[27]

Under Romulus, a woman who had touched wine was killed with impunity by Metennius her husband (Tertullian, *Apol.* 6.4). Finally, a woman that drank wine during the time of Romulus was struck down by her husband Mecennius, who was acquitted (Servius, *Comm. Aen.* 1.737). All four texts agree that Egnatius killed his wife because she had consumed wine, with one authority (Pliny) suggesting that she had done so, not from a cup or a bowl, but rather from a *dolium*, that is, from a large earthenware jar with a wide mouth that was used for storing wine.[28] The image is thus that of conspicuous consumption—like guzzling beer from a keg. The inevitable consequence of such immoderate drinking was intoxication—Valerius' "injured sobriety" (*violate sobrietati*).[29] Two of the texts (Pliny and Valerius Maximus) assert that Egnatius killed his spouse with a club (*fustis*), not with a single blow of

---

27. The translation is that of Dillon and Garland, *Ancient Rome*, 353–54.

28. In a speech condemning Piso, Cicero refers to wine being "poured straight out of the jar" at a dinner party (*Pis.* 67). See also Cicero, *Brut.* 288, where he contrasts old wine that has lost its mellow taste with new wine that is still in a state of ferment and that is drawn from the vat. In both texts the word that he uses is *dolium*.

29. Tertullian, *Apol.* 6. 4, refers to the archaic period when sobriety was protected, then cites two examples when sobriety was lost.

his fist,[30] heightening the heinousness of his act. Strikingly, none of the four texts even hints that she was guilty of adultery. The wife's crime was limited to her immoderate consumption of alcohol.[31]

Three of the texts (Pliny, Tertullian, and Servius) explicitly place this episode in the time of Romulus, thus at the very beginning of Rome's history. A key difference in the accounts is whether Egnatius, as the husband, was entitled to kill his wife unilaterally, without consulting her relatives, and without fear of a trial and punishment. That was Cato's emphatic claim for a wife caught in adultery: the husband, he asserts, may kill his adulterous spouse "with impunity" (*inpune*), that is, without fear of punishment, and "without a trial" (*sine iudicio*) (*ORF4* 222).[32] But if adultery was involved here, the texts—all from authors with moralizing tendencies—are conspicuously silent about it. And in the case of the matron who was starved to death because she had broken open the casket containing the keys to the wine-cellar (Pliny, *Nat.* 14.89; Tertullian, *Apol.* 6.4), that was done by her relatives, not her husband, and it was a sentence carried out over a long time period. She was not brutally bludgeoned to death on the spot by an angry husband. Yet that, according to Tertullian, is precisely what Egnatius did—he killed his wife with impunity (*inpune*) for touching wine.

Valerius' account is more even troubling. Although he begins by calling Egnatius' action a "great crime" (*magno scelere*), Valerius declares that Egnatius was not prosecuted or even censured for this crime. Indeed, he even asserts that there was a consensus that Egnatius' bludgeoning of his wife set an "excellent precedent" (*optimo exemplo*). Pliny, by contrast, indicates that Egnatius was tried and acquitted (*absolutum*) by Romulus, a sequence that is also implied by Servius (*Mecennius absolutus*). That there was a trial implies that the wife's relatives objected to her brutal murder. Yet whether there was a trial or not,[33] Egnatius was not punished for this horrific act, which was

---

30. Contra Bloomer, *Valerius Maximus*, 114.

31. The closest that we come to any hint of adultery is the moralizing conclusion drawn by Valerius when he warns that the immoderate use of wine opens the door to all vices.

32. Treggiari, *Roman Marriage*, 270, tries to evade this conclusion: "Cato's *impune* suggests that the husband would be able to persuade a court that he was not guilty of murder. Some might hold that he had acted *iure*, with justification."

33. Valerius is commonly viewed as the one who altered the story and eliminated the trial before Romulus; see, for example, Münzer, "Egnatius," 1997.

perhaps the first instance in ancient Rome of domestic homicide. In the final analysis, the only "real" crime that male Roman aristocratic society saw committed in this case was the wife's violation of the ban on the consumption of wine; consequently, she was the only one who was punished (*poenas*).

In conclusion, the story of Egnatius helps us to understand why domestic violence continued to be a reality in the centuries that followed. Battering one's spouse was not against the law, and the battered spouse's main hope for relief was intervention by her family. Simple battery of a wife was unlikely to evoke much comment; instances of aggravated assault and homicide were more noteworthy and thus the most likely to be remembered, yet how such incidents were remembered was of crucial importance. Egnatius' killing of his spouse was regarded as justifiable homicide and henceforth functioned for centuries as an *exemplum*. Had he been found guilty of murder and punished accordingly, his *exemplum* would have served as a deterrent to husbands abusing their spouses. But because he either was not tried at all or was tried and acquitted, his example functioned to warn wives of the potentially dire consequences of violating the ban on the consumption of wine, and it authorized husbands to use physical force to enforce the ban. Thus it is no wonder that the beating of wives for violating the prohibition of wine was even incorporated into Roman mythology. Domestic violence appears in one of the answers that Plutarch gives to the question why myrtle was absent from shrines of the Bona Dea (the Good Goddess).[34] He notes that mythologists suggested that the goddess was secretly addicted to wine, and that when her husband, the seer Faunus, detected her addiction, he beat her with myrtle rods.[35] As a consequence, the later women who celebrated the goddess' rites did not use myrtle in the ceremony, and even though they poured libations of wine to the goddess, they euphemistically called the wine "milk" (Plutarch, *Quaest. Rom.* 268d-e). As this anecdote suggests, Roman myth and religion functioned to support and extend the Egnatius *exemplum* by underscoring the perils and penalties of non-compliance with the code of conduct regarding wine.

34. On her cult, see esp. Brouwer, *Bona Dea*.

35. Inasmuch as myrtle was a tree sacred to Venus, it may be that Faunus' beating of his wife with myrtle was intended to suggest a link between her drinking and sexual promiscuity. For this suggestion, see Bettini, "*In vino stuprum*," 229. I owe the reference to Russell, "Wine, Women, and the *Polis*," 79.

Bibliography

Balch, David L. *Let Wives Be Submissive: The Domestic Code in 1 Peter.* SBLMS 26. Chico, CA: Scholars, 1981.
Bettini, Maurizio. "*In vino stuprum.*" In *In Vino Veritas,* edited by Oswyn Murray and Manuela Tecusan, 224–35. London: British School at Rome in association with the American Academy at Rome, 1995.
Bloomer, W. Martin. *Valerius Maximus & the Rhetoric of New Mobility.* Chapel Hill: University of North Carolina Press, 1992.
Brouwer, H. H. J. *Bona Dea: The Sources and a Description of the Cult.* EPRO 110. Leiden: Brill, 1989.
Cairns, Douglas L. *Aīdos: The Psychology and Ethics of Honour and Shame in Ancient Greek Literature.* Oxford: Clarendon, 1993.
Cesare Cassio, Albio. "Two Studies on Epicharmus and His Influence." *HSCP* 89 (1985) 37–51.
Dillon, Matthew, and Lynda Garland. *Ancient Rome: From the Early Republic to the Assassination of Julius Caesar.* London: Routledge, 2005.
Eckstein, Arthur M. *Moral Vision in the Histories of Polybius.* Hellenistic Culture and Society 16. Berkeley: University of California Press, 1995.
Fitzgerald, John T. "Anger, Reconciliation, and Friendship in Matthew 5:21–26." In *Israel's God and Rebecca's Children: Christology and Community in Early Judaism and Christianity: Essays in Honor of Larry W. Hurtado and Alan F. Segal,* edited by D. B. Capes et al., 359–70 (essay) 462–73 (endnotes). Waco: Baylor University Press, 2007.
———. "Domestic Violence in the Ancient World: Preliminary Considerations and the Problem of Wife-Beating." In *Animosity, the Bible, and Us: Some European, North American, and South African Perspectives,* edited by John T. Fitzgerald et al., 101–21. SBLGPBS 12. Atlanta: Society of Biblical Literature, 2009.
———. "Early Christian Missionary Practice and Pagan Reaction: 1 Peter and Domestic Violence against Slaves and Wives." In *Renewing Tradition: Studies in Texts and Contexts in Honor of James W. Thompson,* edited by Mark W. Hamilton et al., 24–44. PTMS 65. Eugene, OR: Pickwick Publications, 2007.
———. "Paul and Paradigm Shifts: Reconciliation and Its Linkage Group." In *Paul beyond the Judaism/Hellenism Divide,* edited by Troel Engberg-Pedersen, 241–62 (essay), 316–25 (endnotes). Louisville: Westminster John Knox, 2001.
———. "Riconciliazone (NT)." In *Temi teologici della Bibbia,* edited by R. Penna et al., 1158–62. Dizionari San Paolo. Cinisello Balsamo: San Paolo, 2010.
Gianakaris, C. J. *Plutarch.* Twayne's World Authors Series. New York: Twayne, 1970.
Jones, C. P. *Plutarch and Rome.* Oxford: Clarendon, 1971.
———. "Towards a Chronology of Plutarch's Works." *JRS* 56 (1966) 61–74.
Keegan, Peter Mark. "Seen, Not Heard: *Feminea Lingua* in Ovid's *Fasti* and the Critical Gaze." In *Ovid's Fasti: Historical Readings at Its Bimillennium,* edited by G. Herbert-Brown, 129–53. Oxford: Oxford University Press, 2002.
Münzer, Friedrich. *Beiträge zur Quellenkritik der Naturgeschichte des Plinius.* Berlin: Weidmann, 1897.
———. "Egnatius (28)." In *PW* 5:1997–98.
Olson, S. D., translator. *The Learned Banqueters,* by Athenaeus, 7 vols. LCL. Cambridge: Harvard University Press, 2006–2011.

Paton, W. R. et al., translators. *The Histories*, by Polybius. 2 vols. LCL. Cambridge: Harvard University Press, 2010–.

Russell, Brigette Ford. "Wine, Women, and the Polis: Gender and the Formation of the City-State in Archaic Rome." *Greece and Rome* 50 (2003) 77–84.

Treggiari, Susan. *Roman Marriage: Iusti Coniuges from the Time of Cicero to the Time of Ulpian*. Oxford: Clarendon, 1991.

Walbank, F. W. *A Historical Commentary on Polybius*. 3 vols. Oxford: Oxford University Press, 1999.

Zetzel, James E. G., editor. *Cicero: On the Commonwealth and On the Laws*. Cambridge Texts in the History of Political Thought. Cambridge: Cambridge University Press, 1999.

9

From Archaeology to Commentary Writing via House Churches

Peter Oakes

David Balch's work has often involved close engagement with archaeological evidence. Recently, this has particularly focused on art in first-century housing, resulting in the essays gathered in his 2008 volume, *Roman Domestic Art and Early House Churches*. A key premise of that book is that an exploration of the material context of ancient accommodation is a valuable route to understanding the lives and ideas of the early Christians who encountered such spaces. "Seeing domestic visual representations that many early believers experienced daily in their own or their masters' or patrons' living spaces assists in comparing and contrasting the gospel with contemporary culture."[1]

In several articles in that volume, Balch studies art that relates to topics in particular New Testament texts. For instance, two articles relate to portrayal of suffering, considered in relation to Paul's depiction of Christ in Gal 3:1. However, the exegetical "pay-offs" from these articles, at least as represented in the articles themselves, are fairly brief and often not especially far-reaching. This raises the question of how far archaeological study can go in shedding exegetical light on the New Testament texts. Should study of the material culture of the first-century world be a fringe activity for New Testament scholars or does it have something crucial and systemic to offer to New Testament study?

---

1. Balch, *Roman Domestic Art*, vi. By "contemporary" Balch here means first-century.

This question finds its sharpest focus in commentary writing. We are all familiar with the brief archaeological sections relating to location found in the introductions of many commentaries. These vary in length, depth, accuracy, and relevance to what comes afterwards. I cut my own academic teeth on assessing whether the archaeological evidence from Philippi supported the frequent commentators' inference that many of the recipients of Paul's letter were veteran soldiers.[2] Commentaries on 1 Corinthians are typically among the fullest in their archaeological introductions and in making use of that evidence in the commentary.[3] Three factors probably contribute to this. First, the reporting of the extensive archaeological investigation of the site has been very effective.[4] Second, several topics in 1 Corinthians have clear potential links to material evidence, for instance, chapters 8–10 on food offered to idols and 11:2–16 on women and head-covering. Third, there is the influential pioneering work of Jerome Murphy-O'Connor in applying study of the Anaploga villa and other parts of the site to issues in 1 Corinthians.[5]

First Corinthians presents a series of relatively easy targets for using archaeology in commentary writing. It is clear, for instance, that archaeological evidence of dining facilities in temple precincts is of interest for studying 1 Corinthians 8. However, most New Testament text does not so obviously relate to material evidence. Can archaeology help in commentating on such less obviously linked text? David Balch himself has had a go at using archaeology in a fairly thoroughgoing way in commentating on a broader text, the Gospel of Luke, in his contribution to the *Eerdmans Commentary on the Bible*.[6] In this substantial and innovative commentary, Balch takes every opportunity to use Graeco-Roman sources to shed light on the text. In most cases, he draws on literary sources, using a wide array of writers to make many interesting and thought-provoking points. However, he also works hard to bring to bear the kind of archaeological work that he and

---

2. A classic instance is Friedrich, "Brief an die Philipper," 92–93, 106. See Oakes, *Philippians*, 50–70.

3. For instance, Thiselton, *First Epistle to the Corinthians*.

4. Reported in the Corinth series. See the series Corinth, edited by Williams and Bookidis.

5. Murphy-O'Connor, *St Paul's Corinth*; cf. Horrell, "Domestic Space."

6. Balch, "Luke," 1104–60.

Carolyn Osiek presented in their 1997, *Families in the New Testament World*. He explains why and how he will do this: "The Gospel was first read in a Mediterranean city to followers of Jesus gathered in a house church to share the Lord's Supper. This commentary makes a special effort to understand how the Lukan Christian communities gathered for worship in Graeco-Roman houses would hear the gospel as they reclined in the dining room (*triclinium*) and sat together in the courtyard (*peristylos*)."[7] This approach has clear effects on Balch's commentary at points in almost all of the chapters that cover Jesus' ministry. Conversely, there is little obvious effect on the birth narratives or the accounts of the crucifixion and resurrection, except for the Emmaus Road story, which is effectively an extension of Jesus' ministry. It will be interesting to reflect later on whether there is material that might go in some of the gaps.

In the conflict-filled ending of Jesus's visit to Nazareth, Balch sees the stories about foreigners like Naaman as potentially carrying a message to some among Luke's hearers who were "resisting inviting just anybody to worship in the dining rooms (*triclinia*) of their house churches."[8] This theme of inclusiveness of invitation then flows through Balch's reading of a range of Lukan passages. Some of these obviously relate to the topic: 5:27–39 on Levi; 14:1–24 on "inviting the indigent to dinner."[9] Others are less obvious. Following Braun[10] he argues that rich Christians are inviting the poor and facing ostracism as a result, for which blessing is pronounced in 6:22 (cf. 21:12–19).[11] Balch sees Luke's Pharisees (11:37–54) as having nothing to do with Pharisaism but instead, being described as "lovers of money", they are symbols for the wealthy in society and church. The Lukan Pharisees' obsession with cleanliness mirrors the architecture of Graeco-Roman houses, in which "dirty" areas such as kitchens are pushed away from the fine spaces. All this coordinates with a reluctance to invite the "dirty" poor.[12] The parables of lost and found (15:1–32) are heard as either a call to welcome others to the house church meals or an evoca-

---

7. Ibid., 1104.
8. Ibid., 1113.
9. Ibid., 1114, 1136.
10. Braun, *Feasting*, 113.
11. Balch, "Luke," 1116, 1149.
12. Ibid., 1130.

tion of the experience of being welcomed. Some readers could have linked the angry elder son with wealthy patrons of the house church, reluctant to admit the poor.[13] At the end of the Gospel, the Emmaus Road story finishes with a meal with a stranger, part of Luke's series of inclusive meals.[14]

In all these meal-related readings, Balch is putting the text into interaction with the archaeology of Graeco-Roman domestic architecture as it pertains to eating. Among other houses, he probably has in mind the House of the Menander at Pompeii, where the division between "show" areas and "menial" areas is particularly clear.[15] One striking effect of Balch's reading strategy is to transpose Luke's "Pharisees" from Galilee to an urban setting such as Pompeii, with Luke seeing them no longer as Pharisees but as symbols of the wealthy. For Balch, this removes the ammunition from those who would use the Lukan Jesus' denunciation of the Pharisees as the basis for anti-Judaism.[16]

Balch visualises the blessings and woes of 6:20–26 being read to the gathered house church, with rich members reclining in the *triclinium* and poor members sitting in the peristyle. This is a powerful picture. He concludes that Jesus claims the property of the rich for the poor.[17] Balch sees the call for love of enemies, in 6:27–36, as applying to masters and slaves eating together.[18] In line with his view of Luke's Pharisees as symbols of the wealthy, Balch sees Jesus' woes against them (11:37–54) as opposition to the social elite. On the other hand, the note in the story of the rich ruler (18:15–30) about all things being possible to God, and the favorable verdict on Zacchaeus (19:1–10), who gave away only part of his wealth, are seen as reassurances to wealthy Christian householders who offer hospitality to house churches.[19] Conversely, the story of the widow's offering (21:1–4) is seen as going against the status divisions enshrined in domestic architecture.[20]

---

13. Ibid., 1137–38.
14. Ibid., 1158.
15. On this house see Ling, *Insula of the Menander*; Osiek and Balch, *Families*, 202; Oakes, *Reading Romans*, 37–42.
16. Balch, "Luke," 1130.
17. Ibid., 1116.
18. Ibid.
19. Ibid., 1144–45.
20. Ibid., 1149.

Going even further, Jesus' farewell speech on slave leadership (22:24–30) reverses the norms represented by the status-related architecture of dining and serving. Scandalously, the Christians behave as though every week saw the celebration of *saturnalia*, with its rituals of social reversal.[21]

Balch also draws on various archaeological points to help the reader understand certain stories. The "sinful woman" (7:36–50) can get access both to the house, because houses were largely public, and to Jesus's feet, because he was reclining, not sitting.[22] Hospitality for the twelve (9:1–17) and seventy (10:1–16) is less surprising than we might think, because crowded houses displayed power.[23] Slave managers (12:41–48; 16:1–13) are well illustrated by evidence on tablets from the Pompeian house of J. Caecilius Jucundus.[24] Lazarus could lie immediately outside the rich man's door (16:19–31) because, in the mixed housing of Graeco-Roman towns, wealthy houses opened immediately onto the street.[25]

Could Balch have gone further in his use of archaeology in commentating on Luke (assuming he had been allowed more pages!)? I think that there are quite a number of points at which this might have been done. Consideration of a few of them will help further in reflecting on the scope of the usefulness of archaeological evidence for commentary writing. A nice starting point for further archaeological input would be Balch's comments on temple access, in relation to Zechariah's vision. Balch supports this with a quotation from Josephus.[26] Archaeological evidence from the Jerusalem temple could also have been used. More subtly, thinking in relation to Luke's audience, reflection on issues of temple access could be broadened by drawing in evidence from temples found in the Graeco-Roman urban context. Work such as that by Jorunn Økland on archaeology and gender in temples at Corinth[27] would raise interesting points not only for this passage but for other temple-related texts in Luke–Acts.

---

21. Ibid., 1152; Oakes, *Reading Romans*, 112.
22. Balch, "Luke," 1118.
23. Ibid., 1121, 1125.
24. Ibid., 1133, 1136.
25. Ibid., 1144.
26. Ibid., 1106, citing Josephus, *Ant.*12.145.
27. Økland, *Women in Their Place*.

Later in the birth narratives, Balch uses the example of Brutus and Coriolanus, drawn from Dionysius of Halicarnassus, to illustrate reversal of fortune, a key theme of the Magnificat.[28] I wonder whether there would have been some wall-paintings that Balch could have drawn on for themes of reversal. More substantively, it would be interesting to bring archaeological evidence of actual reversals of fortune that Luke's audience would encounter. Graeco-Roman urban centers included much epigraphy that illustrated the sudden rise to fortune of certain freed slaves. N. Popidius Ampliatus paid for the restoration of the temple of Isis at Pompeii and thus brought about the election of his very young son to the town council. The freed slave is using his wealth to promote the first freeborn generation of his family, which was typical of a process of new people joining the town elite.[29] There is literary evidence of the converse process, in which elite families fall from grace, seen for instance in Tacitus's accounts of senatorial victims of the depradations of Tiberius in his hunt for money.[30] Archaeological evidence of such falls is inevitably quite hard to find. However, at the extreme end, there is the practice of *damnatio memoriae*, which leaves some monuments with erased names.[31] More subtly, there are very many examples of grand ancient houses that were downgraded in various ways. Cheaper materials or decorations might be used in later periods of a building's existence. Large houses might be divided into apartments.[32] Many different factors could lead to such changes. However, one common cause was the declining fortunes of a particular family. In thinking not only about the Magnificat but about the reversal theme more generally in Luke, it is useful to try to calibrate our thoughts by considering the extent (and limitations) of social mobility in Luke's milieu. Archaeology can help us in thinking about the extent to which Luke's readers would have experience of "the mighty" falling or "the humble" being raised up.

A third example of where archaeological evidence could add significantly to the work that Balch undertakes in his commentary comes in Luke 9:1–6, on the mission of the twelve. Balch talks about Luke's

---

28. Balch, "Luke," 1106, citing Dionysius, *Rom. Ant.* 6.54.1.
29. Zanker, *Pompeii*, 126–27.
30. Tacitus, *Annals*, IV.
31. As happened, for instance, in the case of Domitian.
32. See, for instance, Ling, *Insula of the Menander*, 237.

repeated use of stories of commissioning and puts this in the context of cosmic conflict, mentioning in particular the returning seventy celebrating that demons were subject to them (10:17). He comments in rather general terms, "Mediterranean people often assumed that they were subject to 'fate', to the stars, and salvation is sometimes understood as the defeat of these heavenly powers."[33] Balch backs this only with citations from Ephesians and Colossians. However, I can imagine him itching to put in some of the overwhelming amount of archaeological (and literary) evidence that could be used to make his general comment more concrete and specific. The format of the one-volume commentary would, of course, have prevented this. However, given space, this theme of interaction between salvation and cosmic forces could, with the help of archaeological evidence, have been built into a very substantial stream in the commentary.

These three examples of areas in which archaeological material could contribute to the commentary are all powerfully illustrative because they do not relate to small details of minor importance. Each has the potential to open up a major theme for Luke–Acts: temple and access; social reversal; cosmic conflict. Evidence of first-century material culture can help us gauge something of the author's and audience's experience and expectations in each of these three areas. This helps us improve the sharpness of our observation of what the Lukan text is saying in such a context.

This is not reductionistic. The reversal theme does indeed have a strong socio-economic element, but that is clear in Luke anyway. The temple access theme raises a range of religious questions. In fact it offers a constructive field for consideration of early Christianity and Judaism, as each broad grouping (and varying groups within each grouping) wrestled with living in the aftermath of the destruction of the Jerusalem temple—and the death of Jesus. The cosmic conflict theme is the opposite of reductionistic. Instead of reducing interpretation to a single socio-economic agenda that might be seen as universal, it pushes us to consider the text in relation to concepts that are very alien to the experiences of most of us.

A fourth and final example could be used to point to areas in which archaeology might sometimes support commentary writing without going via house churches. Balch draws on the archaeology of

---

33. Balch, "Luke," 1121.

the house church setting. However, there are still contributions to be made from the archaeology of the Galilean and Judean setting of the events in Luke's narrative. Luke shapes material but he does also transmit material. Take the case of Luke's Pharisees. Balch interestingly links this to the archaeology of "clean" and "dirty" in Graeco-Roman houses. However, it would also be of interpretative value to consider the archaeology of purity and impurity from Galilee and Judaea. I am always struck by the memorable photograph in Yigael Yadin's Masada book, of the orthodox rabbis who had climbed the rock, in heavy overcoats, and were now down in a *mikweh*—a ritual bathing pool—to see if its measurements corresponded to rabbinic norms.[34] My former doctoral student, Diana Woodcock, has explored decoration in a wide range of types of Judean archaeological setting that relate to purity and impurity.[35] Consideration of the archaeology of purity in Galilee and Judaea gives us a way into considering the nature of the narratives that Luke is drawing on in putting his Gospel together. It might even be that in some cases, comparison between the archaeology of clean/unclean in Judaea and that in Graeco-Roman towns might offer help in deciding how heavily Luke might or might not have reshaped his sources to relate to his audience.

For commentary on epistles, the archaeology of the context of house churches (whether meeting in houses or apartments)[36] is clearly a key area to focus on. Epistles not only have a house church audience but generally deal with life in house churches. For commentary on Gospels, the picture is more complex. The texts are written for house churches but narrate the words and actions of Galilean peasants. The text is ultimately the product of both contexts. Commentary writing that draws judiciously on each context, making use, on the one hand, of the archaeology of Galilee, Judaea and peasant life and, on the other hand, of the archaeology of Graeco-Roman domestic life as pioneered by Balch (together with relevant civic archaeology) should substantially enhance our understanding of the Gospel texts.

---

34. Yadin, *Masada*, 166.
35. Woodcock, "Rosette."
36. Balch, "Rich Pompeian Houses," 28.

Bibliography

Balch, David L. "Luke." In *Eerdmans Commentary on the Bible*, edited by James D. G. Dunn, and John W. Rogerson, 1104–60. Grand Rapids: Eerdmans, 2003.

———. "Rich Pompeiian Houses, Shops for Rent, and the Huge Apartment Building in Herculaneum as Typical Spaces for Pauline House Churches." *JSNT* 27.1 (2004) 27–46.

———. *Roman Domestic Art and Early House Churches*. WUNT 228. Tübingen: Mohr/Siebeck, 2008.

Braun, W. *Feasting and Social Rhetoric in Luke 14*. SNTSMS 85. Cambridge: Cambridge University Press, 1995.

Charlesworth, James H., editor. *Jesus and Archaeology*. Grand Rapids: Eerdmans, 2006.

Friedrich, Gerhard. "Der Brief an die Philipper." In *Die kleineren Briefe des Apostels Paulus*, edited by H. W. Beyer et al., 92–130. NTD. Neues Göttinger Bibelwerk 8. Göttingen: Vandenhoeck & Ruprecht, 1962.

Hanson, K. C., and Douglas E. Oakman. *Palestine in the Time of Jesus: Social Structures and Social Contexts*. 2nd ed. Minneapolis: Fortress, 2008.

Horrell, David. "Domestic Space and Christian Meetings at Corinth: Imagining New Contexts and the Buildings East of the Theatre." *NTS* 50 (2004) 349–69.

Ling, Roger. *The Insula of the Menander at Pompeii*. Vol. 1, *The Structures*. Oxford: Clarendon, 1997.

Murphy-O'Connor, Jerome. *St. Paul's Corinth: Texts and Archaeology*. 3rd ed. Collegeville: Liturgical Press, 2002.

Oakes, Peter. *Philippians: From People to Letter*. SNTSMS 110. Cambridge: Cambridge University Press, 2001.

———. *Reading Romans in Pompeii: Paul's Letter at Ground Level*. Minneapolis: Fortress, 2009.

Økland, Jorunn. *Women in Their Place: Paul and the Corinthian Discourse of Gender and Sanctuary Space*. JSNTSup 269. London: T. & T. Clark, 2004.

Osiek, Carolyn, and David L. Balch. *Families in the New Testament World: Households and House Churches*. Louisville: Westminster John Knox, 1997.

Schowalter, Daniel, and Steven J. Friesen, editors. *Urban Religion in Roman Corinth: Interdisciplinary Approaches*. Cambridge: Harvard University Press, 2005.

Thiselton, Anthony C. *The First Epistle to the Corinthians*. NIGTC. Carlisle: Paternoster, 2000.

Williams, Charles K., II, and Nancy Bookidis, editors. *Corinth: The Centenary, 1896–1996*. Corinth 20. Princeton: American School of Classical Studies, 2003.

Woodcock, Diana H. "The Rosette in the Late Second Temple Period: Its Origins and Usage." PhD diss., University of Manchester, 2008.

Yadin, Yigael. *Masada: Herod's Fortress and the Zealots' Last Stand*. London: Weidenfeld & Nicholson, 1966.

Zanker, Paul. *Pompeii: Public and Private Life*. Translated by Deborah Lucas Schneider. Revealing Antiquity 11. Cambridge: Harvard University Press, 1998.

PART TWO

Creating Images—Verbal and Visual

SECTION ONE

Construction of the "Other"

10

Matthew's Others

Scholarly Identity-Construction and Absentee Gentile Great Men (Matt 20:24–27)

WARREN CARTER

DAVID BALCH HAS INSIGHTFULLY OBSERVED IN DIONYSIUS OF HALIcarnassus and Josephus a threefold identity-defining pattern comprising a people's or group's origin, accomplishments or governance, and deeds or way of life.[1] I have profitably utilized Balch's approach elsewhere to discuss Matthean identity-formation in terms of distinctive and competing claims in these three areas.[2]

This approach, though, has not been normative in Matthean studies. Matthean scholars have commonly preferred to construe the gospel's identity-formation in terms of an ingroup-outgroup dyadic that constructs the "other" in negative terms along a "religious," Jewish/synagogal axis (Section 1). That is, assuming the text to be a Jewish religious text, scholars accordingly find that Matthew constructs Jewish religious enemies. In Section 2, I highlight Matt 20:25 to argue that Matthew's othering is more complex and comprehensive. It includes Gentiles and political or imperial structures of rule and slavery that are simultaneously disqualified and mimicked—an argument that reflects my own understandings that the gospel is not an exclusively Jewish religious text but one that constructs identity more broadly in relation to socio-political (imperial) structures.

---

1. Balch, "Two Apologetic Encomia," discussing Dionysius of Halicarnasus, *Rom. Ant.* 1.9—2.29, and Jos., *C. Ap.* 2.145–95.
2. Carter, *Matthew and the Margins*, 9–14.

Section 1: Constructing Identities

It has become somewhat commonplace to recognize that group identities are not essentialist. Rather they are constructed in unstable and fluid processes that involve changing and particular social circumstances mediated or interpreted through language. Frequently these constructions involve dualisms in which the "other" is negatively different, contrasting "what we are not and don't want to be." Matthean scholars have frequently construed the Gospel's identity-constructing work along religious-ethnic lines in a restrictive binary fashion comprising an in-group and an out-group. In his 1985 essay, Sean Freyne employs a double context, first social challenges to the identity of the Matthean community "within the larger Jewish tradition," and second, "the rhetorical tradition of *vituperatio* . . . aimed at destroying the social and political *persona* of one's adversary."[3] He sees Matthew defining his community positively in terms of loyalty to Jesus as *the* authoritative eschatological teacher (23:8–10), rites of admission and expulsion (18:15–19; 28:19), and acts of piety (6:1–6). The latter passage employs *synkrisis* or unfavorable comparisons to distance his community from synagogues. Matthew's rhetoric of *vituperatio* discredits opponents (Jewish leadership) on three counts—failure to interpret scripture adequately, hypocrisy (15:7; chapter 23), and blindness (15:4; 23:16, 17, 19, 24, 26). Freyne identifies in chapter 23 eleven characteristics of scribes and Pharisees against which Matthew polemicizes.[4]

Ultimately, though, Matthew moves beyond denigration to eschatological annihilation, "rhetoric . . . inspired by apocalyptic hatred."[5] Freyne also argues that while this denunciation of opponents differentiates Matthew's group, it also serves to warn and exhort the community about its own practices and identity. Twenty years later, in 2005, Judy Yates Siker sets about "unmasking the enemy" and "deconstructing the 'Other'" in Matthew.[6] She helpfully employs "sociological

---

3. Freyne, "Vilifying the Other," 118–19. Freyne (ibid., 138) refers to Aristotle, *Rhetorica* I.4121b; III.1425b–1427b; Cicero, *De or.* 2.43–46, 345–50; *Ad Herrenium* 1.5. On Cicero, see Booth, *Cicero on the Attack*; also Johnson, "New Testament's Anti-Jewish Slander," 430–41. Johnson samples the invective of, among others, Dio Chrysostom, Plutarch, Epictetus, Apollonius of Tyana, Josephus, and Philo.

4. Freyne, "Vilifying the Other," 143.

5. Ibid., 134–35, 142.

6. Siker, "Unmasking the Enemy," 110.

identity construction theory" especially social constructionist understandings that recognize that identities are commonly constructed by alterity, that is, over against other identities, in binary opposition involving "us/them" tensive relationships.[7] She centers her discussion on relationships between Matthew's Gospel and Judaism, and argues that the Gospel "engages in a polemical construction of Jewish leaders as 'other.'" Employing the notion of "deconstruction" in the sense of "tearing down," she identifies polemic against the leaders' interpretation and teaching of the law, their persecution of prophets, Jesus, and his followers, and self-righteous and hypocritical actions. This polemic de-legitimizes their leadership and denies their authority.[8] Through this binary articulation of difference, Matthew constructs the identity of his own community.

Freyne and Siker offer insightful and engaging constructions of Matthean identity-formation. While Siker's discussion is more theoretically explicit, common emphases on Jewish leaders, interpretation of the Scriptures, and hypocrisy align the two discussions. Centrally both assume that Matthew is a religious text and read it as though its only horizon for identity formation is conflict with Judaism in general and a synagogue in particular. Their constructed Matthean Jesus-followers have interaction with no other worlds. This religious-Jewish reading strategy has pervaded Matthean studies for decades. While religious and ethnic factors undoubtedly play some part in the identities that the Gospel constructs, my argument is that focus on them is too restrictive. Reading Matthew through different glasses complexifies the reconstructions considerably.

For example, the command to love one's enemies constructs the other with the negative term "enemies" that reaches far beyond synagogues (Matt 5:43–44). The dyadic structure, the unspecified plural "enemies" (replacing the singular in Lev 19:18), and the absence of any reference to sympathizers, allies, or neutrals, create a bifurcated world

---

7. For bibliography on ancient and contemporary identity formation, Siker, "Unmasking the Enemy," 110–14; among others, Siker especially uses Woodward, ed., *Identity and Difference*. Siker does not explicitly draw on social science discussions that comprise a Social Identity Approach. For pioneering contributions to this approach, Tajfel, ed., *Social Identity*; Turner, *Rediscovering the Social*; Hinkle and Brown, "Intergroup Comparison"; also Korostelina, *Social Identity*, and Hornsey, "Social Identity Theory."

8. Siker, "Unmasking the Enemy," 116–22.

comprising disciples and pervasive opponents. The following clause's reference to "persecuting" posits animosity between the two groups. Yet disciples are to "love" them, with the next clause specifying love as prayer. The absence of any other specification such as social interaction or material expressions of care reinforces social distance and their identity as other. In 10:36, with a focus on households not synagogues, Matthew's Jesus constructs enemies on the basis of negative responses to Jesus. "One's enemies will be members of one's own household." To not be a disciple is to be an enemy. The passage clearly does not respect a negative response to Jesus and does not repeat the command to love these household "enemies." Matthew's Jesus warns, though, that loving a household member more than loving Jesus indicates that one is not a disciple (10:37). There is, apparently, a clear limit to love for enemies.

The parable of the wheat and the weeds adds a further negative and regrettable dimension to the construction of enemies (13:24–30, 36–43). Pervasive human enemies (non-disciples) are othered by aligning them with a cosmic enemy, the devil, who opposes Jesus's work and God's reign (13:25, 28, 39). Verses 38–39 allegorically interpret the parable of the seeds dualistically, anthropologically, socially, and cosmically. While Jesus the Son of Man produces "children of the kingdom," the "enemy," the devil, produces "children of the evil one." An anthropological and social dualism is created in that people not aligned with Jesus belong to the devil. These enemies will receive eschatological condemnation while the righteous are vindicated. Interestingly, neither parable nor interpretation suggests any interaction, let alone hostility, between the two groups. Wheat and weeds co-exist. Nor are these "weeds" explicitly identified with a particular ethnic, social, or religious group. Nor is anything said about loving them. Rather, their devilish origin, identity, and destiny are their defining and differentiating marks. And interestingly, nothing is said here about the eschatological fate of the enemy/devil. Subsequently, Jesus-believers are assured that the cosmic exalted Christ overcomes all enemies; the only time the word "enemies" is used directly in relation to Jesus (22:44).

The gospel thus constructs "enemies" in a social and cosmic dualism between Jesus-believers and non-believers. This dualism based on response to Jesus is a very neat construction. Interestingly, the narrative of Jesus's ministry is not nearly so clear-cut with interactions between

Jesus and the crowds often depicted as benign and beneficial, but without either understanding or hostility, at least until the Jerusalem crowd, manipulated by the leaders, shouts for Jesus's crucifixion (27:20–23). The narrative also lacks scenes whereby enemies attack disciples. Even in the passion, the enemy is largely within as disciples betray (26:14–25, 47–55), deny (26:31–35, 69–75), sleep (26:36–46), and flee (26:56). Clearly the Gospel's sevenfold use of the term "enemies" contributes significantly to Matthew's complex identity-constructing work. We could consider other language that participates in constructing identity if space permitted (e.g., "[evil] generation," "human beings"). A significant term, not utilized by the religious-synagogue reading, is "the Gentiles"/"nations" (ἐθνικός, ἔθνη).[9] The term significantly destabilizes the limited, dyadic, and conflictual quality of that reading, positing various interactions between Jesus-believers and Gentiles. Only a brief consideration is possible.

Various Gentiles featured in the opening chapters: Abraham and Gentile women contribute to God's purposes (Rahab, Tamar, Ruth, 1:1–3, 5), the Babylonians both resist and advance God's purposes (1:11–12), and the magi worship (2:1–12). The first explicitly identified "Gentiles" are Romans to whom belongs Galilee (4:15), an imperially dominated territory in which Jesus and disciples live in the narrative.[10] Gentiles are also violent in that they war against each other (24:7). At other points, Gentiles are presented as cultural entities with values, practices, and piety at odds with, but not hostile to, Jesus-followers (5:47; 6:7, 32). They are also non-Jewish people to whom Jesus proclaims justice in an unjust imperially-dominated world (12:18). Some participate positively with hope (12:21) and receive God's kingdom (21:43, Jew and Gentile), while others, notably a Roman governor in alliance with Jerusalem's elites, respond with hate in putting Jesus to death (20:19). Jesus-followers are to continue his mission among Gentiles (24:14; 28:19) despite some persecution (10:18; 24:9). Yet as powerful as these nations and people are, they are constructed as ultimately subject to and accountable to the Son of Man in the judgment where they are evaluated on how they have treated the "least of these" (25:32).

---

9. Carter, "Matthew and the Gentiles."
10. Carter, *Matthew and the Margins*, 115.

Gentile identity, then, is constructed as other in terms of political, cultural, and ethnic dimensions, and in relation to God's purposes and Jesus-believers. These interactions comprise variously acceptance, openness, engagement, hope, antithesis, opposition, submission, accountability, and divine condemnation. These dynamics contribute to the construction of the identities of Jesus-believers and Gentiles, and indicate the inadequacy of positing an exclusive Jewish-religious axis for the Gospel's identity-constructing work.

Section 2: The Great Men of the Gentiles (Matt 20:24–27)

Matthew 20:25 constructs a significant contrast between Gentile elites and disciples. After declining to grant the request of the mother of the sons of Zebedee that James and John sit on Jesus's right and left hand in his kingdom, Jesus addresses the angry ten disciples. "You know that the rulers of the Gentiles lord it over them, and their great ones/men are tyrants over them. It will not be so among you; but whosoever wishes to be great among you must be your servant and whoever wishes to be first must be your slave, just as the Son of Man came not to be served but to serve and to give his life as a ransom for many" (20:25b–28a, NRSV). Busy constructing Matthew's other along Jewish-religious lines, Matthean scholars have generally had little use for these verses about Gentile rule apart from theological discussions of "ransom."[11] Those who do wonder about the identity of the Gentile rulers, the nature of their power, its gendered presentation, and the contrast with disciples usually settle for some form of "questing for power" and "greatness, honor, and prestige"[12] or "power and authority"[13] and bending "the wills of others to conform to their own."[14] Such neglect serves only to mask the realities of imperializing power

---

11. For example, Allen, *Gospel*, 217; Sand, *Das Evangelium*, 407; Gnilka, *Das Matthäusevangelium*, 189–90; Gundry, *Matthew*, 403.

12. Hagner, *Matthew 14–28*, 581. Hagner introduces his discussion of 20:20–28 with a bibliography of fourteen scholarly works, ten of which concern the "ransom" saying (576–77).

13. Hill, *Gospel of Matthew*, 288.

14. Garland, *Reading Matthew*, 208.

and to preserve the selective Jewish, religious reading that contemporary scholars have constructed.

Matthew others these Gentiles in terms of power that "lords it over" and, in contrast, constructs disciples with a servile identity. The plural language of "rulers" and "great ones/men" might evoke powerful figures such as Alexander, Antiochus IV Epiphanes, and Pompey, all conquerors of land and people, though I cannot find any Matthean commentator who entertains such a notion except Craig Keener's vague reference to "the tyrants and empires of history."[15] Some identify the Romans[16] though without exploring the dynamics of imperial power either in the capital or among provincial elites.[17] Matthew's negative othering of Gentile elites certainly contrasts with the self-construction of provincial elites such as Plutarch and Dio Chrysostom who present themselves positively as responsibly seeking the good of their cities.[18]

Despite the Matthean prohibition on disciples being like these great men, K. W. Clark argues that the verse constructs Roman power benignly.[19] He rejects the NRSV's translation of the verb κατακυριεύ– ειν in 20:25 as "lord it over," because it constructs the rulers and great men as arrogant, oppressive, and abusive (207), thereby presenting Roman imperial power in an inappropriately negative light. Clark sets about defending the myth of benign imperial power, and rescuing Roman imperialism from such miscasting and the religious Gospel from anything political by examining the occurrences of κατακυριεύ– ειν in the Septuagint, the Oxyrhynchus Papyri, the Apostolic Fathers, and the New Testament. Clark insists that the verb has one constant meaning across this diverse literature, "to rule over, to exercise lordship over, to be lord of, to master, to have dominion over" (212). The appropriate translation "dominion over" constructs Roman rule as "absolute dominion that is exercised strictly yet legally" (208) but is not abusive or oppressive. He names the contrast of Matt 20:25 as: "The Christian virtue is service to his fellows (sic!) rather than political preeminence and power over them. This contrast has no reference

15. Keener, *Commentary*, 487.

16. McNeile, *Gospel*, 289; Hill, *Gospel of Matthew*, 288; Davies and Allison, *Gospel according to Saint Matthew*, 3:93.

17. For provincial elites participating in and negotiating Roman power, Swain, *Hellenism, Classicism*; Salmeri, "Dio, Rome."

18. Salmeri, "Dio, Rome," 60–63.

19. Clark, "Meaning of [KATA]KYRIEYEIN."

to 'lording it over' and there is here no suggestion of arrogance and oppression on the part of Gentile rulers" (210–11).

Clark's discussion suffers from several fatal flaws. The major one is his claim that κατακυριεύειν has one fixed meaning across "so inclusive a sweep of literature from Septuagint to Byzantium, in private documents on papyrus and formal essays, both secular and religious" (210). The texts do not support the claim. The verb does not even appear in the Oxyrhynchus Papyri and the verb κυριεύειν in business contracts hardly replicates the dynamics of imperial power. This is his second major flaw. He fails to take seriously the nature of imperial power constructed by Matt 20:25. Both flaws are evident in a quick examination of the some Septuagintal uses. For example, the divine command to "subdue" (κατακυριεύσατε) the earth (Gen 1:28; 9:1; Sir 17:4) is in no way "legal." It's a divine command that sets humans in a "ruling over" relationship to the earth rather than, for example, a partnership or nurturing relationship. To "subdue" the earth is not a neutral act; it could upon realization by humans be a responsible or an oppressive and abusive act.

Likewise in Jer 3:14 God summons this "faithless or apostate people" Israel to return, declaring "I will rule you" (NRSV: "I am your master"; κατακυριεύσω). From the perspective of the writer of Jeremiah, this divine "rule over" is good and proper. From the perspective of those who have abandoned God's ways it might be a welcome opportunity to return, or an unwelcome intrusion of God's meddling or oppressive power. In Num 21:24, 32:22 and 29, the verb depicts Moses's conquest of the land belonging to the Amorites and Canaanites. This conquest is not legal. While the narrative presents it as consistent with and vindicated by the divine will, it remains an act of aggressive "power over," an abusive and oppressive act for conquered peoples. In the two references of Ps 9:26 and 31 (LXX; Ps 10:5–10, NRSV), the wicked "rule over." In context, this rule comprises persecution of the poor, greed, deceit, oppression, murder of the innocent, spying on the helpless, and seizing the poor. It is not legal or benign. The Psalm constructs the wicked as arrogant, oppressive, and abusers of power.

In two royal Psalms, Israel's king rules in the midst of enemies (109:1 LXX; NRSV 110:2) and represents divine rule. The following verses describe this rule as "shattering kings," and "executing judgment among the nations, filling them with corpses." This is hardly "the strict and legal exercise of dominion" as Clark insists. Rather it depicts the classic imperializing ways of kings in asserting destructive rule over others for the former's benefit, what any subjugated people would call arrogant and abusive power. Psalm 72 presents this "dominion from sea to sea" (71:8 LXX; 72:8 NRSV) much more benignly as the king acts on behalf of God's justice among the poor. But the Psalm cannot maintain this façade. "His enemies" (ἐχθροί) lick the dust, others pay tribute, and all nations serve him (72:9–11). Clark's "legal exercise of dominion" sounds much more like the oppressive and destructive ways of imperialist powers who assert power for their own benefits through conquest. Likewise, in Ps 118:133 LXX (NRSV 119:133), the Psalmist prays that God will "never let iniquity have dominion over me" (κατακυριευσάτω). What is this iniquity? In the next verse he prays, "do not leave me to my oppressors . . . do not let the godless oppress me." The Psalmist prays for deliverance from power that he finds oppressive, arrogant, and abusive. Clark's quest for a consistent and benign meaning for the verb leads him to an unsustainable reading of these Septuagintal uses. Clearly the verb does not have a fixed, stable meaning. It certainly does not construct the exercise of power in a consistently benign, neutral, or legal manner.

How then does Matt 20:25 with its use of κατακυριεύειν construct Gentile rule and the contrast with servile disciples? The othering of Gentile power extends across the whole Gospel, something Clark does not consider.[20] The genealogy constructs the Babylonian empire as contrary to but subjected to God's purposes for the future of Israel (1:11–12). Chapter 2 reveals King Herod, Rome's client king of the Jews, to be replete with a repertoire of imperial tactics: lies, spies, allies, murderous rage, and oppressive power, yet three times it refers to his death as God thwarts his murderous purposes (2:15, 19–20). Chapter 4 constructs Roman power as devilish, as the devil claims possession of all empires (βασιλείας) in offering them to Jesus (4:8–9). In the midst of the Roman Empire, Jesus manifests God's empire (4:17), which provides some rescue from the destructive impact of the unjust imperial structures like diseases (4:23–25) and food shortages (14:13–21). Antipathy between Matthew's Jesus and Roman rule marks Jesus's handing over to the Gentiles for crucifixion (20:19),

---

20. For elaboration, Carter, "Matthew and Empire; Carter, "Matthew Negotiates the Roman Empire."

carried out by the Roman governor Pilate and his allies, the Jerusalem leaders (chapters 26–27).[21] And the Gospel's eschatology constructs Rome's empire as subject to God's judgment which will end its rule (24:29–34).[22] This context does not construct the ruling (κατακυριεύειν) of the "Gentiles"/"great men" as neutral, benign, or legal. It constructs it as obstructive to God's purposes, violent, oppressive, devilish, destructive, and condemned. Yet the Gospel also requires that disciples accommodate its taxing demands (17:24–27; 22:15–22).[23]

By identifying the empire's rulers as "great men" (οἱ μεγάλοι), the verse foregrounds gender in constructing their identity and power. These powerful "great men"—males with elite social status—have the right, position, allies, and means to impose their will on the powerless and dishonored including Jesus and his followers. Jonathan Walters's examination of Roman masculinities suggests they maintain their own corporeal and societal inviolability while their power penetrates the passive, inferior, conquered, womanly nations who are "not great men."[24] Panels from Aphrodisias depict conquered nations as women under attack from manly emperors.[25] Gender, social status, and political power align. Yet the gender lines get blurred partly because the "great ones" must also include powerful (manly) elite women,[26] and partly because the returning Christ will, in very manly style, subdue the Roman legions and destroy the great men's dominating power (24:29–34). The judgment of God—of which Jesus is the agent—penetrates their inviolability.

A further context contributes to the identities constructed by this verse. It concerns the intratextuality between the two verbs κατακυριεύειν and the uncommon κατεξουσιάζειν with their cognate nouns, κύριος and ἐξουσία. In the Gospel, κύριος refers to both God and Jesus. As Lord, God rules heaven and earth (11:25) and manifests God's salvific purposes among humans (1:20, 22, 24). As Lord, Jesus exercises power over eschatological judgment (7:21–22), disease and

21. Carter, *Pontius Pilate*, 75–99.
22. Carter, "Are There Imperial Texts in the Class?"
23. Carter, "Paying the Tax"; also in Carter, *Matthew and Empire*, 130–44.
24. Walters, "Invading the Roman Body."
25. Smith, "The Imperial Reliefs"; Smith, "*Sacra Gentium*."
26. Space prevents elaboration beyond referencing powerful imperial Roman women and provincial elites like Plancia Magna of Perge, Julia Severa of Akmoneia, or Eumachia and Julia Felix of Pompeii.

demons (8:2, 6; 15:22), the sea (8:25; 14:28), disciples (10:24–25), and Sabbath (12:8). The noun ἐξουσία denotes Jesus's authority to teach (7:29), forgive sin (9:6, 8), and share in God's authority over heaven and earth (28:18). That is, the Gospel uses these nouns to construct God and Jesus in imperially imitative terms as the authoritative rulers of heaven and earth. Using the same language for God/Jesus and for the (condemned) Gentile rulers/"great men" sets up a contestive relationship. The Gospel's perspective whereby the authority of God and Jesus trumps all others frames these rulers/great men as usurping rule and authority that rightly belong to God and Jesus, and presents God and Jesus as out-empiring the empire. In this competitive ascribing of power, Matthean theology and Christology compete with, mimic, and trump imperial power.

Having othered Gentile rule as forbidden, oppressive, arrogant, abusive, male, condemned, and devilish, Matthew's Jesus forbids his followers to imitate it among themselves (20:26). Instead he constructs for them a contrasting identity; they are to be slaves of one another (20:26–27). Matthean scholars seem to find this identity admirable, foregrounding in their discussions of it, service, humility, and self-sacrifice.[27] Yet this reinscribing of slavery in terms of "service"—recall Clark's "service to his fellows (sic!) rather than political preeminence and power over them"—is very problematic, since it sanitizes and masks a foundational and brutal structure of Gentile rule, and renders it normative for the identity of Jesus-believers. That is, having othered Gentiles, Matthew utilizes an entity othered by Gentile rule, slavery, to identify Jesus-followers.[28]

Orlando Patterson defines slavery as the "permanent, violent domination of natally alienated and generally dishonored persons."[29] Neville Morley begins his discussion of "forms of exploitation" in Roman economic practices with a discussion of slave labor in which "millions of captives—men, women, and children—were sold into

---

27. Variously, Clark, "Meaning," 210–11; Garland, *Reading Matthew*, 208; Hill, *Gospel of Matthew*, 288; Hagner, *Matthew*, 2:582; Keener, *Commentary*, 486; Talbert, *Reading Matthew*, 241.

28. Seeley ("Rulership and Service,") attempts to trace a Hellenistic tradition of "rule as service" though much of this supporting data suggests that the dominant philosophy comprises benefaction or doing good. Yet note the third century CE Aelian, *Historical Miscellany*, 2.20, who speaks of "kingly rule as honorable slavery."

29. Patterson, *Slavery and Social Death*, 13.

slavery: reduced to the status of property, uprooted from their homes and transported to Italy and Sicily, where they were subjected to the complete dominance of their new owners and the constant threat or reality of violence, usually for the rest of their lives."[30] Matthew assumes slavery (10:24; 22:1–14) and without dissent depicts violence against slaves as normative including torture (18:34), beating (21:35), death (21:35), verbal abuse (25:26), punishment (24:50–51; 25:30) and violent anger (26:51). This ubiquitous societal structure divided free and slave, institutionalized dominance and control, and ensured status and wealth for owners. It deprived slaves of dignity, property, and legal rights, and ensured, for many, corporeal suffering through over-work, branding, poor living quarters, limited nutrition, beatings, sexual availability, and penetration.[31] For certain, slavery is not about chosen self-sacrifice or "service," nor, given its systemic economic, social, political, and imperial dimensions, is it about a personal characteristic of humility.

Bert Harrill sees Matthew following Mark in using the slave metaphor to depict leadership (being "great," "first") in terms of the "slave bailiff" or the *vilicus*.[32] This was a managerial slave with considerable power, who in various rural and urban contexts managed farms or administered urban workshops, inns, baths, stadia etc. The managerial slave appears, for example, in discussions of household management,[33] and functioned as the owner's representative with authority over other slaves and the master's business. Harrill points out that the *vilicus* became a stock bully figure who violently misused his authority in beating other slaves (cf. Matt 18:28–30), as well as a metaphor for freeborn officials serving superiors.[34]

Given these particular dimensions of the slave image, all of which could be developed at length, its use to construct the identity of Jesus-believers is very problematic. Its reinscribing affirms the normalcy and

---

30. Morley, *Roman Empire*, 90.

31. Glancey (*Slavery in Early Christianity*) emphasizes the corporeal experiences of slavery.

32. Harrill, *Slaves in the New Testament*, 85–117.

33. Though he cites in passing Mark 10:43, Harrill's discussion of NT household codes (*Slaves*, 88–89, 103, 113–16) fails to recognize the use of household elements to structure the narratives of Mark 10 and Matt 19–20. See Carter, *Households and Discipleship*.

34. Harrill, *Slaves in the New Testament*, 105.

legitimacy of slavery within the imperial system even though verse 25 appears to reject that system. The image draws from this system and, though seeming to contrast and challenge it, its use sanctions imperial power. Gentile rulers/great men utilize slaves—the ultimate other—to express and enhance their wealth, power, and status. The image constructs discipleship as a perpetually alienated and submissive existence in which disciples, forever "other," are paradoxically both brutalized and brutal. As slaves of Jesus the Lord or master, the image constructs him to be dominant with unlimited access to slave bodies. As slaves, disciples are dominated by him, penetrated, and suffer at his hands. As slaves of one another, disciples not only submit to one another but also dominate and dishonor one another.

Conclusion

I have suggested that in Matthean constructions of identity, the other cannot be reduced to a simplistic notion of synagogues or Jewish leaders as Matthean scholars readily construct it to be. Our brief discussions of Matthew's language of "enemies" show the other to be much more comprehensively and ideologically constructed. His language of "the Gentiles" or "nations" indicates that the Gospel's other is not constrained, as most Matthean scholars seem to be, by Judaeo-centricity and ethnic boundaries, but is very concerned with imperial societal structures and figures of power and status. In discussing 20:25–27, I have suggested that Matthean othering of the Gentile rulers/great men ultimately deconstructs in imitation and contest, as God and Jesus outempire these imperial figures, and as disciples are othered with the brutalized and brutalizing imperial identity of slaves.

Bibliography

Allen, Willoughby C. *The Gospel according to Saint Matthew*. New York: Scribner, 1910.

Balch, David L. "Two Apologetic Encomia: Dionysius on Rome and Josephus on the Jews." *JSJ* 13 (1982) 102–22.

Booth, Joan, editor. *Cicero on the Attack: Invective and Subversion in the Orations and Beyond*. Swansea: Classical Press of Wales, 2007.

Carter, Warren. "Are There Imperial Texts in the Class? Intertextual Eagles and Matthean Eschatology as 'Lights Out' Time for Imperial Rome (Matt 24:27–31)." *JBL* 122 (2003) 467–87.

———. *Households and Discipleship: A Study of Matthew 19–20*. JSNTSup 103. Sheffield: Sheffield Academic, 1994.

———. *Matthew and Empire: Initial Explorations*. Harrisburg, PA: Trinity, 2001.

———. "Matthew and Empire." In *Empire in the New Testament*, edited by Stanley Porter and Cynthia Long Westfall, 90–119. McMaster New Testament Studies Series. Eugene, OR: Pickwick Publications, 2011.

———. "Matthew and the Gentiles: Individual Conversion and/or Systemic Transformation?" *JSNT* 26 (2004) 259–82.

———. *Matthew and the Margins: A Sociopolitical and Religious Reading*. Bible & Liberation Series. Maryknoll, NY: Orbis, 2000.

———. "Matthew Negotiates the Roman Empire." In *In the Shadow of Empire: Reclaiming the Bible as a History of Faithful Resistance*, edited by Richard Horsley, 117–36. Louisville: Westminster John Knox, 2008.

———. "Paying the Tax to Rome as Subversive Praxis: Matthew 17:24–27." *JSNT* 76 (1999) 3–31.

———. *Pontius Pilate: Portraits of a Roman Governor*. Interfaces. Collegeville, MN: Liturgical, 2003.

Clark, Kenneth Willis. "The Meaning of [KATA]KYRIEYEIN." In *The Gentile Bias and Other Essays*, edited by Kenneth Willis Clark, 207–12. NovTSup 54. Leiden: Brill, 1980.

Davies, W. D., and Dale Allison. *A Critical and Exegetical Commentary on the Gospel according to Saint Matthew*. Vol. 3, *Commentary on Matthew XIX–XXVIII*. ICC. Edinburgh: T. & T. Clark, 1997.

Freyne, Sean. "Vilifying the Other and Defining the Self: Matthew's and John's Anti-Jewish Polemic in Focus." In *"To See Ourselves as Others See Us": Christians, Jews, "Others" in Late Antiquity*, edited by Jacob Neusner and Ernest Frerichs, 117–43. Scholars Press Studies in the Humanities. Chico: Scholars, 1985.

Garland, David E. *Reading Matthew*. Reading the New Testament Series. New York: Crossroad, 1995.

Glancey, Jennifer. *Slavery in Early Christianity*. Oxford: Oxford University Press, 2002.

Gnilka, Joachim. *Das Matthäusevangelium*. Vol. 2. Herder: Freiburg, 1992.

Gundry, Robert H. *Matthew: A Commentary on His Handbook for a Mixed Church under Persecution*. 2nd ed. Grand Rapids: Eerdmans, 1994.

Hagner, Donald. *Matthew 14–28*. WBC 33B. Dallas: Word, 1995.

Harrill, J. Albert. *Slaves in the New Testament: Literary, Social, and Moral Dimensions*. Minneapolis: Fortress, 2006.

Hill, David, editor. *The Gospel of Matthew*. NCB. Grand Rapids: Eerdmans, 1972.
Hinkle, Steve, and Rupert Brown. "Intergroup Comparison and Social Identity: Some Links and Lacunae." In *Social Identity Theory: Constructive and Critical Advances*, edited by Dominic Abrams and Michael A. Hogg, 48–70. New York: Springer, 1990.
Hornsey, Matthew. "Social Identity Theory and Self-Categorization Theory: A Historical Review." *SPPC* 2 (2008) 204–22.
Johnson, Luke Timothy. "The New Testament's Anti-Jewish Slander and the Conventions of Ancient Rhetoric." *JBL* 108 (1989) 419–41.
Keener, Craig S. *A Commentary on the Gospel of Matthew*. Grand Rapids: Eerdmans, 1999.
Korostelina, Korina. *Social Identity and Conflict: Structures, Dynamics, and Implications*. New York: Palgrave MacMillan, 2007.
McNeile, Alan Hugh. *The Gospel according to St. Matthew*. London: MacMillan, 1938.
Morley, Neville. *The Roman Empire: Roots of Imperialism*. Roots of Imperialism. London: Pluto, 2010.
Patterson, Orlando. *Slavery and Social Death: A Comparative Study*. Cambridge: Harvard University Press, 1982.
Salmeri, Giovanni. "Dio, Rome, and the Civic Life of Asia Minor." In *Dio Chrysostom: Politics, Letters, and Philosophy*, edited by Simon Swain, 53–92. Oxford: Oxford University Press, 2000.
Sand, Alexander. *Das Evangelium nach Matthäus*. RNT. Regensburg: Pustet, 1986.
Seeley, David. "Rulership and Service in Mark 10:41–45." *NovT* 35 (1993) 234–50.
Siker, Judy Yates. "Unmasking the Enemy: Deconstructing the 'Other' in the Gospel of Matthew." *PRS* 32 (2005) 109–25.
Smith, Roland R. "The Imperial Reliefs from the Sebasteion at Aphrodisias." *JRS* 77 (1987) 88–138.
———. "*Sacra Gentium*: The *Ethne* from the Sebasteion at Aphrodisias." *JRS* 78 (1988) 50–77.
Swain, Simon. *Hellenism and Empire: Language, Classicism, and Power in the Greek World, AD 50–250*. Oxford: Clarendon, 1996.
Tajfel, Henri, editor. *Social Identity and Intergroup Relations*. European Studies in Social Psychology. Cambridge: Cambridge University Press, 1982.
Talbert, Charles H. *Matthew*. Paideia. Grand Rapids: Baker Academic, 2010.
Turner, John C., with Michael A. Hogg et al. *Rediscovering the Social Group: Self-Categorization Theory*. Oxford: Blackwell, 1987.
Walters, Jonathan. "Invading the Roman Body: Manliness and Impenetrability in Roman Thought." In *Roman Sexualities*, edited by Judith Hallett and Marilyn Skinner, 29–43. Princeton: Princeton University Press, 1997.
Woodward, Kathryn, editor. *Identity and Difference*. Media, Culture and Identities. London: Sage, in association with the Open University, 1997.

11

Seeing and Hearing Jesus Christ Crucified in Galatians 3:1 under Watchful Imperial Eyes

Aliou Cissé Niang

Introduction

I WRITE TO EXPRESS MY INCOMMENSURABLE GRATITUDE TO DAVID Lee Balch for being my unfailing teacher and mentor who encouraged me to read Scripture, especially the New Testament, with the Graeco-Roman context in mind. His keen knowledge of Graeco-Roman milieu, literature[1] and domestic art[2] significantly influenced my work.[3] New Testament authors were not impervious to their milieu but lived, exercised their convictions, and died under imperial watchful eyes and tightfisted hands. In his *Roman Domestic Art*, Balch posits that "Graeco-Roman, domestic and tragic art emphasizing *pathos* would have provided a meaningful cultural context for understanding Paul's gospel of Christ's passion."[4] This led him to read Paul's προγράφη with the intriguing myth of the dying Iphigenia, sculptures telling stories of the deaths of the priest Laocoon, and the Dying Suicidal Gaul and his

---

1. Balch, *Let Wives*; Osiek and Balch, *Families*; idem, *Early Christian Families*.

2. Balch, *Roman Domestic Art*; Balch, "Paul's Portrait;" Balch, "Suffering of Isis/Io."

3. Niang, *Faith and Freedom*.

4. Balch, *Roman Domestic Art*, 85; Balch, "Paul's Portrait," 85; Balch, "Suffering of Isis/Io," 25, 24–55.

wife, and paintings enshrining myths that Gauls/Galatians would have readily recognized.

Assuming Balch's thesis, I argue that Graeco-Roman imperial and colonial art may have had both a *negative* and a *positive* influence on the Galatians' seeing Paul's portrayal of Ἰησοῦς Χριστὸς προεγράφη ἐσταυρωμένος, "Jesus Christ publicly displayed as crucified" (Gal 3:1). Thus, "Jesus Christ publically displayed as crucified," like some Graeco-Roman visual art, is a public image that replaces text. Martin Hengel observes that crucifixion is reserved for dangerous criminals, lower class people, slaves, and political and military culprits.[5] Persians (Esth 2:23; 5:14; 7:9; 9:25), Carthaginians and Romans crucified convicts, a practice later abolished by Constantine.[6] Biblical, Dead Sea Scrolls and other Jewish authors knew of capital offenses punished by hanging.[7] Cicero calls crucifixion a "plague" to be removed from the sight of Roman citizens.[8] Crucifixion according to Hengel was a dreadful, cruel, barbaric, and horrific form of punishment that leaves no picture to be desired. Rome crucified Jesus Christ (Josephus, *Ant.* 18.63–64c; Gal 3:1; 2 Cor 13:4; Mark 15:24–27; Matt 27:35–38; Luke 23:33; John 18:18; Acts 2:36; 4:10) whom Paul preaches while admitting that his proclamation is σκάνδαλον, "a stumbling block" to Judeans and μωρίαν, "foolishness" to the non-Judeans (1 Cor 1:23).

---

5. See Hengel, *Crucifixion*, for a detailed discussion.

6. Livingstone, "Crucifix, Crucifixion," 434–35.

7. Deut 21:22–23; Josh 8:29; 10:26–27; 2 Sam 4:12; 21:8–9; 4QpNah; 1 Macc 7:16; Josephus, *JW* 1.97, 113; *Ant* 12.396; 13.380; *GenRab* 65.22; *m. Sanhedrin* 6.4.

8. Cicero, *In Verr.* 2.5.162; *Pro Rabirio* 16. See detailed treatment of the subject in Hengel's *Crucifixion*, 11–14.

162   PART TWO: CREATING IMAGES—VERBAL AND VISUAL

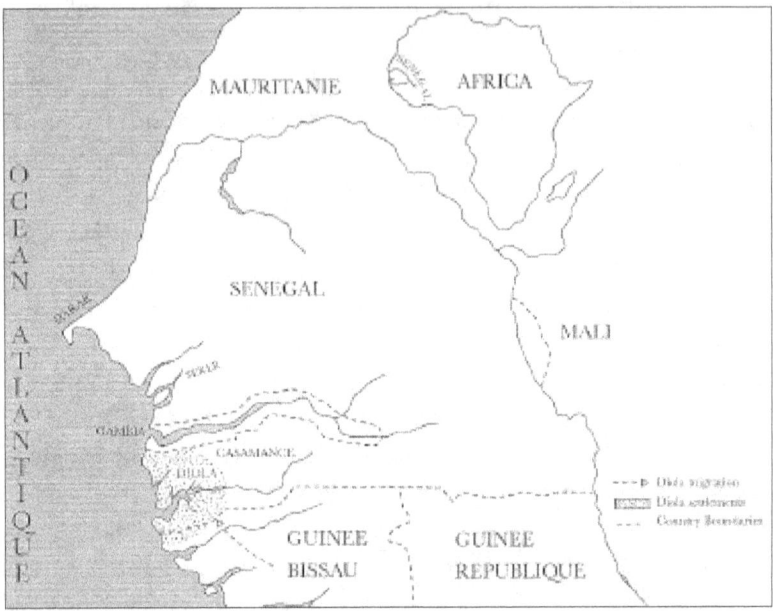

Figure 11.1: Map of Diola settlements on the northern and southern west banks of the Casamance River known as *le Pays Diola* "Diola country." Casamance, a region of Sénégal, West Africa, is the breadbasket of the country. The Casamance River irrigates Diola rice fields and is the fishery for most Diola communities.

As a native of the Diola people of Senegal, West Africa, when I think about crucifixion, this question comes to mind: When the Christian missionaries known as "Holy Ghost Fathers," wearing crucifixes, portrayed Jesus as crucified under the aegis of imperial France, might that have influenced how Senegalese Diola people responded to their message? Postcolonial theoretical adaptations of Lacanian psychoanalysis remind us that colonized subjects often mimic their colonizers in many ways—a life situation engendered by ambivalence[9] in response to overwhelming imperial displacements. As a young village boy in Casamance, Senegal, West Africa (see figure 11.1), I learned about French objectification of Diola people from stories my grandparents often told me. These stories came alive when I entered the French pri-

---

9. Bhabha, *Location of Culture*, 121–44.

mary school where much of my education revolved around French history and culture and little or nothing about mine. French colonists constructed the image of Senegalese people through the French school—a task they proudly called *mission civilisatrice*[10] or *la paix française*. Of course, they were far from being the first colonists to engage in such unhealthy identity constructions. Graeco-Roman colonists defined Gauls/Galatians as "Other," too. I imagine these colonial constructions influenced how the "Other" saw and heard Paul's Jesus Christ publically displayed as crucified.

Greeks and the "Other"

Fifth- and fourth-century BCE Athenians traced their origins to earth-born Ἐρεχθῆος "Erechtheus" and transferred his "chthonic origins" to all Athenians.[11] Isocrates builds on this idea insisting that "Hellenes sprung up from the earth itself" (Iso, *Panath*. 12.124; Iso, *De Pace* 8.49; Plato, *Menex*. 237–239a; Aristotle, *Rhet*. 1.5.5 =1360b31–2). Conceivably, it is "this chthonic origin of the Athenian race" that "became the conventional metaphor for the Athenians' belief that they had lived in Attica since time immemorial," a self-understanding that became an effective dimension of their political ideology for expressing the Greek democratic belief in the equality and superiority of all Athenian citizens.[12] So, Plato's Socrates explains to Menexenus that Athenian ancestors were birthed and "nurtured" by one mother, the "earth," an ancestral origin from which Athenians received an unbroken polity: "democracy" (Plato, *Menex*. 237b–240c).

Benjamin Isaac posits that Greeks constructed the "Other" using their theory of "environmental determinism, the heredity of acquired characters, a combination of these two ideas; the constitution and form of government; autochthony and pure linage."[13] Athenians were taught to believe that climate and geography determine "collective characteristics of groups of people"—a natural phenomenon that permanently

---

10. Lesourd, *L'œuvre Civilisatrice*.

11. Rosivach, "Autochthony and the Athenians," 297, 294–306; Kearns, "Erechtheus," 554–5, refers to Homer, *Il*. 2.547–48, on the myth of Erechtheus.

12. Rosivach, "Autochthony and the Athenians," 297, 305. Some Greek writers did challenge the claim to Greek superiority.

13. Isaac, "Ethnic Prejudice," 331.

affects human genes and thus heredity and activity. This deterministic thinking played a major role in "ancient imperialism" in that "the presumed characteristics that resulted were subject to value-judgments, in which the foreigners were usually rejected as being inferior to the observer. Greeks in the fourth century BCE developed the environmental theory further, adding two elements which made it an essential tool for imperialists. They claimed that Greece occupies the very best environment between Europe and Asia and therefore produces people ideally capable of ruling others."[14] Belief in environmental determinism may have inspired Plato's affirmation of Greek ethnic superiority (Plato, *Menex.* 245d) and unmatched ingenuity (Plato, *Epin.* 987e) and influenced Aristotle's view on how the environment shaped Greeks into "spirited and intelligent" people "able to rule all" (Aristotle, *Pol.* 7.30). To rule all, some Greek authors reshaped their ancestors' texts that described them as founders, colonists or settlers away from home into foundation poems that, according to Carol Dougherty, begin with a civic crisis that forced would-be Greek colonists to consult the Delphic oracle for divine guidance and legitimation.[15] Apollo advises Greeks on their ongoing quests for cultural and economic supremacy and sends them to colonize.[16]

Objectifying the "Other" helps colonists legitimize their actions. For instance, writing under imperial Rome for a Greek audience, Polybius objectifies ancient Celts/Gauls, especially those of Italy, as primitive nomadic unskilled farmers who dwell in unwalled villages (Pol. *Hist.* 2.17. 9–10). He praises Attalus for conquering "the most formidable and warlike nation in Asia" (Pol. *Hist.* 18.41.7), feared for its barbarism (βάρβαρος), lawlessness (παρανομία), (Pol. *Hist.* 3.3.5), and intellectual ineptness "to organize themselves" (Pol. *Hist.* 18.17.9–12) due to a serious primitive moral character flaw he calls ἀθεσία "fickleness."[17] Faithlessness engendered their passion-driven

14. Ibid., 337; idem, *Invention of Racism*, 149–68.

15. Dougherty, *Poetics*, 3–34, ably demonstrates that Apollo sponsors and sanctions most colonial endeavors during the archaic era.

16. Price, "Delphi and Divination," 143–46.

17. Polybius uses this word to characterize both the Celts/Gauls of Italy and well as the Gauls/Galatians of Asia Minor (Pol. *Hist.* 2.32.8; 3.78.2; 24.14.7 compare with Diodorus 18.32.4; 31.45.1). See the verbal equivalent of ἀθεσία, "ἀθετέω," *LSJ*, 31; *BDAG*, 24; "ἀθετέω, ἀθέτησις," *TDNT*, 158–59 which Paul uses in Gal 2:21; 3:15; 1 Thess 4:8 and Mark 6:26. See also the LXX: Jer 20:7; Dan 9:7; 1 Macc 16:17 and 2 Macc 15:10.

irrationality, caused them to suffer consecutive defeats by colonial/ imperial Rome, and alerted their allies (Hannibal and Eumenes the Pergamene) to exercise extreme caution (Pol. *Hist.* 2.32.8; 3.49.3, 70.4; 78.2; 24.14.7). Julius Caesar echoes Polybius's negative description of the Celts, commenting that *cuius consensui ne orbis quidem terrarum possit obsistere,* "a united Gaul forming a single nation animated by the same spirit can defy the universe" (*Gallic War* 7.29, my translation) and Rome vanquished it due to this apparent lack of unity (*Gallic War* 33.17.15). Bibulousness is yet another flaw that impairs their ability to share spoils (Pol. *Hist.* 2.35.3)[18] as well as their bestial eating habits of consuming meat (λεοντωδῶς, "like a lion")—grabbing with both hands and biting the meat off the bone, and afterwards engaging in injurious and lethal fights.[19] In colonial parlance, Gauls/Galatians must be pacified, tamed, and civilized. Pompeius Trogus, a Romanized Gaul, refutes Polybius's negative views on the Gauls/Galatians, insisting "that the lands that bred them could not hold them all; so they sent off 300,000 men, as a 'sacred spring,' in search of new homes."[20]

What texts fail to capture, the Attalids translate into visual representations through the famous Great Frieze—a symbiosis that brilliantly synthesized extant Greek literary characterizations of the "Other" as barbarians into an innovative visual theology of empire (see figures 11.2 and 11.3). In particular, the statue of the "Suicidal Gaul and his Wife" (see figure 11.4) enshrined in the Pergamene Frieze, publicizes Greek socioreligious and cultural supremacy[21] (Pliny, *NH*

---

18. Pol. *Hist.* 2.19.4 (trans. Paton, LCL). Τοῦτο δὲ σύνηθές ἐστι Γαλάταις πράτειν, ἐπειδὰν σφετερίσωνταί τι τῶν πέλας, καὶ μάλιστα διὰ τὰς ἀλόγους οἰνοφλυγίας καὶ πλησμονάς, "This is common among the Gauls, when they have appropriated their neighbour's property chiefly owing to their inordinate drinking and surfeiting." See Diodorus, 5.26.3. Polybius thinks both Celts/Gauls and Romans are savage people (Pol. *Hist.* 12.4.2–3).

19. Athenaeus, *Deipn.* 4.151e–152b.

20. Whereas Justin, *Epit.* 24.4.1–4, says overpopulation led to Celtic/Gallic migrations, Pliny the Elder stresses overpopulation and quest for riches (Pliny, *NH* 12.2.5). Strabo simply says . . . οἱ Γαλάται πλανηθέντες πολὺν χρόνον, "the Galatians wandered for a long time," prior to their settlement in Galatia (*Geogr.* 12.5.1, my translation).

21. Pollitt, *Art,* 79–89; Ferris, *Enemies of Rome,* 1–16; Hartswick, *Gardens of Sallust,* 105–8. See also Balch, "Paul's Portrait," 84–108, who offers a provocative insight on the Pauline counter-colonial message of victorious suffering pictured through the cross of Jesus Christ to the Pergamene frieze.

166   PART TWO: CREATING IMAGES—VERBAL AND VISUAL

Figure 11.2: The dying Gaul or Capitoline Gaul, a Roman copy of the Greek original bronze sculptured between 230–220 BCE. The statue depicts the defeat of barbarism and victory of Greek civilization. Photo: courtesy of David L. Balch.

Figure 11.3: Sculpture of the priest Laocoon in the Vatican Museum, Rome. Photo: courtesy of David L. Balch.

Figure 11.4: A defeated Gaul commits suicide by killing his wife first and then himself—a Roman copy erected to commemorate the victory of the Pergamee Greek kings (Attallus I and Enumenes II) over the Gauls around 240 BCE. Photo: courtesy of David L. Balch.

34.84; Ampelius, *Liber Mem.* 8.14)[22] and proclaims the defeat of uncivilized beasts who threaten Hellenism, namely the civilized world.[23]

Romans and the "Other"

Roman poets, instead of the earthborn Erechtheus and founding ancestor of the Greeks (Homer, *Il.* 2.545), appeal to Aeneas, a divinely sent Asiatic refugee, as founder of Latium-Rome (Virgil, *Aen.* 7.135–60). Displaced by Greeks, Trojan Aeneas, the *new Odysseus*, his progeny and army, head to Latium—*the promised land*. The way to the *promised land*, though *heavenized* (Virgil, *Aen.* 1.259; Horace, *Carm.* 3.5.1), is marred with countless ordeals that only a divinely birthed hero (Virgil, *Aen.* 8.370–453) and sent founder/colonist can surmount. To Dionysius of Halicarnassus, Aeneas is a Greek returning to his ancestral homeland (*Ant. Rom.* 1.31.1–58.2). Whether Aeneas is the father of Romulus and Remus (*Ant. Rom.* 1.72.1) or grandfather,[24] the twin brothers' ancestry is meticulously traced to divine Mars and human Ilia/Rhea.[25] Mars, the god of war, births a warrior-son par excellence (Romulus) who would fulfill the promise of Jupiter/Zeus by founding Rome, the divinely sanctioned to be a limitless empire (Virgil, *Aen.* 1:278).

Greek and Roman colonial lore share key features: divine legitimation, environmental determinism and an idealized concept of civilization. Romans assimilated most Greek colonial features and thus became "honorary Greeks."[26] Greg Woolf notes that Hellenism instilled in the Roman psyche "a growing consciousness that Romans were destined by the gods to conquer, rule and civilize the world."[27]

---

22. Pollitt, *Art*, 79–92; Ferris, *Enemies of Rome*, 1–16 describes how negative typologies work to reduce the foreigners to denigrated objects. See also Kahl, *Galatians*, 31–167 and Lopez, *Apostle to the Conquered*, 1–35. Hartswick, *Gardens of Sallust*, 105–8.

23. Marszal, "Ubiquitous Barbarians," 211–12; Zanker, *Power of Images*.

24. Gruen, *Cultural and National*, 20.

25. Though similar in many ways, accounts of the divine birth of Romulus and Remus by Livy, Dionysius, and Ovid include dissimilar elements (compare *Ant. Rom.* 1.77.1-2 with Livy, *Hist.* 1.3.10–4.3 and Ovid, *Fast* 3.31–40).

26. Champion, "Romans as Barbaroi," 425–44. See Preston, "Roman Questions," 86–119.

27. Woolf, *Becoming Roman*, 48.

Greek authors tried to counter possible objections to barbarians becoming Greeks by affirming that it is possible because "Greekness has no ethnic limit."[28] Pliny spoofs Romans by positing that divine providence ordered the Mediterranean region with its balancing of fire and dampness—a cosmic equilibrium that shaped Mediterranean dwellers, especially Italians, into a superior people apt to rule others (Pliny, *NH* 2.189–90).

By considering Italy "a land which is at once the nursling and the mother of all other lands" (Pliny, *NH*. 3.5.39–40), Pliny echoes the general belief in environmental determinism that pervaded the Graeco-Roman world of his time (*Phys.* 805a–809; see also Plato, *Laws* 5.747d; Aristotle, *Pol.* 7.7, 1327). He believes a well-balanced mixture of cosmic elements (hot, cold, dry, and wet) shaped and placed Rome in a favorable geographical context which, for Pliny, could only mean that Rome is "chosen by the providence of the gods to make heaven itself more glorious, to unite scattered empires, to make manners gentle, to draw together in converse by community of language the jarring and uncouth tongues of so many nations, to give humanity civilization, and in a word to become throughout the world the single fatherland of all races."[29]

As noted earlier, Pliny *heavenizes* Rome, describes Mediterraneans as superior people and considers their milieu the navel of the world, an ideology that shaped the "imperial policy of Rome and the myth underpinning it."[30] Imperial Rome is viewed "as divinely sanctioned with the mission to civilize the barbarians,"[31] and if Rome is divinely chosen so were its Caesars. Julius Caesar and Octavian publically exercised their self-understanding through temples and self-portraits (proclaiming an ideology of dominance).[32] Although Augustus Caesar was deified as *divi filius*, "divine son" symbolizing divine Augustus's

---

28. Balch, "ΜΕΤΑΒΟΛΗ ΠΟΛΙΤΕΙΩΝ," 150.

29. Pliny, *NH* 3.5.39–42. See Woolf, *Becoming Roman*, 54–60.

30. Malina and Neyrey, *Portraits of Paul*, 117, 100–52. See also Winkes, "Physiognômonia," 899–926; idem, "Physiognômonia," 217–42, on ancient cultural stereotypes.

31. Woolf, "Beyond," 1; Woolf, *Becoming Roman*, 48–76. Although Romans viewed their colonial efforts as a mission to receive foreigners, the romanized did not all share equal status.

32. Galinsky, *Augustan Culture*, 312–13; Pleket, "Aspect of the Emperor, 331–47, Price, "Greek Language," 79–95; idem, *Ritual and Power*.

"power" and *praesens*, "presence"³³ after his death, living emperors were deified in Roman Asia Minor.³⁴ It comes then as no surprise that Octavian would consider himself a divinely sent agent to pacify, save the world, and propagate his Imperial good news.³⁵ He reached this conclusion by borrowing soteriological concepts inherent in "Greek and Roman traditions as he was building up his divine aura in Rome."³⁶ His empire/kingdom is therefore an agent through which the gods would conquer, govern and Romanize (civilize) the world.³⁷ Jupiter initiated this ideology, promising Rome limitless boundaries, a promise that Augustus, the Roman imperial agent, would fulfill (Virgil, *Aen.* 1.278–282; 1.231–6.278–83; 6.791–807, 851–53).

Erich S. Gruen observes that early Republican Roman elites did not formulate a clear theory of imperialism. Instead, they assimilated and exercised Greek administrative features.³⁸ This comes as no surprise for Greeks, whose traditions Rome assimilated, to refuse to characterize themselves as imperialists. To circumvent any apparent contradiction, Greeks made a shrewd political move to denounce imperialism as an infringement on the freedom of the *polis* and usurpation of the role of Zeus. Colonial/Imperial Rome, in contrast, is depicted "as divinely sanctioned with the mission to civilize the barbarians."³⁹

Galatians would have experienced Roman imperialism/colonialism through *humanitas/paideia*, or the policy for "receiving all

---

33. Galinsky, *Augustan Culture*, 316–17, 312–18; Horsley, "Introduction," 15–16, who builds on Galinsky's reading of works of Cicero, Pliny, and Ovid on Augustus. On Augustus, see Ovid, *Fast.* 1.315–17, 587–616. Zanker, *Power of Images*, 33–77, notes how images reflected an internal power struggle among emperors but also symbolized their religious powers (297–339).

34. Price, "Gods and Emperors," 79–95.

35. Price, "Rituals and Power," 53; Galinsky, *Augustan Culture*, 318. On Augustus apotheosized, see Philo, *Leg.* 149–51, who calls Augustus σεβαστός. See also *Res Gestae Divi Augusti* 21–22, 24–27, 34–35.

36. Galinsky, *Augustan Culture*, 313; Price, *Rituals and Power*, 23–248; Price, "Rituals and Power," 49, posits that Roman imperial cult adapted Greek traditional religious practices such as sacrifices, rituals, games, and festivals designed to prompt faith toward the emperor whose temples and images permeated daily life.

37. Woolf, *Becoming Roman*, 48.

38. Gruen, *Hellenistic World*, 286.

39. Woolf, "Beyond Romans," 1; idem., *Becoming Roman*, 48–76, thinks Romanized people did not all share equal status. See Carter, *Matthew and Empire*, 9–53.

nations,"⁴⁰ and Paul's Good News as two letters with competing messages: "the *Res Gestae Divi Augusti* as that emperor's 'letter' to the Galatians" and "the *Res Gestae Divi Christi*, Paul's later and alternative letter to those same Galatians. Paul, of course, announced a different savior for a different world, a different salvation for a different earth, a different God and Son of God for a different creation. He proclaimed Jewish covenantal *shalom* against Roman imperial *pax*."⁴¹ Roman *humanitas* was exercised within the bounds of the empire in such a way that "there were so many kinds of Romans to become that becoming Roman did not mean assimilating to an ideal type, but rather acquiring a position in the complex of structured differences in which Roman power resided."⁴² Rome's *humanitas* is not that humanitarian. The peace Rome promises to ensure is experienced by "the Other" as news of violence, terror and death. Those who resist imperial policies were often met with Rome's most effective and feared execution machine: the cross.

The French and the "Other"

In his report to Bonaparte's First Consul in November, 1802, Gabriel Hanotaux described Catholic missionaries as patriotic colonists and "predestined agents of the civilizing empire."⁴³ Like Robert Cushman who appealed to ancestral Biblical accounts as a rationale for settling North America,⁴⁴ G. G. Beslier cites Isa 35:1, 7 to justify French colonial efforts in Senegal⁴⁵ thus collapsing the preaching of the crucified Christ into France's imperial *mission civilisatrice*.⁴⁶ Of course, French colonists traced their ancestry back to the Gauls and defined themselves as missionaries responsible to carry out *la mission civilisatrice de la France*.⁴⁷ The French, as descendants of the ancient Celts/Gauls,

---

40. Balch, "Cultural Origin," 500. See Woolf, *Becoming Roman*, 54–55, for his further discussions of the Roman *humanitas/paideia*.

41. Crossan and Reed, *In Search of Paul*, 183.

42. Woolf, *Becoming Roman*, 245, 238–49.

43. Hanotaux, "Preface," 7–8 (my translation).

44. Cushman, *Historical Genealogy*, 34, cites Gen 13:6, 11–12; 34:21; 41:20, to justify the colonization of the Americas.

45. Beslier, *Sénégal*, 93. (Isa 35:1, 7).

46. Nemo, *Mission et Colonisation*, 171.

47. Dietler, "'Our Ancestors the Gauls,'" 589. Froelicher, *Colonisateurs*, 7: "France's civilizing mission."

are then divinely sent to imprint a French personality on vanquished nations, convert them to French ways, "sword in hand, and after the battle, in part smugly and in part sympathetic, he will reveal to them all that they gain by becoming French."[48]

Of course, France's mission was confused with the proclamation of the crucified Jesus Christ. As in the case of the Galatians, though in a quite a different era, French colonists readily described Senegalese people, especially the Diola, as superstitious, *ivrognes*, "drunks" and savages.[49] Les Pères du Saint Esprit, "the Holy Ghost Fathers," who came to Senegal with the first French colonial administrators considered their Eurocentric version of Christianity as a normative and effective tool with which to civilize Diola barbarians, when opposed by Diola elders and priests. For this, they described Diola religion as a satanic path and its *ouwasena* "priests" as savages.[50] French colonists did not hesitate to label Diola people bibulous, fickle, and driven by an uncontrollable anger and passion,[51] thus echoing Polybius's characterization of the Gauls/Galatians.[52] Disputes over property such as rice fields often invite bloody brawls that could linger for generations and old grievances are revived with an excess of palm wine.

Echoing the words of Polybius and Caesar, Christian Roche notes that in spite of their bravery in battle, "Diola people often suffer defeats due to their lack of unity before a common enemy."[53] Louis-Vincent Thomas confuses Diola resistance to French hierarchical rule with

---

48. Michelet, *Autobiographie*, 220–21 (my translation). See also Lesourd, *L' Oeuvre Civilisatrice*, 11, on the role of missionaries.

49. Beslier, *Sénégal*, 66, 77. See also Mark, "Fetishers, 'Marybuckes,'" 91–99.

50. Baum, "Emergence of Diola," 386, rightly says that labeling started as a result of a conflict between elders and the Holy Ghost Fathers over the resistance of Diola elders to the message being inculcated in the minds of their children, especially those who were catechumens. Elders, especially the *ouwasena*, responded by accusing Holy Ghost Fathers of "poisoning their children's ears"—a countervoice that recalls the Athenian charge against Socrates.

51. Roche, *Histoire de la Casamance*, 34–35.

52. Polybius, *Hist.* 35.3, uses negatively the word θυμός, "passion," to depict the behavior of the Gauls/Galatians—a word expressive of τὰ ἔργα τῆς σαρκός, "the works of the law," in Gal 5:19–20, Rom 2:8 and Eph 4:31.

53. Roche, *Histoire de la Casamance*, 35 (my translation). Polybius and Caesar made similar remarks about the Gauls/Galatians. Polybius blames their lack of unity and defeats in battle to their fickle character, a thought that probably influenced Caesar's comments.

what he thinks is a natural flaw he calls "mentalité," deeply entrenched in the Diola psyche.[54] Roche believes Diola people simply "had an original society that associated freedom and the fierce desire for liberty to the traditional virtues of African solidarity. Hostile to any foreign authority, they would mount a lively resistance—active or passive—to any attempt of foreign domination."[55] Sure, Diola people would oppose any intrusive power to preserve their freedom, wouldn't any oppressed social group? It is striking to see how the above mentioned contumelies follow a common thread from antiquity to the present.

Galatians Hearing and Seeing Jesus Christ Publically Displayed as Crucified

Celts/Gauls/Galatians displaced by stasis (overpopulation and internecine conflicts), migrated across the Hellespont into Asia Minor in 278/77 BCE, where they were defeated and confined to the Phrygian region of Galatia (235–232 BCE)[56] by Attalus I, named after that region as Galatians,[57] and later colonized by Rome.[58] The Attalid kings commissioned a Frieze fossilizing these brave Celts/Gauls/Galatians, "the Other," into statues publically displayed as vanquished for all to see and fear. Those once textually objectified as "Other" are now placarded. Image replaced text. Given the above discussion, when Paul portrays Jesus Christ as publically crucified before their eyes, what possible images would have been evoked by his word pictures? Strikingly, scholarly debates tend to focus solely on textual rhetorical elements of speech, thus reducing Paul's image-laden language to a mere skillful figurative expression of Paul's own "display of the Crucified Christ."[59] Paul's Jesus Christ προεγράφη ἐσταυρωμένος, "publically displayed as

---

54. Thomas, "Mentalité," 253–72.

55. Roche, *Histoire de la Casamance*, 36; Thomas, *Diola*, 2.539.

56. Strabo, *Geogr.* 12.5.1., records the three tribes' settlements: Τρόκμοί "Trocmi," Τεκτοσάγες, "Tectosages," and Τολοστοβώγιοι, "Tolostobogii."

57. Polybius, *Hist.* 21.38.2, called them τοὺς ἐν Ἀσίᾳ Γαλάται "Asiatic Gauls" or οἱ Γαλλογραικοί "Gallogricians" (Strabo, *Geogr*, 12.5.1).

58. Sherk, "Roman Galatia," 954–63.

59. Davis, "Meaning of ΠΡΟΕΓΡΆΦΗ," 194–212, especially 212. I am unsure how this would have persuaded Paul's converts if all they saw were τὰ στίγματα τοῦ Ἰησοῦ, "the marks of Jesus," he bears on his body, as Davis maintains. On προγράφη, see Betz, *Galatians*, 131.

crucified,"⁶⁰ must have evoked distasteful memories of gruesome images of crucifixions they probably saw and invectives they heard.

Christian Strecker rightly observes that "Paulus erscheint so als göttlich legitimierte Schwellenperson" ("Paul appears thus as a heavenly legitimized liminal person")⁶¹ who reinterprets and drops⁶² centuries old traditions (of observance of circumcision and food laws) that οἱ ἐκ περιτομῆς "those of the circumcision" read, preach and enforce (Gen 17:10-27; Lev 11-15; Ezra 10:3; 1 Macc 1:62-63; 2 Macc 2:21; 4:13; 7:1, 36-37; 8:1; Let. Aris. 139-42; Jub. 22:16; Jdt 10:5; 12:2, 17-19; Tob 1:10-11; Add Esth 4:17 LXX). Of course, the Apostle Paul claims that his birth, mission, and message are all divinely orchestrated, he says (Gal 1:11-15).⁶³ Unlike Greek and Roman colonists who found colonies, God called Paul before his birth (Gal 1:15-16) and sent him to create not "colonies or cities but houses (Luke 10:5; 19:9; Acts 2:46; 8:3; 11:14; 16:15, 31; 18:8; 20:20) and churches (ἐκκλησίαι; Acts 8:3; 9:31; 15:3, 41; 20:28)."⁶⁴ Cleansed, transformed and empowered as an apostolic hermeneut (Gal 1:13-16; 1 Cor 15:9b), Paul reinterprets his former socioreligious and parochial ethnocentric convictions (Gal 1:13-14, 23; 2:15) to describe the "Other," his Galatian converts, as υἱοθεσίαν "adopted children" and future heirs of βασιλεία θεοῦ, "God's empire/kingdom/reign" (Gal 5:21) through faith in Jesus Christ. This new identity in Christ would inevitably run counter to the faiths,

60. See "προγράφῃ," BDAG.

61. Strecker, Liminale Theologie, 111.

62. Gal 2:11-14; 3:26-29; 4:1-31; 1 Cor 8:1-9:20; 10:25-27; Phil 3:2-10; Rom 10:3.

63. Gal 1:15 ὁ ἀφορίσας με ἐκ κοιλίας μητρός μου "[God] separated me from my mother's womb" and Gal 1:16 ἵνα εὐαγγελίζωμαι αὐτὸν ἐν τοῖς ἔθνεσιν "in order that I may preach him among the Gentiles." He argues that James, Peter, and John are aware of the divine origin of his message (Gal 2:7-9). This confirms Luke's account (Acts 9:3-20) that characterizes Paul as a potential murderer (Acts 9:1), who sees a theophany (Acts 9:17; 22:6; 26:13), hears a divine voice, divinely disabled (Acts 9:3-6) and ritually cleansed [not in a temple but in a house (Acts 9:17-18)], and guided by God (Acts 9:16) to κηρύσσειν (announce) God's liberating message (Acts 9:20). Wilson, "Urban," 77-99, discusses crucial parallels between Graeco-Roman colonization and Luke's account of early Christian missions.

64. Balch, "ΜΕΤΑΒΟΛΗ ΠΟΛΙΤΕΙΩΝ," 163. The founding of house churches suggests a return to the basic family-community concept which, in Diola parlance, is called *hank* (community). Many Diola houses are built to include different families living under the same roof.

freedoms, and community constructions championed by some of his fellow Judeans and imperial Roman rulers.

This new reality rests on the gory publically displayed *votive offering* of God (Gal 3:1–2, 10–13, 26–29): the crucified Jesus Christ whose redemptive work they initially received (Gal 1:1–9; 3:4). Galatians are not beast-like warriors and unreliable vanquished barbarians, as empires portrayed them with text and image; rather, they are children of the God revealed in Jesus Christ (Gal 3:26–27). Balch observes that "the early baptismal confession—'there is no longer Jew or Greek' (Gal 3:28a)—is an assertion from below: '[we] Jews [Asians, non-Europeans] are not inferior!'"[65] This new experience of freedom and empowerment aims at proclaiming the continuous power of the cross-event to crucify Graeco-Roman binarism that legitimizes colonization, repression, oppression, derogatory labeling, exclusivism advocated by James's emissaries, the "false believers" (Gal 2:4), and even French claims to supremacy over Diola people centuries later.

Paul, much less his Galatian converts, did not witness the actual crucifixion of Jesus but he uses words with no crucifix around his neck, to paint a vivid historical picture. That is risky. As a colonized people, they probably recalled Roman crucifixions of some of their loved ones or neighbors. Conceivably, some of them, after hearing the reading of the epistle exclaimed: *Aha! He, like us, must have been an innocent victim of Rome* and a majority murmured, *He was one of those political insurrectionists Romans crucified.* They may have been ambivalent about Paul's language of the cross given the negative sentiments it might have engendered in the Graeco-Roman context. What does this have to do with Diola people living in a non Graeco-Roman world?

Diola People Hearing and Seeing Jesus Publically Displayed as Crucified

The dawn of French colonialism in Senegal significantly altered the Diola socioreligious world governed by *Ala Emit* "the Owner of Heaven or God." Gripped with ambivalence, Diola people scrambled for ways to cope with the crushing effect of imperial France. Baum posits that "the quest for spiritual unity had become a central problem of *awasena*

---

65. Ibid., 153.

religion as missionaries prepared to bring a new religion to Esulalu."[66] Before the arrival of Christians and Moslems, Diola warriors relied on their traditional shrines and medicines for healthcare[67] and protection against evil spirits, sorcery and war.[68] Amulets (gris-gris), later purchased from Muslim merchants, crucifixes, and medals of Christian saints served the same purpose. As Baum rightly observes, with "the arrival of Portuguese traders in the sixteenth century, vigorous trade in Christian medicines also developed. Crucifixes and saints' medals were seen as having the same type of properties as gris-gris and Diola medicines. Such medicines were particularly valued against cannon and muskets which were introduced by European Christians."[69] The striking irony is that the cross empire once employed to intimidate and kill the "Other" is now used by the "Other" against imperial lethal weapons.

Unlike Paul, when the Holy Ghost Fathers preached Jesus Christ crucified they were probably wearing crucifixes on their necks, hanging them on catechism and literacy classroom walls or giving them to Diola people. Initially, they sought to adapt their message to key extant dimensions of the Diola socioreligious world: praying for abundant rain and bountiful harvest and health.[70] Teaching uninitiated Diola catechumens about the birth and death of Jesus was strongly opposed by Diola elders and priests (only through initiation to adulthood did I learn about childbirth and women). Missionaries responded by forcing European Christian marriage, banning catechumens from attending Diola religious ceremonies, and lampooning Diola priests as uncivilized savages whose religion is satanic.[71]

Most catechumens dropped out as a result and many catechism schools closed down[72] because Christ was portrayed as a French imperialist proud of his European civilization rather than publically

66. Baum, "Emergence of Diola," 378. Esulalu is the name of a Diola settlement. See pp. 370–78, 392–95 for the various Diola responses to the Holy Ghost Fathers' Christianity.

67. Madge, "Therapeutic Landscapes," 295–98; 294–311.

68. Baum, "Shrines, Medicine," 274–88; Madge, "Therapeutic Landscapes," 295–98; 294–311.

69. Baum, "Shrines, Medicine," 283.

70. Baum, "Emergence of Diola," 380.

71. Ibid., 381–89.

72. Ibid., 386.

displayed as crucified for Diola people. In 1942, the prophet Aline Sitoé opposed and denounced Imperial France and its version of Christianity and promised her followers that *Emitai* ("one who owns Heaven") will deliver them from imperial shackles.[73] For this, the empire moved quickly silencing her and her followers who were never to be heard from again. Whether unconscious or conscious, the Holy Ghost Fathers mimicked empire by forcing their European values on Diola people, thus dangerously equating Christianity with colonialism, instead of assuming their call as divinely sent to create households of God.

Conclusion

I concur with Balch that Graeco-Roman representational art would have helped Paul fuse the socioreligious horizons of his Galatian converts to the Christ event—a fusion that would have had a vivid effect on how Gauls/Galatians appropriated the message of the cross. The deafening silence of Pauline churches in Galatia left scholars wondering: "What happened to Galatia?"[74] Could it be that Paul's vivid portrayal of the crucifixion of Jesus recalled shameful memories of being objectified as "Other," inferior and Roman crucifixion of their loved ones? Did Galatians find Judaism safer than Paul's Jesus Christ crucified, given that they themselves suffered humiliation in texts, images and invectives?

In contrast to the Galatians, a Diola Christianity emerged led by a native clergy (soon after the Holy Ghost Fathers relinquished their colonial *mentalité*) that could portray Jesus Christ publically displayed as crucified before Diola eyes. My question then is what portraits of Jesus Christ Crucified should the Holy Ghost Fathers have used in a non Graeco-Roman context to convey their message? Would there be words portraying Diola ritual life other than those of *Ala Emit* raining, sustaining and healing people in community? Would images of the Diola domestic art such as the "dancing Mask"[75] or the bull that sym-

---

73. Niang, *Faith and Freedom*; Baum and Waldman, "Innovation as Renovation," 252–53.

74. Crossan and Reed, *Search of Paul*, 216.

75. Mark et al., "Ritual and Masking," 36–96.

bolize death and new life in Diola socioreligious world[76] have helped the Holy Ghost Fathers fuse their portrayal of Jesus Christ publically displayed as crucified with Diola socioreligious world? Probably, but that is a topic for another project.

---

76. Diatta, *Taureau symbole*.

Bibliography

Balch, David L. "The Cultural Origin of 'Receiving all Nations' in Luke-Acts: Alexander the Great or Roman Policy?" In *Early Christianity and Classical Culture: Comparative Studies in Honor of Abraham J. Malherbe*, edited by John T. Fitzgerald et al., 483–500. NovTSup 110. Leiden: Brill, 2003.

———. "ΜΕΤΑΒΟΛΗ ΠΟΛΙΤΕΙΩΝ Jesus as Founder of the Church in Luke-Acts: Form and Function." In *Contextualizing Acts: Lukan Narrative and Graeco-Roman Discourse*, edited by Todd Penner and Caroline Vander Stichele, 139–88. SBLSymS 20. Atlanta: Society of Biblical Literature, 2003.

———. "Paul's Portrait of Christ Crucified (Gal 3:1) in Light of Paintings and Sculptures of Suffering and Death in Pompeiian and Roman Houses." In *Early Christian Families in Context: An Interdisciplinary Dialogue*, edited by David L. Balch and Carolyn Osiek, 84–108. Religion, Marriage and Family. Grand Rapids: Eerdmans, 2003.

———. "The Suffering of Isis/Io and Paul's Portrait of Christ Crucified (Gal 3:1): Frescoes in Pompeian and Roman Houses and in the Temple of Isis in Pompeii." *JR* 83 (2003) 24–55.

———. *Let Wives Be Submissive: The Domestic Code in 1 Peter*. SBLMS 26. Chico, CA: Scholars, 1981.

———. *Roman Domestic Art and Early House Churches*. WUNT 228. Tubingen: Mohr/Siebeck, 2008.

Balz, H., and G. Schneider Baumgarten, editors. *Exegetical Dictionary for the New Testament*. 3 vols. Grand Rapids: Eerdmans, 1990–1993.

Bauer, Walter et al., editors. *Greek-English Lexicon of the New Testament and of other Early Christian Literature*. 3rd ed. Revised and edited by Frederick William Danker. Chicago: University of Chicago Press, 2000

Baum, Robert M. "Emergence of Diola Christianity." *Africa* 60 (1990) 371–98.

———. "Shrines, Medicines, and the Strength of the Head: The Way of the Warrior among the Diola of Senegambia." *Numen* 40 (1993) 274–92.

Beslier, G. G. *Le Sénégal*. Collection d' Études de Documents et de Témoignages Pour Servir à l' histoire de Notre Temps. Paris: Payot, 1935.

Betz, Hans Dieter. *Galatians: A Commentary on Paul's Letter to the Churches in Galatia*. Hermeneia. Philadelphia: Fortress, 1979.

Bhabha, Homi. *The Location of Culture*. London: Routledge, 1994.

Brown, Colin, editor. *New International Dictionary of New Testament Theology*. 4 vols. Grand Rapids: Zondervan, 1975–1985.

Brunt, P. A. "Introduction." In *Paul and Empire: Religion and Power in Roman Imperial Society*. Edited by Richard A. Horsley, 25–35. Harrisburg, PA: Trinity, 1997.

Carter, Warren. *Matthew and Empire: Initial Explorations*. Harrisburg, PA: Trinity, 2001.

Champion, Craige. "Romans as Barbaroi: Three Polybian Speeches and the Politics of Cultural Indeterminacy." *CP* 95 (2000) 425–44.

Crossan, John Dominic, and Jonathan L. Reed. *In Search of Paul: How Jesus' Apostle Opposed Rome's Empire with God's Kingdom*. New York: HarperCollins, 2004.

Cushman, Henry Wyles. *Historical Genealogy: The Descendants of Robert Cushman, the Puritan, From the Year 1617 to 1855*. Boston: Little, Brown, 1855.

Davis, Basil S. "The Meaning of ΠΡΟΕΓΡΆΦΗ in the Context of Galatians 3:1." *NTS* 45 (1999) 194–212.

Diatta, Nazaire Ukëyëng. "Participation du Joola chretien aux rites Traditionels." *Telema* 46:2 67–81.

———. *Le Taureau symbole de Mort et de Vie dans l'initiation de la circoncision chez les Diola (Sénégal)*. Mémoire pour l' obtention du Diplôme de l' École des Hautes-Études en Sciences Sociales, Mai 1979.

Dietler, Michael. "'Our Ancestors the Gauls': Archaeology, Ethnic Nationalism, and the Manipulation of Celtic Identity in Modern Europe." *African Arts* 96 (1994) 584–605.

Dougherty, Carol. *The Poetics of Colonization: From City to Text in Archaic Greece*. New York: Oxford University Press, 1993.

Ferris, I. M. *Enemies of Rome: Barbarians through Roman Eyes*. Stroud, UK: Sutton, 2000.

Froelicher, Capitaine. *Trois Colonisateurs: Bugeaud, Faidherbe, Galliéni*. Paris: Lavauzelle, 1904.

Galinsky, Karl. *Augustan Culture: An Interpretive Introduction*. Princeton: Princeton University Press, 1996.

Girard, Jean. *Genèse du pouvoir charismatique en basse Casamance (Sénégal)*. Dakar: IFAN, 1969.

Gruen, Erich S. *The Hellenistic World and the Coming of Rome*. 2 vols. Berkeley: University of California Press, 1984.

———. *Culture and National Identity in Republican Rome*. Cornell Studies in Classical Philology 52. Ithaca, NY: Cornell University Press, 1992.

Hanotaux, Gabriel. "Preface." In *L' Oeuvre Civilisatrice et Scientifiques des missionnaires Catholiques dans les colonies Françaises*, by Paul Lesourd, 7–9. Paris: Sous le patronage du commissariat général de l' exposition coloniale internationale de Paris, 1931.

Hartswick, Kim J. *The Gardens of Sallust: A Changing Landscape*. Austin: University of Texas Press, 2004.

Hengel, Martin. *Crucifixion in the Ancient World and the Folly of the Message of the Cross*. Philadelphia: Fortress, 1977.

Isaac, Benjamin. "Ethnic Prejudice and Racism." In *The Oxford Handbook of Hellenic Studies*, edited by G. R. Boys-Stones et al., 328–39. Oxford Handbooks. Oxford: Oxford University Press, 2009.

———. *The Invention of Racism in Classical Antiquity*. Princeton: Princeton University Press, 2004.

Justin Martyr. *Epitome of the Philippic History of Pompeius Trogus*. APACR. Translated by J. C. Yardley. Classical Resources Series. Atlanta: Scholars, 1994.

Kahl, Brigitte. *Galatians Re-Imagined: Reading with the Eyes of the Vanquished*. Paul in Critical Contexts. Minneapolis: Fortress, 2010.

Lesourd, Paul. *L' Oeuvre Civilisatrice et Scientifiques des missionnaires Catholiques dans les colonies Françaises*. Paris: Sous le patronage du commissariat général de l' exposition coloniale internationale de Paris, 1931.

Liddell, Henry George, and Robert Scott. *Greek-English Lexicon with a Revised Supplement*. Rev. ed. Oxford: Clarendon, 1996.

Lopez, Davina C. *Apostle to the Conquered: Reimagining Paul's Mission*. Paul in Critical Contexts. Minneapolis: Fortress, 2008.

Madge, Clare. "Therapeutic Landscapes of the Jola, The Gambia, West Africa." *Health and Place* 4/4 (1998) 293–311.
Malina, Bruce J., and Jerome H. Neyrey. *Portraits of Paul: An Archaeology of Ancient Personality*. Louisville: Westminster John Knox, 1996.
Mark, Peter. "Fetishers, 'Marybukes' and the Christian Norm: European Images of Senegambians and Their Religions, 1550–1760." *ASR* 23 (1980) 91–99.
Mark, Peter, et al. "Ritual and Masking Traditions in Jola Men's Initiation." *African Arts* 31.1 (1998) 36–47, 94–96.
Marszal, John R. "Ubiquitous Barbarians: Representations of the Gauls at Pergamon and Elsewhere." In *From Pergamon to Sperlonga: Sculpture and Context*, edited by Nancy T. de Grummond and Brunilde S. Ridgway, 191–234. Berkeley: University of California Press, 2000.
Martinez, Florentíno García. *The Dead Sea Scrolls Translated: The Qumran Texts in English*. Translated by Wilfred G. E. Watson. New York: Brill, 1992/1994.
Martyn, J. Louis. *Galatians: A New Translation with Introduction and Commentary*. AB 33A. New York: Doubleday, 1997.
Michelet, Jules. *Autobiographie et Introduction a L'historie Universelle*. Oeuvres de Michelet 1. Paris: Larousse, 1930.
Mitchell, Stephen. *Anatolia: Land, Men, and Gods in Asia Minor*. Vol. 1, *The Celts in Anatolia and the Impact of Roman Rule*. Oxford: Clarendon, 1993.
Nemo, Geneviève Lecuir. *Mission et colonisation: Saint Joseph De Cluny: La première Congrégation de femmes au Sénégal de 1819 à 1904*. Memoire de Maîtrise. Université de Paris I, October 1985.
Niang, Aliou C. *Faith and Freedom in Galatia and Senegal: The Apostle Paul, Colonists and Sending Gods*. Biblical Interpretation Series 97. Leiden: Brill, 2009.
Osiek, Carolyn, and David L. Balch. *Families in the New Testament World: Households and House Churches*. The Family, Religion and Culture. Lousville: Westminster John Knox, 1997.
Pleket, H. W. "An Aspect of the Emperor Cult: Imperial Mysteries." *HTR* 58 (1965) 331–47.
Pollitt, J. J. *Art in the Hellenistic Age*. Cambridge: Cambridge University Press, 1986.
Polybius. *The Histories*. Edited by Jeffrey Henderson. Translated by W. R. Paton. Vol. 2. LCL. Cambridge: Harvard University Press, 1922.
Preston, Rebecca. "Roman Questions, Greek Answers: Plutarch and the Construction of Identity." In *Being Greek under Rome: Cultural Identity, the Second Sophist and the Development of Empire*, edited by Simon Goldhill, 86–119. Cambridge: Cambridge University Press, 2001.
Price, S. R. F. "Rituals and Power." In *Paul and Empire: Religion and Power in Roman Imperial Society*, edited by Richard A. Horsley, 47–71. Harrisburg, PA: Trinity, 1997.
———. *Rituals and Power: The Roman Imperial Cult in Asia Minor*. Cambridge: Cambridge University Press, 1984.
Roche, Christian. *Histoire de la Casamance: Conquête et résistance: 1850–1920*. Paris: Editions Karthala, 1985.
Rosivach, Victor. "Autochthony and the Athenians." *CQ* 37.2 (1987) 294–305.
Sherk, Robert K. "Roman Galatia: The Governors from 25 B.C. to A.D 114." In *ANRW* Band II.72, edited by Hildgard Temporini, 954–963. Berlin: de Gruyter, 1980.

Strecker, Christian. *Die liminale Theologie des Paulus: Zugänge zu paulinischen Theologie aus Kulturanthropologischen Perspektive*. FRLANT 185. Göttingen: Vandenhoeck & Ruprecht, 1999.

Thomas, Louis-Vincent. "La mentalité du Diola (de l' anthropologie culturelle à l' ethno-psychologie)." *RPP* 14/3 (1959) 253–72.

Waldman, Marilyn Robinson and Robert Baum. "Innovation as Renovation: 'The Prophet' as an Agent of Change." In *Religious Traditions: Essays in the Interpretation of Religious Change*. Religion and Society 31. New York: Monton De Gruyter, 1992.

Wilson, Walter T. "Urban Legends: Acts 10:1—11:18 and the Strategies of Graeco-Roman Foundations Narratives." *JBL* 120/1 (2001) 77–99.

Winkes, Rolf. "Physiognômonia: Probleme der Charakterinterpretation Römischer Porträts." In *ANRW* II.1.4, edited by Hildgard Temporini, 899–929. Berlin: de Gruyter, 1973a.

———. "Physiognômonia: Probleme der Charakterinterpretation Römischer Porträts." In *ANRW* II.1.4, edited by Hildgard Temporini, 217–42. Berlin: de Gruyter, 1973b.

Woolf, Greg. *Becoming Roman: The Origins of Provincial Civilization in Gaul*. New York: Cambridge University Press, 1998.

———. "Beyond Romans and Natives." *WA* 28 (1997) 339–50.

Zanker, Paul. *The Power of Images in the Age of Augustus*. Ann Arbor: University of Michigan Press, 1988.

12

Rhetoric and the Art of Persuasion in the Wisdom of Solomon

Leo G. Perdue

Introduction

THE SOCIAL LOCATION OF THE RHETOR WHO WROTE THE WISDOM OF Solomon is not identified in the text, but there are clues to suggest that he may have attended a *gymnasion* and its school of rhetoric in Alexandria in Roman times, perhaps during the period of 30 to 40 CE.[1] His command of Hellenistic Greek, especially with a Hebraic tint, his knowledge of Greek rhetoric, and his awareness of certain philosophical teachings, including in particular those of Stoicism, suggest a highly educated author. Certainly he shared many literary expressions with Philo, even though neither cites the other. The author's presumption that his audience understood the various cultural and social facets of Hellenism at a rather sophisticated level, and the longstanding tensions between Jewish and Egyptian and Jewish and Greek populaces that emerged particularly in Alexandria, would point to this urban center as the likely location for this text. There are other intimations of this time frame and cultural location that will be laid out in the course of this essay.

During the Hellenistic period, the *gymnasia* became locations of intellectual activity for older citizens, philosophers, and students. While physical exercise continued, these centers became the equiva-

1. Kolarcik, "Book of Wisdom," 438–40.

lents of institutions of secondary education, while some even took on the character of universities in a few locations, including Athens and highly cultured Alexandria.[2]

Greek *paideia* permeated Hellenistic and Roman schools of the diaspora, and became the primary means of influencing the cultures of the colonies brought within the empires of Alexander and Rome. *Paideia* involved two related features: education that culminated in a young man's taking his place in society, and character instruction, meaning that the educated person became both virtuous and civilized.[3]

Philo Judaeus, who belonged to an aristocratic and extremely prominent Jewish family in Egypt, likely would have studied in a Hellenistic *gymnasion* in Alexandria, even though *gymnasia* were under the patronage of pagan gods. If this was the case, this study would have meant that he enjoyed Alexandrian citizenship. Yet he was also intimately familiar with Judaism, suggesting that he was the student of Hellenistic Jewish teachers (*Spec.* 1.314) and received the tradition handed down by the "elders of the nation" (*Mos.* 1.4). He gives indications that he studied Palestinian Judaism's *haggadah* and *halakhah*.[4] In his essay *On the Preliminary Studies*, he describes in detail a Greek *paideia* that includes a curriculum of philosophy, grammar, geometry, and music. However, philosophy was ranked highest and was known as the "lawful wife" (*Prelim. Studies*, 74–76). The other disciplines were philosophy's "handmaidens." Ethics and physics (especially cosmology) were the chief subjects of philosophy.[5]

Philo refers to the "rounded education" of students from wealthy families in *Spec.* 2.230, *Prov.* 2.44–46, and *Congr.* 74–76, which included both the humanities and the sciences.[6] Philo also speaks of "Sabbath schools" where the general Jewish population was taught virtue: good sense, temperance, courage, justice, and so on (*Spec.* 2.62). He notes that Sabbath schools, likely attached to synagogues, were present in the thousands in every city (*Mos.* 2.216). Indeed, the people devoted

---

2. Doran, "High Cost," 94–115. Also see Nilsson, *Die hellenistiche Schule*; Marrou, *History of Education*; Kah and Scholz, *Das hellenistische Gymnasion*; Delorme, *Gymnasion*, 253–315; Pélékidis, *Histoire de l'Éphebie Attique*; and Miller, *Arete*.

3. Mendelson, *Secular Education in Philo*, 1.

4. Neusner, *Early Rabbinic Judaism*, 100–36.

5. Kah and Scholz, *Das hellenistische Gymnasion*.

6. Barclay, *Jews in the Mediterranean Diaspora*, 161.

their Sabbaths to study to improve their character and to examine their consciences (*Opif.* 128). He notes in *Spec.* 2.63–64 that the faithful on the Sabbath study both duty to God and duty to others.

The curriculum of the *gymnasia* came to include the study of rhetoric in classical Greece. After formal education in Greek grammar from ages seven to fourteen, students entered a rhetorical school to study theory, listen to lectures, and learn from the declamation of their instructor and famous orators.[7] Those seeking a higher level of achievement spent five to six years in these rhetorical schools in order to cultivate the finer skills of language. These schools considered declamation and its composition as the primary objective and the crowning achievement of an education. The student began with the *progymnasmata*, which were the preliminary rhetorical exercises that taught him the basic techniques of writing and how to select themes to develop.[8] Exercises of impersonation (or imitation, *mimēsis*) and praise were also common.[9] The former involved declamations proclaimed by students who played the roles of mythological, heroic, or literary figures (see Lysias, *Orations* 1, 7, 9, and 21). These impersonations encouraged students to use their imaginations and skills in rhetoric to develop the arguments of these figures within a particular context. The latter was a prose or poetic panegyric that praised a significant person, thing, or idea (see Aristotle, *Rhet.* 2.20, 1393a23–1394a18).[10] This was occasionally combined with the historical recounting of the past through the praise of ancestors, gods, and cities.

It is important to recall that the "audience" of educated hearers was surpassed by literate readers, perhaps as early as 300 BCE, so that rhetoric was no longer limited to public speaking. Rather it was embodied in texts, including especially the classics, which were read and appreciated for their literary elegance and persuasive qualities by those educated and well placed people who had access to them.[11] This does not suggest the demise of oratory or that the written text replaced the spoken word. Indeed, texts that were composed often incorporated the

---

7. Kennedy, "Historical Survey," 18–19.

8. Cribiore, *Gymnastics of the Mind*, 222.

9. Ibid., 228.

10. Aristotle, *Rhet.* See Lee, *Form of Sirach*; and Mack, *Wisdom and the Hebrew Epic.* Cf. Wis 10:1—11:1.

11. Cole, *Origins of Rhetoric.*

speech or speeches of the rhetors. Thus, while there was a movement from the artistic craft (*technē*) of speaking to the literary reading of educated people, oratory remained a prominent skill. Speeches and texts were presented to be imitated by students learning to speak or to write texts of artful persuasion that would serve as verbal embodiments of the rhetor's argument.[12] The Wisdom of Solomon was not intended for the common masses of uneducated Jews who lacked the resources and thus the time to study and learn.

Rhetoric and the Wisdom of Solomon

The primary group to which Wisdom's rhetor spoke likely consisted of Jews, most probably a highly educated *gerousia* charged with leadership of the Jews in Alexandria.[13] What intensifies the occasion of this *protreptikos logos*, or hortatory speech, appears to be the suffering generated by a pogrom (perhaps that of Flaccus). The Jewish community requires encouragement to continue to maintain their heritage of faith and practice. Some in the audience appear to have wavered in their commitment to Judaism. Thus, this speech of exhortation provides confirmation that the Jews have a rich and noble history and may expect immortality if they remain righteous. Some in the audience may have witnessed members of the community who had crossed the line into the acceptance of features of Hellenism that Judaism opposed, including, for example, the worship of other gods and the honoring of pagan images.[14] Thus, these are to be warned of the punishment, in particular the loss of immortality, which comes to those who forsake the key features of their religious identity and teaching. The rhetor exhorts them to return to the practice of the primary features of Judaism.[15]

Apologetic elements suggest the rhetor also sought to provide a justification of Jewish faith and life to Greek and Egyptian intellectuals who would have been at least sympathetic to, if not supportive of, Alexandrian Jews and their practices. Further, there may have been in the city "god-fearers," i.e., non-Jews sympathetic to and followers of Judaism, if this is the major connotation of the term. Judeophobia and

---

12. Ibid., 27.
13. Larcher, *Le Livre de la Sagesse*, 179–81.
14. Wolfson, *Philo*, 73–74. See also Goodenough, *Philo Judaeus*.
15. Gammie, "Paraenetic Literature," 52.

a pogrom unleashed against the Alexandrian Jews, due in part to their state granted privileges and their continuing quest for citizenship in the *polis*, may have led to the anti-Jewish actions of Avillius Flaccus—and especially his collaborator Isodoros the Hellene—during the reigns of the emperors Gaius Caligula and Claudius. Urged on by other prominent Egyptian Hellenes who harbored a deep-seated xenophobia against Jews in Alexandria, Flaccus instigated a wide-ranging pogrom against the Jews of Egypt.[16] Flaccus, perhaps seeking to gain the favor of Caligula, whom he had foolishly failed to support in his quest to obtain the throne, yielded to the Alexandrian citizens and Egyptians who sought to lower Jewish social status and remove their privileges. In the pogrom he launched, the Jews were attacked physically and some were murdered, while their homes were ransacked and burned, their shops plundered, and their synagogues desecrated. Jewish women were forced to eat pork or suffer the humiliation of physical abuse. Even members of the *gerousia* were flogged. Philo indicates that this pogrom was the work of three Hellenes—Dionysus, Lampon, and Isidoros—who incited Flaccus to take action against the Jews.

Greek and Egyptian anger boiled over from what they considered to be illegitimate Jewish efforts to obtain Greek citizenship, and from resentment of the special privileges Jews had enjoyed since the reign of the Ptolemies. Flaccus denied Jews civic privileges and declared them to be foreigners and aliens (Philo, *Flacc.* 65–72; and *Leg.* 127–131). Flaccus even had Jews executed to celebrate Caligula's birthday. Due to the strong reaction of the Jewish community against Flaccus and his supporters, which became uncontrollable, Caligula had him arrested, tried, dispossessed of his property, exiled, and soon thereafter murdered. However, the decree of Flaccus that the Jews were aliens and strangers, and not privileged residents who could follow their own laws, became an issue of great concern. Its resolution required two trips to Rome by delegations of Jews, led in both instances by Philo. The first, to Caligula, resulted in nothing but the emperor's threat to install his image in the Jerusalem temple; the second, to Claudius, ended hostilities against the Jews and restored their ancient rights to worship and to follow their own customs without interference. However, Jews,

16. The Egyptian population earlier carried out a pogrom against the Jewish community at Elephantine during the reign of Darius (424–405 BCE). The Jewish temple there was destroyed (see Modrzejewski, *Jews of Egypt*, 21–44). For an overview of the Alexandrian pogroms against the Jews, see Gruen, *Diaspora*.

unless they already were citizens, could not receive citizenship in the *polis* of Alexandria from the time of the decree of Claudius.

Types of Rhetoric in Wisdom

The three types of rhetoric, as identified and described by Aristotle, are present in Wisdom: deliberative speech, which consists of exhortations or opposition to a course of action; judicial rhetoric, which consists of either accusation or justification about what has been done in the past, based on the criterion of justice; and epideictic oratory, in which a person is praised or blamed due to actions considered to be either honorable or shameful. From these come both an assessment of the past and a possible prognostication of the future.

The book is filled with exhortations, which may be summarized as urging the audience to remain faithful to their Jewish heritage and to justice, and to avoid wickedness that leads ultimately to eternal death (thus, deliberative rhetoric). Examples include exhorting the audience to avoid the deeds and words of the ungodly in order to allow Wisdom to dwell within them, so that they may receive immortality (1:12–15), govern nations and peoples under the kingship of God in the eschatological age (3:8), and avoid divine punishment and everlasting death (3:1–7, 10).

The arrangement of rhetoric often consists of an introduction, a narrative, a proof, and a concluding summary.[17] One may see these features in the logical movement of the rhetorical structure of the "Book of History" (11:2—19:22) in Wisdom:

A. A narrative: wisdom saves her own (10:1—11:1)

B. Introduction to the antithetical diptychs (11:2–4)

C. Theme: Israel is benefited by the very things that punish Egypt (11:5)

D. Proof of the theme in five antithetical diptychs (11:6—19:22)

  1. Water from the rock instead of the plague of the Nile (11:6–14)

  2. Quail instead of the plague of little animals (11:15—16:14)

     (Digression: critique of pagan religions, 13:1—15:19)

---

17. De Brauw, "Parts of the Speech," 187–202.

3. A rain of manna instead of the plague of storms (16:15–29)
4. The plague of darkness and the pillar of fire (17:1—18:4)
5. The tenth plague and the exodus (18:5—19:21)
6. Conclusion (19:22)

Further, the judicial character of this *protreptikos logos* is also seen in the initial *prooimion*, where the divine spirit that "fills the earth" will inquire into the counsels of the ungodly and make a report to the Lord, who, as judge, will render a verdict of punishment. Indeed, the purpose of the report is "to convict them (i.e., the ungodly) of their lawless deeds" (1:6-9). Further, judicial rhetoric is pronounced in the speech of the ungodly who seek to undo the "righteous man" who accuses them of sins against the law (i.e., the civic code in effect in Alexandria) and against their education (*paideia*; 2:12). This *paideia* is likely the education of the wicked (perhaps apostate Jews). That the ungodly had some status in the *polis* is suggested by the rhetor's claim that they have decided to "try his forebearance" and "condemn him to a shameful death." This judicial rhetoric blends into the apocalyptic judgment, when the lawlessness of the unrighteous will convict them (4:20). This indictment extends even to the kings who rule over the nations, because as servants of the kingdom of God they did not rule with righteousness or keep the law. One final example of the judicial character of Wisdom is the reference to the Canaanites who have no one to accuse God for the destruction of the nations through his judgment, and no advocate or legal representative to plead their case before the righteous Lord (12:12).

Then there is epideictic speech, which involves the blame or praise of a person or persons. Wisdom, as will be noted below, receives frequently the praise of the rhetor in the form of both the panegyric and the encomium. Yet there are humans who are praiseworthy. In particular, the rhetor extols the righteous, who, though they may die young, will stand in judgment to condemn the aged among the unrighteous (4:16, 5:1-2) and rise up in the presence of the oppressor who will be amazed at their salvation. The righteous will live forever and receive a glorious crown from the Lord, while the wicked will be overthrown by an angry God who brings them to destruction (5:15-23). By contrast the unrighteous and the ungodly receive considerable blame in this *protreptikos logos*. Because they held the righteous in derision and did not know the way of the Lord, their arrogance and wealth have not brought them anything of consequence, but only the finality of death. The wicked, including especially the Canaanites (= the Greeks who worship Dionysus and other false gods, 12:1–11), the Egyptians (12:13-27, 17:1—19:21), and the worshippers of nature (13:1-9) and of idols (13:10-19), and Israelites who were faithless (16:5) are held in blame.

The important features of rhetoric in Wisdom comprise, first of all, the major rhetorical parts of the author's *protreptikos logos*: prologue (the general exhortation to justice, 1:1-15), narrative (the encomium in 10:1—11:1 and the history of the exodus in 11:2—19:22), argument and counter-argument (found throughout the book; the debate with the wicked in 1:16—2:24 is especially illustrative), and epilogue (briefly stated in the abrupt ending in 19:22).[18] Second, the basic classifications of rhetoric mentioned above (forensic, deliberative, persuasive, and epideictic) are reflected in this Jewish text. Wisdom is a combination of the second and third types with features of epideictic that enhanced its literary artistry and included features of praise and blame. Third, *heuresis* (invention), which sets forth the means by which to discover things to say to respond to the issues under discussion, and to refute the argument of opponents, also includes conjecture, definition, quality, and transference. These are found throughout the exhortation of Wisdom. The rhetor's refutation of the reasoning of the "wicked" in 1:16—2:24 demonstrates the inconsistency of their arguments. In 2:21-22, he argues that they were wrong in their view that God will rise up to defend the righteous man from torture and a shameful death, and defend and deliver him from the wicked. The rhetor counters that they erred, because their wickedness blinded them and they did not know the hidden counsels of God or discern the innocent soul's reward, which is immortality (see 3:1-13). Conjecture is discovered in his argument that the origin of death is due to the envy of the devil. He defines wisdom in terms of its many characteristics and major functions, based partially on tradition and outside texts, as well as his own speculation. Quality, which has to do with the nature of an action, is seen in the example of the argument that immortality comes to the righteous one who acts faithfully, while the deeds of the wicked intended to bring harm to the righteous lead to destruction. Finally, transference is evident in his explanation that the

---

18. Russell, "Rhetoric, Greek," 1313.

Egyptians suffered the devastation of the plagues due to their sinful actions and oppression of God's people. Thus the destruction caused by the plagues is due, not to their inherent power as diseases and natural catastrophes, but rather to God, who punishes the sinful oppressors of the enslaved Hebrews.

The Means of Persuasion

According to Aristotle, the means of persuasion may be divided into "non-artistic" and "artistic" categories. Non-artistic or direct evidence includes written, legal materials such as contracts and the testimony of witnesses, while artistic means of persuasion characterize the speaker as trustworthy by what is said in the speech itself, whether this be by logical argument or appeal to the emotion of the audience. For the author of Wisdom, God is the "witness" of people's innermost feelings, the observer of their deeds, and the hearer of their words. While this witness crosses over into the arena of the imagination of the rhetor of Wisdom, this aspect of the formal character of rhetorical persuasion is used, although theologically nuanced (1:6). At the same time, the divine spirit of the Lord, which permeates the cosmos, will take note of their unrighteousness and report moral violations to God in order to "convict them of their lawless deeds." And as judge the Lord will bring punishment.

The Ethical Trustworthiness of the Rhetor

When speaking to a Jewish audience, the trustworthiness and ethical character of the rhetor is to be revealed through his speech. The accuracy of his knowledge of Jewish tradition—especially the deliverance of the chosen from slavery during the exodus, and their salvation by protection and provision during the wilderness wandering—achieves in part the desired effect of bolstering his arguments of persuasion. In addition, the rhetor uses the Septuagint as it was taking shape as the canon of Greek-speaking Jews, especially in Egypt. Further, he even takes on the role of Solomon (chapters 7–9), the paragon of wisdom and the builder of the temple in Jewish history, who says his love for wisdom beyond all else led him to pray to obtain her. The rhetor thus assumes the ethical qualities of this revered king of tradition.

As Solomon he also speaks of God's providential direction of him as a sage, for both the wise and their words are in the Lord's hand. God and wisdom, who fashioned all things, provided him (the rhetor as Solomon) unerring knowledge of the cosmos, including the activity of the elements, the times and seasons, the constellations, the natures of animals, the thoughts of humans, the varieties of plants, and the medicinal value of roots (7:15–22). While it was not considered good form among the rhetoricians to praise oneself or to engage in a self-defense, save as a means to respond to the slandering of the speaker's character, the rhetor of Wisdom may have used the guise of Solomon to prove his reliability to a sympathetic audience. Thus, as Solomon he shall be found "keen in judgment," the beneficiary of honor among the elders, and receive admiration from rulers who will listen to his speech even though it may continue at length (8:12). Finally, the values that he affirms and makes central to his discourse are those that the faithful share: righteousness (1:1, 15), truth (1:4), justice (3:10–13; 5:18–23), punishment of the wicked (1:7–11; 11:15—12:2) including the final judgment (4:20—5:14), the sure reward of the righteous, the goodness and protection of God (1:13–14), the hopeful anticipation of divine salvation of those who persevere in righteousness and loyalty to God (4:7–19; 19:22), and immortality (1:15; 3:4; 5:15–23).

The Appeal to the Emotions of the Hearers

Assuming the Egyptian and specifically Alexandrian location of this rhetor, his emotive appeal to his audience of Jewish leaders is based in large part on his selection of the tradition of the Egyptian persecution of their ancestors, who were able to prevail over their oppressors due to the salvific work of divine Wisdom. The first is Joseph, who rises to a position of everlasting honor because the witness of his accusers proved to be false (10:14). The second is Wisdom's deliverance, by signs and wonders, of a holy and blameless people from "a nation of oppressors." She provided them with guidance and shelter during their journey to the land promised to them, led them through the Red Sea while their enemies drowned, and guided their travels through the treacherous wilderness when they were beset by foes and thirst (10:15—11:14). Another tradition that would have awakened the sacred memory of the rhetor's audience and appealed to their emotions is that of the wickedness of the Canaanites, who are vilified as an accursed race of practitioners of sorcery and unholy rites, merciless slaughterers of children, murderers of the helpless, and eaters and drinkers of human flesh and blood (12:3–11).

Rhetoric and Rhetorical Forms in the Wisdom of Solomon[19]

Wisdom participates in the various dimensions of Greek rhetoric. The author of the text is well educated in the characteristic features of this discipline and uses rhetorical features rather often. This is especially clear when he enters into the mind of the young Solomon, who aspires to obtain from Wisdom eloquence beyond mere ornamentation (8:8c, 12). The rhetor has the ability to compose an expressive and clear discourse, to proceed logically in moving his arguments forward, to make transitions from one topic to the next in an orderly fashion, to return to his main subject after a series of digressions, to engage in questions to which he provides appealing and provocative answers, to construct a harmonious balance of words and phrases, and to make use of engaging images (4:3–5, 5:9–12, 13, 7:9–10, and 17:18–19). These are but a few examples that point to a well crafted *protreptikos logos* merged with his own Jewish form of Hellenistic Greek.[20]

One also notes a number of instances where forms of rhetoric are used with exquisite skill. As mentioned above, the student of rhetoric began with the *progymnasmata*, preliminary rhetorical exercises that taught the basic techniques of writing and how to select themes to develop.[21] As in the exercise of imitation (*mimēsis*), the rhetor assumes the role of the wise and noble king, Solomon, allowing his mind to engage one of the most notable personages of Jewish history and legend. He enters into the mind, voice, and life of Solomon at a time when he has excelled in an education that has prepared him to rule justly and well (chapters 7–9).

---

19. While the rhetor of *Wisdom* uses numerous Greek forms common to rhetorical speeches and texts, he also at times gives his own distinctive meanings to Greek words (Larcher, *Le Livre de la Sagesse*, 182).

20. Ibid., 185–87.

21. The exercises listed in *Attributed to Hermogenes* included the studies of fable, narrative, chreia, maxim, common-place, encomion, syncrisis ethopoeia, ecphrasis, thesis, and introduction of a law (see Kennedy, *Progymnasmata*, 73–88, and Cribiore, *Gymnastics of the Mind*, 222).

Numerous other figures reflective of preliminary exercises also occur. The *gnōmē* was a proverb or saying that expressed a truth about existence or some insight into moral behavior.[22] It appears frequently in the literary and oratory works of Greeks from the earliest period into the first centuries of imperial Rome. Drawing on similar types of sayings and lists from Jewish wisdom, the rhetor makes use of two blessing sayings in 3:13 (the barren woman) and 3:14 (the eunuch) in a manner that contravenes normal understanding: barrenness is not sterility that is due to sin, and the righteous eunuch will have a reward far beyond that of the gift of children. Similar forms are found in 4:1 and 5:9–14.

The *panēgyrikos* ("for an assembly") was a public formal oration, verse, or narrative of praise regarding a person, virtue, event, city, state, or deity.[23] A related expression was the *engkōmion* (see Aristotle, *Rhet.* 2.20, 1393a23–1394a18). This was occasionally combined with a historical recounting of the past through the praise of ancestors, gods, and cities. The rhetor of Wisdom engages in praise of Wisdom (6:12–16; 7:22b—8:1), including her acts of salvation of ancestors from Adam to Moses (10:1—11:1). In the role of Solomon, he engages in royal self-praise (7:1–22), along with a panegyric in praise of Wisdom (8:2—9:18).

Perhaps the most noticeable feature of Greek literary influence on the book is its overarching form, which combines elements of exhortation, declamation, exhibition, display, and "praise, eulogy, panegyric."[24] In addition, other common forms and elements of Greek rhetoric present in this book include the diptych ("doubled, folding") and *synkrisis* ("comparison of opposite or contrary things"), which in Wisdom places in opposition the features of creation that brought salvation to Israel but that effectuated disaster for the Egyptians (16:1–4, 5–14, 15–29; 17:1—18:4; 18:5–25; and 19:1–12). The literary form of the text is a speech of persuasion that has as its purpose the convincing of an audience to pursue a particular course of life (e.g., 6:12).[25] While

22. Silk, "gnōmē," 640.

23. See Russell and Wilson, *Menander Rhetor*. Menander made frequent use of panegyrics in his treatises.

24. Gilbert, "Wisdom Literature," 283–324; Winston, review of *Il libro della sapienza*, 527.

25. Winston, *Wisdom of Solomon*, 18–20, and Reese, *Hellenistic Influence*, 117–18. Reese explains: "The protreptic, then, is not a formal treatise on the abstract aspects of

the panegyric is a major form in Wisdom (cf. 19:2), the rhetor also makes use of additional types of oratory, including the "accusation" (e.g., 2:21–24), "apology" (11:15—12:2; 12:3–18), and the funeral oration (cf. 3:1–9).[26]

A final form that occurs in Wisdom and draws from Greek oratory is that of the *periautologia* ("self-praise") issued by Solomon in chapters 7–9.[27] While self-praise is to be avoided, it is acceptable in defense of one's good name. Further, Plutarch justifies legitimate boasting to enhance one's reputation in order to achieve a greater good.[28] This would be the case with Solomon, who presents himself in the text as the paragon of royal virtue and righteous rule for pagan kings, and as a model of virtue for youth in Jewish schools to emulate.

Conclusion

The literary character of this *protreptikos logos* points to a rhetorical adeptness acquired by one whose skills of combining content with elegant language (epideictic) are reasonably well presented in both judicial and deliberative oratory. This suggests that the author was a rhetor, who had studied in a rhetorical school, while his audience consisted of Jews, likely the *gerousia*, present in an assembly in a synagogue. The rhetor writing the Wisdom of Solomon merged a variety of Greek rhetorical forms and ethics with Jewish teachings of creation and redemptive history, in particular the plagues and the exodus, along with elements of Philonic mysticism.[29] While he affirms the superiority of Judaism in comparison with the pagan religions of the Hellenists, he still uses Greek rhetoric and morality to aid in the coalescing of these two different cultures.[30] The primary intention of the rhetor's use of exhortation becomes obvious from

---

philosophy, but an appeal to follow a meaningful philosophy as a way of life." See also Burgess, *Epideictic Literature*, 229–30, and Stowers, *Letter Writing*, 92.

26. The last two mentioned are examples of epideictic oratory.

27. Plutarch, "On Praising Oneself Inoffensively," *Mor.*, 7; Dio Chrysostom, *Fifty-seventh Discourse*; and Quintilian, *Inst.* 11.1.15–28. See Betz, "De Laude kipsies," 367–93.

28. Watson, "Paul and Boasting," 77–100.

29. Winston, "Sage as Mystic," 383–97.

30. Modrzejewski, *Jews of Egypt*, 67; and Collins, *Between Athens and Jerusalem*, 13.

the content of the text. He admonishes Jews to remain steadfast in loyalty to their traditions ethnicity, and religious identity, especially when they are suffering ridicule and abuse at the hands of their opponents. The occasion appears to be one of violence, in which the Jewish community is undergoing a period of intense persecution. The references to the explanation of the origins of death and the immortality of the righteous suggest that this persecution may have taken place in a state sponsored pogrom, and, if so, the one initiated and pursued by Flaccus in 38 CE would be the obvious one.

The rhetor's hope for the future is based on his faith in the salvific acts of God in the past (19:22). Thus in his exhortation he admonishes the faithful to endure, knowing full well they shall receive the gift of immortality.

Bibliography

Barclay, John M. G. *Jews in the Mediterranean Diaspora: From Alexander to Trajan (323 BCE—117 CE)*. Edinburgh: T. & T. Clark, 1996.
Betz, Hans Dieter. "De Laude kipsies (*Moralia* 539A-47F)." In *Plutarch's Ethical Writings and Early Christian Literature*, edited by Hans Dieter Betz, 367-93. SCHNT 4. Leiden: Brill, 1978.
Burgess, Theodore C. *Epideictic Literature*. Ancient Greek Literature. New York: Garland, 1987.
Cole, Thomas. *The Origins of Rhetoric in Ancient Greece*. Ancient Society and History. Baltimore: John Hopkins University Press, 1991.
Collins, John J. *Between Athens and Jerusalem: Jewish Identity in the Hellenistic Diaspora*. New York: Crossroad, 1983.
Cribiore, Rafaella. *Gymnastics of the Mind: Greek Education in Hellenistic and Roman Egypt*. Princeton, NJ: Princeton University Press, 2001.
De Brauw, Michael. "The Parts of the Speech." In *A Companion to Greek Rhetoric*, edited by Ian Worthington, 187-202. Blackwell Companions to the Ancient World. Literature and Culture. Malden, MA: Blackwell, 2007.
Delorme, Jean. *Gymnasion: Étude sur les Monuments consacrés à l'éducation en Grèce (des origins à l'Empire romain)*. Paris: Boccard, 1960.
Doran, Robert. "The High Cost of a Good Education." In *Hellenism in the Land of Israel*, edited by John J. Collins and Gregory E. Sterling, 94-115. Christianity and Judaism in Antiquity 13. Notre Dame: University of Notre Dame Press, 2001.
Gammie, John G. "Paraenetic Literature: Toward the Morphology of a Secondary Genre." In *Paraenesis: Act and Form*, edited by Leo G. Perdue and John G. Gammie, 41-77. *Semeia* 50. Atlanta: Scholars, 1990.
Gilbert, Maurice. "Wisdom Literature." In *Jewish Writings of the Second Temple Period: Apocrypha, Pseudepigrapha, Qumran Sectarian Writings, Philo, Josephus*, edited by Michael E. Stone, 283-324. Philadelphia: Fortress, 1984.
Goodenough, Erwin Ramsdell. *Introduction to Philo Judaeus*. 2nd ed. Oxford: Blackwell, 1962.
Gruen, Erich S. *Diaspora: Jews amidst Greeks and Romans*. Cambridge: Harvard University Press, 2002.
Kah, D., and P. Scholz. *Das hellenistische Gymnasion*. Wissenkultur und Gesellschaftlicher Wandel 8. Berlin: Akademie, 2004.
Kennedy, George A. "Historical Survey of Rhetoric." In *Handbook of Classical Rhetoric in the Hellenistic Period (330 B.C.—A.D. 400)*, edited by Stanley E. Porter, 3-42. Leiden: Brill, 1997.
———. *Progymnasmata: Greek Textbooks of Prose Composition and Rhetoric*. SBLWGRW 10. Atlanta: Society of Biblical Literature, 2003.
Kolarcik, Michael. "Book of Wisdom." In *NIB* 5:435-600. Nashville: Abingdon, 1997.
Larcher, Chrysostome. *Études sur Le Livre de la Sagesse*. EBib. Paris: Gabalda, 1969.
Lee, Thomas R. *Studies in the Form of Sirach 44-50*. SBLDS 75. Atlanta: Scholars, 1986.

Mack, Burton L. *Wisdom and the Hebrew Epic: Ben Sira's Hymn in Praise of the Fathers*. Chicago Studies in the History of Judaism. Chicago: University of Chicago Press, 1985.

Marrou, H. I. *A History of Education in Antiquity*. Translated by George Lamb. New York: Sheed & Ward, 1956.

Mendelson, Alan. *Secular Education in Philo of Alexandria*. Monographs of the Hebrew Union College 7. Cincinnati: Hebrew Union College Press, 1982.

Miller, Stephen G. *Arete: Greek Sports from Ancient Sources*. 3rd ed. Berkeley: University of California Press, 2004.

Modrzejewski, Joseph. *The Jews of Egypt: From Rameses II to Emperor Hadrian*. Translated by Robert Cornman. Princeton: Princeton University Press, 1997.

Neusner, Jacob. *Early Rabbinic Judaism: Historical Studies in Religion, Literature and Art*. SJLA 13. Leiden: Brill, 1975.

Nilsson, Martin P. *Die hellenistiche Schule*. Munich: Beck, 1955.

Pélékidis, Chrysis. *Histoire de l'éphébie Attique des origines à 31 avant Jésus-Christ*. École française d'Athènes. Traveaux et mémoires 13. Paris: Boccard, 1962.

Reese, James M. *Hellenistic Influence on the Book of Wisdom and its Consequences*. Analecta Biblica 41. Rome: Biblical Institute Press, 1970.

Russell, D. A. "Rhetoric, Greek." In *Oxford Classical Dictionary*, edited by Simon Hornblower and Antony Spawforth, 1312-14. Oxford: Oxford University Press, 1996.

Russell, D. A., and N. G. Wilson, editors and translators. *Menander Rhetor*. New York: Oxford University Press, 1981.

Silk, Michael S. "Gnōmē." In *Oxford Classical Dictionary*, edited by Simon Hornblower and Antony Spawforth, 640. Oxford: Oxford University Press, 1996.

Stowers, Stanley K. *Letter Writing in Greco-Roman Antiquity*. LEC 5. Philadelphia: Westminster, 1986.

Watson, Duane F. "Paul and Boasting." In *Paul in the Greco-Roman World: A Handbook*, edited by J. Paul Sampley, 77-100. Harrisburg, PA: Trinity, 2003.

Winston, David. Review of *Il libro della sapienza: Struttura e genere letterario*, by Paolo Bizzeti. *CBQ* 48 (1986) 525-27.

———. "The Sage as Mystic in the Wisdom of Solomon." In *The Sage in Israel and the Ancient Near East*, edited by John G. Gammie and Leo G. Perdue, 383-97. Winona Lake: Eisenbrauns, 1990.

———. *The Wisdom of Solomon: A New Translation with Introduction and Commentary*. AB 43. Garden City, NY: Doubleday, 1979.

Wolfson, Harry Austryn. *Philo: Foundations of Religious Philosophy in Judaism, Christianity, and Islam*. 2nd rev. printing. Cambridge: Harvard University Press, 1948.

13

Standing Together

The Murder of Lesbians and the Martyrdom of Saints Perpetua and Felicity

Stephen V. Sprinkle

*"You may forget but
Let me tell you
this: someone in
some future time
will think of us."*
   —Sappho of Lesbos[1]

"How could we tell a hate crime if we were murdered by one?"
   —Karla Mantilla[2]

JUXTAPOSING DIFFERING GENRES IS A PROVOCATIVE ACT. DOING SO across seventeen centuries intensifies the provocation by several magnitudes. The *Passion of Saints Perpetua and Felicitas* was written in the third century CE as a testimony to the public execution of Perpetua, a Roman matron, and Felicitas, a slave woman, in the amphitheater of Carthage on March 7, 203. News reports of the murder of lesbian partners Julianne "Julie" Williams and Laura "Lollie" Winans began to appear in early June 1996, soon after their bodies were discovered at a secluded campground in Shenandoah National Park, Virginia. The stories of these two pairs of women are strangely similar. Both stories

---

1. Sappho, *Sappho: New Translation*, 60.
2. Mantilla, "Murder on the Appalachian," 1.

are epistemologically transgressive, challenging accepted canons of culture on gender, sexuality, and heteronormativity. The task of this essay will be to "stand them together," as stories and as strangers to the societies that aided and abetted their deaths. Using each story as a lens through which to examine the other, new insights about these narratives and the stranger-communities that produced them emerge, causing a re-examination of the sexual ideologies haunting late antiquity and late twentieth century America alike. These are not safe texts[3] for the status quo of either era. They harbor dangerous memories.[4]

After Perpetua and Felicitas died in the amphitheater of Carthage, the written account of their martyrdom took shape. The *Passion* text was written in the third century, presumably very early. This *Passion of Saints Perpetua and Felicitas*, according to Amat, was originally written in Latin and translated into Greek.[5] Its form consists of three sections: a brief introductory narration by an editor or redactor; the so-called "diary" of Vibia Perpetua, presumably written while under house arrest and in prison as she awaited execution; and finally, back matter including an account of the martyrdom by a witness to the execution, who may have been the same as the narrator of the introduction. By the fifth century, a couple of theological abridgements of the *Passion*, called the *Acta*, were written to satisfy certain ecclesial dissatisfactions in the original. These *Acta* never succeeded in supplanting the *Passion*

---

3. Stone, *Practising Safer Texts*, 12–14.

4. In a broad sense, "dangerous memory" refers to the persistent and obdurate cultural memories of the oppressed. Postcolonial hermeneutics employs cultural memories of colonized people in order to resist the hermeneutic strategies of conquering colonial powers. Renny Golden uses the work of Eduardo Galeano in just such a way: "Can a people's spirit be killed off? Galeano says not as long as someone remembers. Remembers who they are by knowing who they came from. Remembers their people's struggle. This is the danger of cultural memory. It contains spiritual visions and historical lessons which contest the vision of the dominator. Dangerous memory is a weapon of the colonized," (Golden, "Dangerous Memories and Cultural Resistance," paragraph 2). In a more specifically textual sense, Bruce T. Morrill has employed the political theology of Johann Baptist Metz to say that anamnesis, liturgical memory, is "dangerous memory." See Morrill, *Dangerous Memory*, 159; and Metz, *Faith in History and Society*, 109–10, 195–96.

5. For a detailed discussion of Latin and Greek manuscripts and editions of *The Passion of Saints Perpetua and Felicitas*, see Amat, *Passion de Perpétue*, 84–90. In this chapter, the form of notation for the Latin texts of the *Passion* and the *Acta* is that devised by Amat, i.e., *Pass.* 20.7; *Act* I.V.6, etc.

in the popular mind of the western church.⁶ Gail P. C. Streete and Jacqueline Amat argue that the *Passion* received a virtually immediate and wide diffusion in the province of Africa.⁷ Veneration for the sacrifice of Perpetua and Felicitas increased throughout the third and fourth centuries due to the reciprocal effect of devotion to the relics of the saints and the powerful text which was read at least annually on the anniversary of the martyrs' deaths at their shrine in Carthage.⁸ By 313, the anniversary was on the official calendar of the Church of Rome.⁹

The identity of these young Roman wives and mothers captured the imagination of the faith community, especially the fascinating personal portrait of Perpetua. While Felicitas, the slave, is a relatively minor character in the *Passion*, with more writing by far assigned to several other characters in the narrative,¹⁰ her identity is tied to Perpetua's strongly and decisively enough that the "titular focus" which seized the popular imagination of the early Christian community in Africa (and later of the whole Latin church) was of both Perpetua *and* Felicitas.¹¹ The men who died in the arena with the women have received considerably less commemoration throughout the centuries, an indicator of the significance and intriguing ambiguity surrounding the way these socially unequal female martyrs were remembered by the faith community.¹²

Scholars have debated how the successive communities who remembered these women passed their memories along. One school of thought suggests that some objective historical data can be discovered about these women, especially in the "diary" of Perpetua, such as a durable biographical kernel of the "real" Perpetua despite the overlay

---

6. Salisbury, *Perpetua's Passion*, 172. See also Amat, *Passion de Perpétue*, 82–83.

7. Streete, *Redeemed Bodies*, 56, and Amat, *Passion de Perpétue*, 82–83.

8. Salisbury, *Perpetua's Passion*, 166–70.

9. Ibid., 170.

10. For example, Saturus, Perpetua's father, Governor Hilarianus, and even Perpetua's deceased little brother, Dinocrates.

11. Osiek, "Perpetua's Husband," 290. Osiek writes, "Nothing explains the titular focus on Felicitas." The pairing of two women facing death for their Christian faith together would seem to supply rather ample reason, however. See Boswell, *Same-Sex Unions*, 140; and Salisbury, *Perpetua's Passion*, 174.

12. Salisbury, *Perpetua's Passion*, 171, writes that by the fourth century, the martyrdom of Perpetua and Felicitas had been granted a festival day in their honor as a part of the annual cycle of feast days for the church in Carthage.

of male ideologies (Brent D. Shaw), or enough reliable dream material in Perpetua's visions to determine her psychological or psychosocial state of mind (Marie Louise von Franz and Aviad Kleinberg).[13] Others are skeptical of any claim of autobiography in the *Passio*.[14] Stephanie Cobb, for example, writes "The martyr acts are better understood as educational propaganda than objective history."[15] No matter how the *Passio* is debated, however, the way in which communities who believe they have a stake in the narrative remember the story is more significant than what may or may not actually have happened.[16] The construal of this memory is particularly important when the relationship of the slave and the young matron who died together in the amphitheater is considered.[17]

What was the tie that bound Perpetua and Felicitas together? In the narration of the execution of the women, the witness-narrator gives a hint of what it might have been. The moment described is made all the more provocative because until this point in the narrative, the women have had very little engagement with each other. The ordeal with a wild, crazed heifer, has just passed. Perpetua comes to her senses after being tossed by the cow. She sees Felicitas on the floor of the amphitheater, who has been gored and knocked down by the same beast. Perpetua approaches Felicitas, offering her hand to help Felicitas get to her feet. In 20.7 of the *Passio*, the witness to the martyrdom writes, *Et ambae pariter steterunt*, "And they both stood together."

Carolyn Osiek suggests that more is implied here than a freeze-frame of two women standing side-by-side. Indeed, Perpetua, the woman of higher social status, has acted in accord with her class. She has taken the cultural initiative in an unsurprising way. Then, however, Osiek opens the possibility that cultural norms in a threshold moment

---

13. For example, Shaw, "Passion of Perpetua," 3–45; von Franz, *Passion of Perpetua*; Farina, *Perpetua of Carthage*; and Kleinberg, *Flesh Made Word*, 56–90.

14. Castelli, *Martyrdom and Memory*, 85–92; Castelli, "I Will Make Mary Male," 38; and Cobb, *Dying to Be Men*, 4–5, 131–32.

15. Cobb, *Dying to Be Men*, 5. Building on the work of Castelli, that the text of the martyrdom is a means of "culture making," Cobb argues that the *Passio* is not concerned with the identity of the women, but instead with the formation and identity of the Christian community. See Cobb, 131 n. 18, for the suggestion that Perpetua may be a fictitious construct.

16. Salisbury, *Perpetua's Passion*, 2–3, 16.

17. D'Angelo, "Women Partners in the New Testament," 85.

for these soon-to-die women have perhaps slipped their moorings into something unexpected. She writes, "but perhaps the author knew more than we suspect and was telling of a solidarity that had grown between the two women of unequal social status, who stood together as equals facing death."[18]

Could this "solidarity" of which Osiek writes include a homoerotic dimension? At first glance, this suggestion seems unlikely. Perpetua and Felicitas were subject to a stratified, patriarchal moral system that both described and prescribed gender and sexual roles for women, bond and free alike. As Bernadette Brooten writes, "Roman-period writers presented as normative those sexual relations that represent a human sexual hierarchy. They saw every sexual pairing as including one active and one passive partner, regardless of gender."[19] Irrespective of biology, the Roman sexual world was dualistically divided into active (masculine) and passive (feminine) actors. This binary reached further into Roman life than sexuality and gender, extending to the age, nationality, economic standing, legal status (slave or free), and social position of the partners.[20] Women were always supposed to be passive, though throughout the *Passio*, Perpetua assumes "manly," or active, prerogatives and roles such as sharing leadership of the small band of incarcerated Christians along with Saturus, demanding better prison quarters and rations, setting the place and time for suckling her infant son, resisting the wishes of her father and mother, and, on the day of her execution, successfully refusing to wear the costumes of a priestess of Ceres[21] that she and Felicitas were expected to wear into the arena. In her fourth dream-vision, she becomes a man [*sum masculus* (*Pass.* 10.7)] and assumes the role of a gladiator in the deadly contest with the Egyptian wrestler.[22]

18. Osiek, *Woman's Place*, 153–54.

19. Brooten, *Love between Women*, 2.

20. Ibid., 3.

21. Ceres was goddess of the circus and the games. Smith, *Fools, Martyrs, Traitors*, 111.

22. Countering the suggestion that Perpetua strips herself of her feminine identity in both the dream-state of her fourth vision and in her successive attainments of spiritual growth, Kleinberg argues that she never ceases to be a woman in the fourth vision. Instead, she has added a masculine identity to her feminine one. He writes, "During the battle, Jesus is with Perpetua, and she is with Jesus." After the battle, Kleinberg says she had no need to explain how she became a woman again: "She never stopped being one." See Kleinberg, *Flesh Made Word*, 76.

Finally, at the moment of her actual death in the amphitheater, she willingly dies by taking the trembling hand of the inexperienced gladiator assigned to kill her, guiding his sword to cut her own throat. Though Felicitas as a slave is presumed passive in all things, because of her close identification with Perpetua in Christian martyrdom, something for which she devoutly prayed,[23] she is associated with all these active characteristics, dying with the courage of a man in the arena, as well.[24] In all these "manly" deeds, Felicitas and Perpetua remain Roman women. Cobb argues that this very paradox, the paradox of the "manly woman," is the reason the story of Perpetua and Felicitas was so meaningful for early Christian communities.[25]

Though the muscular words and deeds of these women martyrs are praiseworthy, and though the testimonies of their deaths hijacked the very state-sponsored executions that sought to humiliate them and discredit their faith claims, turning them to the purposes of the Christian gospel instead,[26] Perpetua and Felicitas were still "slaves to the penalty" of the law that condemned them and the stratified social system that utterly encompassed them.[27] Whatever manly deeds they had done in the name of Jesus notwithstanding, because they were still women, wives, and young mothers, every gawker in the amphitheater likely believed their acts were "unnatural." According to Streete, "in the world of late antiquity, the home of emerging Christianity, manly women are no better than effeminate men."[28] Attendance in the amphitheater on that March day in 203 may have been higher than normal[29] because the execution of rebellious Christian women had a certain exotic, sadistic, or even pornographic attraction to it. The responses of the audience recorded in the *Passio*—an inordinate need to humiliate the women sexually to please the crowd, strong reactions to the nudity of the women wrapped in a net for the heifer's charge, strange atten-

---

23. Salisbury, *Perpetua's Passion*, 115–16.
24. Amat, *Passion de Perpétue*, 36.
25. Cobb, *Dying to Be Men*, 60–91, 93, 111.
26. Young, *Procession before the World*, 12.
27. Freeman, *New History of Early Christianity*, 208. Freeman contends that the victims in the arena were mere puppets on the string of the state, "just an object to be played with."
28. Streete, *Redeemed Bodies*, 71.
29. Even taking into consideration that the March 7 games were "special" on account of the Emperor Geta's birthday.

tion to the dripping breasts of Felicitas, sexist concern with Perpetua's uncovered thigh, and even the mocking choice of a cow[30] to match the gender of the victims—seem to make room for this possibility.

There is, however, something different about this moment of solidarity between Felicitas the slave and Perpetua the Roman matron—something that goes beyond the explanations of outlaw sympathy and Christian social solidarity—that transcends the confines of the norms of social and sexual stratification common to traditional Romans and Christians alike. William Farina writes, "The martyrs not only stood together, but more importantly, *did so when they were not expected to* [emphasis his]."[31] Such instances of surprise are destabilizing to traditional gender identity. Elizabeth Castelli writes that they are "moments of slippage, spaces where the self-evidency of gender conventions and relationships for which they were foundational might have been thought otherwise."[32] To the "queer eye,"[33] this moment is saturated by a thin coating of eroticism, making the separate identities and social boundaries that had held these women apart throughout their lives supple enough to touch and adhere.

Admittedly, the affective lives of women in antiquity remain largely a mystery. Yet hints, like the glimpse of an unusual physical closeness between Perpetua and Felicitas in the arena, while slender evidence of how two ancient women may have loved each other, at least do not foreclose on the possibility that they did. The fact that they were both wives who shared the experience of pregnancy in difficult circumstances, and that they shared the births of their children "in the

---

30. Salisbury, *Perpetua's Passion*, 141: "The choice of the beast and the change in the animal's expected gender would have added further dimensions to the symbol of sexual degradation," Salisbury writes, suggesting there may have been room interpretively to introduce an element of homosexual degradation. See also Shaw, who writes that the cow may have indicated that the women had "some different sort of sexuality" ("Passion of Perpetua," 8).

31. Farina, *Perpetua of Carthage*, 93.

32. Castelli, "I Will Make Mary Male," 47.

33. A habit of noticing oppressive, denigrating heterosexist binaries, that establish controls over individuals and social groups, such as "slaves make the master; women make men; women make God the Father; Queers make straights; sinners make 'the saved.'" These binaries are identified by the queer interpreter in order to "invert, disperse, and disrupt" the heteronormative relationships they engender. Althaus-Reid, *Queer God*, 80.

valley of the shadow" apparently without benefit of their husbands,[34] does not foreclose on the possibility of their having formed a strong affective bond in the month or so they shared in prison. While the dearth of information about Perpetua's relationship with Felicitas during incarceration forces us to remain agnostic about the subject,[35] we cannot shut off our minds. As John Boswell suggests, "A young woman's marriage in second- or third-century Rome did not necessarily indicate anything about the direction of her affections."[36] Taboo relationships in antiquity must often be sleuthed out by close attention to fleeting mentions or single artistic depictions, as Mary Rose D'Angelo has famously shown from developing her understandings of female partnerships in the New Testament from the depiction of two women clasping right hands on a funerary monument. Of that single handclasp, she writes of a commitment between the partners that "may have involved a recreated family relationship, a partnership in work, a religious commitment, or some combination of these."[37]

Brooten cautions us not to impose our dualistic assumptions about sexual orientation on women in late antiquity. "Whereas we often dualistically define sexual orientation as either homosexual or heterosexual," she writes, "they saw a plethora of orientations."[38] Brooten's and D'Angelo's insights into the bonding of ancient pairs of women comport well with the influential work of Adrienne Rich in the 1980's, proposing a spectrum of ways in which women stand in solidarity and affection with each other—ways that need not be genital to be found along her "lesbian continuum."[39] Broadening the embrace of "woman-identified experience" as Rich does, to include "forms of primary intensity between and among women," regardless of whether

---

34 While Perpetua's husband is unnamed and virtually ignored throughout her "diary," among the possibilities that exist for who he was is Osiek's proposal that Saturus, the probable catechist of the small band of Christians, is the most likely candidate. See Osiek, "Perpetua's Husband," 287–90. The *Passio* is silent about Felicitas's mate. Since she was arrested with Revocatus, a fellow-slave, speculation has fallen on him. But in the first of the *Acta*, Felicitas calls Revocatus her "brother" (*Act* I.V.6). When the proconsul questions her about her husband, she admits she has one, but she "despises" him (*Act* I.V.3).

35. Salisbury, *Perpetua's Passion*, 116.
36. Boswell, *Same-Sex Unions*, 139.
37. D'Angelo, "Women Partners in the New Testament," 71.
38. Brooten, *Love between Women*, 3.
39. Rich, "Compulsory Heterosexuality," 121.

a woman has sought genital experience with another women, room is made for a range of erotic[40] bonding possibilities that Perpetua and Felicitas may have known as they stood together side-by-side facing their fate. This would also hold true for a deeply felt religious commitment, such as the one that undoubtedly united the women as they sought martyrdom in Carthage. D'Angelo argues, "In the early Christian pairs, it is the women's participation in the Christian mission that takes the foreground. But that should not obscure the recognition that their commitment to the mission can also be seen as the commitment to each other."[41]

If Christian women were already condemned as unnatural, impious rebels and gender outlaws by the Severan empire as Felicitas and Perpetua indeed were since their confession, *Christiana sum* (*Pass.* 6.4), before the proconsul, then whatever the amphitheater audience suspected about their affective inclinations was possibly no more than the momentary attention of the narrator in 20.6–7, or than the darkly ironic choice of the crazed heifer by the organizers of the games. According to Donald G. Kyle, the entertainment value of Christians, even exotic ones like these women, was limited. After a series of executions of these *noxii* who had no honor, rights or privileges, but were only the playthings of imperial "justice," the crowd would have most likely become bored.[42]

But there were people who would have been intensely invested in the drama taking place in the arena for these two women: the Vibii, Perpetua's family; the Carthaginian Christian community, as we have already seen; and those keen enough to recognize the bond of solidarity they were witnessing. We know there were long-term homoerotic relationships among females in late antiquity,[43] and there is reason to believe they would have seen or heard enough of the nuanced behavior of these female martyrs to be intrigued by them. We do not know

---

40. "Erotic" here is taken in its broadest meaning, the attraction in amatory desire and experience. According to Rich these might include "the sharing of a rich inner life, the bonding against male tyranny, the giving and receiving of practical and political support," 121.

41. D'Angelo, "Women Partners in the New Testament," 72.

42. Kyle, *Spectacles of Death*, 247–48.

43. D'Angelo, "Women Partners in the New Testament," 70; and Brooten, *Love Between Women*, 3. Brooten cites the existence of Ptolemaic magical texts and incantations intended to secure love between women.

any of the names of these proto-lesbians[44]—fear would have seen to that.[45] Romans and North African Christians alike loathed "homoerotic women." As Brooten points out, the ancient writer who took first note of Perpetua and Felicitas and honored them, Quintus Septimius Florens Tertullianus, or Tertullian (ca. 160—after 220), classified such women "with prostitutes or castrated men—traitors to the stratified order of [his] world."[46]

Male authors of the period besides Tertullian knew of primary same-gender relationships among women, ranging from the Platonic to the sexually active.[47] Boswell, in his controversial landmark study, *Christianity, Social Tolerance, and Homosexuality*, contended that the pairing of two female martyrs whose relationship transcended social inequality and gender appealed to the Christians of late antiquity. "The popularity of the story of Saints Perpetua and Felicitas . . . was largely due to the appeal of the love between two women," he wrote. Though their male companions died as gloriously as the women, Boswell notes, "only Perpetua and Felicitas captured the fancy of the Christian community, apparently because the tale of two women comforting each other in jail, suffering martyrdom together as friends, and bestowing upon each other the kiss of peace as they met their end, charmed the tastes of the age."[48] In any case, as Salisbury notes, "Perpetua's diary . .

---

44. As a host of queer scholars has pointed out, the assignment of the terms "lesbian" and "gay" to the ancients is anachronistic, since the type of homoerotic relationships developed in the twentieth and early twenty-first centuries was unknown in late antiquity. Boswell has drawn considerable fire for his choice to designate ancient Greeks and Romans by identities coined and framed in modern times. But the very ambiguity and fluidity Brooten suggests were characteristic of sexual orientations in late antiquity seem to open the possibility that something like the terms "lesbian-identified" and "gay-identified" may be usefully employed, so long as we use them with caution and humility, as lesbian biblical scholar Deryn Guest writes. See Guest, *When Deborah Met Jael*, 56. For Guest, "lesbian," rather than indicating an identity thick and stable with reality, means "a perpetually unclear signifier that carries a diversity of different identifications depending on who is doing the positioning." Further, Guest chooses to use "lesbian," "lesbianism," and "lesbian-identified" to nominate a chastened reading and writing position hallmarked by "epistemological inadequacy, psychological coarseness, and historical contingency" (Guest, *Deborah Met Jael*, 58)—in other words, truly "queer"—as this article attempts to do.

45. Brooten, *Love between Women*, 16.

46. Ibid., 15.

47. Ibid., 16. She calls this awareness on the part of male authors, "wide ranging."

48. Boswell, *Christianity, Social Tolerance*, 135.

. became one of the corpus of respected readings that was read in the Carthage communities for centuries."[49]

The ideal of martyrdom had to change in order to fulfill the formation and education of succeeding Christian communities, and the interpretation of the *Passio* changed along with it. The context of the Christian church shifted from cultural hostility or indifference in the third century to state assimilation in the fourth and fifth centuries. By 381, Christian orthodoxy had not only become a *religio licita*, but by decree of Emperor Theodosius was imposed upon citizens of the eastern empire by threat of force.[50] Any other interpretation of God than the Athanasian version of the Trinity endorsed by the Council of Constantinople was considered unlawful and insane. Martyrdom, once considered to be the "seed of the church," had become agitprop for correct Christian behavior and belief. But the story of Perpetua and Felicity with its vivid drama and gender ambiguity had become the property of the public. The *Passio* retained its popularity even in the face of attempts to modify the story and tone down the role of the women.[51] Salisbury writes that the continuing reinterpretation of the *Passio* is essentially a good thing: "We use the memory of [Perpetua's] actions and her words to enhance the meaning of our own experience."[52]

This has certainly been true of the lesbian, gay, bisexual, transgender, and queer community. The "queer eye" has seen much in the story that compels the LGBTQ[53] community to ask, following Althaus-Reid, "What would this story sound like if it were told as a rumor in a gay strip club, or overheard as Latinas talked about it in a smoky salsa bar?"[54] What new meanings or possibilities might open up along the fault lines, seams, and slippages already identified in the *Passio*, if the story were juxtaposed with the disruptive sexual stories of marginalized lesbians and gay men? Regardless of the genital desires of this

---

49. Salisbury, *Perpetua's Passion*, 74.

50. Freeman, *A.D. 381*, 91–104.

51. Salisbury, *Perpetua's Passion*, 170–72.

52. Ibid., 179.

53. Lesbian, Gay, Bisexual, Transgender, and Queer (henceforth referred to as LGBTQ). This designation, like all other nomenclature for the sexual minority community, is in flux. LGBTQ is generally accepted, and indicates the diversity of the community, which is more like a loose alliance of affinities rather than a "people." "Gay community" is also used to designate the collective, as well as "queer community."

54. Althaus-Reid, *Queer God*, 2.

unlikely pair of women, did they, *do they*, stand *queer* as they witness to their truth, shoulder-to-shoulder?[55]

Indeed, conversations like this do go on in gay stripper bars and over drinks at salsa clubs, where communities of queer folk gather to share the news of their lives in the midst of an often hostile world.[56] While internet chat rooms have augmented the bar scene as sites where LGBTQ people contact each other, local bars and clubs remain primary locations where women and men share web news, stories from the local press, and word-of-mouth of gay interest. Often the clubs are venues for lively theological conversation, a surprise to many straight people. Many patrons of these clubs live at the crossroads of a series of sexual, personal, political, and theological localities. They come from all walks of life in the early twenty-first century: by necessity they have learned how to live and negotiate the difficulties inherent in a heterosexist/homophobic world. As Althaus-Reid notes, "There are many sexual dissenters whose theological community is made up of the gathering of those who go to gay bars with rosaries in their pockets, or who make camp chapels of their living rooms simply because there is a cry in their lives, and a theological cry, which refuses to fit life into different compartments."[57]

Threshold experiences[58] are familiar to LGBTQ people, who encounter them to a degree the majority communities in American life may find extraordinary.[59] Like everyone else, members of the gay community need to talk about these events and experiences, to help make sense of them in the context of their everyday lives. It is unsurprising, then, that violence perpetrated against the LGBTQ community comes up on a relatively regular basis. In the United States, the queer community is the last great social group that is still socially permissible to despise openly.[60] Though organized religion continues to be a source

---

55. Idem., "Queer I Stand," 109.

56. Sprinkle, "God at the Margins?" 57–83. See particularly the NB comment on 83 acknowledging "dancer-theologians."

57. Althaus-Reid, *Queer God*, 2.

58. The verge or beginning of a critical or new experience, i.e., birth, rite of passage or initiation, coming of age, life crisis, catastrophic illness, commencement or cessation of a significant relationship, confronting death, and the like.

59. Stuart, *Gay and Lesbian*, 65–77. Stuart chronicles the challenges and losses the gay community faced in the plague years of the AIDS crisis.

60. Cobb, *God Hates Fags*, 1–14, calls the LGBTQ community, "Last Safe Group To Hate."

of pain, frustration, and (all-too-often) violence against them, LGBTQ people have developed resources to help them wrestle with the hate rhetoric and physical violence that impinges on this community.[61] One of these resource strategies is to tell the stories of the victims,[62] and to cast them in the light of a sort of secular martyrdom.[63] Michael Cobb writes insightfully about the targets of hate crimes as *homo sacer*, the sacred or accursed victim.[64] Murdered LGBTQ people are indeed "sacrifices, martyrs." But the rhetorical goal in the way these stories of queer martyrs is told is not to politically sacralize either these victims or the queer community. Instead, the goal is to make the targeted community more esteemed by society through a perception of solidarity in suffering, and harder therefore to do away with: "Then," Cobb concludes, "we become a bit more valuable and make it harder to make us *homo sacer*, to make it harder to dispose of us as if we don't matter."[65] The moves the LGBTQ community makes by reading and interpreting the stories of their martyrs in this fashion is according to the best canons of queer interpretation, as put forth by Althaus-Reid and others.[66] It decenters the heteronormative sexual ideology lying behind the rhetoric of violence, exposes and weakens its oppressive, xenophobic power, opens up safe theological space for difference, and produces a form of transgressive memory that the reigning ideologies of power must deal with or be shut outside this significant hermeneutical circle. This strategic re-reading of narratives also causes the interpretation of other pertinent texts to be reconsidered in light of this new, queer analysis.

In the queer spaces of bars and clubs where the strangers to heteronormative religion gather, then, the juxtaposition of a contemporary story of anti-lesbian hate crime murder with the story of Perpetua and Felicitas would "queer" both narratives, and open them both to new interpretive possibilities for the LGBTQ community. To that end, the

---

61. Comstock, *Violence Against Lesbians and Gay Men*, 95–140; and Comstock, *Unrepentant, Self-Affirming*, 49–85.

62. One such resource providing an anthology of stories of representative LGBT hate crimes murder victims is Sprinkle, *Unfinished Lives*.

63. Cobb, *God Hates Fags*, 22–42.

64. Ibid., 33–35.

65. Ibid., 148. See also Metz, *Faith in History*, 90. The queer martyr localizes, incarnates, and performs the "dangerous memory" of a powerful, new political theology.

66. Sprinkle, "God at the Margins?," 67, 70–72.

story of the hate crime murder[67] of Julianne "Julie" Williams and Laura "Lollie" Winans in May 1996 deserves to be told, and "stood together" with the martyrdom of the paired saints of Carthage.

There is no unified text for the story of the unsolved murder of Julie and Lollie. Like the vast majority of anti-LGBTQ murders that have taken place in the United States since 1984, most of the information we have about it exists in news stories, blog posts, and word of mouth. Accounts of violence against queer folk are shockingly ephemeral. Physical violence against LGBTQ people is the most savage and the least likely to be reported of any hate crime in the United States.[68] When the victims are female, poor, marked by disability, non-white, young, or gender non-conforming, then the stories fade even more rapidly. Typically, then, no book has yet recorded the story of Julie and Lollie. The investigation into their brutal murder in Shenandoah National Park is still open, though law enforcement has made a fruitless arrest in the case. The main sources for the story are found in an article for the now-defunct journal, *Off Our Backs*, "Murder on the Appalachian Trail," written in July 1996;[69] another for *Out Magazine* in November 1996, titled "Murder on the Mountain;"[70] and an annotated web site kept current until 2004 that lists links to news reports, many of which have decayed into uselessness.[71]

A narrative compiled from these sources provides the story. Julie Williams, 24, a natural scientist from St. Cloud, Minnesota, and her partner, Lollie Winans, 26, a student at Unity College in Maine who would have received a degree in outdoor recreation at the end of the academic year, went to hike the Appalachian Trail[72] for a long

---

67. "Hate crime murders" differ from other homicides in that they are message killings, assassinations intended not only to target individuals in a community, but to terrorize the members of the group. They are characterized by "overkill" of the sort reported in the murders of Billy Jack Gaither and Scotty Joe Weaver in Alabama. See Herek, "Overkill in Alabama." The usual characteristics of an anti-LGBTQ hate crime are all there in the homicides of Williams and Winans.

68. National Coalition of Anti-Violence Programs, "Report of Hate Violence Against Lesbian, Gay, Bisexual, Transgender and Queer (LGBTQ) Communities in the United States in 2009."

69. Mantilla, "Murder on the Appalachian Trail."

70. Yeoman, "Murder on the Mountain."

71. "Tragedy in Shenandoah."

72. The Appalachian Trail is an unbroken footpath, starting in Katahdin, Maine, and ending approximately 2,160 miles later at Springer Mountain, Georgia.

Memorial Day weekend. They took along Lollie's golden retriever, Taj, for company. Both were avid outdoorswomen who met in 1995 while working for a Minneapolis-based organization, Woodswomen, Inc., and fell in love. In Burlington, Vermont, where Julie was working at a bookstore, they quietly became lovers, and planned to move in together later in the summer. Julie and Lollie dreamed of opening an outdoor program together that would provide "healing experiences" for women who had been sexually abused, according to mutual friends and co-workers.

On May 18, 1996, they headed south from Burlington to central Virginia, the heart of Blue Ridge Mountain country, to hike the Trail. Both Julie and Lollie were experienced backpackers, so they chose a primitive campsite near Skyland Lodge where they would be undisturbed. Using photos the women had taken themselves, found in a camera left at the site, the FBI and the National Park Service Rangers were able to put together a timeline of their last days in the wilderness. On Thursday, May 23, a Park Ranger drove them to the head of the path leading down to the campsite. He was the last person, besides their killer, to see them alive. The final photograph of them was taken the next day, May 24. Sometime between May 24 and 8:30 a.m. on June 1, they were savagely murdered.

The women had intended to do a five-day hike, and had extended their stay for a couple of days longer. When they were overdue, Park Rangers began looking for them on May 31. Early on June 1, Lollie's dog, Taj, was found wandering near Skyland Lodge alone. Rangers combed the area, and found a grisly scene. They had chosen a perfect spot for two lovers: a secluded site near the stream, sheltered under a canopy of big trees. Julie's body was found where it had been dragged forty feet from the camp, down a hill. She was beside her sleeping bag, her hands tied and her mouth gagged. She had been stabbed multiple times, and her throat had been slit. Lollie was found inside the tent. Like her lover, she had been bound and gagged with duct tape. Her throat had also been cut. Both women were partially stripped of their clothes, but there was no evidence of sexual assault.

Julie in particular had been reticent about declaring her sexual orientation, though among friends in Burlington, it was an open secret. The Rev. Rebecca Strader, Julie's pastor at Christ Church, the

"More Light" Presbyterian Church,[73] broke the news of the nature of the relationship between the two women in the interest of furthering the investigation. Neither set of parents knew of their daughters' lesbianism at the time of their murder. As Julie and Lollie's relationship became known to authorities, suspicion that the slaying was an anti-lesbian hate crime mounted, eventually issuing an arrest and indictment in 2001 for hate crime murder against Darrell David Rice, a convicted felon with a prison history of bragging about murdering the lesbians. The case against him proved inconclusive, and charges against Rice were dismissed in February 2007. No further arrests have been made, and the murder of Julie and Lollie, like so many lesbians and gay men before them, remains unsolved. Both families and officials at the highest levels of the federal government, including former Attorney General John Ashcroft, still believe the murder was an anti-lesbian hate crime.

Was the murder of Julie and Lollie martyrdom? Juxtaposing their narrative with the story of Perpetua and Felicitas opens us to that possibility. While the lesbians never specifically chose to expose themselves to mortal danger, they must have understood that same-sex coupling in the late twentieth century had potentially dire consequences. Love was not to be denied, however, and the effects of societal bias against LGBTQ people proved fatal to them. They did not die as a sacrifice for a faith, but for a love. Neither did they die publicly in a stadium *ad bestias*, with the American mob crying out for their blood. But it is arguable that the third-century amphitheater that claimed the lives of Perpetua and Felicitas metamorphosed through time, diffusing such that the political boundaries of the United States became the arena for Julie and Lollie. Thousands of queer folk have paid for their affective commitments in every state of the union, and from every demographic group. It is no safer to be a queer in America today than it was to be a catechumen during the Severan persecutions. Like the Christians of Carthage, a community keeps the memory of the two lovers alive. The Women's Professional Group dedicates their Women's Outdoor Gatherings to Julie and Lollie each Memorial Day weekend.[74] Among the purposes of the memorial weekends is to "honor women who

---

73. "More Light" refers to the open and affirming program of the Presbyterian Church (USA).

74. See "Women's Outdoor Memorial." No pages.

have been victims of violence in the outdoors and develop strategies to prevent future attacks." With the stories of Perpetua and Felicitas, and Julie and Lollie standing side-by-side, the reasons for remembering these hate crimes victims become clearer—as well as for honoring them in a reverential way.[75] The deaths of these women form community identity in the face of the amnesia and pervasive disapproval of their respective cultures and societies. The LGBTQ community needs to create a queer political theology of martyrdom to keep the "dangerous memories" of their dead alive, and to subvert the reigning sexual ideologies that seek to drive out the lives and loves of the Other.

Was the execution of Perpetua and Felicitas a hate crime murder? Standing the stories side-by-side casts the deaths of the African martyrs in a queerly revealing light. Not only is there room for interpreting the killings of Felicitas and Perpetua as an amatory pair, as the LGBTQ community has thought for decades, but it also seems possible to call their martyrdom a state-sponsored hate crime, perpetrated against "unnatural" gender outlaws. It is unnecessary to ascribe genital eroticism to them. Their commitments fit well into the continuum of woman-identified relationships Rich and D'Angelo describe. William T. Cavanaugh has shown that state-sponsored acts of terror intend to "disappear" faith community, to isolate adherents from each other through fear by making examples of some.[76] Anti-LGBTQ hate crimes function in the same fashion. Similar forces are at work to atomize community, and then make their former members come to the state for "protection" from perils the state least condones, if not outright enacts against them.

Out of martyrdom and hate crime comes a new community, of which Julie and Lollie, Felicitas and Perpetua are founding mothers, lovers, saints, and sisters. They stand together. Their queer memory is the seed of a new sexual praxis.

---

75. See Sprinkle, *Unfinished Lives*.
76. Cavanaugh, *Torture and Eucharist*, 21–71.

Bibliography

Althaus-Reid, Marcella. *From Feminist Theology to Indecent Theology: Readings on Poverty, Sexuality, and God*. London: SCM, 2004.

———. *The Queer God*. London: Routledge, 2003.

———. "Queer I Stand: Lifting the Skirts of God." In *The Sexual Theologian: Essays on Sex, God and Politics*. Queering Theology Series. London: T. & T. Clark International, 2004.

Amat, Jacqueline. "Introduction." In *Passion de Perpétue et de Félicité suivi des Actes*, 19–94. Sources Chrétiennes 417. Paris: Cerf, 1996.

Boswell, John. *Christianity, Social Tolerance, and Homosexuality: Gay People in Western Europe from the Beginning of the Christian Era to the Fourteenth Century*. Chicago: University of Chicago Press, 1980.

———. *Same-Sex Unions in Premodern Europe*. New York: Vintage, 1995.

Brooten, Bernadette J. *Love between Women: Early Christian Responses to Female Eroticism*. Chicago: University of Chicago Press, 1996.

Castelli, Elizabeth. "I Will Make Mary Male." In *Body Guards: The Cultural Politics of Gender Ambiguity*, edited by Julia Epstein and Kristina Straub, 29–39. New York: Routledge, 1991.

———. *Martyrdom and Memory: Early Christian Culture Making*. New York: Columbia University Press, 2004.

Cavanaugh, William T. *Torture and Eucharist: Theology, Politics, and the Body of Christ*. Challenges in Contemporary Theology. New York: Wiley-Blackwell, 1998.

Cobb, L. Stephanie. *Dying to be Men: Gender and Language in Early Christian Martyr Texts*. Gender, Theory and Religion. New York: Columbia University Press, 2008.

Cobb, Michael. *God Hates Fags: The Rhetorics of Religious Violence*. Sexual Cultures Series. New York: New York University Press, 2006.

Comstock, Gary David. *Unrepentant, Self-Affirming, Practicing: Lesbian/Bisexual/Gay People within Organized Religion*. New York: Continuum, 1996.

———. *Violence against Lesbians and Gay Men*. Between Men—Between Women. New York: Columbia University Press, 1991.

D'Angelo, Mary Rose. "Women Partners in the New Testament." *JFSR* (1990) 65–86.

Farina, William. *Perpetua of Carthage: Portrait of a Third-Century Martyr*. Jefferson, NC: McFarland, 2009.

Freeman, Charles. *A.D. 381: Heretics, Pagans, and the Dawn of the Christian State*. Woodstock, NY: Overlook, 2010.

———. *A New History of Early Christianity*. New Haven: Yale University Press, 2009.

Golden, Renny. "Dangerous Memories and Cultural Resistance." No pages. Online: http://www.epica.org/Library/indigenous/golden.htm.

Guest, Deryn. *When Deborah Met Jael: Lesbian Biblical Hermeneutics*. London: SCM, 2005.

Herek, Gregory M. "Overkill in Alabama: All the Rage." No pages. Online: http://www.beyondhomophobia.com/blog/2007/09/13/antigay-overkill/.

Kleinberg, Aviad. *Flesh Made Word: Saints' Stories and the Western Imagination*. Translated by Jane Marie Todd. Cambridge: Belknap, 2008.

Kyle, Donald G. *Spectacles of Death in Ancient Rome*. Approaching the Ancient World Series. London: Routledge, 1998.

Mantilla, Karla. "Murder on the Appalachian Trail." *Off Our Backs*, July 1, 1996, 1. http://www.proquest.com.ezproxy.tcu.edu/ (accessed August 13, 2010).

Metz, Johann Baptist. *Faith in History and Society: Toward a Fundamental Practical Theology*. A Crossroad Book. New York: Seabury, 1980.

Morrill, Bruce T. *Anamnesis as Dangerous Memory: Liturgical and Political Theology in Dialogue*. A Pueblo Book. Collegeville: Liturgical Press, 2000.

National Coalition of Anti-Violence Programs. "Report of Hate Violence Against Lesbian, Gay, Bisexual, Transgender and Queer (LGBTQ) Communities in the United States in 2009." Online: http://www.avp.org/documents/NCAVP2009HateViolenceReportforWeb.pdf/.

Osiek, Carolyn, et al. *A Woman's Place: House Churches in Earliest Christianity*. Minneapolis: Fortress, 2006.

———. "Perpetua's Husband." *JECS* 10 (2002) 287–90.

Rich, Adrienne. "Compulsory Heterosexuality in Lesbian Experience (1980/1986)." In *Public Women, Public Words: A Documentary History of American Feminism*. Vol. 3, *1950–Present*, edited by Dawn Keetley, 121–26. Lanham, MD: Rowman & Littlefield, 2005.

Salisbury, Joyce E. *Perpetua's Passion: The Death and Memory of a Young Roman Woman*. New York: Routledge, 1997.

Sappho. *Sappho: A New Translation*. Translated by Mary Barnard. Berkeley: University of California Press, 1958.

Shaw, Brent D. "The Passion of Perpetua: Christian Woman Martyred in Carthage in A.D. 203." *Past & Present* 56 (May 1993) 3–45.

Smith, Lacey Baldwin. *Fools, Martyrs, Traitors: The Story of Martyrdom in the Western World*. Evanston: Northwestern University Press, 1997.

Sprinkle, Stephen V. "A God at the Margins?: Marcella Althaus-Reid and the Marginality of LGBT People." *Journal of Religious Leadership* 8.2 (Fall 2009) 57–83.

———. *Unfinished Lives: Reviving the Memory of LGBTQ Hate Crimes Victims*. Eugene, OR: Resource Publications, 2011.

Stone, Ken. *Practising Safer Texts: Food, Sex and Bible in Queer Perspective*. Queering Theology Series. London: T. & T. Clark, 2005.

Streete, Gail P. C. *Redeemed Bodies: Women Martyrs in Early Christianity*. Louisville: Westminster John Knox, 2009.

Stuart, Elizabeth. *Gay and Lesbian Theologies: Repetitions with Critical Difference*. Hampshire, England: Ashgate, 2003.

"Tragedy in Shenandoah National Park (VA) in the A.T. Vicinity." Online: http://www.fred.net/kathy/at/tragedy.html (Accessed August 12, 2010).

von Franz, Marie-Louise. *The Passion of Perpetua*. Jungian Classics Series 2. Irving: Spring Publications, 1980.

"Women's Outdoor Memorial Gatherings." No pages. Online: http://www.aee.org/leadership/affiliationGroups/WPG/gatherings/#proaction/.

Yeoman, Barry. "Murder on the Mountain." *Out* (November 1996). Online: http://www.barryyeoman.com/articles/murderonmountain.html/.

Young, Robin Darling. *In Procession before the World: Martyrdom as Public Liturgy in Early Christianity*. Père Marquette Lecture. Milwaukee: Marquette University Press, 2001.

14

Image and Religion
A Christian in the Temple of Isis at Pompeii

FREDERICK BRENK

AS THE ONLY TEMPLE FROM ANTIQUITY WITH ITS FRESCOES AND MOST of its furnishings almost completely preserved or drawn *in situ*, the Isis temple at Pompeii is a unique treasure and ideal for comparative purposes.[1] One might, then, compare this temple with early Christian churches in which frescoes and furnishings survive.[2] However, on second thought it seemed appropriate, like a traveler in the snow, to follow more closely in David's footsteps.[3] So I have attempted to examine, not the possible effect of the frescoes on a devotee of the Isis cult, but rather that upon a hypothetical Christian of the time, who might have visited the temple (see figure 14.1).

---

1. I am grateful to Valeria Sampaolo, Director of the Museo Archeologico Nazionale of Naples for permission to use photos taken in the Museum (henceforth referred to as MNN), and to Professors Giuseppina Capriotti Vittozzi and Molly Swetnam-Burland for helpful suggestions and corrections. On the temple, see Sampaolo, "decorazione pittorica" and "Tempio di Iside;" Moormann, "Temple of Isis in Pompeii;" Brenk, "Gleaming Ray," and "'Great Royal Spouse.'"

2. On the Christian churches, see Yasin, *Saints and Church Spaces*.

3. Articles on Pompeian painting now collected in Balch, *Roman Domestic Art*. Of particular interest is chapter 2, "Sufferings of Isis/Io."

Figure 14.1: Piranesi, Tempio di Iside.

The Isaeum was tucked away in the "Hellenistic Quarter" of Pompeii, which contained, besides the temple, a theater and an *odeion*.[4] In fact, to be built, the Isaeum had to be squeezed against the rounded back of the theater, something which gave it a peculiar ground plan. Whether the temple existed in the second or first centuries BCE is still a matter of dispute.[5] In any case the final infrastructure belongs primarily to the Augustan age.[6] The stucco and painting programs, though, pertain to a restoration after the damage caused by the earthquake of 62, just two years before the fire in Rome and the persecution of the Christians under Nero. The frescoes were completely redone, mainly in the contemporary "Fourth Pompeian Style," but some traces of the Augustan paintings seem to have been preserved in some "*quadretti*," (small inset paintings), many of them of warships, which seem out of place.[7] All ended with the eruption of Vesuvius in 79 until the temple

---

4. For maps, see, e.g., Cantilena, "Tavole," 86–87, pls. I and II; Sampaolo, "Tempio di Iside," 732, and Gasparini, "Santuari Isiaci," 85, fig. 1; for theaters, 86.

5. Blanc et al., "'*fundamento restituit*'?"; rejected by D'Alessio, *I culti a Pompei*, 76–77, and Gasparini, "Santuari Isiaci," 67.

6. For Augustus's involvement with Egypt, see Swetnam-Burland, "*Aegyptus Redacta*."

7. References to the painting are to Sampaolo, "Tempio di Iside." Esposito, *officine*

rose from the ashes in 1774–1776, creating a sensation in Europe, not only stimulating Mozart to write *The Magic Flute*, but also Masonic and other movements looking for an alternative to Christianity.

Let us now imagine a Christian of the time just before the eruption in 79, whether of Jewish or Graeco-Roman religious heritage. We presume he or she had absorbed much of the Jewish background of Christianity and at the same time was fairly well instructed in Graeco-Roman culture. Perhaps our imaginary Christian would first notice the contradiction between the somewhat obscure location of the temple, the excellent quarter in which it was located, and the beauty of its art and architecture. Our Christian would be aware of how, as in Acts of the Apostles (16:10–13), both the Jewish and Christian places of worship tended to be relegated to the periphery of the city, and how worship frequently even occurred in a "house church" or very small synagogue.[8] Our Christian was somewhat encouraged when the guide related how humble and troubled were the beginnings of the Isis cult in Rome and in Italy, how Isiacs had even seen their temples torn down, the statue of Isis thrown into the Tiber, and their priests crucified.[9] The Christian hoped that such a turnaround might happen to Christians too in the future.

On entering the temple precinct, our Christian was astounded to discover, contrary to all his expectations, that the temple was tiny and not very Egyptian looking. The guide accepted the observation, but claimed it was normal and that the basic architecture with its high podium, high steps in the center of the temple, and flanking "prostyle" columns for a small porch, even in Egypt would be recognized as an Isaeum.[10] Our Christian was then struck by the small altars, one in front of the *Purgatorium*, and others in front of the temple. This suggested that sacrifice and a common sacrificial meal must have been offered, but on a small scale.[11] The Christian then continued around the courtyard with its surrounding porticoes on three sides. The guide

---

pittoriche, 56–57, sees touches of Vespasianic painting. Bricault, "Fonder un lieu de culte," 64, suggests the warships refer to the protection of the grain supply from Egypt.

8. On this see Osiek and Balch, *Families*, esp. 91–103.

9. Gasparini, "Santuari Isiaci," 69–71; and Takács, *Isis and Sarapis*, 56–70.

10. See, e.g., Golvin, "L'architecture de l'Iseum à Pompéi;" Naerebout, "Temple at Ras el-Soda;" and Gasparini, "Santuari Isiaci," 84–86.

11. Gasparini and Sampaolo, "Tempio di Iside," plan, 732, 12a and 12b, and 798–99, for the altars; See also Osiek and Balch, *Families*, 193–214.

told him they must go now to the southwest corner, and then examine things in a counterclockwise fashion. His eye first caught sight of an *aediculum* on the wall at the center of the east portico. An Isiac priest in the painting was venerating a statue of a handsome athletic-looking youth in the style of the famous sculptor Praxiteles.[12] He was informed that the statue represented Harpocrates, the Graeco-Roman version of Horus, the son of Isis and Osiris. The painted sanctuary within which the priest was practicing his ritual struck the Christian as greatly resembling the very one he was standing in. He was surprised at such veneration of a statue, but was told of its importance in Egyptian religion as requiring a considerable part of their day.

Moving on, he noticed that to follow the paintings of the portico, whether on the south side or the north, one had to proceed counterclockwise toward the west, that is, past the small temple with its altar in the center of the courtyard, to the "Ekklesiasterion."[13] Small vignettes of sacral-idyllic scenes alternated with those of Isiac priests, a priestess, and a boy priest or acolyte. The figures, judging by the heads of all but the last figure, with one exception, before entering the Ecclesiasterion, were pointed toward the viewer's left, as though in a procession toward the Ecclesiasterion, the largest room, on the west side. He asked the guide if west had some special significance for Egyptians, and was told that the souls of the dead traveled to the west, as was the place of the afterlife, and that the burial place of Osiris was on an island called the Abaton (or Bigga) just to the west of Philae. The Christian learned that Philae was one of the greatest temples, and perhaps the greatest, of Isis in Egypt, and that every year the ritual body of Osiris was carried from Philae to the Abaton.[14]

In the vignettes our Christian could make out nine liturgical figures: one woman priestess, one boy, and seven Egyptian-looking priests with shaven heads.[15] One could not tell, though, whether they

---

12. Sampaolo, "Tempio di Iside," National Archaeological Museum of Naples, inventory number (MNN inv.) 8975. See Corso, *Art of Praxiteles* III.

13. The names are not ancient but given by the early excavators.

14. For the west, see Griffiths, *Plutarch's*, 563–64. De Vos, *Aegyptus Romana*, 136–39, was the first to notice this for the Isaeum at Pompeii. See also Brenk, *With Unperfumed Voice*, 353, 356–57, 378–79, 385–90. For the rites at Philae, see Meyboom, *Nile Mosaic*, 61, 64, figs 81–83, pl. IV no. 113, Appendix, 8–11 (136–46).

15. According to Sampaolo, "decorazione pittorica," 26.

were real Egyptians, or Romans or Greeks dressed like Egyptians.[16] The boy, though, who carried a mammiform *situla* in his hand, seemed decidedly Graeco-Roman and had a full head of hair.[17] The guide explained that the boy was a *spondophoros* and was carrying the milk of Isis in a *situla*.[18] The priestess looked especially Graeco-Roman, since she had a "melon" type hairdo, like Cleopatra's (see figure 14.2).[19]

Figure 14.2: Priestess.

16. In "'Egyptian' Priests," Swetnam-Burland argues that most of the priests were Graeco-Romans, esp., 337, 348.

17. Sampaolo, "Tempio di Iside," 775, no. 66, MNN (Museo Archeologico Nazionale di Napoli) inv. 8529. The *pterophoros* (ibid., 745, no. 18, MNN inv. 8925) has a golden *bulla* around his neck, suggesting he is Roman.

18. Ibid., 775, no. 66, MNN inv. 8529.

19. Ibid., 772, no. 62, MNN inv. 8923, the only representation of a woman devotee in the temple. An engraving shows her with a *"Melonenfrisur"* hairstyle, an offering dish, and bracelets on her arm.

One priest carried a cobra (see figure 14.3), while another, the *pterophoros*, who had two plumes in his headdress, evidently carried a sacred scroll. Three of the priests held palms.[20]

Figure 14.3: Priest with cobra.

The Christian remembered the procession with palms in the life of Jesus, but the guide explained the special significance here and how the word *phoinix* could mean either a palm or the sacred bird of Osiris, who rose from the ashes.[21] Certain animals were represented as perched on the wall-like backdrop behind the figures. A lion was resting on the wall, behind the priest carrying the cobra in a crown of roses.[22] The magpies on the wall behind one priest supposedly symbolized the *ba*, one of the souls of the deceased. The *zakoros* was holding a palm in his right hand and in the other what looked like a handful of wheat.[23] The guide explained that the black cat with a lotus crown behind the *pterophoros* was the goddess Bastet who protects the god

---

20. For the palms in Egypt and relationship to the phoenix, see Capriotti Vittozzi, "La palme e il loro significato."

21. Sampaolo, "Tempio di Iside," 758, no. 41, MNN inv. 8921.

22. Ibid., 702, no. 48, MNN inv. 8922.

23. Ibid., 758–59, no. 41, MNN inv. 8921.

Re (the sun) from the primordial serpent.[24] Another priest, whom the guide called a *lychnophoros*, carried a golden oil lamp in the shape of a boat.[25]

Most disturbing to the Christian was a figure wearing a brilliant scarlet toga, but with the head of a jackal, so realistic that it made him shudder (see figure 14.4).[26]

Figure 14.4: Anubis.

24. Ibid., 745, no. 18, MNN inv. 8925.

25. Ibid., 779, no. 75, MNN inv. 8969. The *lychnophoros* leads the procession, and Anubis with a mask and *caduceus* (Hermanubis) appears in the procession of Apuleius, *Metamorphoses* 11.10–11. See Griffiths, *Apuleius of Madauros*, 80–85, 194–215.

26. Sampaolo, "Tempio di Iside," 784, no. 84, MNN inv. 8920. The background resembles an Egyptian temple.

The guide explained that this represented Anubis. This was the only representation of a god with an animal head and human body in the whole temple. Our Christian remembered that funerary rites were extremely important for Egyptians, something he thought excessive. He also believed that their portrayal of gods as animals and worship of living animals was idolatry, contrary to the Ten Commandments and condemned by Jews such as Philo of Alexandria.[27] On the east side of the north portico was a panel with two beautiful facing peacocks.[28] He learned that the peacocks were used for the phoenix in the Graeco-Roman world, and signified rebirth and immortality. Our Christian and his guide now moved to the Ekklesiasterion, the largest room, evidently used for meetings and meals.[29] The painting was of extraordinary quality. Running along the top of the room was a long "peopled frieze" containing Egyptian animals and a delightful pygmy girl wearing a diaphanous dress, flanked by ibises, and sitting on an acanthus crown held up by swirling crocodiles.[30]

The guide explained that to appreciate the paintings one should again move in a counterclockwise direction. On each of the three walls there was one very large triptych in *tromp l'oeil* style. The side panels depicted sacral-idyllic scenes of temples on islands.[31] According to the guide they represented the "Dodekaskoinos," a stretch of the Upper Nile near the great temple of Isis at Philae. The central panels were quite different, mythological paintings of great masters of the Classical and Hellenistic periods but meant to fit Ptolemaic ideology and the Isis cult.[32] The guide had trouble explaining the exact meaning for Isiacs, but claimed that essentially they represented freedom from bestiality and salvation through Isis.[33] On the north wall, Argos was about to be slain by Hermes, and Io turned into a cow (see figure 14.5)."

27. See Pearce, *Land of the Body*; and the review by Brenk.

28. North portico, east side, Sampaolo, "Tempio di Iside," 749, no. 23, MNN inv. 8577.

29. For the importance of the meal, see Taussig, *In the Beginning*; and Alikin, *Earliest History*.

30. Sampaolo "Tempio di Iside," 757, no. 39, MNN inv. 8545.

31. For ideal views of Egypt, see Parkinson, *Reading Ancient Egyptian Poetry*, 4–5.

32. Sampaolo, "Tempio di Iside," 824–45, no. 188, MNN inv. 9548 on the center of the north wall. Other copies have been found at Pompeii, Herculaneum, and in the Casa di Livia on the Palatine. See Balch, *Roman Domestic Art*, 59–83 and 213–15.

33. The myth and painting might have inspired Apuleius's Isis book (XI) of the *Metamorphoses*, in which Lucius is restored from ass to human form. For salva-

Figure 14.5: Io, Argo, and Hermes.

On the west wall was another triptych belonging to the story of Io.[34] On one of the side panels of the triptych, bulls or cows were grazing (see figure 14.6).[35]

---

tion, see also Sfameni Gasparro, "Hellenistic Face," esp. 40, 56, 72; and Belayche and Rebillard, "'Cultes orientaux,'" 137–38.

34. The central panel was destroyed before or during the excavation.

35. Sampaolo, "Tempio di Iside," 841, no. 213, MNN inv. 8558.

Figure 14.6: Bulls Grazing.

They seemed absurd on a tiny island in the Nile. The guide ventured that the scene alluded to the raising of the sacred Apis bulls for the sanctuary at Memphis. This made the Christian uneasy since once again he recalled the condemnation of idols in Exodus and the terrible punishment meted out by God to the Jews in the Sinai for venerating a golden calf (Exod 32).

As they moved to the last triptych, that on the south wall, the myth and its *raison d' être* became clearer. Here Isis was returning Io to her human form (see figure 14.7).[36]

---

36. For depiction of myths at Pompeii, see Hodske, *Mythologische Bildthemen*.

Figure 14.7: Io at Canopus.

In the background, one could see Isis's sister Nephthys, Hermanubis (Anubis-Hermes/Mercury), a combination of Anubis and the god who accompanied the souls of the Greeks into the next life, and Harpocrates at her feet. The beauty and warm humanity of Isis, who apparently knew what suffering was and reached out her hand to the suffering, was overwhelming. The Christian wished that his religion had such beautiful art to express the love and compassion of Christ and his mother.[37]

Just as he was about to enter the last room, the "Sacrarium," something struck his eye on the left side panel of the "Isis at Canopus" fresco, the closest panel to the door as one proceeded to the Sacrarium. In this quite extraordinary scene among the other sacro-idyllic paintings, an actual scene of funerary ritual seemed to be occurring (see figure 14.8).

37. For Isis's "corkscrew locks" in the painting, see Bianchi, "Images of Isis," 482–87. Oddly, no representations of Isis Fortuna, the most popular at Pompeii, or of Isis Lactans were found in the temple. In contrast see Capriotti Vittozzi, "L'Egitto a *Praeneste*," 80–82.

Figure 14.8: Adoration of the Mummy.

An Egyptian priest, *hierodoulos* or *pterophoros* was making an offering on an altar before a mummy case. Five or seven high steps ascended to the mummy case, just like those in front of an Isis temple. Over the mummy case was a stone lintel in the form of a low triangular pediment, itself resting upon two large slabs in the form of anthropoid mummy cases. But the strangest sight of all was an incredibly large bird with a lotus crown on its head perched on top of the mummy case.[38] Tied around each slab was a large, long yellow ribbon and around the mummy case, a smaller white one, according to the Greek custom. In the background a huge cylindrical Roman style temple or tomb appeared, and possibly high up on a cliff in the background an Egyptian tomb.

The guide explained that this probably represented the Island of Bigga, or the Abaton, the final resting place of Osiris and the source of the Nile, at which each year there was a funerary procession carrying the clay "body" of Osiris from Philae, and the enacting of funerary rites for him there.[39] The island was famous for its giant falcons

38. In a relief from Abydos, Isis as a hawk sits on the mummy Osiris's midriff, and a giant Horus with a falcon head stands at the foot, but nothing in Egyptian art seems to resemble the Pompeian scene.

39. Meyboom, *Nile Mosaic*, 60–61, 64, IV no. 113, app. 8–11 (136–46); Brenk, *Unperfumed Voice*, 353, 356–57, 378–79, 385–90.

230   PART TWO: CREATING IMAGES—VERBAL AND VISUAL

brought from Africa, but this bird, judging by its lotus crown, was surely divine, neither exactly a falcon nor a phoenix (the symbol of rebirth in the Osiris cult), nor any other bird.[40] In the foreground a large amphora suggested the source of the Nile, and in the background a herm with an erect penis possibly suggested the resuscitated Osiris, though in this iconography he was represented as supine. The guide added that Osiris was worshipped in the form of water carried in the processions. In Egyptian iconography, too, Osiris was resuscitated from the dead by Isis and her sister Nephthys in the form of birds flapping their wings over the corpse, and Isis as a hawk sometimes sat upon the mummy. Our Christian was confused by all this polyvalent symbolism, which nonetheless made a deep impression.

They now proceeded to the "Sacrarium," a room which looked quite different from the others.[41] Instead of the exquisite paintings of the Ekklesiasterion, these were rather crudely done.[42] The east wall was covered with animals, some obviously divine, since they wore lotus crowns and two of them wore solar disks (see figure 14.9).

Figure 14.9: Animals.

40. Sampaolo, "Tempio di Iside," 836, no. 205, MNN inv. 8570, interprets the bird as the sacred bird of Osiris, the phoenix, symbol of the sun, rebirth, and the Nile flood. Meyboom, *Nile Mosaic*, 130, notes that the Tomb of Osiris on the Abaton was called the "House of the Phoenix" (in Egyptian art usually represented as the *benu* bird).

41. A somewhat similar inferior style appears in the "Egyptian" Sepolcro Z of the Vatican necropolis (beginning of III cent.). See Liverani and Spinola, *le necropoli vaticane*, 84–87, no. 46, but *pace* the authors, Toth (or Anubis) has been filtered through Graeco-Roman imagery.

42. Moormann, "Temple of Isis," 153–54.

The whole scene looked something like a zoo, but the guide explained that the animals represented different Egyptian gods.[43] Most, but not all, were easy to identify. The ibis was Toth; the cobra, Wadjet, goddess of lower Egypt; the jackal, Anubis; the bull with the solar disk, Apis; the ram, Khnum, god of the cataract; the lion, possibly Maahes; the vulture, Nekhbet, primordial goddess of Upper Egypt; the crouching ichneumenon, Horus; the seated baboon, Toth.[44] The guide was embarrassed, however, in being unable to identify the rat. The most unusual scene of all was something like a *"lararium,"* covering the whole north wall (see figure 14.10).[45]

Figure 14.10: Isis in a Barque.

In the center was Isis in a boat, flanked by two river gods. These looked looking somewhat like the god Serapis, but represented the Lower and Upper Nile, a true Egyptian concept as the guide declared.[46] Just below them in heraldic form was a *cista mystica* resting on something like a stone altar. On either side were flanking serpents and, below, flanking acanthus stems. The crescent moon on the *cista mystica* was supposed

---

43. See the map in Sampaolo, "Tempio di Iside," *sacrarium* (5), and the photos, 815–19, nos. 172–79. The east wall had an arched doorway on the south end, 816–17, no. 177 and 178. From the courtyard portico at least part of the "Isis and Osiris Enthroned," could be made visible.

44. Ibid., cobra 816, no. 174, MNN inv. MDXII; white ibis, 816, no. 175, MNN inv. 8562; vulture, 816, no. 176 (no MNN inv. number); baboon, rat, ichneumenon, vulture, jackal, ram, 818. no. 178; Apis bull, 818, no. 179, MNN inv. 8565.

45. For the *mélange* of objects see Swetnam-Burland, "Egyptian Objects," and for the effort to obtain real objects, Capriotti Vittozzi, "Frammento di statua."

46. Sampaolo, "Tempio di Iside," 815, no. 172, MNN inv. 8929.

to be the symbol of Isis. To the far left (from the viewer's standpoint) Bes was sitting on a chair or throne, and not quite as high as the busts of the river gods.[47] He looked taller and more human and kindly than the usual grotesque representations of him at Pompeii. Next came an *aediculum* with a faience "idol" inside.[48] To the right of the Nile gods and about as high as their busts, one could see a lion, with a cobra below, and an ibis, while a vulture flew over the space between them. The Christian had often seen snakes around a *cista mystica* on coins, but never a complete scene like this. The snakes made him uncomfortable, as they did not have the best reputation in the Old Testament, especially in Genesis, though he also remembered Moses using a snake to heal the Israelites in the desert.[49]

The woman in the reed barque, presumably Isis, judging by the lotus crown on her head and her clothing, was towing behind her another barque with a man's head at the prow.[50] On the second barque was a large box, with a depiction of a bird with a white or yellow breast and a dark back and wings, looking more like a swallow than a falcon.[51] The guide explained that after Osiris had been murdered by his brother, Seth dispersed his members in the Nile, but Isis, having found them, recomposed the pieces and succeeded in resuscitating Osiris. The story of passion, death, and resurrection seemed similar to the passion and resurrection of Christ, and the important role of the women in his funerary rites. After Osiris was resuscitated, the guide continued, Osiris in some versions became the father of Horus or Harpocrates, who avenged his death.[52] Afterwards, Osiris became king of the dead,

---

47. See Sampaolo, "Tempio di Iside," 813, no. 170, MNN inv. 8929 (engraving by N. Billy after drawing by G. Casanova), and 814, no. 171, MNN inv. 8916. For types of Bes, see Capriotti Vittozzi, "Bes dal Quirinale a Piazza."

48. The inscriptions with the donor's name appears in Bricault, *Recueil des inscriptions*, 602–5.

49. In the New Testament Satan is not identified with a serpent, outside of Revelation, e.g. 12:7.

50. Sampaolo, "Tempio di Iside," 813, no. 170, and 815, no. 172, MNN inv. 8929.

51. Ibid., 815, no. 172, MNN inv. 8929, who sees a falcon depicted on the box, claims it represents the transport of the sacred water.

52. In Plutarch, *On Isis and Osiris* 358D, Harpocrates, not Horus is born at this time but see Griffiths, *Plutarch's*, 307, 338–39.

but some people were now saying that Osiris went not to the west nor to the underworld but had risen to the heavens.[53]

Moving again counterclockwise from the north side to the west side, to the last of the painted Sacrarium walls, the Christian observed another remarkable but somewhat familiar scene. The guide called it "Isis and Osiris Enthroned" (see figure 14.11).[54]

Figure 14.11: Isis and Osiris Enthroned.

Isis was in the center of the composition, seated upon a throne, while a benevolent looking Osiris, at her right side, sat upon a padded stool, or chair like that used by Bes, and looking inferior to Isis (see figure 14.12).[55]

---

53. Suggested in Plutarch, *On Isis and Osiris*, 382E-383E, where Osiris is not in the underworld, but belongs to the intelligible sphere.

54. Sampaolo, "Tempio di Iside," 820, no. 182 (no MNN inv. number).

55. Ibid., 821, nos. 182–83, MNN inv. 8927, sees the snakes as symbols of eternal regeneration, but they were common in *lararia*.

Figure 14.12: Osiris.

Neither of the pair looked very Egyptian. Both had lotus crowns on their heads, as did some of the snakes in the painting, but Osiris also wore a strange flat hat. Both Isis and Osiris wore a narrow black sash running from their left shoulder to the right of their waists, like those worn by Isiacs. There were numerous snakes with lotus crowns in the painting, suggesting that this was the underworld. There was a strong resemblance to scenes of Persephone and Plouton reigning in the underworld, as depicted on Greek vases.[56] It did appear, though, as a scene of triumph over suffering and death, and of benevolence to those who worshipped these gods, especially Isis. Our Christian, nonetheless, felt that his own faith offered a more joyous and better life in the next world, and that the death of Osiris did nothing in itself to save him.

56. See Clarysse, "Egyptian Religion," 577–84.

Our Christian wanted to make some further inquiries, but the guide informed him that his time had expired. In leaving the temple, as he recollected what he had observed, there were some elements the Christian did not like, such as the absence of a strong male figure. He also believed that the paintings architecturally were not too focused, or if focused could only be seen in one room. There was a movement to a deeper understanding of a mystery, but one had to begin over in another room. Also the painting varied in style from Classical to Hellenistic, to Pompeian IV style, to a somewhat untrained popular style, which also seemed to be the most religious. But he marveled, nonetheless, at the magnificent use of art to convey religious ideas. He was astounded at how wonderfully Egyptian religion and art had been incorporated into the Graeco-Roman scene, so that simultaneously everything seemed completely Egyptian and completely Graeco-Roman. One could think of the procession of religious dignitaries, the beautiful sacro-idyllic landscapes, the narration of great religious events through masterpieces of painting, scenes of ritual and suffering, the expression of the bond between humans and the gods, "paintings of suffering and death" followed by a luminous, triumphal blessed afterlife.[57] Above all he admired the image of Isis, the mother and queen, reaching out her hand to mortals like us, struggling through the vicissitudes of life with both its joyous moments its crises, though seemingly far far away, always near.[58]

---

57. Balch, *Roman Domestic Art*, 84.

58. Not all the paintings had a religious dimension, and two in the bedroom (*cubiculum*) were even erotic. See Sampaolo, "Tempio di Iside," map, 732, nos. 7, 8, 9, and 843–49.

Bibliography

Alikin, Valeriy A. *The Earliest History of the Christian Gathering: Origin, Development and Content of the Christian Gathering in the First to Third Centuries.* Supplements to Vigiliae Chrstianae 102. Leiden: Brill, forthcoming.

Balch, David L. *Roman Domestic Art and Early House Churches.* WUNT 228. Tübingen: Mohr/Siebeck, 2008.

Belayche, Nicole, and Eric Rebillard. "'Cultes orientaux' et pluralisme religieux: introduction thématic." In *Religioni in contatto nel Mediterraneo antico: modalità di diffusione e processi di interferenza,* edited by Corinne Bonnet et al., 137–50. Mediterranea 4. Pisa: Serra, 2008.

Bianchi, Robert S. "Images of Isis and Her Cultic Shrines Reconsidered: Towards an Egyptian Understanding of the *Interpretation Graeca.*" In *Nile into Tiber: Egypt in the Roman World,* edited by Laurent Bricault et al., 470–505. RGRW 159. Leiden: Brill, 2007.

Blanc, Nicole et al. "'*A fundamento restituit*'?: refections dans le temple d'Isis à Pompéi." *RAr* 2 (2000) 227–309.

Brenk, Frederick E. "A Gleaming Ray: Blessed Afterlife in the Mysteries." In *Relighting the Souls: Studies in Plutarch, in Greek Literature, Religion, and Philosophy, and in the New Testament Background,* 291–308. Stuttgart: Steiner, 1998.

———. "'Great Royal Spouse who Protects Her Brother Osiris': Isis in the Iseaum at Pompeii." In *With Unperfumed Voice: Studies in Plutarch, in Greek Literature, Religion and Philosophy, and in the New Testament Background,* edited by Frederick E. Brenk, 346–70. PAwB 21. Stuttgart: Steiner, 2007.

———. Review of *The Land of the Body: Studies in Philo's Representation of Egypt,* by Sarah J. K. Pearce. *JEA* 94 (2008) 340–42.

———. "'Great Royal Spouse Who Protects Her Brother Osiris:' Isis in the Iseaum at Pompeii." In *Mystic Cults in Magna Graecia,* edited by Giovanni Casadio and Patricia A. Johnston, 217–34. Austin: University of Texas Press, 2009.

Bricault, Laurent. *Recueil des inscriptions concernant les cultes isiaques (RICIS).* Mémoires de l'Académie des Inscriptions et Belles-Lettres 31. 2 vols. Académie des Inscriptions et Belles-Lettres, 2005.

———. "Fonder un lieu de culte." In *Religioni in contatto nel Mediterraneo antico: modalità di diffusione e processi di interferenza,* edited by Corinne Bonnet et al., 49–64. Mediterranea 4. Pisa: Serra, 2008.

Cantilena, Renata. "Tavole." In *Alla ricerca di Iside: analisi, studi e restauri dell'Iseo pompeiano nel Museo di Napoli,* edited by Stefano De Caro, 86–87. Rome: Arti, 1992.

Capriotti Vittozzi, Giuseppina. "Bes dal Quirinale a Piazza Vittorio: 'alia Aegyptiaca Romana.'" *BCAR* 100 (1999) 155–65.

———. "Le palme e il loro significato." In *Tra le palme del Piceno: Egitto, terra del Nilo,* edited by Alessandro Roccati and Giuseppina Capriotti Vittozzi, 119–22. Piceno: Riviera delle Palme, 2002.

———. "Frammento di statua di Sethi I." In *Sculture antiche nell'Abbazia di Grottoferrata,* edited by Annarena Ambrogi et al. 50–52. Rome: Comitato Nazionale per le Celebrazioni del Millenario della Fondazione dell'Abbazia di S. Nilo a Grottaferrata, 2008.

———. "L'*Egitto a Praeneste: alcune note.*" *Mediterranea* 6 (2009) 79–98.

Clarysse, Willy. "Egyptian Religion and Magic in the Papyri." In *The Oxford Handbook of Papyrology*, edited by Roger S. Bagnall, 561-89. Oxford Handbooks. Oxford: Oxford University Press, 2009.
Corso, Antonio. *The Art of Praxiteles III: The Advanced Maturity of the Sculptor*. Studia archaeologica. Rome: L'Erma di Bretschneider, 2010.
D'Alessio, Maria Teresa. *I culti a Pompei: divinità, luoghi e frequentatori (VI secolo a.C.—79 d.C.)*. Archeologia del territorio. Rome: Libreria dello Stato, 2009.
De Vos, Mariette. "Aegyptica Romana." In *Alla ricerca di Iside*, edited by Pia De Fidio et al., 130-59. Naples: Gaetano Macchiaroli, 1994.
Esposito, Domenico. *Le officine pittoriche di IV stile a Pompei: dinamiche produttive ed economico-sociali*. Studi della Soprintendenza archeologica di Pompei 28. Rome: L'Erma di Bretschneider, 2009.
Gasparini, Valentino. "Santuari Isiaci in Italia: criteri e contesti di diffusione." In *Religioni in contatto nel Mediterraneo antico: modalità di diffusione e processi di interferenza* (= *Mediterranea* 4 [2007]), edited by Corinne Bonnet et al., 65-89. Pisa: Serra, 2008.
Golvin, J.-C. "L'architecture de l'Iseum à Pompéi et les characteristiques des édifices isiaques romains." In *Hommage à Jean Leclant III: Études isiaques*, edited by Catherine Berger et al., 235-46. Cairo: Institut Français d'Archéologie Orientale, 1999.
Griffiths, J. Gwyn, editor and translator. *Plutarch's De Iside et Osiride*. Cardiff: University of Wales Press, 1970.
———. *Apuleius of Madauros: The Isis-Book (Metamorphoses: Book XI)*. EPRO 39. Leiden: Brill, 1975.
Hodske, Jürgen. *Mythologische Bildthemen in den Häusern Pompejis: die Bedeutung der zentralen Mythenbilder für die Bewohner Pompejis*. Stendaler Winckelmann-Forschungen 6. Rutzen: Ruhpolding, 2007.
Liverani, Paolo, and Giandomenico Spinola. *Le necropoli vaticane: la città dei morti di Roma*. Monumenta Vaticana Selecta. Vatican City: Libreria Editrice Vaticana, 2010.
Meyboom, Paul G. P. *The Nile Mosaic of Palestrina: Early Evidence of Egyptian Religion in Italy*. EPRO 121. Leiden: Brill, 1995.
Moormann, Eric M. "The Temple of Isis in Pompeii." In *Nile into Tiber: Egypt in the Roman World*, edited by Laurent Bricault et al., 137-54. RGRW 159. Leiden: Brill, 2007.
Naerebout, F. G. "The Temple at Ras el-Soda. Is it an Isis Temple? Is it Greek, Roman, Egyptian, or Neither? And So What?." In *Nile into Tiber: Egypt in the Roman World*, edited by Laurent Bricault et al., 506-54. RGRW 159. Leiden: Brill, 2007.
Osiek, Carolyn, and David L. Balch. *Families in the New Testament World: Households and House Churches*. The Family, Religion, and Culture. Louisville: Westminster John Knox, 1997.
Parkinson, R. B. *Reading Ancient Egyptian Poetry: Among Other Histories*. Chichester, UK: Wiley-Blackwell, 2009.
Pearce, Sarah J. K. *The Land of the Body: Studies in Philo's Representation of Egypt*. WUNT 208. Tübingen: Mohr/Siebeck, 2007.

Sampaolo, Valeria. "La decorazione pittorica." In *Alla ricerca di Iside: analisi, studi e restauri dell'Iseo pompeiano nel Museo di Napoli*, edited by Stefano De Caro, 23–62. Rome: Arti, 1992.

———. "VIII 7, 28, Tempio di Iside." In *Pompei: Pitture e mosaici VIII. Regio VIII–Regio IX Parte I*, edited by Ida Baldassare et al., 732–849. Rome: Enciclopedia Italiana, 1998.

Sfameni Gasparro, Giulia. "The Hellenistic Face of Isis: Cosmic and Saviour Goddess." In *Nile into Tiber: Egypt in the Roman World*. RGRW 159, edited by Laurent Bricault et al., 40–72. Leiden: Brill, 2007.

Swetnam-Burland, Molly. "*Aegyptus Redacta*: The Egyptian Obelisk in the Augustan Campus Martius." *Art Bulletin* 92 (2010) 135–53.

———. "Egyptian Objects, Roman Contexts: A Taste for Aegyptiaca in Italy." In *Nile into Tiber: Egypt in the Roman World*, edited by Laurent Bricault et al., 113–36. RGRW 159. Leiden: Brill, 2007.

———. "'Egyptian' Priests in Roman Italy." In *Cultural Identity in the Ancient Mediterranean*, edited by Erich S. Gruen, 336–53. Los Angeles: Getty Research Institute, 2011.

Takács, Sarolta A. *Isis and Sarapis in the Roman World*. EPRO 124. Leiden: Brill, 1995.

Taussig, Hal. *In the Beginning Was the Meal: Social Experimentation and Early Christian Identity*. Minneapolis: Fortress, 2009.

Yasin, Anne Marie. *Saints and Church Spaces in the Late Antique Mediterranean: Architecture, Cult, and Community*. Greek Culture in the Roman World. Cambridge: Cambridge University Press, 2009.

15

The Shadow of an Ass

On Reading the Alexamenos Graffito

Oliver Larry Yarbrough

THE ALEXAMENOS GRAFFITO FOUND ON THE PALATINE HILL IN 1856 is frequently described in current literature as "well known." It is, but only if the phrase refers to the image's existence and a few basic assumptions about its meaning. In fact, however, questions abound with regard to almost every aspect of the graffito, so that discovering, or perhaps better, constructing its meaning is difficult.

In his essay "Paul's Portrait of Christ Crucified (Gal. 3:1) in Light of Paintings and Sculptures of Suffering in Pompeiian and Roman Houses," David Balch notes some of the questions related to the Alexamenos graffito and addresses one of them: Was there a Christian precedent for its image of the crucifixion?[1] In what follows, I examine some of the other questions and reflect on approaches to finding the graffito's meaning. I begin, however, with a description of the graffito and an analysis of its setting, both of which affect the reading of it.

Description[2]

The graffito is composed of two crudely drawn figures and an inscription etched between and below them, in equally crude letters (see figure

---

1. In Balch and Osiek, *Early Christian Families*, 84–108. For his comments on the Alexamenos graffito, see 103–4. See also the companion essay "Suffering of Isis/Io."

2. The most thorough treatments of the Alexamenos graffito are Solin, *Graffiti*; and Riemann, "Paedagogium." Since I have not had occasion to see the original, I have consulted several reproductions. The best are the plate in Solin, *Graffiti*, 209 and, though small, the photograph reproduced in Spier, *Picturing the Bible*, fig. 2, p. 227.

240 PART TWO: CREATING IMAGES—VERBAL AND VISUAL

Figure 15.1: Graffito of a crucified figure. From the Domus Gelotiana, Palatine, Rome. 2nd CE. Location: Antiquarium del Palatino, Rome, Italy. Photo Credit: Scala/Art Resource, NY.

15.1). Above and to the right of the central figure the Greek letter upsilon appears etched more deeply and exactingly than any of the other letters. The more prominent figure, both in terms of size and placement, is a human body with the head of an ass.[3] Seen from the rear (as

3. I hold with this identification even though the ears do not appear to be those of an ass, at least when compared to the ears of the figure in graffito 289, which is explicitly identified in its inscription as an ass. See below. Observing how the Alexamenos artist draws hands, however, it is not surprising that he does not do ears well.

evidenced by the exposed buttocks), it is attached to a T-shaped cross with arms outstretched and feet resting on a cross beam. The head of the figure is turned to the left, in the direction of (and perhaps looking toward) the other figure. The left eye and mouth are identifiable, as is the muzzle. The figure appears to be wearing a short, sleeveless garment that extends from the shoulders to the mid-buttocks. A curved line on each leg appears to mark the knee joint. Lightly etched lines extended from the forearms to the upper crossbeam perhaps represent ropes. Neither hand is discernible.

The second male figure is situated to the left of the central one and appears to be standing level with the bottom of the vertical post of the cross. He is slightly shorter than the central figure. He too appears to be seen from the rear, though the buttocks are not exposed beneath the garment he is wearing. The head, which is large for the body, is turned and raised slightly toward the central figure so that it is seen in profile. The right eye and mouth are discernible. Hair appears to be represented by jagged lines beginning at the forehead and extending to the back of the skull. There are no ears. The right arm is extended upward toward the central figure and is bent at the elbow; the curved left arm is extended downward and away from the body. Notably, only the right arm is drawn with a hand, and its fingers are splayed.

The inscription runs to four lines, with the first word being divided. It reads ALE / xAMENOS / SEBETE / QEON, or so it would seem.[4] If this is the correct construal of the inscription, it can be translated either "Alexamenos, worship God" or "Alexamenos worships God," with the latter being more likely.[5]

---

4. I am working with this rendering of the inscription for this essay. But I find the last word very problematic. The third letter could be read as a *W*; the last letter is poorly etched, being three times larger than the other letters on this line and quite different from the N on the second line. The *E* is also ill formed. All this leads to the conclusion that the last word in the inscription should be carefully reexamined. Might the last word originally have been a form of IAO that was later reworked? This would involve revisiting treatments of the letter *U* in light of recent treatments of magical amulets using divine names and such passages as *The Apocryphon of John* (NHC II.1.11), though there Yao is identified with a serpent's head and Eloaiou with an ass's.

5. In Greek the subject and verb do not agree. The latter translation is more easily derived by taking se/bete as an itacism for σέβεται.

Setting

The Alexamenos graffito was discovered in a building[6] probably belonging to the imperial palace complex designed by Domitian's architect Rabirius and completed in 92 CE, with several renovations over the course of the next two centuries and significant expansion under Septimius Severus.[7] Though not enough of the *paedagogium* survives to allow certainty in assessing the full range of its functions, the building's scale, proximity and relation to the palace, and the types of graffiti in its various rooms suggest that it served as living or working quarters (or both) for imperial slaves and freedmen.

Three hundred sixty-nine graffiti from the *paedagogium* survive.[8] The vast majority of them are simply the names (or the fragments of names) of slaves and freedmen who lived or worked in the building. Occasionally, a term related to a profession or geographic origin is appended to the name.[9] In addition, there are some twenty-five drawings, the range of which is rather narrow: palm branches, horses, asses, and various human figures.[10] With regard to the human figures, there are

---

6. Due to the use of the phrase *exit de paedagogio* in several of the graffiti, the building is commonly referred to as a *paedagogium* (school). For discussion, see Solin, *Graffiti*, 72–78. Itkonen-Kaila provides a detailed treatment of the architecture in the same volume, 3–34. For convenience I will use the term *paedagogium* as shorthand for the building.

7. For a survey of the palace complex, see MacDonald, *Architecture of the Roman Empire*, 47–74; for floor plans of the building in which the graffito was found, see Solin, *Graffiti*, 5, 10, and 11. I use Solin's numbering for the rooms and the individual graffiti. His edition includes a chart correlating his numbers with earlier versions (263–264). The Alexamenos graffito was removed shortly after discovery and is now in the Palatine Museum. The preserved piece of plaster with the graffito measures 33.5 x 38 cm (13.2 x 15 in).

8. Most of them were found rooms 5, 6, 7, and 8. The Alexamenos graffito was in room 7. Solin identifies three other graffiti which he considers spurious (*Graffiti*, 250–51). One of these (*2) refers to Alexamenos (written in Greek) as "faithful" (in Latin); another (*3) is a chi-rho.

9. For discussion of the names, see Solin, *Graffiti*, 57–67. Interestingly 18 of the 30 names mentioning geography refer to Africa (Latin, *Afer*). Most have a form or abbreviation of *Afer*; some, however, mention a specific city. For a list of the geographic references, see Solin, *Graffiti*, 259.

10. The range of topics is considerably narrower than those in Pompeii, though as Solin points out (46) the *paedagogium* is a relatively confined space, to which only a few had ready access.

gladiators,[11] athletes (?),[12] and isolated heads and busts.[13] Compared to the graffiti at Pompeii, there are remarkably few erotic examples, phalluses being the most common.[14]

Most of the drawings in the *paedagogium* are even more crudely rendered than the figures in the Alexamenos graffito. Two, however, are clearly better in their execution. In the same room as the Alexamenos drawing there is an etching of a horse that is more detailed and aesthetically pleasing.[15] In an adjoining room (8), there is a drawing of an ass turning a millstone that is more competently and realistically rendered.[16] Like the Alexamenos graffito, this one also has an inscription: *labora aselle quomodo ego laboravi/et proderit tibi* ("Work, little ass, as I have worked—and it will go well for you.").[17]

Questioning the Graffito

If we wonder how a graffito admonishing a little ass to work hard ends up in the slave quarters of the imperial palace, how many more questions does the Alexamenos graffito raise in such a context? While its execution accords well with the relatively low artistic standards of the *paedagogium*, what of its content? What of its purpose? Who was its "artist"?[18] Who was his target? What reaction was he trying to effect? And, the question that has exercised historians of early Christian art, what were his precedents?

To some extent, such questions apply to all art—the wall paintings and sculptures Balch has examined, for example. Nor are they significantly different from the questions that drive the exegesis of ancient texts, like the letters of Paul. But in the case of a graffito like the one we are examining here, the questions seem more pointed.

11. Solin, *Graffiti,* numbers 277, 304, 306.
12. Ibid., number 97.
13. Ibid., numbers 228 (?), 71 (?), 300, and 302.
14. Phalluses: Ibid., numbers 92, 96 (?), and 134. Solin finds homosexual references in 121, 230, 232, and 364.
15. Solin, *Graffiti,* number 243.
16. Ibid., number 289.
17. Translations in the essay are my own, unless otherwise indicated.
18. Two of the graffitists refer to themselves as "painters" (298 [an African] and 304). But the term hardly applies to the person who drew the Alexamenos figures. So I use the term artist loosely.

One reason for this is that even though the "artist" who executed it likely had few artistic pretensions, he nonetheless used an artistic form common in Roman urban settings—drawing on walls. Thus, though crudely drawn, the graffito should not be seen as simple or naïve. Indeed, there are numerous levels of meaning to it and the whole piece works because the artist combined image and word so evocatively and so precisely. One is tempted to say he "nailed it." In contrast to "the little ass" graffito, at any rate, it has considerably more bite (to change metaphors). For whereas the exhortation to work in "the little ass" graffito seems generalized and moralistic, the Alexamenos graffito is more pointedly direct, so that we are almost certainly to see its target as a real person.

Still, the artist who composed the Alexamenos graffito chose to "speak" in a public place—not the forum or marketplace, to be sure, nor even a public street or alley. In fact, it was public in only a narrow sense, since those who frequented the rooms in the *paedagogium* were most likely the artist's fellow laborers—other members of the *familia Cæsaris*. Thus Alexamenos was not the only one who would see the drawing and read the inscription. This makes the question of the artist's purpose all the more acute. Would he have been content to embarrass Alexamenos in the presences of his fellows or was he after some more concrete result? Was the artist exposing Alexamenos, or did everyone know of his religious views? Does the graffito give vent to anger? Frustration? Fear? Was it the product of a private feud or was it commentary on larger social questions? To some extent, answering these questions depends on another—what did the artist know about the iconography he uses in his drawing?[19]

In wrestling with these questions, it is important to remember that the graffito consists of both image *and* word. If all we had were the drawings in this graffito, it would still be significant as the first graphic

---

19. On similar questions related to erotic graffiti, see Richlin, *Garden of Priapus*, chaps. 3-4. For graffiti more generally, see Baird and Taylor, *Ancient Graffiti*, which is appearing too late for consideration here, but promises both theoretical and contextual insight for a closer reading the Alexamenos graffito. I have also found helpful discussions of various forms of satire in the work by Richlin just mentioned; Highet, *Juvenal the Satirist,* chapters 6 and 25 (the latter on Satire 15, which treats Juvenal's view of Egypt and Egyptian animal worship); and Rudd, *Themes in Roman Satire,* chapter 1. Mime, a popular Roman form of entertainment and commentary, also appears in discussions of the Alexamenos graffito. For a provocative (and neglected) essay on this and related issues in early Christian art see, Colwell, "Fourth Gospel."

representation of crucifixion, even if the identify of the figures and their relationship to one another was even more unclear. Likely as not, there would still be numerous references to the graffito in studies of early Christian art and many of the interpretations would be much as they are.[20] As it is, however, the artist was not content simply to draw a scene. He also chose to comment on it, not only by naming the figures but also by identifying the action that is taking place. The artist makes sure that anyone who sees his creation will know:

1. That he has depicted Alexamenos worshiping his god;
2. That Alexamenos's god has the head of an ass; and
3. That this ass-headed god is crucified.

Whatever else the artist may have known (or meant to convey) about Alexamenos and his god, these three things are fundamental. They are what give the graffito its punch.

The Head of an Ass

From early on discussion of the ass-headed figure has focused on claims that Jews and Christians worshiped the head of an ass.[21] Tertullian *Apology* 16.1–3 and *Ad Nationes* 1.14 and Minucius Felix *Octavius* 9.3 are commonly cited as the primary evidence. Minucius Felix has Caecilius report, "I hear that [Christians] worship the head of an ass, the ugliest of animals, and consecrated for I don't know what absurd reason—but appropriate enough for a religion with such morals!"[22] Caecilius's condescending aside links the Christians' worship of an ass's head to all the other immoral acts in which they are

---

20. But not all. The inscription indicates Alexamenos *worships*. It is not clear from the drawing itself, however, that the gesture of the person raising his right hand would have been interpreted as worshiping, since the normal gesture for this was to raise both arms. See Aldrete, *Gestures and Acclamations in Ancient Rome*, 11–13. And note the frequent appearance of the *orans* position in early Christian sepulchral art. Nor is the gesture the same as putting hand to mouth in recognition of the image of a god that Minucius Felix has Caecilius perform when seeing a statue of Serapis (calling it a superstitious practice). See *Octavius* 1.2.

21. For the history of interpretation, see Riemann, "Paedagogium," 2205–6 and Solin, *Graffiti*, 210–12. I will refer to some of the more recent literature here, but cannot undertake a full survey in the space allowed.

22. Minucius Felix, *Audio eos turpissimae pecudis*.

said to take part.²³ But he does not address the origin of the charge or explain it further.

Tertullian's references to the charge that Christians worship the head of an ass are fuller, but enigmatic. In both *Apology* and *Ad Nationes*,²⁴ his defense begins with a statement of the charge: *[S]omniastis caput asininum esse deum nostrum*, "You dream that our God has an asinine head." He then notes that Tacitus is the source of the idea. Tertullian apparently quotes the passage from memory, however, for in his first account he mistakenly refers to *Histories* 4²⁵ and in both alters Tacitus's language. First, in recounting Tacitus's story of the Jews' following "a herd of wild asses" to find water in the desert, he changes *grex asinorum agrestium* to *onagris*.²⁶ Then, referring back to the story of the wild asses to explain Jewish rites in the Temple, Tacitus writes that the Jews "consecrated the image of the animal" (*effigiem animalis . . . sacrevere*) and placed it in their shrine. Tertullian turns Tacitus's phrase into *consimilis bestiae superficiem . . . consecrasse*.²⁷ Finally, when summarizing Tacitus and extending what he had said about Jews to the charges against Christians Tertullian himself is addressing, he uses yet another phrase: Christians and Jews are so closely related, he writes, that according to common opinion they worship "the same image" (*eidem simulacro*). Thus, Tacitus and Tertullian use three separate terms in reference to the "image" supposedly worshiped by Jews and Christians, with none expressly refers to the *head* of an ass.

Moving beyond his treatment of Tacitus, there is yet another layer to Tertullian's consideration of the charge that Christians worship the head of an ass. At the end of *Apology* 16, Tertullian refers to a rumor he has heard regarding a new notion of the Christian god be-

---

23. Caecilius goes through a long list of shameful practices in 9–10. The story of "the Golden Ass," known through the versions of Lucian and Apuleius, illustrates the erotic use of the ass in ancient fiction.

24. Both were written in 197 in Carthage; *Apology* is the more polished of the two accounts and is probably the later version. See Quasten, *Patrology* 2:255–64.

25. Tertullian, *Ad Nationes* 1.14. He correctly identifies Book 5 in *Apology* 16.

26. To be sure, the change is rather insignificant, since both *onager* and *asinus agretsis* refer to a wild ass. Tertullian's term is used in Dan 5:21 LXX, which may have influenced him.

27. Here Tertullian stretches the meaning of *superficies*, whether he takes it as head (extending its meaning as the part of a building extending above ground) or "shell." See the entry in the *OLD*. The latter usage, which is late, at least allows for Glover's translation of it as "image" (LCL).

ing spread abroad in Rome (16.12). A charlatan, he writes, is parading around the city carrying a *pictura . . . cum eiusmodi inscriptione Deus Christianorum Onokoites* ("a picture with the explanatory inscription: 'The God of the Christians, ass-begotten'").[28] Since the inscription is not descriptive, without the picture we have no idea of its image. Fortunately, however, Tertullian does provide a description: *Is erat auribus asininis, altero pede ungulatus, librum gestans et togatus* ("He has the ears of an ass and a hoofed foot, carries a book, and is dressed in a toga."). Here then is evidence that Christians are said to worship the *head* of an ass, though, to be precise, the figure in the picture had only the *ears* of an ass. Furthermore, it had an ass's hoofed foot. Thus, the picture must have represented an essentially human figure with two asinine features. Interestingly, Tertullian also refers to the rumor of this picture in *Ad Nationes* 14, noting details left out of the later version: the charlatan was an apostate Jew; and "the ass-begotten god is proclaimed in all the city *(in tota ciuitate Onocoetes praedicatur)*."[29]

Like Minucius Felix, therefore, Tertullian makes the claim that Christians were reviled for worshiping the head of an ass. For our purposes, however, Tertullian is more useful, since he plays with language of representation, beginning with general terms for "images" and ending with an explicit reference to a *pictura*. We also have Tertullian's description of the picture and his report that it was being paraded around Rome in the last decade of the second century. It seems, therefore, that the Alexamenos graffito was not unique, at least with regard to the representation of the Christian god as a human form with asinine features.

Interestingly, Tertullian never mentions Josephus, the other major source for the claim that Jews worshiped the head of an ass. Josephus warrants attention, however, since there are aspects of his story that pertain to the Alexamenos graffito, filling in some of what is missing from Minucius Felix and Tertullian. Josephus writes of the charge that Jews worship the head of an ass in his address *To Apion*,

---

28. Tertullian, *Onokoites* is a difficult term. I have used Glover's translation here, but rendered *eiusmodi* as "explanatory" (literally, "of the same sort") to suggest the close relationship between the picture and the inscription. I wonder, moreover, if *onokoites* is Tertullian's imaginative translation of whatever term appeared on the placard he had heard about, perhaps playing off of Paul's ἀρσενοκοῖται in 1 Cor 6:9.

29. The phrase could also mean that the picture of the *onocoetes* was *displayed* throughout the city.

stating that Apion had learned of it from Mnaseas of Patara and, perhaps, Posidonius and Apollonius Molon.[30] In an examination of "Ass-Worship" in his extended treatment of Greek, Roman, and Egyptian attitudes toward Jews in antiquity, Peter Schäfer has called Josephus's understanding of Apion into question, not with regard to the charge *that* Jews worshiped (the head of) an ass but with regard to Apion's source for it. His argument is more detailed than I can treat here, since it examines the whole range of ancient sources and recent attempts to interpret them. But his final conclusion is worth noting. Schäfer argues that prior to Apion, there is no explicit reference to Jews worshiping the head of an ass, and only the most general attempts to link Jews and ass-worship. He points out that according to Diodorus Siculus's account Antiochus IV Epiphanes entered the Temple in Jerusalem and discovered "the marble statue of a heavily bearded man seated on an ass." Schäfer suggests Diodorus is not concerned with the ass at all but with Moses "who is responsible for the strange Jewish law and who is depicted in the Temple sitting on an ass."[31] This is quite different from Apion's account, which states that Jewish worship of the head of an ass was revealed when Antiochus entered the Temple and found "the head [of an ass], made of gold and worth a high price."[32] Thus, Schäfer argues, "it was none other than Apion himself who gave the story its peculiar tone and thereby invented the fable of Jewish ass-worship. He may have had an Egyptian source on some connection of the Jews with Typhon-Seth and the ass, but the sharp anti-Jewish bias with its emphasis on the absurdity of actually *worshipping* an ass may well have been his invention and therefore belong to the milieu of the Alexandrian anti-Semites."[33]

30. For the reference to Josephus's use of Mnaseas, see Jos. *C. Ap.* 2.112–14; for Posidonius and Apollonius, see Jos. *C. Ap.* 2.79–80.

31. Since Schäfer accepts the view that Diodorus was dependent on Posidonius and argues that his account must have echoed Posidonius's, he rejects the notion that Posidonius could have been a source for Apion. *Judeophobia*, 58. The quotation is from the LCL translation as cited by Schäfer, 59.

32. Josephus, *C. Ap.* 2.80. I cite the LCL translation as quoted by Schäfer, *Judeophobia*, 60.

33. Schäfer, *Judeophobia*, 60–61. For Schäfer's arguments concerning "the Alexandrian anti-Semites," see chapter 8. He deals with Egypt more broadly in chapter 9. Schäfer's treatment of Tacitus (*Judeophobia*, 61–62) is less satisfying, since he fails to explain how the *effigies animalis* in Tacitus's account of Antiochus's entry to the Temple could have derived from Apion. Still, Schäfer is probably correct in ar-

Locating the notion of Jewish (and Christian) ass-worship in the anti-Semitism of Alexandria (and Egypt more broadly) opens other avenues for our consideration of the Alexamenos graffito. The first is admittedly tenuous, but still worth noting. As mentioned above, a significant number of references to Africa shows up in the graffiti in the *paedagogium* on the Palatine Hill.[34] Although the artist of the Alexamenos graffito does not sign his name and thus there is no way of knowing whether he is among those who identify themselves as an African in any of the other graffiti, the presence of such a strong anti-Semitic element to his drawing makes a connection to Alexandria (or at least to Egypt) worth considering.

A Crucified God

The second avenue is a possible link between Alexandria and one of the most insightful critics of Judaism and Christianity in antiquity—Celsus. Here, too, the link is somewhat tenuous, for Celsus's identity and origin are uncertain. But there is much to be said for Henry Chadwick's comments in support of Alexandria as his home.[35] And if he is right about the dating of *The True Doctrine* (177–180), we have another anti-Semitic voice pointedly dealing, in part at least, with one of the Alexamenos graffito's primary concerns, the absurdity of a crucified god. Even if the African/Egyptian/Alexandrian connection does not hold, however, Celsus still warrants careful consideration because of the concerns he shares with the Alexamenos artist.

Celsus does not deal with the claim that Jews and Christians worship an ass—in any form. So we cannot link him to the Alexamenos graffito on that score. The only reference to anything approximating the head of an ass (or ass-worship) is in 6.30, where he describes "the seven archontic daemons" who are doorkeepers to the heavens. The seventh of these, Celsus says, "has the face of an ass, and . . . is called

---

guing that "[i]t is the [Jew's] mocking of the Egyptian cult which is the focal point of [Tacitus's] passage," showing Jewish disrespect for other religious traditions. The quotation is on page 62. Note also Schäfer's admission on page 168 that Artaxerxes III Ochus (who captured Egypt in 343 BCE) worshiped the ass associated with Seth.

34. See n. 9 above.

35. Chadwick, trans. *Origen: Contra Celsum*, xxiv–xxix. But his treatment of Celsus's theology (xvi–xxii) is also important in placing him geographically as well as intellectually.

Thaphabaoth or Onoel."[36] He returns to the doorkeepers in 7.40, where he writes bitingly: "It is because of such gross deceit and those wonderful counselors and the miraculous words addressed to the lion and the animal with double form and the one shaped like an ass and the other superhuman doorkeepers, whose names you poor unfortunates have wretchedly learnt by heart so that terrible madness has taken hold of you, . . . that you are crucified."[37]

This is not an attack on ass-worship; nor is it an attack on the Christian notion of God, at least directly. But it does introduce us to Celsus's concern with crucifixion, which is one of his points of attack on Christian belief and practice. The range of Celsus's attack on Christian attention to crucifixion is broad. At times the ridicule can be sharp, but humorous. In 6.34, for example, he writes, "And everywhere [Christians] speak in their writings of the tree of life and of resurrection of the flesh by the tree—I imagine because their master was nailed to a cross and was a carpenter by trade. So that if he had happened to be thrown off a cliff, or pushed into a pit, or suffocated by strangling, or if he had been a cobbler or stonemason or blacksmith, there would have been a cliff of life above the heavens, or a pit of resurrection, or a rope of immortality, or a blessed stone, or an iron of love, or a holy hide of leather."[38]

More substantively, he argues that Christian claims that Jesus's suffering and death on the cross were predicted by Jewish prophets signify nothing (7.14). "[T]he prophets could not have foretold this. For it is wicked and impious." He continues: "So we should not consider either whether they did or whether they did not foretell it, but whether the act is worthy of God and is good. And we should disbelieve what is disgraceful and evil, even if all men should seem to predict it in a state of frenzy. How, then, is it anything but blasphemy to assert that the things done to Jesus were done to God." If Jesus had been a god, Celsus writes (here in the name of a Jewish critic of Christianity), "he ought, in order to display his divinity, to have disappeared suddenly from the cross." (2.68) As it is, (now writing from his own perspec-

36. Origen of course dismisses this line of attack by saying it does not apply to true Christians but to Ophites. All translations from *Contra Celsum* are Chadwick's.

37. On the lacuna, see Chadwick, trans., *Origen: Contra Celsum*, 428 n. 2.

38. As Wilken observes, Origen did not see the humor in this passage (*Christians*, 96). By comparison, note that Tertullian laughs at the *pictura* of the Christian god on display in Rome (*Apology* 16).

tive) Christians "worship not a god, nor even a daemon, but a corpse" (7.68).

The crucifixion of their god is not all that Celsus ridicules in his assessment of the Christians. Indeed, it was only one of several epicenters of his critique; he weighed in on almost every aspect of Christian belief and practice.[39] I emphasize it here to show that Celsus and the Palatine artist held in common the view that the notion of a crucified god was preposterous and that he and his followers were fitting targets of ridicule. One aspect of their view was doubtless the shame of the cross, which has been the focus of many treatments of the Alexamenos graffito and of the absence of the crucifixion (and cross) in early Christian art.[40] Celsus mentions it explicitly and it would certainly have contributed to the intended effect of the graffito. Tertullian's picture also strikes at the center of Christian notions of themselves and their god by joining the parody of ass-worship with the mocking of intellectual pretensions (the book) and aspirations to status (the toga).

Toward a Conclusion

But while the intent to shame Christians may be a sufficient explanation of Tertullian's picture, it does not sufficiently explain the point of Celsus's attack and the Alexamenos graffito.[41] For both of these the target of the ridicule is worship of a crucified god. Celsus clearly has a more sophisticated, or a least a more comprehensive, delineation of the issues. He is intent on defending the notion of "the highest God" of the philosophical (and elitist) tradition.[42] Whether the Palatine artist had such an intent, we can never know. But in some respects his

39. For an overview, see Wilken, *Christians*, chap. 5.

40. The classic treatment of crucifixion is Hengel, *Crucifixion*, though there is a growing number of more recent studies, most notably Chapman, *Ancient Jewish*. Two recent contributions to the discussion from different, and very promising perspectives are Conway, *Behold the Man* and Sheckler and Leith, "Crucifixion Conundrum." In addition to Balch's comments on the reticence of Christians to use the cross/crucifixion in art in the two essays mentioned above, see especially Mathews, *Clash of Gods*; and Finney, *Invisible God*. Jensen, *Understanding Early Christian* and *Face to Face*, surveys the issues and offers significant insight into resolving them.

41. Nor do I think it is sufficient to address the larger question about Christian avoidance of the cross in art. But I cannot address this here.

42. See Chadwick's comments in *Contra Celsum*, xvi–xxii and Wilken, *Christians*, chapter 5.

grasp of the issues was as perceptive as Celsus's—and it may have been more poignantly presented. His graffito, at any rate, has generated a thousand words many times over.

At a turning point in Celsus's argument in *The True Doctrine,* he moves from his purported Jewish attack on Christianity to his own by noting that "Christians and Jews quarrel with one another very foolishly," making his point with reference to a proverb about "the shadow of an ass." The proverb means, he writes, "there is nothing worthy of attention in the dispute of Jews and Christians."[43] As he himself demonstrated, however, the Jewish-Christian debate was about more than *whether* the prophesied savior had come. It also involved Christian claims of who he was and what he did. And as Celsus's detailed critique shows, he regarded these claims as worthy of considerable attention. The charge that Jews and Christians worshiped the head of an ass means that Celsus's reference to the shadow of an ass may be read differently than what he meant and that the ass actually cast quite a long shadow.

---

43. Chadwick, trans., *Origen: Contra Celsum* 3.1.

Bibliography

Aldrete, Gregory S. *Gestures and Acclamations in Ancient Rome*. Ancient Society and History. Baltimore: Johns Hopkins University Press, 1999.
Baird, J. A., and Clair Taylor, editors. *Ancient Graffiti in Context*. Routledge Studies in Ancient History 2. New York: Routledge, 2011.
Balch, David L. "The Suffering of Isis/Io in Paul's Portrait of Christ Crucified (Gal 3:1): Frescoes in Pompeiian and Roman Houses and in the Temple of Isis in Pompeii." *JR* 83 (2003) 24–55.
Balch, David L., and Carolyn Osiek, editors. *Early Christian Families in Context: An Interdisciplinary Dialogue*. Religion, Marriage and Family. Grand Rapids: Eerdmans, 2003.
Chapman, David W. *Ancient Jewish and Christian Perceptions of Crucifixion*. Grand Rapids: Baker Academic, 2010.
Coleman, K. M. "Fatal Charades: Roman Executions Staged as Mythical Enactments." *JRS* 80 (1990) 44–47.
Colwell, E. C. "The Fourth Gospel and the Struggle for Respectability." *JR* 14 (1934) 286–305.
Conway, Colleen M. *Behold the Man: Jesus and Greco-Roman Masculinity*. Oxford: Oxford University Press, 2008.
Ferris, Iain. "Suffering in Silence: The Political Aesthetics of Pain in Antonine Art." *JCA* 1 (2005) 67–92.
Finney, Paul Corby. *The Invisible God: The Earliest Christians on Art*. New York: Oxford University Press, 1994.
Hengel, Martin. *Crucifixion*. Translated by John Bowden. Philadelphia: Fortress, 1977.
Highet, Gilbert. *Juvenal the Satirist: A Study*. A Galaxy Book. New York: Oxford University Press, 1961.
Jensen, Robin Margaret. *Understanding Early Christian Art*. London: Routledge, 2000.
———. *Face to Face: Portraits of the Divine in Early Christianity* Minneapolis: Fortress, 2005.
MacDonald, William L. *The Architecture of the Roman Empire*. Vol. 1, *An Introductory Study*. 2 vols. Rev. ed. Yale Publications in the History of Art. New Haven: Yale University Press, 1982.
Mathews, Thomas F. *The Clash of Gods: A Reinterpretation of Early Christian Art*. Princeton: Princeton University Press, 1993.
Origen. *Contra Celsum*. Translated with an Introduction and Notes by Henry Chadwick. Cambridge: Cambridge University Press, 1965.
Quasten, Johannes. *Patrology*. Vol. 2. Christian Classics. Louisville: Westminster John Knox, 1984.
Richlin, Amy. *The Garden of Priapus: Sexuality and Aggression in Roman Humor*. New Haven: Yale University Press, 1983.
Riemann, Hans. "Paedagogium Palatini." In *PW* 18.1 (1942) 2205–18.
Rudd, Niall. *Themes in Roman Satire*. Norman: University of Oklahoma Press, 1986.
Schäfer, Peter. *Judeophobia: Attitudes toward the Jews in the Ancient World*. Cambridge: Harvard University Press, 1997.

Sheckler, Allyson Everingham, and Mary Joan Winn Leith. "The Crucifixion Conundrum and the Santa Sabina Doors." *HTR* 103 (2010) 67–88.

Solin, Heikki, and Marja Itkonen-Kaila. *Graffiti del Palatino*. Vol. 1, *Paedagogium*. Edited by V. Väänänen et al. Acta Instituti Romani Finlandiae 3. Helsinki: Helsingfors, 1966.

Spier, Jeffrey. *Picturing the Bible: The Earliest Christian Art*. New Haven: Yale University Press, 2007.

Wilken, Robert L. The *Christians as the Romans Saw Them*. New Haven: Yale University Press, 1984.

SECTION TWO

Constructing the Visual World

16

Constructing the Spaces of Epiphany in Ancient Greek and Roman Visual Culture

JOHN R. CLARKE

WHAT DOES IT MEAN WHEN A BELIEVER "SEES" A DEITY AND THE DE-
ITY "sees" him or her? Like the ancient Greeks, we call the appearance of the divinity "epiphany."[1] However, we lack an adequate word for the other side of the equation, that is, the believer's reception of the divinity's gaze—and the effects of that reception. The Sanskrit word *darśan* best encompasses the experience of the divinity's gaze, and the continuity of the tradition of seeking and receiving *darśan* best in modern Hinduism helps us understand ancient Mediterranean behaviors in regard to seeing and being seen by the gods.[2] My current project investigates the ways that visual representation encodes this reciprocal visual and spiritual exchange between human worshiper and divinity.[3] I use the term "visual representation" rather than "art," "works of art," and "visual art," because there is a whole range of visual phenomena not covered by our contemporary conception of "art." We tend to think that ancient visual art is what we display in museums or the buildings and objects we see when we visit an archaeological site. The sculptures, paintings, ceramics, and other objects that have come down to us constitute relatively permanent visual representations, whereas an ancient believer saw many impermanent representations created to open him or her to communication with the deity. These included the

---

1. Particularly useful for the definition and range of *epiphany*: Marinatos and Shanzer, "Divine Epiphanies."

2. Eck, *Darśán*.

3. Clarke, *Seeing Gods*, forthcoming.

visual phenomena associated with pilgrimage, processions, pageants, religious rites, theatrical performances, and much more.

Indeed, consideration of these myriad visual representations opens the question of their location within a larger matrix. It is the aggregate of visual experiences of individuals and groups in a community that constitute what we call visual culture. In this essay I concentrate on the ways that architecture, considered broadly as the construction or framing of place, not only locates epiphany but also sets out the rules of engagement for both the devotee and the deity.

Pilgrimage

First we must consider the locations of epiphany. Pausanias's *Periegesis*, as a kind of pilgrimage journal, reminds us that to communicate with the deity one must go to the place he or she has chosen to bless with his or her presence. Jaś Elsner and Ian Rutherford, editors of an excellent collection of essays on ancient pilgrimage, address the problems surrounding the term even while proposing a typology of ancient Greek, Roman, Jewish, and Christian pilgrimage from earliest times to the fourth century CE.[4] Particularly fitting for our exploration of epiphany here are their questions about the identity of the pilgrim, what the pilgrim does at the sanctuary, and his or her motivation.

Along her path the pilgrim, prompted by sacred texts, songs, priests, and the activities of other devotees, seeks signs of the deity in the configurations of mountains, cliffs, valleys, and rivers -in a word, in the landscape. Vincent Scully is one of the few modern scholars to examine fully the connections between the sacred landscape and the temple in the ancient Mediterranean, with special emphasis on Greece. His central hypothesis is that ancient people first recognized and worshipped the deity as inhabiting a striking landscape feature, then later built a temple.[5] The ways to these sacred places, as well as the connections between one sanctuary and another, imprint themselves upon the devotees. These paths constitute a psychomotor stimulus that prepares the devotee for the vision of the deity. The way to the place is, in this sense, part of the epiphanic experience.

---

4. Elsner and Rutherford, *Pilgrimage*, 1–30.
5. Scully, *Earth, the Temple*.

Mysterious, wondrous places reveal themselves slowly, as the pilgrim takes one of several well-trodden paths to the sacred spot. On the way to the oracle of Delphi, marvelous natural features, like the Castalian Spring, or the view from the platform of the sanctuary of Athena *Pronaia*, "spoke" to the believer of the wonders of the gods both through their own beauty and through the rituals performed there.[6] Once the devotee reached the sanctuary, he entered the *temenos* and began to climb the Sacred Way (see figure 16.1).

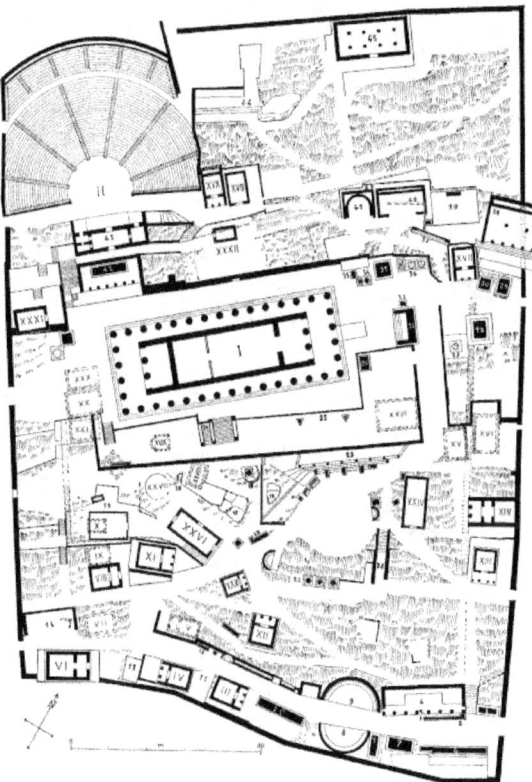

Figure 16.1: Delphi, Sanctuary of Apollo, plan. Drawing by the author.

6. Ibid., 109–10.

This approach was always sacred, even well before the city-states built their treasuries and other impressive monuments, for its main purpose was to convey the pilgrim to the rocky platform perched up against the cliff formed by the twin peaks of the Phaedriades, the "Shining Ones" (see figure 16.2).

Figure 16.2: Delphi and the Phaedriades.
Photo by Michael Larvey.

It was the cleft in this platform beneath the temple that emitted the vapors that inspired the oracle. The various forms of the Temple of Apollo itself, as well as the sanctuary and Theater of Dionysus, constitute built responses to this amazing natural landscape of oracle. The architects sited the temple and created forms that would both complement and oppose the mass of the Phaedriades at Delphi.

At Delphi, as at other great sanctuaries, the primary epiphany of the deity was the sight of the sacred landscape that first evoked him or her, long before the architectural elaboration of the sanctuary. Sacrifice on ash-cone altars, and later festivals as well as athletic and theatrical contests celebrated that Ur-epiphany. These human actions in the sacred landscape gave the deity his or her particular flavor or quality, expressed in epithet: the Ephesian Artemis, the Olympian Zeus, the Pythian Apollo, and so on. Striking landscape configurations themselves constituted or manifested the presence of the deity.

Mystery, Oracular, and Healing Epiphany

If the Greeks built temples as both markers of the presence of the deity in the sacred landscape and as the embodiment of the god or goddess him/herself, it is because they thought of the temple building as a prismatic solid, each stone, each tightly-spaced column a part of the deity.[7] Anyone who has contemplated the god-sized steps of a well-preserved temple, like those at Paestum, feels the power of the stone masses, pushing the mortal back from entry. The spaces of the temple are first and foremost for the deity alone; at Olympia we read that the head of Phidias's statue of Zeus seemed to graze the ceiling.[8] The viewing of such a powerful, sacred image was a special experience, temporally and ritually limited.[9]

Spaces for oracles and healing cults are a different matter; architects construct them to create the ritual paths of devotees seeking more intimate contact with the deity. Such buildings take us from the simple siting of the temple in relation to the deity's command of the natural landscape to inner landscapes of surprising complexity. Even

---

7. Kaschnitz-Weinberg, *Mittelmeerische Grundlagen*.

8. Frazer, *Pausanias* 3:530–36.

9. By Pausanias's time, in the mid-second century CE, access to the cella of this and other temples to view famous works of art had become routine.

so, there is a much larger scholarly literature concerning the texts that record the oracles given or the cures received than on the construction and use of these spaces.

At times the texts suggest answers to questions surrounding the built form. Excavations of the building housing the Mysteries of Demeter at Eleusis, in sharp contrast to the exteriority of the canonical Greek temple, was a huge interior space (about 177 by 177 feet), a veritable forest of columns of square plan (see figure 16.3).

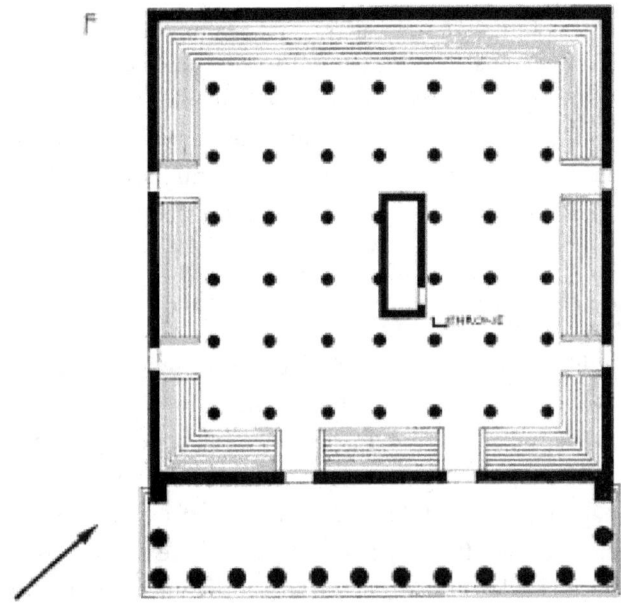

Figure 16.3: Eleusis, Sanctuary of Demeter, plan. Drawing by the author.

Flights of eight steps, like those of a theater, lined the interior walls; six gangways cut through the steps.[10] Recently Kevin Clinton has reconstructed the staging of the epiphany at Eleusis. The culminating experience of the Eleusinian Mysteries was the revelation to the initiates of an extraordinary and unforgettable light. Clinton has shown how the built forms, as far as we can know from modern excavations, accommodated this epiphany.[11]

10. Berve and Gruben, *Greek Temples*, 399–404.
11. Clinton, "Epiphany," 85–101.

The oracular sanctuary of Apollo at Didyma enshrined a venerable holy place. There, as at Delphi, flowed a spring whose waters inspired prophecy, and Apollo's sacred bush, the laurel, was worshipped there. A processional way, a little over eight miles long, connected the sanctuary with Miletus, its patron city. We know little of the original temple, destroyed in 494 BCE, and it is not until the oracle prophesied Alexander's future victory (331 BCE) that the sanctuary began to be rebuilt on a grand scale that rivaled its most splendid competitors, the Artemesium at Ephesus and the Heraeum at Samos. It never reached completion, despite extravagant patronage—even by the emperor Hadrian. It measured 358 by 167 feet, and its high platform of seven steps carried a double peristyle of 108 columns, each over 64 feet tall (see figure 16.4).

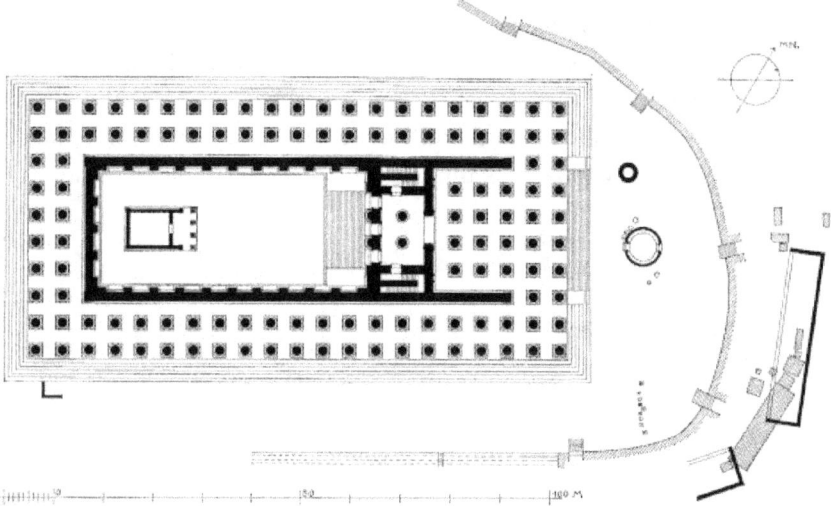

Figure 16.4: Didyma, Temple of Apollo, plan.
Drawing by the author.

The peristyle enclosed a huge court, fifteen feet below the level of the temple platform and enclosed by high walls. It was there that the spring, the laurel grove, and a small temple with the archaic cult statue of Apollo were to be found—all in open air.

A stairway on axis with the ancient ash cone altar guided the devotee into this columnar forest. In the hot months its deep shade and coolness vividly contrasted with the sharp light and baking heat of the flat plain that it occupies. A first-time visitor had little clue where to go as he entered this virtual forest, save for the knowledge that in most temples the colonnade preceded the fore-temple (*pronaos*), always placed on the central axis of the building. At Didyma, the long arms of the *pronaos*, filled with twelve columns, cast the devotee even deeper into the shade. Normally the cella, home of the cult image, lay at the back of the *pronaos*. But not so at Didyma, where in place of the cella a visitor found a tall doorway (18 1/2 x 46 feet) opening to a hall with two columns, completely inaccessible because its sill was nearly five feet above the pavement. Was it from this doorway that Apollo spoke through his priests to the crowd assembled in the *pronaos*?[12] It seems likely that the faithful saw sacred tableaux or pantomimes here; twin staircases concealed behind the walls at either side of the hall lead to the roof. The stairways, called "labyrinths" in the inscriptions, their ceilings decorated with meanders, may have allowed cult functions to extend to the roof.

Those permitted to enter the huge court behind had to find their way to one of the long, dark tunnels that led down to the inner area of the temple (see figure 16.5).

---

12. The jambs of this "door of manifestation" were 46 feet long and weighed some 70 tons, the biggest monoliths to have been set in position in antiquity: Berve and Gruben, *Greek Temples*, 469.

Figure 16.5: Didyma, Temple of Apollo, view of corridor. Photo by Ufuk Soyoz

After experiencing the darkness of porch and tunnel a devotee's eyes must have been blinded by the burst of light that revealed the huge courtyard, open to the sky. At the rear of this hypaethral space was the goal of her journey: a small freestanding temple housing the cult statue of Apollo. Yet even here the devotee's expectations were reversed. It was in turning her back to the temple that Apollo presented himself yet again—and here we can only conjecture what forms this apparition took (see figure 16.6).

Figure 16.6: Didyma, Temple of Apollo, view of stairway from west. Photo by Michael Larvey.

A huge stairway rises up from the depths of the courtyard's pavement to reveal the other side of the two-columned hall with its door of apparition facing the front porch. Here, on the courtyard side, the hall opens the full width of the stairway, providing a bigger and more brightly lit stage. If this space housed the actual oracular process, as some scholars have proposed; or if it was a space for performance of rituals beyond the usual sacrifices that would be offered before the cult statue in its little temple below, we cannot know. What is clear is that the architects, working at a huge scale and with equally large budgets, were charged to create an experience of disorientation, mystery, and surprise. Scholars have studied the oracles written by temple priests and handed to the faithful for their social and political content.[13] Yet if we look at the remains of the huge temple and the unusual layout of its spaces, we begin to understand what an ancient devotee might have experienced while seeking the epiphany of Apollo.

The surviving elements in the architecture of the sanctuary of Asklepios at Pergamon suggest that a devotee seeking the blessings of the god would have experienced similarly disorienting visual and

13. Fontenrose, *Didyma*; Oesterheld, *Göttliche Botschaften*.

motor stimuli—but this time within a regimen aimed at healing (see figure 16.7).

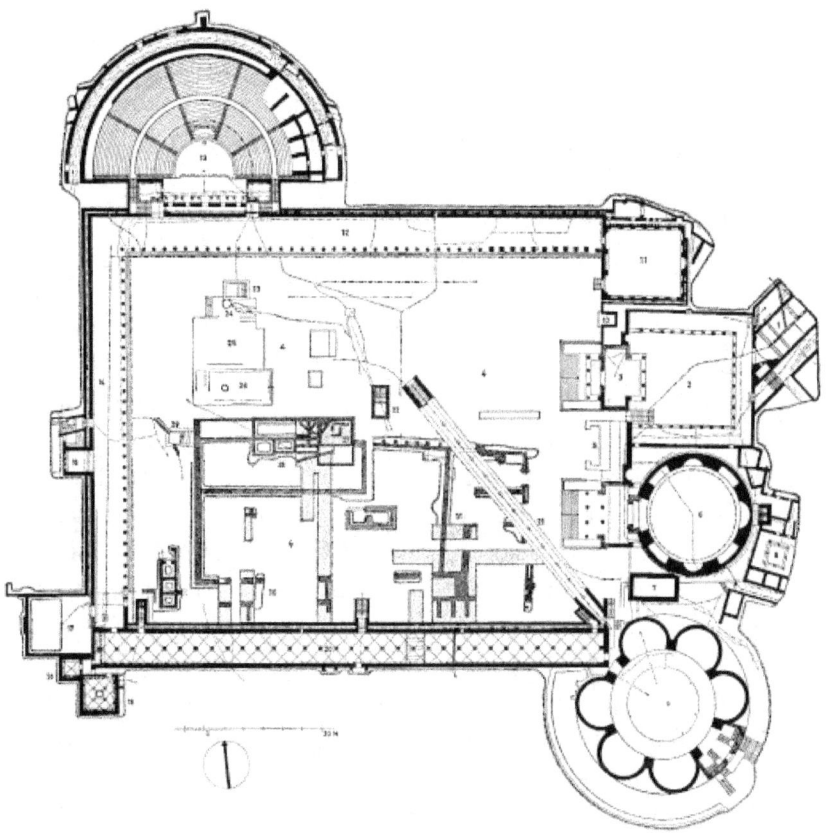

Figure 16.7: Aisklepieion at Pergamon, plan. Drawing by the author.

Alexia Petsalis-Diomidis emphasizes that the prescribed behaviors as set forth in the *lex sacra* of the Asklepieion constituted a way of ordering the bodies of the pilgrims through ritual and choreography. The *lex sacra* specifies the nature of offerings as well as the time and place to make them, mentioning specific cult statues and altars. It mandated dress codes, abstinence from certain foods and from sex, as well as a communal religious procession before the night of incubation.[14] If

---

14. Petsalis-Diomidis, "Body in Space," 198–204.

we put these costumed processions and rites performed before cult statues and at altars back into the spaces of the sanctuary, we begin to appreciate how the architecture framed rituals that orchestrated the desired epiphany: the appearance of Asklepios to the suppliant in his or her dream.

Although a rather modest sanctuary at its foundation in the beginning of the fourth century BCE, under the patronage of Antoninus Pius (138–161 CE) it took on a grand scale. Stoas defined the ceremonial square, now measuring 362 x 497 feet, on the north, west, and south sides, while symmetrical temple fronts masked surprising forms behind them on the east: a great propylon (2) leading to the sacred way that linked the Asklepieion with the city and a rotunda, a reduced scale-model of the Pantheon housing the cult statue of Asklepios (6). Behind the northern stoa was yet another surprise: an elegant theater capable of hosting 3,500 spectators. The most unusual building is the elegant rotunda with six apses (called by archaeologists the "Pump-room" or the *Kursaal*, 9) set into the southeast corner of the complex.[15] Although all of the structures of the Asklepieion deserve analysis in terms of their ability to induce epiphanic experience, one is particularly evocative. It is the tunnel leading from the apsidal rotunda (9) to the area of the ceremonial square housing the core of the old sanctuary: the two Hellenistic temples (25 and 26) and the incubation complex (27 and 28). At the southeast corner of the plan two stairways provide access to the underground passage, while a single, grand stairway concludes its course and leads up to the level of the ceremonial square. The configuration of the tunnel suggests that it may have allowed the sudden "apparition" of priests, actors, or even images of the god—seemingly from nowhere. The audience for these epiphanies, whether at Eleusis or in the Pergamene Asklepieion, was the devotees; they would have been familiar with such staged epiphanies not only in sacred settings but also in the theater. We can imagine a devotee seeing sacred dramas enacted in the theater attached to the Asklepieion and then re-enacted within the sanctuary itself as part of the rituals of healing.

The architectural language of the Asklepieion, leading devotees from open spaces through dark passageways and into enclosed geometries encouraged and prompted the god's appearance. Even more so the cult statues themselves. The god's image would have been burned

---

15. See Soyoz, "Paths to Ritual Dreams."

into the devotee's brain, especially if we consider that she had come on pilgrimage, been fasting, taken part in long rituals and processions, and had probably endured a regimen of drugs and perhaps even bloodletting, as described in the written sources. Visual representations of the Asklepios himself, as well as many related deities, were everywhere. They prompted epiphany both in the dream state and in waking, to judge from the accounts of Aelius Aristides and others.[16] As Fritz Graf has noted, the distance between the statue of a god and the epiphany of that god is "shorter than we think." Artemidorus, in his *Dream Book*, reminds us that to dream of a statue of a god was equivalent to dream of the god (Artemidorus Daldianus *Onirocritica* 2.39).[17] It was not only cult statues accumulating through the long life of the sanctuary that prompted epiphany, but also the countless votives set up in and around the sanctuary. These testimonies to the power of the Asklepios used texts—and often arresting images—to tell the story of a person's experience of the deity. They must have competed for the viewer's attention, considering their often startling visual forms, like the bronze eyes attached to a plaque by Tapari, or the ear plaque of Fabia Secunda.[18] During his sojourn at the sanctuary, a suppliant seeking the god's help would have come to expect the miraculous through what Elsner has called the "ritual viewing" of these votives.[19]

Roman Epiphany: Finding and Losing the Axis

The sanctuary of Apollo at Didyma and the Asklepieion at Pergamon take a fundamentally different approach to the visual culture of epiphany from that of the earlier Greek sanctuaries. No matter how many treasuries and other features crowded the Sacred Way at Delphi, the ultimate architecture was the sacred landscape itself: the steep ascent from the Valley of the Itea to the cliffs of the Phaedriades: Apollo and the Pythia inhabited the place itself as much as they did the successive forms of the temple.[20] A different relationship between devotee and

16. Petsalis-Diomidis, "Body in Space," 208–17.
17. Graf, "Trick or Treat?," 125.
18. Petsalis-Diomidis, "Body in Space," figs. 12–13.
19. See especially his account of the guided reading of the Tabula of Cebes: Elsner, *Art and the Roman*, 39–48.
20. See especially the articles on the topography and features of Delphi in Maass, *Delphi*, 79–110.

divinity had always characterized Roman epiphany and it prompted built forms that situated the deity on the axis of the devotee's gaze even while cueing, containing, and constraining his or her movement.

The late Republican oracular sanctuary of Fortuna Primigenia at Praeneste is an artificial mountain at least 300 feet high.[21] Constructed of vaulted concrete forms that adhere to the natural mountain, it presents an absolutely regular, axially-symmetrical form (see figure 16.8).

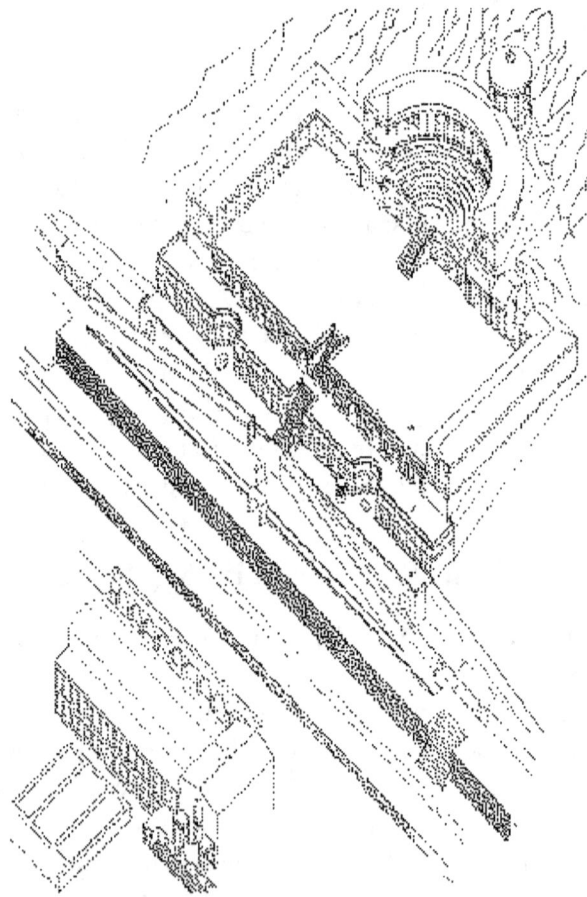

Figure 16.8: Praeneste, Sanctuary of Fortuna Primigenia, axonometric. Drawing by the author.

21. Calculated from the propylon to the lower sanctuary to the level of the road running behind the rotunda of the upper sanctuary, the height is 113 meters, or 370 feet; I give the measurements from the beginning of the upper sanctuary to the road behind the rotunda at 92 meters or 301 feet. See Merz, *Heiligtum der Fortuna*, fig. 17.

Nothing in Greek architecture compares. Closest to it in form is the Sanctuary of Asklepios at Kos with its successive terraces approximately tracing an axial path to the Temple of Asklepios framed by a porticus on the top terrace. What makes the devotee's quest for the Fortuna dramatic is the way that the built forms announce the goddess from the beginning yet set up an arduous path to reach her.

From a distance the pilgrim could see the upper sanctuary, all forms symmetrically arranged to right and left of the dominating "Fortuna axis" that culminated in the tholos that constituted her temple. Yet to reach that epiphany, features of the successive terraces invited her to leave the steep stairs that defined the axis. Even the most steadfast had to veer radically off-axis to climb one of the ramps connecting terrace III with terrace IV. These long tunnels took the viewer from bright light to relative darkness. The "light at the end of the tunnel" was literally the goddess-axis. As the pilgrim climbed under the cover of the ramping barrel vault, the columns that supported it on the outboard side framed views of the countryside below.

Terrace IV, perched about halfway up, pulled the devotee off the axis with the strongest possible magnet: Fortuna herself was framed in front of the right-hand hemicycle. Cicero describes this famous statue of Fortuna Primigenia, as well as the cleft in the rock where Numerius Suffustius found the oak lots (Cicero *De divinatione* 2.41.85–87). Excavators found a plinth for the statue on axis with the hemicycle.[22] The statue showed Fortuna, first-born daughter of Jupiter, as mother: Jupiter and Juno, appearing as babies in her lap, reach for her breast. As both daughter and mother, Fortuna Primigenia was the quintessential goddess of motherhood. Next to the plinth excavators found what looked like a well 25 feet deep. But there was not a drop of water in it, and remains of an elaborate round building around its perimeter led them to identify the "well" as the miraculous cleft.[23] The oak lots with ancient writing needed a proper container; where the temple now stands, Cicero tells us, honey flowed from an olive tree. The devotees made a chest from the olive tree to house the oak lots. Cicero ridicules the believers, certainly not magistrates or people of importance, who hoped that the statue of Fortuna would nod or give some sign. If the

---

22. Kähler, "Fortunaheiligtum," 201–2.
23. Ibid., 202–3, fig. 4.

goddess obliged, the priest would instruct a boy to open the chest and pull out the lot that would answer the suppliant's question.[24]

While on this terrace, a pilgrim would perhaps wish to sacrifice at the altar dedicated to an unknown deity and placed at the matching hemicyle on the west (left-hand) side of the terrace. In fact, as in most Greek and Roman sanctuaries, the devotee prayed and sacrificed to many deities; attested at Praeneste are Jupiter Arcanus, Jupiter Imperator, Juno, Apollo, Hercules, Mater Matuta, and Minerva.[25]

What of the temple mentioned by Cicero that marked the place where the miraculous olive tree stood? To reach it the devotee had to return to the axis and climb to the top of the structure, taking in the many sights, including dramatic views out across the plain such as that provided by terrace VI, measuring 46 x 110 m and the novel space of the theatral area comprising terrace VII (see figure 16.9).

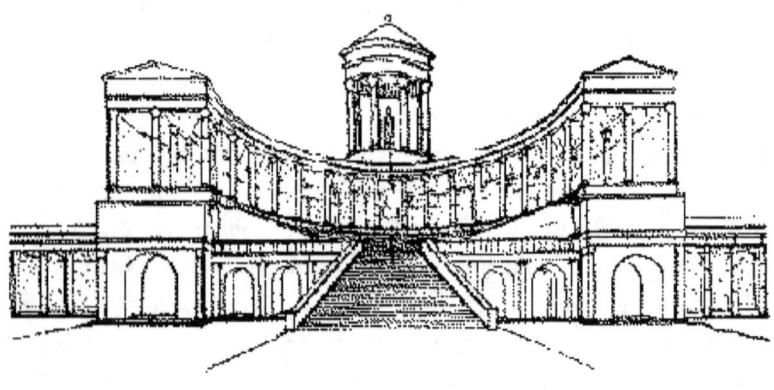

Figure 16.9: Praeneste, Sanctuary of Fortuna Primigenia, view of theatrical area, terrace VII. Drawing by the author.

We do not know exactly how the devotee would have reached the round temple of Fortuna, since modern construction has destroyed evidence, yet it is clear that sight of the goddess in her tholos must have been a welcome reward for the climb. From this point there was

---

24. On inscriptions and dedications, as well, see Suetonius, *Tiberius* 63, see Romanelli, *Palestrina*, 30–31.

25. Romanelli, *Palestrina*, 29.

another reward, especially for the devotee of Fortuna who had visited her shrine at Antium. Looking across the plain on a clear day he could have another epiphany: the axis of the sanctuary at Praeneste seems to have aligned across many miles with the sanctuary of a Fortuna, worshipped as two sisters, the Fortunae Antiates, who also gave oracles by lots.[26]

To the modern visitor, there is something of the tease in the constructed spatio-motor experiences that we can still experience if we climb the sanctuary at Praeneste today. Yet to reconstruct an ancient devotee's subjective feelings, focused as they are upon a mutual exchange of gaze between devotee and deity, we need to dig deeper. Several striking parallels appear in the forms taken by the traditional aristocratic house, the *domus* (see figure 16.10).

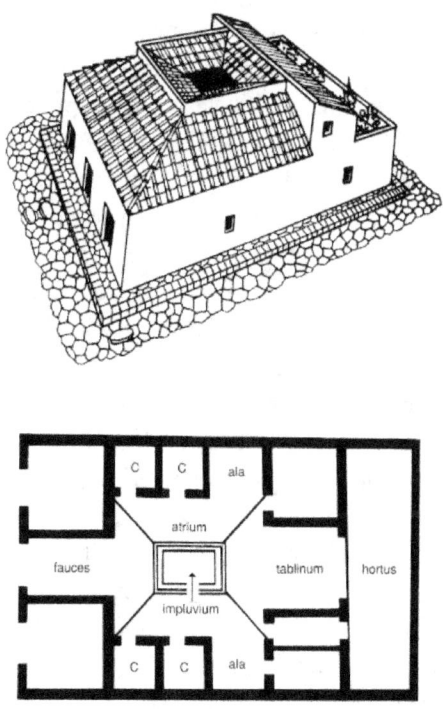

Figure 16.10: Plan of typical atrium house of the third century BCE. Drawing by the author.

26. Ibid., 32; Merz, *Heiligtum der Fortuna*, 17.

Domestic Epiphanies

Scholars have noted that the spatial configuration of the *domus*, by imposing a rigid axis of power between *paterfamilias* and client, relates to similar axial configurations in temples and their precincts.[27] Its principal entry on the street front is a narrow, tunnel-like, ramping space centered on the axis of the house that begins the articulation of a long axis running through the atrium, or central hall, to the *tablinum*, or principal reception space. A downward-sloping roof covered most of the space of the atrium, but the center of the roof was open. The *compluvium*, a square or rectangular opening in the center of the roof of the atrium, funneled rainwater from the roof into a catch basin directly beneath it, called the *impluvium*. A client first sees the focus of his visit, the *paterfamilias* standing in the *tablinum* (see figure 16.11). Although the *paterfamilias* stands on the visual axis as the goal of the "view-through," to reach him the client must veer from that axis in his walk around the *impluvium*.[28] In like fashion, a suppliant approaching the goddess Fortuna Primigenia at Praeneste sees the goal, the round temple of Fortuna, on axis and from afar, but must follow a path that repeatedly loses and finds that axis on the way to the goal.[29]

What of the point of view of the *paterfamilias* standing in the *tablinum*? He is not a deity, yet his position in relation to the client resembles that of the Roman temple, axially positioned in a symmetrical space bounded by its enclosure walls. He is not a cult statue, yet the spaces are analogous. Just as, from the point of view of the faithful, the high temple platform framed the cult image (and priestly activities such as sacrifice and augury), so the *tablinum* defined the seat of power in the *domus*. From the *tablinum* the *paterfamilias* controlled the very axis of entry that manifested his power to his clients. Indeed, the ritual that caused the Romans to structure the *domus* around the *fauces-atrium-tablinum* axis was the *salutatio*, the daily visit by dependents to the *paterfamilias*, their patron (*patronus*). Although the *paterfamilias* is not a deity, his powers, especially the *patria potestas*, are great, and his epiphany, as it were, occurs in an architectural and ritual framework that emphasizes those powers.

27. Clarke, *Houses*, 6.
28. Hales, *Roman House*, 107–13; Drerup, "Bildraum," 145–74.
29. Scully, *Earth, the Temple*, 210–12.

Figure 16.11: House of the Menander, view from fauces.
Photo by Michael Larvey.

It is interesting to note in this connection that a cult image frequently worshiped in domestic rituals represents the powers of the *paterfamilias*.[30] It is the image of the *genius* of the *paterfamilias*, found in domestic shrines to the *Lares*, the twin protector-deities of the household.[31] He is togate, head veiled, and extends a *patera* in his right hand; sometimes, as in the painting from the kitchen of the House of Sutoria Primigenia at Pompeii, the guardian spirit of the *materfamilias*, the *Juno*, appears at his side (see figure 16.12).

Figure 16.12: Pompeii, House of Sutoria Primigenia, room 17, east wall, detail. Photo by Michael Larvey.

---

30. Orr, "Roman Domestic Religion," 1577–91.
31. For Pompeii, see Fröhlich, *Lararien- und Fassadenbilder*.

The sacrifice carried out on appointed days was to the Lares but *also* to the *genius* of the man who conducted the sacrifice. The Lares, aside from their visual representations in paintings and sculptures, are invisible, but the *paterfamilias* is not. Is not the very construction of the shrine, whether under the high roof of the atrium or, as here, in a humble kitchen, not an invitation for the Lares to appear and bless the house? If so, the representation of the *genius* is a different kind of invitation, certainly for the *paterfamilias* himself to recall his great male ancestors who founded his *gens*, (loosely translated "clan") and through whose procreation he stands there, accompanied by the latest representatives of the *gens*—himself included. As he and his *familia* looked at the image that represented the potency of the gens and hopes for its prosperity, did they imagine that they were calling on the *genius* to appear? Did the artist paint or sculpt the *genius* (and the *juno*) to look like the current representatives of the *gens*? As humble as it is, this is yet another space tailor-made for epiphany.

Throughout this essay, my emphasis has been on how architecture and the rituals that it frames encode belief systems. For the ancient viewer the act of looking—whether at the sacred landscape, ritual, or the image of the deity—was also the experience of being looked at. Sacred looking, to be effective, had to be reciprocal, a kind of *darśan*. The creation, use, and contemplation of sacred places and images brought the deity to life so that he or she could bestow benefits upon the faithful. It always was, it seems, a case of *do ut des*. Pilgrimage, prayers, song, choreographed movement, and sacrifices invoked the deity; they temporarily transformed the material of landscape, temple, or image into the deity. When successful, together, they constructed epiphany.

Bibliography

Berve, Helmut, and Gottfried Gruben. *Greek Temples, Theatres, and Shrines.* Translated by Richard Waterhouse. London: Thames & Hudson, 1963.

Clarke, John R. *Houses of Roman Italy, 100 B.C.—A.D. 250: Ritual, Space, and Decoration.* Berkeley: University of California Press, 1991.

———. *Seeing Gods: Epiphany in Ancient Mediterranean Visual Culture,* forthcoming.

Clinton, Kevin. "Epiphany in the Eleusinian Mysteries." *ICS* 29 (2004) 85–101.

Drerup, Heinrich. "Bildraum und Realraum in der römischen Architektur." *RM* 66 (1959) 145–74.

Eck, Diana L. *Darśán: Seeing the Divine Image in India.* 3rd ed. New York: Columbia University Press, 1998.

Elsner, Jaś. *Art and the Roman Viewer: The Transformation of Art from the Pagan World to Christianity.* Cambridge Studies in New Art History and Criticism. Cambridge: Cambridge University Press, 1995.

Elsner, Jaś, and Ian Rutherford, editors. *Pilgrimage in Graeco-Roman Antiquity and Early Christian Antiquity: Seeing the Gods.* Oxford: Oxford University Press, 2005.

Fontenrose, Joseph. *Didyma: Apollo's Oracle, Cult, and Companions.* Berkeley: University of California Press, 1988.

Frazer, J. G., translator and editor. *Pausanias's Description of Greece.* Vol. 3. London: Macmillan, 1898.

Fröhlich, Thomas. *Lararien- und Fassadenbilder in den Vesuvstädten: Untersuchungen zur "volkstümlichen" pompejanischen Malerei.* RMSup 32. Mainz: Von Zabern, 1991.

Graf, Fritz . "Trick or Treat? On Collective Epiphanies in Antiquity." *ICS* 29 (2004) 111–27.

Hales, Shelley. *The Roman House and Social Identity.* Cambridge: Cambridge University Press, 2003.

Kähler, Heinz. "Das Fortunaheiligtum von Palestrina Praeneste." *AUSP* 7 (1958) 189–240.

Kaschnitz-Weinberg, Guido von. *Die mittelmeerischen Grundlagen der antiken Kunst.* Frankfurt: Klostermann, 1943.

Maass, Michael. *Delphi: Orakel am Nabel der Welt. Exh. cat. Badisches Landesmuseum Karlsruhe.* Sigmaringen: Thorbecke, 1996.

Marinatos, Nanno, and Danuta Shanzer. "Divine Epiphanies in the Ancient World." *ICS* 29 (2004) 25–42.

Merz, Jörg Martin. *Die Heiligtum der Fortuna in Palestrina und die Architektur der Neuzeit.* Römische Forschungen der Bibliotheca Hertziana. Munich: Hirmer, 2001.

Oesterheld, Christian. *Göttliche Botschaften für zweifelnde Menschen: Pragmatik und Orientierungsleistung der Apollon-Orakel von Klaros und Didyma in hellenistisch-römischer Zeit.* Göttingen: Vandenhoeck & Ruprecht, 2008.

Orr, David. "Roman Domestic Religion: The Evidence of the Household Shrines." In *ANRW* 2.16.2 (1978) 1577–91.

Petsalis-Diomidis, Alexia. "The Body in Space: Visual Dynamics in Graeco-Roman Healing Pilgrimage." In *Pilgrimage in Graeco-Roman Antiquity and Early*

Christian Antiquity: Seeing the Gods, edited by Jaś Elsner and Ian Rutherford, 183–218. Oxford: Oxford University Press, 2005.

Romanelli, Pietro. *Palestrina*. Naples: Di Mauro, 1967.

Scully, Vincent J. *The Earth, the Temple, and the Gods: Greek Sacred Architecture*. New Haven: Yale University Press, 1962.

Soyoz, Ufuk. "Paths to Ritual Dreams: The Sanctuary of Asklepios at Pergamon—The Design of the Cure Building." In *The Classical World in Medical Terminology*. Department of the Classics, The University of Texas at Austin. Online: http://sites.la.utexas.edu/medterms/greek-and-roman-essential-terms/.

Melancholy, Colonialism, and Complicity

Complicating Counterimperial Readings of Aphrodisias's Sebasteion

HAL TAUSSIG

THE SEBASTEION IN THE ANCIENT CITY OF APHRODISIAS WITH ITS stunning collection of large sculptural reliefs has only within the last two years been placed on permanent exhibition, after more than twenty years in on-site storage. The sculpture collection which now occupies most of the new wing of the Aphrodisias museum lies within a short walk of the ruins of the more than two-story, ninety-meter-long parallel porticos that originally housed the plates. This new complex offers an especially rich ensemble of images from the prodigious sculptural workshops of ancient Aphrodisias and one of the most intact sculptural statements of Greco-Roman Asia Minor.

Even more promising, Aphrodisias's Sebasteion is just in its initial stages of interpretation. Although R. R. R. Smith's series of articles[1] during the 1980s and 90s have provided strong description of the actual plates while they were not available for viewing by wider circles of scholarship or the public, the limited access has certainly inhibited analysis of the impressive sculptural ensemble near its impressive structural home. Smith and the New York University archeological team[2] have made progress in grasping the circumstances of the first century construction of the large structure and its 100-some sculp-

---

1. Smith, "Imperial Reliefs"; Smith, "*Simulacra Gentium*"; Smith, "Archeological Research."

2. New York University's teams have worked at the site since the mid-1960s. Cf. Erim, *Aphrodisias*, for a description of the work in the first three decades.

tural plates. The structure of two parallel extended facades near the entrance of a temple seems to have been built collaboratively in honor of the Julio-Claudian emperors by two local families in two stages about seven years apart in the first half of the first century CE (see figure 17.1).

Figure 17.1: The remnants of the upper storey of the south portico of the Sebasteion with inserted copies of the sculpted reliefs, whose originals now are housed in the adjacent Aphrodisias museum. Photo by H. Taussig.

New Testament Empire Critical Studies and the Sebasteion

Very recently extremely significant study of the Sebasteion has been done by a number of New Testament scholars through an empire critical lens. John Dominic Crossan and Jonathan Reed's *In Search of Paul: How Jesus' Apostle Opposed Rome's Empire with God's Kingdom* discusses the reliefs to illustrate the point made in the book's title. Laura Nasrallah has also reviewed the Sebasteion from a similar point of view, and provided some methodological reflections on the use of architecture as public discourse in the second century.[3] Harry O. Maier's essay on "Barbarians, Scythians, and Imperial Iconography in the Epistle to the Colossians" in *Picturing the New Testament: Studies in Ancient Visual Images* situates the reliefs within Paul Zanker's notion of "visual language" and post-Pauline language. Even the book, *The Historical Jesus in Context*[4] contains an essay by Reed citing this Asia Minor building in reference to Jesus in Galilee.

Davina Lopez has provided perhaps the most sustained examination. In her *Apostle to the Conquered: Reimagining Paul's Mission*, Lopez analyzes a number of images in the Sebasteion through an empire critical lens. She surveys the topics of the Sebasteion's sculptural reliefs and takes note of the prominence of "emperors and members of the imperial family, personifications, military trophies, and several barbarians in various postures of defeat" on the upper story of the south portico.[5] On the lower level of the same portico she highlights mythological images of "a more specifically Roman connotation."[6] And, on the upper story of the northern portico, Lopez shows, there are some fifty figures of "nations that the Romans had conquered[7] and incorporated, from the Callaeci in western Spain to the Judeans and Egyptians in the south."[8]

Lopez concludes:

---

3. Nasrallah, *Christian Responses*.
4. Reed, "Archeological Contributions."
5. Lopez, *Apostle to the Conquered*, 43.
6. Ibid.
7. Contra Smith, "*Simulacra Gentium*," 58–59.
8. Lopez, *Apostle to the Conquered*, 45.

The Sebasteion at Aphrodisias shows that worship of the emperor and imperial dynasty is equated with worship of the imperial victory that generates peace and stability, even (perhaps especially) for relatively wealthy eastern client cities. Victory here is specific to that result awarded following the defeat of various far-flung nations of the inhabited world. While Britannia is a particularly graphic representation of a woman being vanquished, the portico of *ethne* signifies the numbers and variety of peoples who might have endured the same fate. At least, in the Roman imperial imaginary, they are presented as such. The women shown standing in line represent diverse points in a whole world dominated by Roman *imperium*. Thus, there is a consistency and continuity to the representation of conquered territories and peoples being displayed in and on these diverse media.[9]

Lopez's analysis includes a ground-breaking analysis of how gendered imagery in the Sebasteion underlines the dominance of Rome over the conquered peoples. And the book itself goes on to integrate this reading of the Sebasteion and other Roman public art into a larger interpretation of the writings of Paul.

The work of this recent scholarship—along with the new availability of the sculpted reliefs—almost certainly makes the Sebasteion a key Roman monumental example for the ever-growing empire critical field of New Testament study. The extent of the Sebasteion reliefs and site itself, its new accessibility, and the clear insight that this monument to the empire shares an imaginal vocabulary with the New Testament provide an important new focus of scholarship bound to explore more specific dimensions of this Aphrodisias expression. It is in this spirit that I write this essay.

The Specifics of Aphrodisias

In relationship to Roman imperial domination of Asia Minor, Aphrodisias played a relatively unique role. As a result of some prior connections to the Julio-Claudian family, an unclear, yet persistent, shared devotion to Aphrodite, and what appears to have been a geographical attraction, Augustus's affection for the city resulted in both his and his successors' benefaction and the declaration of Aphrodisias as a free

---

9. Ibid., 51.

284 PART TWO: CREATING IMAGES—VERBAL AND VISUAL

city. This meant that the city had intense commercial, religious, and artistic connection to Rome itself, even while being "free" of the many forms of explicit political obligations. Both the growing repute of its sculptural work (because of the quality of sculptors and quantity and quality of nearby quarries) and the nuanced combination of political independence and commercial connections allowed the city to flourish economically in the first and second centuries CE, despite lack of precedent for this and an otherwise undistinguished location.

The Sebasteion itself was neither a central location in the city nor most likely an original art work. It is true that the porticos served as a walkway to a temple of Aphrodite, but they stood at a curious angle and were not particularly close to the forum, the theaters, or governance centers. Some of the sculpture on the porticos is quite accomplished, while other is relatively clumsy. Most observers think that it was a copy of the Fora of Caesar and Augustus in Rome, significant not for its originality,[10] but for its translation of the form and images into a more Greek milieu[11] and a model for later monuments in Asia Minor.[12]

Without in any way disputing the New Testament empire critical projects relative to the Sebasteion, it is also important to note that there is no evidence of any "Christian" presence in Aphrodisias for almost two centuries into the common era. This, of course, does not mean that there were no "Christians" there, since epigraphic evidence of Christians in the first two centuries is nearly non-existent. There is a rather well known epigraphic list of synagogue members in Aphrodisias from around 200. This list contains mention of so-called "God-fearers," and has played a significant role in both on-going discussions of this category and imaginations of 'Christians" at Aphrodisias.

The Relief of Achilles and Penthesilea

Among the many mythological figures represented in these reliefs is a nearly complete plate showing the warrior Achilles carrying the mortally wounded (or dead) queen of Amazons, Penthesilea. Upon even the most cursory examinations this portrait is quite gripping. The

---

 10. Cf. Kuttner, *Dynasty and Empire*, 92–94, and Smith, "*Simulacra Gentium*," 50–77.

 11. Cf. the very detailed case made by Smith in "Imperial Reliefs," 88–138.

 12. Cf. Erim, *Aphrodisias*, 122.

story itself is, of course, dramatic; charting Achilles's saving the Greek army from defeat by Penthesilea and the Trojans to whose aid she had come; and then Achilles's falling in love with her upon her death at his own hands. This story attracted both a number of written versions and a wide range of visual representations from as early as the sixth century BCE. The Sebasteion's portrait is striking in a number of ways. First, uncharacteristically, Penthesilea is larger and more muscular than Achilles. Her body stretches diagonally across the whole plate, dominating the very muscular and large body of Achilles, who is supporting her. Her posture also seems to indicate that she is still living or perhaps just having died, and in any case, evoking the emotional connection of Achilles to her. Her large head with its Amazon hair and cap/helmet claims center stage, as Achilles seems to struggle to hold her. In contrast to most other portraits of the pair, Achilles is not above her. Rather he stares straight into her face. His look is desperate and sad, imaging not the triumph of the Hellenic portraits, but the attachment in the latter part of the story (see figure 17.2).

Figure 17. 2: Photo by H. Taussig

What is this mournful portrait of muscularity and attachment doing in the Sebasteion's ensemble of glorification of the Julio-Claudian imperial dynasty and the submission of the nations to Roman emperors? I propose that it indeed belongs to a point of view in the larger ensemble, which carries significant nuance and reflects the history and positionalities of the colonization of Asia Minor. By this, I do not reject the important advance in the analysis of the Sebasteion's reliefs in empire critical terms. Rather, my aim is to undergird and use the empire critical perspective by showing permutations of life in the Roman empire that do not rely only on oppressor-oppressed categories. This has mostly to do with an acknowledgement of the complex history of colonization of Asia Minor by Greece and Rome. That this portrait of Achilles and Penthesilea, so full of the drama of Greek imposition on Asia Minor, is found in Aphrodisias's Sebasteion cannot be ignored. First of all, Achilles could embody for Aphrodisias both its longer history of submissions to Greece and in the Roman imperial situation of the relief's production Aphrodisias's own connections to dominant Rome. Perhaps even more telling, the long history of Greek and Roman rhetoric against the barbarian Asia Minor places Aphrodisias close to the Amazon Penthesilea.[13]

Aphrodisias, especially as a city that does not have a reputation of its own political strength, knows at some level the force of an argument against its importance in the eyes of the Greeks and the Romans. The beautiful dying Amazon[14] could evoke for Aphrodisias its own mixed sense of alienation, power, and defeat. The cost and irony of being powerful as a city designated as "free" by the Romans could hardly go completely unnoticed by Aphrodisias. In other words, this relief that brings Achilles and Penthesilea together in one picture could serve Aphrodisias's subliminal sense of itself well in its semi-hidden acknowledgement of much gone unspoken. This—especially when this particular sculptural expression is acknowledged—may not really be simply an evocation of Greco-Roman connection and grandeur. Rather, the possibility that this relief reflects the complex melancholy

13. Cf. the extensive case made for this in Kahl, *Galatians Re-imagined*, 31–204.

14. My gratitude to Professor Brigitte Kahl for this insight on the connection between Amazons and Asia Minor. Kahl's work on the public images of imperial Rome and her larger project of "critical reimagination" of the New Testament world through critical analysis of public imperial images is clearly a pivotal new contribution to all of New Testament studies.

of an Asia Minor city at the crossroads of its own colonization and complicity needs to be considered. Rather than see Aphrodisias simply as a Roman tool or ally, the relief allows for a possible hybrid processing of the situation.

In the late 1980s Smith already began to suggest that the Sebasteion had its own version of the grandeur of Rome's empire. In two essays, he lays out the interpretational agenda of Aphrodisias's own Sebasteion in comparison to other grand sculptural projects of the Roman imperium. On the one hand, he recognizes this as perhaps the fullest (although not the earliest) extant example of "something new in Roman art . . . distinctively . . . representing their empire visually."[15] On the other hand, he pays close attention to the way the Sebasteion is a "provincial representation of the emperor," noting that "(t)he Aphrodisias Sebasteion is the first major complex in which this process of adaptation and innovation can be fully analyzed."[16] Although connecting the Sebasteion clearly to the imperial cult and in this way a forerunner of the recent empire critical scholarship, Smith insists on understanding it as a regional work whose "purpose here is to evoke, through a series of its familiar and authorized images, the world of Greek culture and religion, into which the Roman emperors are to be incorporated . . ."[17] As such, he proposes that the Sebasteion "does not . . . constitute a body of propaganda."[18] "Instead, the relief panels as a whole present a detailed and broadly expressed vision of the fortunate position of the Greek world under Roman imperial rule."[19]

Smith, of course, was not in conversation with recent New Testament empire critical studies, and cannot be considered to be taking positions on the issues raised by these scholars. I, however, think that his work can help nuance and (therefore) strengthen such empire critical interest in the Sebasteion. This essay wants to take seriously his regionally-based analysis of the Sebasteion in order to provide the next level of empire critical analysis of the Sebasteion. I find Smith's insight that the Sebasteion exhibits a provincial appreciation of the benefits of Roman imperial rule important, but I wish to refine that conclu-

15. Smith, "Imperial Reliefs," 88.
16. Ibid., 89.
17. Ibid., 97.
18. Ibid., 138.
19. Smith, "*Simulacra Gentium*," 50.

sion in two ways. First, such appreciation needs to take seriously the particularity of Aphrodisias's "free city" status. Second, as noted in this analysis of the Achilles and Penthesilea relief, Aphrodisias's complex position relative to the longer history of both Greek and Roman colonization of Asia Minor needs also to be kept in mind. When these two additional Aphrodisias factors are taken into consideration, new dimensions of regional expression emerge, particularly relative to a complex consciousness that not only appreciates the benefits of Roman rule, but also experiences ambivalence and melancholy about it. Indeed, the loving look for Penthesilea from the murderous Achilles seems to correspond dramatically and hauntingly to the complexities of affection, resentment, regret, and honor that Aphrodisias must have experienced as it acknowledged the "favor" Rome had dispensed on this city in Asia Minor.

A Second Look at the Sebasteion's Nations

The work of Lopez, Crossan, and others on the Sebasteion's large set of portrayals of nations has produced a clear insight that the Sebasteion glorifies Rome's conquest of the nations of the Mediterranean basin. All of these portraits of nations personify them as women. Lopez's work focuses particularly on this dimension of the Sebasteion's reliefs. She focuses on the portrait from the south portico of "the divinely nude Claudius"[20] standing menacingly over a femininely personified Britannia (see figure 17.3).

---

20. Lopez, *Apostle to the Conquered*, 43.

Figure 17.3: Photo by H. Taussig

Lopez summarizes:

> Britannia's Amazonian and captive imagery designates her as a worthy opponent, but one who should predictably lose. In this sense, she is related to other depictions of Hellenistic Amazon warriors . . . Britannia seems posed to be sexually conquered by Claudius, illustrating his impenetrability and her vulnerability. Sexual conquest is inferred by the choice of weapon used to subdue this nation—presumably a sword, an instrument of penetration . . . Claudius' possible sexual conquering of Britannia also infers a relationship involving Roman state fertility and the resurrection of conquered peoples to serve it

> ... Children born of this union are descendants of the attractive and powerful Roman emperor and the debased native nation, now forming part of the extended family inclusive of the entire world.[21]

After reviewing the rest of the reliefs of the nations her conclusion is similar to that of Crossan, Reed, and Maier, but with nuanced attention to the gender dynamics: "The widespread dissemination of images to the public depicting Roman men conquering female nations, and conquered nations arranged in deferential line following their conquest, served to justify and naturalize not only Roman territorial expansion and imperial domination, but also patriarchal gender constructs."[22]

As noted at the beginning of this essay, these empire critical insights bring a major new perspective to the analysis of the Sebasteion (and the New Testament). They can, however, be extended and nuanced to include discrete voices of Aphrodisias and Asia Minor. The complexity of perspective which has surfaced in the examination of the Achilles and Penthesilea plate is actually complemented by further examination of other portraits of the nations in the Sebasteion.

Another dimension that complicates the empire critical conclusions above has been noted by Smith before the empire critical scholarship began. This has to do with several exceptions to the idea that all of the reliefs in the (north) portico of the nations at the Sebasteion are nations that were conquered by Rome. As Smith observes about the status of nations at the time of the construction of the Sebasteion, "Arabia and Dacia were not parts of the empire at all until later . . . The Bosporans (and Ethiopians) were never" a part of the Roman empire (see figure 17.4).[23]

---

21. Ibid., 44- 45.
22. Ibid., 55.
23. Smith, "*Simulacra Gentium*," 58.

Figure 17.4: The base of Bospara. Photo by H. Taussig, 2596.

In other words, that four nations were not under Rome's domination at the time of the Sebasteion's construction (or ever) eliminates a construal that the reliefs together form a portrait of conquered nations.[24] On the other hand, the larger emphasis of the Sebasteion on Roman power and glory is also unavoidable. Here is where the interesting space created by the Achilles and Penthesilea relief may help imagine the insertion of reliefs of non-conquered nations as a particular way of Aphrodisias thinking about its own particular ("free") status. Inside a monument dedicated to Roman glory are placed exceptions not unlike the way citizens of Aphrodisias might have liked to think of their own city.

A similar note is struck in surveying the north portico plates of the various feminine nations. It is true that some of the nations are

---

24. Contra Lopez, *"Apostle to the Conquered."* She describes the portico images as being of "nations that the Romans conquered" (45). Cf. Joyce Reynolds' proposal that all of the reliefs represent places where Augustus had military victories ("Further Information on the Imperial Cult," 115), and Smith's challenge to this proposal in *"Simulacra Gentium,"* 58–59.

portrayed in ways that demonstrate the defeated character of the nations. For instance, the nation with a bull (no. 2), perhaps Dakon, has her right breast and shoulder exposed in ways similar to the victimized nations Lopez describes (see figure 17.5).

Figire 17.5: Photo by H. Taussig

But most of the other "women" in the portico of the nations are portrayed with dignity. Indeed as Smith has noted, the reliefs in the portico generally seem interested in portraying elements of the particular nation for which they are recognized. By and large, there is little interest here in the humiliation of the nations (see figure 17.6).

Figure 17.6: Photo by H. Taussig

This dimension of the portico of the nations, along with the pointed exceptions to the generalization that all the nations were conquered by Rome, also provides nuance to empire critical generalizations. Here too one might recognize both that this portico is interested in the nations conquered by Rome and that the portico also shows this mix of nations with energetic appreciation and only hints of humiliation. Again this more complex mix fits the exceptional situation of Aphrodisias itself, caught in the web of imperial domination, yet "free." Upon close examination the Sebasteion's portico of the nations exhibits a complexity of consciousness similar to the relief of Achilles and Penthesilea, confirming the centrality of empire critical issues and complicating them with the specificity of the position of Aphrodisias.

Professor David Balch

This essay has sought to follow the first and second generations of pioneering scholarship on the Sebasteion upon the occasion of the reliefs becoming available to scholars in general and the public, after a long wait. The NYU archeological teams and the subsequent empire critical interest have laid an important foundation for what promises to be another round of exciting examination of the reliefs. This essay has found itself interested in what nuanced attention to specifics of the collection can contribute to understanding a multiplicity of empire critical conclusions. It is this kind of persistence to the specifics of a material culture and its relationship to the larger trends of New Testament studies that characterize the stunning career and contributions of professor David Balch. The field is deeply indebted to him.

Bibliography

Crossan, John Dominic, and Jonathan L. Reed. *In Search of Paul: How Jesus's Apostle Opposed Rome's Empire with God's Kingdom: A New Vision of Paul's Words and World*. San Francisco: HarperSanFrancisco, 2004.

Erim, Kenan T. *Aphrodisias: City of Venus Aphrodite*. New York: Facts on File, 1986.

———. "De Aphrodisiade." *AJA* 71 (1967) 233–43.

———. "A New Relief Showing Claudius and Britannia from Aphrodisias." *Britannia* 13 (1982) 277–81.

Galinsky, Karl. "Venus, Polysemy, and the *Ara Pacis Augustae*." *AJA* 96 (1992) 457–75.

Kahl, Brigitte. *Galatians Re-imagined: Reading with the Eyes of the Vanquished*. Paul in Critical Contexts. Minneapolis: Fortress, 2010.

Kuttner, Ann L. *Dynasty and Empire in the Age of Augustus: The Case of the Boscoreale Cups*. Berkeley: University of California Press, 1995.

Lopez, Davina C. *Apostle to the Conquered: Reimagining Paul's Mission*. Princeton Readings in Religions. Minneapolis: Fortress, 2008.

Maier, Harry O. "Barbarians, Scythians, and Imperial Iconography in the Epistle to the Colossians." In *Picturing the New Testament: Studies in Ancient Visual Images*, edited by Annette Weissenrieder et al., 385–406. WUNT 193. Tübingen: Mohr/Siebeck, 2005.

Mitchell, Stephen. Review of *Aphrodisias and Rome: Documents from the Excavation of the Theatre at Aphrodisias Conducted by Professor Kenan T. Erim, Together with Some Related Texts by Joyce Reynolds*. *CR* 34 (1984) 291–97.

Nasrallah, Laura Salah. *Christian Responses to Roman Art and Architecture: The Second- Century Church amid the Spaces of Empire*. Cambridge: Cambridge University Press, 2010.

Reed, Jonathan. "Archeological Contributions to the Study of Jesus and the Gospels." In *The Historical Jesus in Context*, edited by Amy-Jill Levine et al., 40–54. Princeton Readings in Religions. Princeton: Princeton University Press, 2006.

Reynolds, Joyce. "Further Information on the Imperial Cult at Aphrodisias." *Studii Clasice* 24 (1986) 101–17.

Smith, R .R. R. "Archaeological Research at Aphrodisias in Caria, 1993." *AJA* 99 (1995) 33–58.

———. "The Imperial Reliefs from the Sebasteion at Aphrodisias." *JRS* 77 (1987) 88–138.

———. "*Simulacra Gentium*: The *Ethne* from the Sebasteion at Aphrodisias." *JRS* 78 (1988) 50–77.

Welch, Katherine. "The Stadium at Aphrodisias." *AJA* 102 (1988) 547–69.

18

Nudity in Early Christian Art

Robin M. Jensen

The Vatican's Museo Pio Cristiano houses the most extensive collection of extant third- and fourth-century Christian sarcophagi. These objects display relief sculptures depicting biblical figures from both Old and New Testaments, some of them represented nude. Usually males—Eve is an exception—these nudes are not insignificant or sketchy, but have clearly rendered genitalia and often occupy the central or dominant position in the visual frame (see figures 18.1 and 18.2).

Figure 18.1: Daniel with Noah, fourth-century Christian sarcophagus (right end). Now in the Vatican Museo Pio Cristiano, used with permission. Photo: Author.

Figure 18.2: Jonah with orant, late third-century sarcophagus from the church of Sta. Maria Antiqua, Rome. Photo: Author

The most common examples are representations of Daniel and Jonah who appear similarly naked in the Roman Catacombs. As on the sarcophagi, other Old Testament notables join these two: Abraham, Noah, Moses, and the three young men in the fiery furnace who, by contrast, are modestly clothed. While nude (or nearly nude) presentations of Adam and Eve are consistent with the Genesis narrative of their shameless nakedness, the reason for Jonah and Daniel's nudity is less apparent. Nothing in their stories alludes even to their physical appearance, much less to their being unclothed. But this is how they appear in early Christian art, looking not a bit embarrassed and, even, a bit alluring.

The ancient Christian viewers of these attractive heroes would have tended to eschew public (and even private) nudity. In this respect, they were not altogether different from most of their non-Christian neighbors. In general, Romans disapproved of public nudity. They did, however, tolerate nudity in certain social contexts as well as in their works of art. Although a seeming disconnection between art and life, statuesque nudes in Roman sculpture, painting, and mosaic tended to be limited to certain kinds of persons, deities, or mythological characters, just as they were limited to particular figures in early Christian art. Nudity in Roman art signifies heroic prowess (e.g., Hercules), corresponds to narrative episode in which nudity plays an intrinsic role (e.g., Endymion), or celebrates physical beauty (e.g., Adonis). Christian artworks that originated in the same general time and place also used nudity as a signifying element, but giving it a different set of meanings. This essay argues that nudity of certain early Christian figures was not meant to identify them as singularly heroic or attractive, but having been rescued from death and raised to new life. In order for this idea to have been effectively expressed, Christian iconography strategically employed particular visual idioms drawn from their contemporary social and artistic contexts.

The Social Context: Roman and Christian Attitudes toward Nudity in Daily Life

To a great degree, attitudes and practices of bodily modesty were markers of social rank or status. Generally, Romans were inhibited in this regard. Although working men might strip to their underclothes to work in the fields or on their fishing boats, nearly all citizens (pagans, Christians, and Jews alike) would have kept their clothes on in most social situations. In fact, to do otherwise might have subjected them to certain legal penalties for indecent exposure.[1] Nevertheless, three particular cultural contexts for nudity may also play a role in these depictions: the abuse of certain groups of individuals (e.g., slaves and condemned criminals), the baths, and the games.

Land-owning aristocrats or higher ranking citizens were somewhat more accepting of public nudity in certain contexts. Slave owners were unashamed to be nude in front of their servants of either sex as they bathed and dressed. Unashamedly appearing nude before a slave would have been a common experience for elite class men and women alike. The former slave and Christian seer Hermas described just such a situation. His owner, Rhoda (also a Christian, but a high-ranking woman), once asked him to assist her out of river where she was bathing. As she was naked, he noted both her beauty and his own fear of unruly and unacceptable sexual desire. It was not only that he was a slave and she a lady, but also that even unspoken and unconsummated desire was sinful. In fact, a few verses later, Hermas recounts Rhoda's

---

1. Plut., *Rom.* 20:3. See the excellent work of Hallett, *Roman Nude*, esp. 61–101. Also see Bonfante, "Nudity as Costume," 543–69.

reprimand for looking at him lustfully.[2] Moreover, the story demonstrates her disregard of his gaze, as if he were no more than an animal.

Parallel to this, public nudity was required or imposed upon slaves or other unfortunates in certain circumstances. Slaves were displayed nude in the marketplace so that their bodies would be fully exposed to potential buyers.[3] Entertainers (acrobats, dancers, and mimes) performed in scanty and revealing costumes. Captured soldiers were paraded nude in triumph processions and condemned criminals who were crucified or subjected to the beasts in the arena were stripped prior to execution. Nudity-or at least near nudity—was, in these situations, intended to be either erotic or humiliating.[4] Nevertheless, Roman reticence about public nudity inhibited some of these displays. For example, the account of the martyrdoms of Perpetua and Felicity reports that the crowd was so offended to see two young matrons (and mothers) so exposed, that the women were returned to the prison to be given loose tunics. And, when Perpetua was tossed onto her back by a beast, she quickly sat up and pulled down her skirt since, according to the text, she cared more for her modesty than for the pain of her wound.[5]

Yet, in other contexts, freeborn citizens could appear nude without shame; when nudity was accepted, appreciated, or necessary. For example, most Romans patronized public baths and, for at least part of the time, were nude while they soaked or even worked out in the exercise yard (*palaestra*). However, even here Romans tended to observe some rules of modesty. Some historians suggest that Romans avoided full nudity while bathing, perhaps even donning special garments for the occasion.[6] Certain Roman moralists objected to full nudity at the baths or in the gymnasium, some even judging it a depraved Greek practice that was not only exhibitionism but could lead to pederasty.[7]

2. Herm., *Vis.* 1.1

3. On slaves' bodies see Glancy, *Slavery in Early Christianity*, 9–38.

4. On soldiers see Livy, 3.28.11–29.1, quoted in Hallett, *Roman Nude*, 64. See also the story of Livia's intervention against the threatened execution of men who had accidentally come into her presence while nude, Dio Cassius, 58.2.4.

5. *Passio Perp.* 20. Thecla is stripped before being thrown into the arena as well. When she emerges alive, the governor orders clothing to cover her: *Acts of Paul and Thecla*, 32–38.

6. See Yegül, *Baths and Bathing*, 34–35. On Roman Baths generally see Fagan, *Bathing in Public*.

7. See Hallett, *Roman Nude*, 71–76, citing Cicero, *Tusc.* 4.70.

These same moralists also objected to mixed-sex bathing (suggesting that was not unknown).[8] Roman women probably bathed with some kind of covering and, for the sake of modesty, would have attended the baths at times reserved only for them or gone to a bath which had a special women's side.[9]

Cicero, for example, believed that Nature intended certain parts of the body to be covered and approved the modesty even of stage actors, as well as the proper reticence of fathers to bathe with their adult sons:

> Our face and figure generally, in so far as it has a comely appearance she [Nature] has placed in sight; but the parts of the body that are given us only to serve the needs of Nature and that would present an unsightly and unpleasant appearance she has covered up and concealed from view. Man's modesty has followed this careful contrivance of Nature's; all right-minded people keep out of sight what Nature has hidden and take pains to respond to Nature's demands as privately as possible. As for stage people, their custom, because of its traditional discipline, carries modesty to such a point that an actor would never step out upon the stage without a breech-cloth on, for fear he might make an improper exhibition, if by some accident certain parts of his person should happen to become exposed. And in our custom grown sons do not bathe with their fathers, nor sons-in-law with their fathers-in-law. We must, therefore, keep to the path of this sort of modesty, especially when Nature is our teacher and guide.[10]

Christian authorities, like their conservative Roman counterparts, urged their followers to avoid indulging in the public baths. In particular, they cautioned against bathing in mixed company. For example, Clement of Alexandria (ca. 200) denounced the "morally lax" women who allowed men other than their husbands to see them naked in their baths and criticizes them for going to such places, where

---

8. Condemnation of mixed bathing: Quintilian, *Inst.* 5.9.14. See Fagan, *Bathing in Public*, 26–29.

9. On women's segregated bathing (or special facilities) see: Pliny, *Nat.*, 33.153; Plutarch, *Cat. Maj.* 20.6.

10. Cicero, *Off.* 1.126–29 [trans. LCL XXI (1913)], 129–31. Also cited by Hallett, *Roman Nude*, 75.

"they strip for licentious indulgence (for from looking men get to loving) as if their modesty had been washed away in the baths."[11]

Cyprian regards the baths as "promiscuous" and warns women (especially dedicated virgins) against these places where they would see naked men and be seen naked by men. Rather than cleansing the body for healthful purpose, he says that these washings actually make the body dirty, since the baths themselves are as defiling as the theatre or the arena. There, he says, "all modesty is put off together with the clothing of garments, the honor and modesty of the body is laid aside; virginity is exposed to be pointed at and to be handled."[12]

Other early writers were concerned even about nudity in the sex-segregated baths. Ambrose, writing on the duties of the clergy, warns against immodesty and reminds his audience that the ancient Romans would avoid bathing nude with their grown children and urges that his congregants retain some clothing in the baths so that the body be at least partially covered.[13] Jerome's epistle to Laeta likewise deplores any kind of public nudity, "I know that some people have laid down the rule that a Christian virgin should not bathe along with eunuchs or with married women, inasmuch as eunuchs are still men at heart, and women big with child are a revolting sight. For myself, I disapprove altogether of baths in the case of a full-grown virgin. She ought to blush at herself and be unable to look at her own nakedness."[14]

A third context in which public nudity was approved was the arena. Games and shows were occasions for different sorts of bodily exhibitionism. Athletes competed in the nude, or at least wearing little more than a loincloth (*sigularium*) sometimes covered by a brief apron-like garment (*perizoma* or *campestre*). During the Augustan period, however, women were prohibited from attending these events, probably because they would have been exposed to the sight of nude (or nearly nude) contestants.[15] Yet, despite the popularity of the games,

---

11. Clement, *Paed.* 3.5, ANF 2:279. But see *Paed.* 3.9–10, where Clement gives instructions on how to use the baths properly: not for pleasure or indulgence, but instead for health and external cleansing. See also the *Apos. Const.*, 1.3.9, which proscribes mixed bathing for women and suggests that they even use the women-only baths infrequently.
12. Cyprian, *Hab. virg.*, 19, trans. ANF 5:435.
13. Ambrose, *Off.* 1.18.79.
14. Jerome, *Epist.* 107.11 (trans. Wright, LCL).
15. See Hallett, *Roman Nude*, 68–71.

athletes were not viewed as entirely respectable. Men of the elite upper classes would not have participated since it would have been degrading to be displayed before a public audience.[16] Like the Greeks, Romans could appreciate a beautiful (and nude) athletic body, but only as an object and not as a person who might be their social equal.

Tertullian condemns spectacles for their associations with idolatry and their cruelty. He also rails against their ability to arouse the passions. Although he does not single out athletes for their immodesty, he complains that the titillating performances of the dancing girls and mimes make them the victims of public lust. He fulminates, "Let the Senate, let all ranks, blush for shame!"[17] He notes that the man who scarcely would lift up his tunic to urinate in public is willing to strip before an audience, and that fathers who otherwise protect their daughters from vile speech or sights think it all right to bring them to the theatre where they will see and hear all kinds of disturbing things.[18]

The Artistic Context: Nudity in Roman and Christian Visual Art

Romans adapted the concept of honorific statue from the Greeks. However, unlike their predecessors, beginning in the late second or first century BCE, Roman sculptors frequently rendered some of their (especially male) subjects as heroic nudes with idealized bodies.[19] These were portraits of prominent citizens or civic benefactors who had held important offices or to whom a populace owed some debt of gratitude. During the Empire, emperors and princes might be portrayed nude as often as wearing military garb or a proper Roman toga. Artistic presentations of leading citizens or rulers as nudes emphasized their virility and strength and also implied certain divine characteristics. Depicting a man with an attractive physique reflected a belief that beauty and virtue were linked.

---

16. See examples given in Hallett, *Roman Nude*, 70, 76–77. These include Cicero's reproach of Mark Antony for acting as a lupercus while consul and the ejection of M. Palfurius Sura from the senate for participating as a wrestler in the games.

17. Tertullian, *Spect.* 18.

18. Ibid., 21.

19. Women were rarely portrayed nude, although there are exceptions, which are assumed to have been private portraits (not intended for public view).

Veristically rendered heads of emperors, generals, or ordinary businessmen were commonly attached to athletic torsos, sometimes creating an almost comically discordant presentation (at least to the eyes of a modern viewer—cf. fig. 18.3).

Figure 18.3: Statue of the Emperor Vespasian, first-century CE, from the Shrine of the Augustales. Now in the Museum of the Castello di Baia. Photo: Author.

And even while the practice was fairly common, it had its critics. Pliny the Elder claimed that nude statues were a foreign, Greek, invention. In the old days, he asserted, Romans portrayed their honored men only as wearing togas and their military heroes in battle dress.[20]

A beautiful body (often artificially attached to an aging face) also suggested the eternal youthfulness or immortality associated with the

20. Pliny the Elder, *Nat.* 34.18.

gods who may have been their iconographic prototypes. Almost any male god could be depicted nude, but Jupiter, Hercules, Apollo, Sol, Dionysus, Endymion, Achilles, and Admetus were the most common (see figure 18.4).[21]

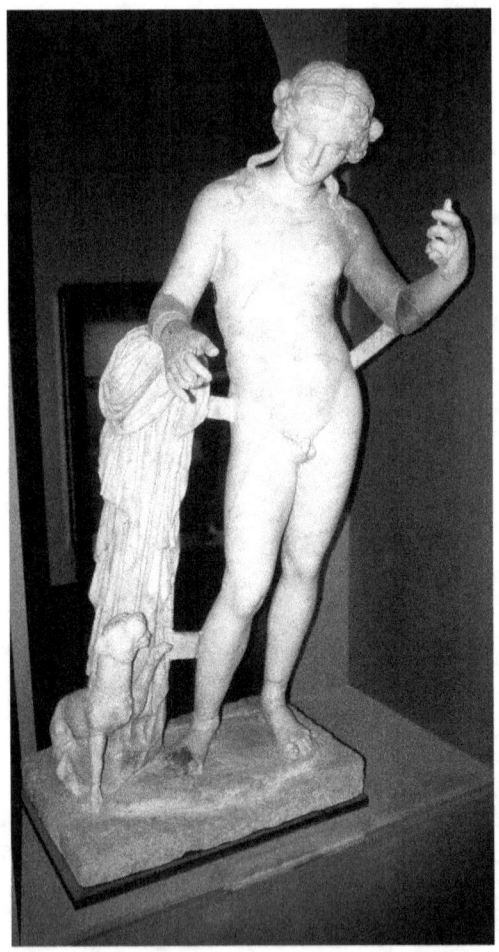

Figure 18.4: Dionysius with panther, first century, CE. Now in the Archeological Museum of the Phlegraean Fields, Castello di Baia. Photo: Author.

21. Female divinities are generally clothed, with the usual exception of Venus/Aphrodite.

Sometimes the alignment between mortal and divinity was more than subtle, as when the emperor adopted the props or attributes of the god being depicted.[22] Unlike the emperor or honored patron, however, gods appeared nude in a wider range of monuments: paintings, mosaics, coin reverses, and engraved gems, for example (see figure 18.5).

Figure 18.5: Triumph of Neptune, third-century Roman mosaic, now in the Archeological Museum, Sousse (Tunisia). Photo: Author.

Christians, of course, objected to all statues of the gods, avoiding them when possible. That they were vain or false or demonically inspired was the main objection to them. However, the nudity of many of the images was also a reason to reject them, along with depictions of drunken satyrs, phallic tokens, and scenes of lovemaking or more lascivious debauchery that they associated with the pagan deities. Clement of Alexandria, for example decries these kinds of artworks, insisting that they are reasons for shame: "Not only the use of them, but the sight of them, and the very hearing of them, we denounce as deserving the doom of oblivion. Your ears are debauched, your eyes commit fornication."[23]

22. See Maderna, *Iuppiter, Diomedes*; Hallett, *Roman Nude*, 237–40.
23. Clement of Alexandria, *Protr.* 4, trans. ANF 2:189.

Considering the official ecclesial disapproval of nudity in daily life, not to mention depictions of the "demonic" pagan gods, it seems inconsistent that Christians would have tolerated nude figures in artworks depicting biblical narratives. Explaining this phenomenon simply as an iconographic transferral from classical depictions of nude heroes and demigods overlooks the Christian rejection of those depictions as idolatrous and disregards the apparent inconsistency of showing some biblical heroes clothed while others as naked.

One key aspect of the Christian depiction of nudity is its context. As noted above, these nude figures are commonly found on Christian funerary monuments from the late third to mid-fourth century, and most frequently on objects found in or near the city of Rome, or that may have been manufactured there.[24] These were costly objects, no doubt reflecting the tastes and values of the elite classes and designed not only to honor the dead but also to allude to the state of the deceased after death. The subjects or themes used to decorate them should be considered in this light.

Although Christians would have denounced them as idolatrous, most of the figures that appear on pagan sarcophagi would have been familiar to them, as they were part of a more or less common visual vocabulary. This vocabulary, usually drawn from popular mythological motifs, lent itself to Christian adaptation. For example, the popular visual renderings of cherub-like naked *putti* harvesting or otherwise engaged in playful activities, regularly featured in Roman (pagan) art, appear as well on third- and fourth-century Christian sarcophagi, where they are shown milking sheep or harvesting wheat and grapes, perhaps an allusion to eucharistic bread and wine. Hermes Criophorus and the Orant figures are two others that appear in Roman art and were easily adapted by Christians, since their meanings were not substantially transformed. Like Hermes, the Good Shepherd was a caretaker and guide to souls as they journeyed into the underworld. However, a more complex process was required in the adaption of the figure of the sleeping Endymion into the resting Jonah. Presuming that viewers knew the basics of both stories (Endymion's and Jonah's), they would also need to be able to see the relevance of the one for the other. This

---

24. For example, a Jonah sarcophagus now in the British Museum, although found near Bath, was likely produced in Italy. Similarly, the so-called Sarcophagus of the Chaste Suzanna in the Arles Antiquities Museum was probably manufactured by a Roman workshop.

would not have been obvious unless they had been introduced to an interpretive strategy that made the links for them.

The Endymion-Jonah Adaptation

The figure of the beautiful shepherd Endymion frequently appears on second and third-century Roman sarcophagi. He normally appears nearly nude; his lower body usually is lightly draped. He reclines, ordinarily on his left side with his left arm supporting him and his right arm bent over his head (see figure 18.6).

Figure 18.6: Endymion, third-century Roman sarcophagus. Now in the Museo Capitolini, Rome. Photo: Author.

This pose is often associated with sexual availability, which makes sense since he is about to be paid a conjugal visit by Selene, the goddess of the moon.[25] Selene, according to the myth, fell hopelessly in love with the handsome youth and persuaded Zeus to cast him into eternal slumber, so that she might have endless sexual intercourse with him while he slept. However cruel this sexual exploitation might seem to modern viewers, the popularity of the scene on Roman sarcophagi suggests that it may have referred to a bliss-filled afterlife (being eter-

---

25. Compare the presentations of Ariadne as Dionysus comes to her on other Roman sarcophagi, for example.

nally loved by a beautiful goddess) or, perhaps, to a happy marriage that the couple hoped would continue even beyond death. Michael Koortbojian provides several sources to support this interpretation.[26] Furthermore, depicting the hero as sleeping might have been a way of indicating that he was in a state of divine receptivity; dreams were thought to be the gods' vehicles of communication.[27]

Art historians have long noted that the presentation of a nude Jonah, resting (sleeping) under his gourd vine as it appears in Christian catacomb painting and sarcophagi from the late third and early fourth centuries bears strong similarities with the depiction of the sleeping Endymion.[28] This, the third scene of a visual narrative sequence that starts with the sailors throwing the prophet overboard into the waiting jaws of the sea creature, and the creature's subsequent regurgitation of the prophet, completes the visual narrative. Significantly, the iconography omits the beginning and ending of the biblical story; God's call to preach to the Ninevites and their ultimate conversion. Nor does the picture cycle depict Jonah praying within the sea creature's belly; rather, the composition simply shows Jonah's being swallowed, regurgitated, and resting (nude) in the shade, under a still-leafy gourd vine.

Jonah was one of the most popular characters in Christian funerary art, although episodes from this narrative sequence also appear in other contexts as well (e.g., gems, redware bowls, lamps, glasses, and a mosaic pavement from the early fourth-century basilica at Aquileia). Nevertheless, historians tend to emphasize the sepulchral setting of the Jonah cycle, some concluding that the figure must refer to the soul, now at rest in the *refrigerium interim*, others that it references a phrase in an ancient Christian prayer for the dead (*ordo commendationis animae*).[29] However, a striking difference between the sleeping

26. See Koortbojian, *Myth, Meaning, and Memory*, where he also notes that some sarcophagi bore portraits in the features of Endymion and Selene, presumably of husbands and wives who commissioned them (106 and n. 21).

27. See ibid., 107–8 for relevant texts.

28. On the Endymion-Jonah parallels see (for example) Balch, "Endymion in Roman *Domus*," 273–301; Snyder, *Ante Pacem*, 90–96; Ferrua, "Paraliapomeni di Giona," 7–69; Lawrence, "Three Pagan Themes," 323–24; Stommel, "Zum Problem der frühchristlichen," 112–15. Snyder's book includes a helpful bibliography of other scholarly analyses.

29. On Jonah as a figure of the soul see Stuiber, *Refrigerium Interim*, 136–51; on the *commendatio anima* see Ferrua, "Paralipomeni." For a summary of the latter see Jensen, *Understanding Early Christian Art*, 71.

Endymion and the reclining Jonah is Jonah's complete nudity; he lacks Endymion's skimpy veil. Nothing in Jonah's source narrative offers an explanation for such a presentation (later iconography of Jonah almost always portrays him fully clothed). Interestingly, it may be that the lack of the veil makes his nudity less erotic, perhaps to Roman eyes at least.[30] This is underscored by the lack of any sexual partner in the iconography.

The striking parallels between Jonah and Endymion in Roman funerary art must have been evident to contemporary viewers; even though its meaning has puzzled modern interpreters. If one views Endymion as a figure of eternal, blissful sleep, it seems reasonable to surmise that Jonah's idyllic rest was meant to allude to the Christian soul comfortably awaiting the general resurrection. Such a scene would have been a consolation to those who mourned their deceased brother or husband. Still, Jonah's exposed nude body seems an unnecessary augmentation. Moreover, on at least one famous monument from Asia Minor: the so-called Cleveland Jonah (see figure 18.7).

Figure 18.7: Jonah under the Gourd Vine, Late Roman statuette from Asia Minor (280-90), now in the Cleveland Museum of Art. Photo: copyright The Cleveland Museum of Art, John L. Severance Fund, 1965.239.

---

30. See many of the illustrations in Clarke, *Roman Sex*, in which prostitutes are scantily clad (but not fully naked).

This Jonah wears a tunic, even though his posture is the same as elsewhere (reclining, right arm crooked over his head, right leg crossed over left).

The reference to Jonah in the Gospel of Matthew is not incidental to Christian perceptions of the prophet. Here Jonah is made the type of Jesus's own resurrection following three days in the belly of the earth (Matt 12:40). Early commentaries on this passage make it proof of the resurrection of the body. For example, Irenaeus and Tertullian both insist that Jonah's three-day sojourn in the creature's belly demonstrates the possibility of bodily incorruptibility in the grave or following the resurrection.[31] Jonah was a symbol of Christ's resurrection, and Christ's resurrection the prototype, seal and promise of the future raising of all humanity (cf. 1 Cor 15:20–26). Referring to that promise with a symbol of the promised general resurrection makes the same kind of sense on a Christian sarcophagus as Endymion's blissful slumber does on a pagan one. But apart from positing the straightforward adaption of a visual prototype, the question of why a figure of resurrection would necessarily be nude—even more nude than its iconographic prototype—remains.

The answer may lie in the fact that early Christians believed they obtained access to resurrection through baptism. That baptism is the primary ritual of resurrection is clear from Christian documents beginning with Paul's epistle to the Romans (cf. Rom 6:4–5) and continuing in the writings of later exegetes, homilists, catechists, and theologians. For example, in his second mystagogical lecture Cyril of Jerusalem emphasizes the ways that recipients imitate Christ's passion in the baptismal ritual. First, by entering the baptistery chamber and removing their clothing they are like him, naked on the cross.[32] Next, as they are led to the pool they represent Christ being laid in the tomb. Finally, their triple immersion in the water signifies Christ's three days in the tomb. Cyril concludes with a quote from Eccl 3:2: "In that same moment you were dying and being born, and that saving water was at once your grave and your mother. What Solomon said in another context is applicable to you: 'A time for giving birth, a time for dying;' although for you, contrariwise, it is a case of a 'time for dying

---

31. Irenaeus, *Haer.* 5.5.2; Tertullian, *Res.* 58. See also *Apos. Const.* 5.7.
32. Cyril of Jerusalem, *Myst.* 2.1.

and a time for being born.' One time brought both, and your death coincided with your birth."³³

Ambrosiaster, writing in Rome sometime in the third quarter of the fourth century, also explains baptism as the way Christians appropriate the benefits of Christ's sacrificial death and the expectation of sharing his resurrection, asserting that baptism kills sin and destroys death, which gives the recipient hope of rising again to new life. He reasons that as the baptismal water washes dirt from the physical body, the invisible and incorporeal body is spiritually cleansed and renewed. Baptism is, he concludes, both the image and the pledge of resurrection.³⁴ Similarly, Basil of Caesarea urged the unbaptized among his flock to accept burial with Christ in baptism. Citing Romans 6, he insists that if they do not, they cannot rise with Christ.³⁵ In a treatise on the Holy Spirit he reiterates this same idea, but here citing Phil 3:10–11, urges them to become like Christ in his death, so that they might attain resurrection from the dead. And baptism, he asserts, is the manner of this death and burial that puts an end to the old life and the regeneration that inaugurates the new one. For bodies, he says, are buried in the water—the water becomes their temporary tomb.³⁶ Furthermore, Basil was one who explicitly noted the baptismal significance of the Jonah story, asserting that it typifies both Christ's descent into Hell as well as the triple immersion in baptism.³⁷ Jonah goes into the water, just as the candidate goes into the font. Both of them emerge, delivered from death and reborn to new life.

Certain ritual practices are also relevant to viewing nude Jonah in early Christian art specifically as a baptismal figure. Although Christians were warned away from the public baths and entertainments in order to preserve their modesty, they were expected to remove all of their clothes for the initiatory ritual. Being baptized nude signified several theological ideas or life transitions. Primarily, baptismal nudity expressed the concept of regeneration or being born again by shedding an old life with its sins and earthly vanities. And just as babies emerged naked from their mothers' wombs, so neophytes rose from the water

33. Ibid., 2.4–5.
34. Ambrosiaster, *Comm. in ep. ad Rom.* 6.1–6.
35. Basil of Caesarea, *Prot. bapt.* 2.
36. Basil of Caesarea, *Spir.* 15.35.
37. Ibid., 14.32.

in the same state. Nudity also signaled the return of the baptized to the innocence of Adam and Eve, before their disobedience when they were unaware of their nakedness.[38] And, as noted above, nudity also signified participation in Christ's crucifixion, as he was naked on the cross. Significantly, Jesus himself is never shown as nude in Christian art, except at his baptism (see figure 18.8).

Figure 18.8: Dome mosaic, Arian baptistery, early sixth century. Ravenna. Photo: Author.

Among the earliest testimonies to the practice of nude baptism is the *Apostolic Tradition*, which specifies that candidates disrobe, and that women specifically should loosen their hair and lay aside any jewelry (gold ornaments), lest they enter the font with an alien object on their bodies.[39] Thus, candidates' being stripped of their clothing had a practical as well as symbolic purpose. Unless the water could reach

---

38. This association may also account for the frequency of nude Adam and Eve in early Christian funerary art. On this symbolism of nudity in Christian art see Smith, "Garments of Shame," 220–24; and earlier, De Bruyne, "L'imposition des mains," 239, 245.

39. Hippolytus, *Trad. ap.* 21.3, 5, 11.

every part of the body, it would not be fully sanctifying.[40] Additionally, the removal of jewelry and other adornments would have been a representative act of embracing humility and rejecting personal vanity, worldly wealth, and markers of social superiority.

The Case of the Naked Daniel

This explanation of Jonah's nudity in early Christian art may help to account for why Daniel is also shown naked, especially on third- and fourth-century Roman artifacts.[41] Although art historians have tended to characterize Daniel's nudity as "heroic" and thus patterned after conventional, classical presentation of youthful heroes who performed feats or defeated wild beasts (e.g., Hercules and Meleager), this does not explain why other biblical heroes are depicted as clothed (e.g., Noah, the three youths in the fiery furnace, and Moses).[42] In sarcophagus friezes with a broad selection of biblical narrative scenes, Daniel's nudity is almost startling. Moreover, unlike Jonah's recumbent pose, no close parallel to Daniel's posture or presentation (facing forward in the prayer stance with a lion on either side) exists in contemporary (or near contemporary) Roman art. The reason for Daniel's nudity must account, not only for his particular selection, but also for his posture.

Early Christian interpretations of the Daniel narrative most frequently view Daniel as a martyr and, as such, prefiguring Christian men and women who were willing to die rather than betray their faith.[43] According to the story in the Old Testament, Daniel refused to

40. See for example, Hippolytus, *Trad. ap.* 21.3, 5, 11; Zeno of Verona, *Inv. font.* 6; *Ep. Paul Sen.* 6; Cyril of Jerusalem, *Myst. Cat.* 2.2; Theodore of Mopsuestia, *Hom. bapt*.3. 8; Chrysostom, *Catech. illum.* 2.24, and *1 Ep. Innoc.*, and *2 Ep. Innoc.*; and Ps. Dionysius, *Ecc. Hier.* 2.2.7.

41. Images of Daniel with clothing are more common from the eastern part of the Empire, although a sarcophagus from Gaul (Aire sur L'Adour) also shows Daniel with clothing. The Junius Bassus sarcophagus's figure of Daniel as an older (garbed) prophet is a late replacement of an earlier, nude Daniel.

42. See, for example, Leclercq, "Nu," 1783; Swift, *Roman Sources*, 54; and Weitzmann, *Age of Spirituality*, 413. A close parallel might be the depiction of Hercules in the Garden of Hespirides from the Dino Compagni hypogeum of Rome's Via Latina Catacomb. Hercules stands in three-quarter view, holding his club and, performing his eleventh labor, tries to retrieve an apple from the tree guarded by the dragon, Ladon. In this instance the parallels to Adam are probably stronger than to Daniel.

43. For example, see Clement of Rome, *1 Cor.* 45.6; Tertullian, *Scorp.* 8.7; *Idol.* 15.10.

obey the Babylonian King's interdict that forbade prayer to anyone but himself. Daniel, caught in prayer to God, was cast into a den of lions (Daniel 6). Cyprian, in particular, believed Daniel to be an inspiring model for Christians facing torture and death for refusing to offer prayers or incense to idols. A reply written by him, along with thirty-six other bishops, to letters from Spanish communities regarding the lapse of certain local bishops, presents certain Old Testament heroes as exemplary, among them Daniel who never wavered in bravely witnessing to his faith, despite being isolated in an alien land and subjected to constant persecution.[44] A century later (and fifty years past the time of the last persecution), Cyril of Jerusalem admonishes candidates for baptism to be constant in their faith, like Daniel, whose fortitude "stopped up the mouths of lions" (Dan 6:22).[45]

As noted above in the case of Perpetua, as a way of increasing their degradation, martyrs may have been sent into the arena stripped of their clothing. A fifth-century mosaic from Borj El Youdi (Furnos Minus), about 40 km outside of Carthage and now in Tunis's Bardo Museum, presents a naked figure surrounded by four lions (see figure 18.9).

Figure 18.9: Blossos family mausoleum, from Furnos Minos. Now in the Bardo Museum, Tunis. Photo: Author.

---

44. Cyprian, *Ep.* 67.8.2. See also *Laps.* 19, 31; *Ep.* 61.2.1; *Fort.* 2.11.

45. Cyril of Jerusalem, *Cat.* 5.4. See also Gregory of Nazianzus, *Or. Bas.* 48.74

The figure, usually identified as Daniel, might also have been intended to depict a martyr facing the beasts while praying to God for deliverance. The inscription identifies the monument as being set up to someone named Blossus, by Honoratus, an agent for (and perhaps member of) the Blossus family.[46]

Thus Daniel is the figure of the Christian hero, condemned to face the lions, and here shown like a martyr in a Roman arena. Here he also signifies the reward of that martyr: immediate resurrection from death. At the end of the Book of Daniel, the seer receives a revelation of the end time, when all the dead will be raised, the righteous to everlasting life and the wicked to eternal shame and contempt (Dan 12:2–3). He sees a man clothed in linen, standing by the bank of a stream who tells him that he must keep the vision secret, and in the meantime "go your way and rest; you shall rise for your reward at the end of the days" (Dan 12:12). In his full commentary on the Book of Daniel, Hippolytus emphasizes the connections between Daniel's rescue from death and his vision of bodily resurrection. Noting that the prophet received his supernatural strength by one who appeared in "human form" (Dan 10:15–19), he sees the narrative as signifying the body's future restoration. Hippolytus puts these words into Daniel's mouth: "But while I was in this position, I was strengthened beyond my hope. For one unseen touched me and straightway my weakness was removed, and I was restored to my former strength. For whenever all the strength of our life and its glory pass from us, then are we strengthened by Christ, who stretches forth his hand and raises the living from among the dead, as it were from Hades itself, to the resurrection of life."[47]

Daniel, thus, both received a vision of the end time, when all the dead would be restored, and also had an advance experience of it. Furthermore, his rescue from the lions not only prefigured the martyrs' liberation from their tortures but also Jesus's resurrection. According to the story, Daniel was sealed in his tomb by a stone, brought and laid over its entrance (Dan 6:17). At dawn the king got up and hurried to the den where he found Daniel alive. The parallels between these narrative details and the events of Easter morning as presented in the

---

46. The inscription reads: MEMORIA BLOSSI HONORATUS INGENUS ACTOR PERFECIT.

47. Hippolytus, *Comm. Dan.* 10.16 (trans. *ANF* 5:190).

New Testament Gospels may have been apparent to those who first compiled, heard, or commented on accounts of Christ's empty tomb.[48] In any event, Daniel's rescue undoubtedly signified several things that were intricately connected: Christ's resurrection on Easter morning, the martyr's reward, and the end time rising of the rest of the dead.

The image of this end time resurrection may be seen on other early Christian sarcophagi, which show Jesus pointing a staff toward a pile of bodies in order to revivify them (see figure 18.10).

Figure 18.10: Adam and Eve, Jesus raising the dead from a fourth-century Christian sarcophagus, Vatican Museo Pio Cristiano, used with Permission. Photo: Author.

This image, probably an allusion to Ezekiel's vision of graves opening and dry bones rising (Ezek 37:1–10), shows Jesus as the life-giver. In each instance, the iconography shows the resuscitated ones as nude—like newly born children. Significantly, the closest parallel to these little nudes in Christian art are depictions of a newly baptized Jesus and the raised Lazarus (see figure 18.11).

48. See Keener, *Commentary on the Gospel of Matthew*, for some discussion of this.

Figure 18.11: Jesus raising Lazarus, arrest of Peter, from a fourth-century Christian sarcophagus, Vatican Museo Pio Cristiano, used with permission. Photo: Author.

In some cases, this scene is juxtaposed with nude figures of Adam and Eve, perhaps chosen deliberately in order to imply the beginning as well as the final chapter of the creation story.

Daniel, unlike these other nude figures, stands in the prayer posture, presumably because he is giving thanks for his deliverance. In most of the images, in addition to the two symmetrically placed lions, Habakkuk also appears, bearing food to comfort Daniel while he was in the pit, based on the apocryphal book Bel and the Dragon (vv. 33–39). If Daniel is interpreted as a figure of baptism (and thus of the resurrection promised through baptism), Habakkuk's meal could signify the heavenly banquet, prefigured by the eucharist. Thus, the figure of Daniel not only signifies the promised afterlife, but one of its components (a happy meal).

Conclusion

In summary, nudity in the Roman cultural world—the world in which Christians lived—was associated with humiliation (slavery), martyrdom, athletic contests, and the baths. In visual art (as opposed to life) nudes were generally heroic or divine figures, in at one case a blissfully sleeping object of divine love. Both of these contexts are relevant for understanding nudity in Christian art. It was appropriate, in one instance, for a heroic martyr who faced combat with wild beasts and who was miraculously rescued from death. It was apt, in another instance for a figure who, by virtue of his (nude) baptismal bath, enjoyed a peaceful rest while awaiting the general resurrection.

Moreover, the nudes in early Christian art, while based upon contemporary pagan models, were selected because their narratives had particular associations with resurrection which had obvious meaning on a funerary monument. Even the figures of Adam and Eve may be best understood, on these monuments, as symbols of restoration, rather than reminders of the fallen human state. Like Adam and Eve returned to the Garden, neophytes did not feel shame at being naked.

This idea is expressed in the *Gospel of Thomas*, when Jesus admonishes the disciples not to be anxious about clothing and to consider the lilies of the field (cf. Matt 6:28–29). His disciples then ask when he will be revealed to them so that they can see him, and he responds: "When you undress without being ashamed, and take off your clothes and put them under your feet like little children do and trample on them, then you will see the Son of the Living One and you will not fear."[49]

---

49. *Gos. Thom*, log. 37 (trans. *ANT* [Elliott, 140–41]).

Bibliography

Balch, David. "From Endymion in Roman *Domus* to Jonah in Christian Catacombs." In *Commemorating the Dead: Texts and Artifacts in Context*, edited by Laurie Brink and Deborah Green, 273–301. Berlin: de Gruyter, 2008.
Bonfante, Larissa. "Nudity as Costume in Classical Art." *AJA* 93 (1989) 543–69.
Clarke, John. *Roman Sex*. New York: Abrams, 2003.
De Bruyne, Lucien. "L'imposition des mains dans l'art chrètien ancienne." *RivAC* 20 (1943) 113–266.
Fagan, Garrett G. *Bathing in Public in the Roman World*. Ann Arbor: University of Michigan Press, 2002.
Ferrua, Antonio. "Paraliapomeni di Giona." *RivAC* 38 (1962) 7–69.
Glancy, Jennifer. *Slavery in Early Christianity*. Minneapolis: Fortress, 2006.
Hallett, Christopher H. *The Roman Nude*. Oxford Studies in Ancient Culture and Representation. Oxford: Oxford University Press, 2005.
Jensen, Robin M. *Understanding Early Christian Art*. London: Routledge, 2000.
Keener, Craig. *Commentary on the Gospel of Matthew*. Grand Rapids: Eerdmans, 1999.
Koortbojian, Michael. *Myth, Meaning, and Memory on Roman Sarcophagi*. Berkeley: University of California Press, 1995.
Lawrence, Marion. "Three Pagan Themes in Christian Art." In *De Artibus Opuscula*. Vol. 40. Edited by M. Meiss, 323–24. New York: New York University Press, 1961.
Maderna, Caterina. *Iuppiter, Diomedes und Merkur als Vorbilder für römische Bildnisstatuen*. Heidelberg: Archäologie und Geschichte, 1988.
Smith, Jonathan Z. "Garments of Shame." *HR* 5 (1966) 220–24.
Snyder, Graydon. *Ante Pacem: Archeological Evidence of Church Life before Constantine*. Macon: Mercer University Press, 2003.
Stommel, Eduard. "Zum Problem der frühchristlichen Jonasdarstellungen." *JAC* 1 (1958) 112–15.
Stuiber, Alfred. *Refrigerium Interim, die Vorstellungen vom Zwischenzustand und die frühchristliche Graveskunst*. Theophaneia: Beiträge zur Religions- und Kirchengeschichte des Altertums 11. Bonn: Hanstein, 1957.
Swift, Emerson. *Roman Sources of Christian Art*. New York: Columbia University Press, 1951.
Weitzmann, Kurt, editor. *The Age of Spirituality*. New York: Metropolitan Museum of Art, 1979.
Yegül, Fikret. *Baths and Bathing in Classical Antiquity*. New York: Architectural History Foundation, 1995.

19

Bible Translation and Ancient Visual Culture

Divine Nakedness and the "Circumcision of Christ" in Colossians 2:11

Yancy W. Smith

As a teacher, David L. Balch changed his students' paradigm for reading Scripture by linking it with relevant yet hidden cultural assumptions. He helped them uncover those assumptions by bringing a broad array of ancient Hellenistic and Jewish texts, as well as art and household remains, into a mutually critical dialogue with modern social science models of culture. Balch advocated a bold approach, "Take a position and defend it." His own bold approach to the household codes[1] liberated those of us who had previously read Paul through the lenses of the deutero-Pauline epistles to reverse the order. I remember often coming from his lectures with the dizzying thought, "This changes everything." Balch constantly reminded his students and readers that in the nitty-gritty of biblical exegesis the gaze falls almost exclusively upon written texts as the primary means to reconstruct the ancient visual context.

The ancient urban readers' gaze most often fell upon art and monuments. Texts were secondary. For those of us who have been and

---

1. Balch, "Household Codes," 3:318 summarizes: "In the mid-seventies, three scholars—D. Lührmann, K. Thraede, and D. Balch—independently rejected ... [previous] hypotheses [about the origin and meaning of the household codes], suggesting instead that the NT codes are related to the stereotypical Hellenistic discussion of 'household management' *(peri oikonomias)*, especially as formulated by Aristotle (*Pol.* 1.1253b.1–14). This Aristotelian text (cf. *Mag. Mor.* 1.1194b.5–28) is parallel to the form of Col 3:18–4:1 and Eph 5:21–6:9."

are his students, Balch engineered many escapes from the intensity of our textual worlds. To do so often is healthy for our textual endeavors. But I also recall Balch's care for the individual student, his concern for the oppressed and the marginalized. Perhaps his greatest achievement was to make our reading of Scripture more humane and, thus, more godly.

The Problematic Text as Theoretical Journey

Reading Col 2:11–12 is disconcerting, like taking a pilgrimage, a θεωρία,[2] to observe the religion and customs of a strange land. The difficulty of this text, with all its multiple possible meanings and referents, however, goes beyond the tortuous metaphor. It equates conversion to Christ with "circumcision." In this way it applies a well-known symbol of barbarism and slavery to the conversion of both males and females.[3]

Balch and Osiek argued that the author of Colossians belonged to a second generation of Paul's followers.[4] A clear difference in Paul's and Colossians' approach to gender relations may be seen in the translation[5] in Colossians of the baptismal confession represented in Gal 3:27–28: "As many of you as were baptized into Christ have clothed yourselves with Christ. There is no longer Jew or Greek, there is no longer slave or free, there is no longer male and female; for all of

---

2. See LSJ, "θεωρέω," "θεωρία."

3. Thus the shift, observed also in *Gos. Thom.* 21–22, of reconceptualizing the female as male, serves the interest in seeing humanity eschatologically as one new creation. The difference between *Gos. Thom.* and Colossians is that the latter thereby endorses male dominated hierarchy. The female becoming male may symbolize the transformation of the earthly and perishable (i.e., the female) into the heavenly and imperishable (i.e., the male). See Meyer, "Making Mary Male," 554–70.

4. Balch and Osiek, *Families*, 123.

5. I use "translation" here not simply in its modern linguistic sense, but in the way Cicero "translated" the Greek rhetors and recontextualized their Greek ideas to a Latin audience. In effect, the author(s) of Colossians and Ephesians are "translating" an iconic Paul, domesticating his texts to fit the authoritarian structure of the Hellenistic household and imperial values. The text of Paul himself acheived an unassailable iconicity from ancient times (2 Pet 3:15, 16). As Denzey, *Bone Gatherers*, 150–51, 170, 188, 203, shows, the Latin word *translatio* was early used among Christians as holy, ceremonial transference of the bones of saints to centers of power that could benefit from accumulating such relics.

you are one in Christ Jesus." The confession is repeated in Col 3:10–11 but "no longer male and female" has gone missing. The change, they argue, is in line with the Augustan moral revolution that emphasized traditional, hierarchical family values.[6] The procedure Colossians uses to transform the earlier, more radical confession is the adoption of the typical Aristolean household code with its structure of three interconnected relationships within the household: (1) masters and slaves, (2) husband and wives, (3) parents and children.[7] That code contradicts the earlier confession and asserts that the differences in the household still exist and are still important for the proper function of the household.[8] They explain: "As the eschatological urgency wanes and the church acculturates socially, the social reversals that Jesus and Paul's eschatological thought had hoped for disappear, with corresponding changes in both baptism and Christian ethics."[9] In its adaptive translation of the previous confessional statement, Colossians especially expands the part of the code on the master/slave relationship; the world would have to wait for the industrial revolution for Christians to effectively challenge the justice of that relationship.[10]

The text is a doorway to a foreign social world.[11] I propose to look at this short but problematic text in terms of the visual *realia* of what I take as its references based upon reflections of metaphorical themes found in Galatians 6:11–17, that is circumcision, crucifixion, new creation, and the rhetorical power of nudity connected with circumcision and suffering.

---

6. The Augustan moral revolution included more rigid social stratification, submission of wives to husbands and slaves to masters. See Balch and Osiek, *Families*, 63–119. The idealized structure of the Aristotelian household code reinforced by Augustus called for, in the words of Octavian "to conquer and rule all mankind, to allow no woman to make herself equal to a man" (Dio Cassius, *Roman History* 50.28).

7. See Balch, *Let Wives Be Submissive*, 14–15.

8. Balch and Osiek, *Families*, 120.

9. Ibid.

10. While Colossians and Ephesians represent an acculturation to some Augustan values, they may retain some of the challenge to imperial values by Jesus and Paul.

11. See Balch, "Acculturation in 1 Peter," 79–101 for a judicious approach to social science theories to biblical interpretation.

"Reality is a cliché from which we escape by metaphor."[12]

To borrow another thought from Aristotle, metaphors breathe the air of unfamiliarity: τὸ ξενικόν, (cf. Aristotle, *Rhet*. 3.2.9 [1405a8]). They are memorable because of their novelty and emotional impact. They strike the reader with a sense of clarity and aptness or, perhaps, obscurity, and revulsion. Aristotle's appeal primarily to the visual sense to explain metaphor gives priority to the compelling argument in metaphors that sets something "before the eyes" (πρὸ ὀμμάτων 3.2.10 [1410b]).[13] In a similar vein, Hellenistic writers like Dionysius of Halicarnassus described a well-known stylistic effect they observed in the court speeches of Lysias known as "vivid description" or ἐνάργεια. The speaker appeals to the senses of the listener and he describes attendant circumstances in such a way that the listener will be beguiled into thinking he or she has become an eyewitness.[14] The listener identifies with the speaker, is persuaded, and transformed by that identification.

Dionysius of Halicarnassus suggests that readers who cannot respond to a speech or text in this way are "clumsy, fastidious, and slow-witted." Quintilian discusses effectual ἐνάργεια in Cicero's *Verrine Orations* in which Cicero gave a brief sketch of Verres's relationship with his mistress. He readily admits that *his mind adds details that are not in the text*; however, he also explains that such *imaginative* reading is, in fact, normative. He asks, "Is there anyone so incapable of *forming images* of things that he does not seem to see?"[15] That is, Quintilian presents such reading and hearing as the *kind of participation speakers and authors expect of their ideal audience*.[16] Quintilian thus associates ἐνάργεια with painting (*Training of the Orator* 8.3.61; 12.10.6), a quality of good oratory he admires and discusses at length (6.32; 6.2.34-36; 8.3.64-65).[17] Jesus himself tells his disciples, "*See* what you

---

12. Stevens, *Opus Posthumous*, 204.

13. See the important study by Collins, *Power of Images in Paul*, 1–10, for a discussion of Paul's use of metaphor. This is a very helpful book. It is puzzling, however, that not one reference can be found in the book to any artifacts of ancient visual culture, despite the similarity to the title of Zanker, *Power of Images*.

14. Dionysus of Halicarnassus, Lysias 7; [Usher, *Critical Essays*, 1:14, 17] cited and discussed in Zanker, "Enargeia," 297.

15. Emphasis mine.

16. Webb, *Ekphrasis*, 21.

17. Benediktson, *Literature and the Visual Arts*, 175–76.

hear" (Mark 4:24), and Paul declared that the effect of his preaching of the gospel in Galatia was that "before [their] eyes . . . Jesus Christ was graphically portrayed as crucified!" (Gal 3:1).[18]

In the aesthetic world of the New Testament visual communication was more important than textual.[19] Adding an appreciation of relevant visual culture brings life to the text. With the appropriate visual dimension texts like Col 2:11 may take on new meaning.[20] Surely visual culture is relevant to phrases like "circumcision" or "stripping off the body of flesh." Such questions about the visual registry of reference in a text helps *the translator better approximate the profile of the ideal reader that ancient authors expected to meet*. Such knowledge may greatly enhance the translator's ability as an exegete to enjoy textual endeavors and to produce a text that is both helpful and enjoyable for her readers. Visual references (in both metaphor and in figured speech [Greek, ἔμφασις]) are a significant part of the relevant cognitive environment of the source text, even when the direct discussion of artifacts of visual culture, a rhetorical genre known as ἔκφρασις, is not the topic of the source text.[21]

In Col 2:11 is a delicate case of the Greek rhetorical figure known as ἔμφασις, which quite different from the English "emphasis." The figure of ἔμφασις is speech that depends for its rhetorical power upon indirectness, avoiding explicit statements. Irony and indirectness is very difficult for translators and exegetes because it is so difficult to identify. When a speaker or author uses ἔμφασις, he speaks indirectly and may even appear to speak unwittingly using the rhetorical virtue of δεινότης, or "craftiness," a virtue greatly admired and cultivated, if not always feared, in the ancient world. Demetrius (*Style* 287) says: "That which is called 'figured' in speech present day orators use for humorous effect. They combine it with vulgar and *suggestive emphasis*. But genuine figured speech has these two goals in mind: good taste and the [speaker's] safety (ἀσφάλεια)."

---

18. Balch, *Roman Domestic Art*, 86.

19. Most people could not read well or did not read at all and made their way through life by means of visual and oral cues. See ibid., 109–36.

20. The problem is not only a pressing issue in translation studies, but is a live issue in ethnography. See Banks, "Visual Anthropology," 9–23; Harper, "Argument for Visual Sociology," 24–41.

21. On *ekphrasis*, see Aune, *Westminster Dictionary*, 143–45.

Demetrius saw two legitimate uses for ἔμφασις, the maintenance of good taste (in discussing delicate matters) and preserving the speaker's safety in situations in which a speaker may offer critique of people that have the power to retaliate against him.[22] Quintilian notes that ἔμφασις is used "a great deal nowadays" (*Inst.* 9.2.65), and he adds a third use to Demetrius's two uses of ἔμφασις. It is similar to a third (but non-"genuine") use of ἔμφασις suggested by Demetrius, when ἔμφασις is adopted for pleasurable effect (9.2.66). ἔμφασις, then would be a way of speaking that operates by depending on implicitness for social and rhetorical reasons.

Crucifixion and Nakedness

The mention of "circumcision" and "putting off the body of the flesh" is vivid, emphatic speech, in the Greek sense. As such both figures are simply ways of describing death by crucifixion. Public crucifixions were common in the period from Julius Caesar to Nero,[23] and it is likely that the mention of crucifixion conjured up for the readers an image, not simply of a man hanging in pain on a cross, but stripped naked to die in shame.[24] Crucifixion was an exemplary punishment to dissuade

22. Not genuine, he says, is the ἔμφασις used by orators for humorous effect.

23. It was the "slaves' punishment," *Valerius Maximus* 2:7.12. Appian reports that during the slave rebellion of Spartacus, Crassus had six thousand slaves crucified on the Via Appia leading into Rome (*Bella Civilia* 1:120). Josephus tells that the Roman General Titus had five hundred Jews a day crucified (Jos. *JW.* 5.11.1).

24. Whether or not the historical Jesus himself was crucified naked is perhaps debatable but plausible (Mat 27:35; Mark 15:25; John 19:23). For Mark, the nudity (partial or total) fulfills Scripture (Ps 21:16 LXX). John states: ἐλαβόντα τὰ ἱμάτια αὐτοῦ, "they took his clothing." Matt 27:28 (cf. Luke 10:30) states that the Roman soldiers "stripped" (ἐκδύσαντες) Jesus prior to the crucifixion. That may mean they took away all of his clothing, including his loincloth, but not necessarily. Two reasons might seem to support a more modest crucifixion: (1) John 21:7 records another man who was naked but probably with a loin cloth: "That disciple whom Jesus loved said to Peter, "It is the Lord!" When Simon Peter heard that it was the Lord, he put on some clothes, for he was naked (ἦν γὰρ γυμνός), and jumped into the sea" (NRSV). Working in the nude on a boat is disadvantageous and dangerous. "Naked" is not necessarily totally naked. (2) Out of respect for the sensibilities of the Jews the Romans might have allowed those they crucified a loincloth. These reasons, however, seem rather weak in the face of rapacious Roman brutality in Judea during the first century. Hadrian (76–138 CE) limited what torturers and executioners could confiscate from those condemned for treason (*maiestas*) only to what they had on their body. Before that time all a condemned person's goods were supposed to be taken into the imperial

dissent and foster acquiescence during the monstrous regime of the *Pax Romana*.[25] In *The Interpretation of Dreams*, Artimedorus (2nd century CE) considered it particularly inauspicious for a wealthy man to dream of crucifixion, since, "the crucified are stripped naked and lose their flesh," τὰ δὲ κρυπτὰ ἐλέγχει· ἐκφανὴς γὰρ ὁ σταυρωθείς. τοὺς δὲ πλουσίους βλάπτει· γυμνοὶ γὰρ σταυροῦνται καὶ τὰς σάρκας ἀπολλύουσιν οἱ σταυρωθέντες.[26] What is more the cross "exposes things that are hidden: because the person who is crucified is disclosed."[27] One may compare this language with Col 2:11 ἐν τῇ ἀπεκδύσει τοῦ σώματος τῆς σαρκός, "in the stripping of the body of the flesh" as a verbally graphic depiction of death on a cross. Thus, both shameful nakedness and the loss of flesh (an image of death and disfigurement either through rotting, violence or to vermin) were likely part of crucifixion.

Early Christians were apparently certain that Jesus was naked on the cross, or so they appear to have imagined him. For example, Melito of Sardis, *On the Passover* 740–43 writes: "The Lord was made a mockery, 'dressed' in his naked body. And it is not even deemed worthy of any covering at all so that no one would look upon it. For this reason the stars went out and the day became darkened, so that the one stripped naked on the cross might be covered, though not to darken the body of the Lord, but to keep the eyes of human beings from seeing these things" (see figure 19.1).[28]

---

treasury. (Tacitus, *Ann.* 6.29; Justinian *Digest* 48.4.11 [critical text and translation in Mommsen, Krueger, and Watson, eds., *Digest of Justinian*, 4:804].) See the discussion in Collins, *Mark*, 745. Hadrian's rescript codifies the informal practice. In all likelihood the emperors before Hadrian were not concerned with insignificant belongings, but with collecting substantive wealth from those deemed traitors. The point is that the law gave cover for soldiers to practice wholesale looting of the condemned.

25. On the systematic use of violence for pleasure and profit in ancient Rome, see Auguet, *Cruelty and Civilization*. Images of violence and oppression were common themes in the wall paintings of Roman homes. See Balch, *Roman Domestic Art*, 132–6, 202–13.

26. Pack, "*Artemidori Daldiani onirocriticon libri v*," 1963.

27. My translation.

28. My translation. Ὁ δεσπότης παρεσχημάτισται γυμνῷ τῷ σώματι καὶ οὐ δὲ περιβολῆς ἠξίωται ἵνα μὴ θεαθῇ. Διὰ τοῦτο οἱ φωστῆρες ἀπεστράφησαν καὶ ἡ ἡμέρα συνεσκότασεν, ὅπως κρύψῃ τὸν ἐπὶ ξύλου γεγυμνωμένον, οὐ τὸ τοῦ κυρίου σῶμα σκοτίζων, ἀλλὰ τοὺς τούτων ἀνθρώπων ὀφθαλμούς. Text from Perler, ed. *Meliton de Sardes*.

Figure 19.1: Tracing of Palatine Graf

The earliest graphic representations of Christ crucified are from the late second or early third century CE[29] and they emphasize a naked Christ on the cross.[30]

---

29. Some have objected to the early dating of the Palatine inscription on the supposition that Christians did not revere the cross until the fourth or fifth century. It is impossible to establish that supposition either way; early Christians like Alexamenos did not necessarily have to worship images in order to be caricatured as worshiping a crucified Jesus. See Balch, *Roman Domestic Art*, 104–5.

30. Solin and Itkonen-Kaila, "Graffiti del Palatino I," 209–12; Snyder, *Ante Pacem*, 60. A second image, comparable to the Palatine graffito is on an amulet from Syria in the late second or early third century (British Museum, o5–01.1]). Jesus is portrayed as nude, bearded and with long hair, arms stretched out beneath the *patibulum* and tied to it by strips at his wrists. He is shown body forward but in profile, turned to the left and bent at the knee as if seated upon a bar or peg (see figure 19.2). See the high resolution images and discussions in Spier, *Picturing the Bible*, 227–28.

Figure 19.2: Amulet

In these representations the starkness of the positioning of the body, emphasizing his nudity, is antithetical to the triumphal symbolism of Christ that appears in later centuries.³¹ It is natural, then, to assume that the body references in Col 1:20, 22 and in 2:11 depend upon a graphic imagination of the crucifixion of a naked Jesus.³² "Graphic

31. Spier, *Picturing the Bible*, 228.

32. For a discussion of ancient attitudes toward the complex symbolism of nudity, see Hallett, *Roman Nude*, chapters 1–3. Hurwit, "Problem With Dexileos," 35–60. See also Zanker, *Mask of Socrates*, 4, 6, 24–25, 28–30, 33, 63–64, 136, 163, 176, 178, 226, 299, 368 n60. The treatment and exposure of the penis, as seen in Greco-Roman art, was the object of care and a means of non-verbal communication. On the κυνοδέσμη, pin or tether for binding up the penis, see ibid., 28–30. An uncircumcised male ran the risk of being abusively called κόλλοψ, or ψωλός "penis head," "hard-on-bare glans" (ibid. 28, 374 n44). (For ψῶλος see the following note.)

imagination" does not depend on whether the historical Jesus was crucified naked or not, but on whether the writer of Colossians and the readers were likely to have imagined him so. Whether or not every mention of circumcision in 2:11 refers to what happens to believers who experience union with Christ, circumcision is mentioned because the death of Jesus involved him being stripped, exposing what Romans would consider his barbaric and shameful, circumcised penis.[33]

Since the metaphorical nexus of circumcision, crucifixion and ancient Christian baptism is *nakedness* (total or partial, real or metaphorical) on the level of the human experience of honor and shame,[34] perhaps it is a clue to understanding the significance and complexity of the argument of the letter to the Colossians. Indeed, given the concrete references to the physicality of crucifixion in 1:15–22 ("the blood of the cross," "reconciled in his fleshly body through death"), an implied nakedness links 1:15–22 and 2:9–15. In this context the reference to circumcision and putting off the body of flesh represents "emphatic" or "figured" speech that would have a powerful, evocative vividness in its context. Its dependence upon a visual register well known to the audience suggests a vital, if neglected, strategy for understanding the rhetorical force of the passage.

---

33. See Hodges, "The Ideal Prepuce," 375–405. His comment on 392–93 is particularly apt: "In the classical era, the association between the denuded glans and criminal impropriety is reflected in the vernacular, for in the plays of Aristophanes [Aristophanes, *Birds* 502–9, in *Aristophanes: Birds*, 81; Aristophanes, *Knights* 963–64, in *Aristophanes: Acharnians, Knights*, 347. See the commentary on *psolos* in Henderson, *Maculate Muse*,110–11 n. 16; 111 n. 17.] we find use of the derisory adjective *psolos* (ψωλός). The scoliasts suggest that *psolos* can simply mean 'having an erection,' a situation that can inadvertently cause the prepuce to evert, exposing the glans, but this definition does not take into account the varied contexts in which the word is used. The *psolos* male need not necessarily be circumcised either, as in the following slander: 'He's come back here with an old man who's filthy, hunchbacked, wretched, wrinkled, bald, toothless, and, by God, I think he's *psolos* too!' [Aristophanes, *Wealth* 265–67] When applied to certain foreigners of ill repute, however, *psolos* can very well imply that circumcision is the cause of the offender's lewdness." See additional references in item, 393.

34. Guy, "Naked Baptism in the Early Church," 133–42. Guy argues that, though baptism was not likely commonly practiced with the baptizand totally in the nude, the language of nudity connected with it in the patristic sources was the only language adequate to match the dramatic power of the ritual and the radical change it signified.

Artistic, Rhetorical Functions of Nudity and Circumcision

Nudity in Greco-Roman art and life is a rhetorically complex issue.[35] Nudity with various functions immediately confronts the person who enters a Roman *domus*. Abundant wall art represents nudity for a wide variety of purposes: comical and apotropaic effect, to portray ranges of meaning including sexual innocence or experience, vulnerability or divinity, nobility or venality, virtue or eroticism and dissipation, *joie de vivre* or tragic loss, strength and victory in battle, or loss and cowardice.[36] Art historians have often considered as a stylistic failure the Roman habit of copying the Greek ideal nudity of the human body and placing atop such sculptures realistic, but mismatched, heads of men and women.[37] Nevertheless, nudity conceived in the way Roman portraiture represents it is a type of costume, a means of communicating social values and status.

In his *Wars of the Jews*, Josephus recounts how Antigonus, the son of Aristobulus, tried to cast Antipater in a bad light. Though both these men had been enemies of Caesar, they tried to ingratiate themselves to him. Antipater, at a climactic moment, "threw away his garments, and showed the multitude of the wounds he had, and said, that as to his good-will to Caesar, he had no occasion to say a word, because his body cried aloud, though he said nothing himself" (*JW* 1.10.2). Nudity in this case functions as an artistic proof of heroic, even Herculean, virtue, and loyalty. In a similar way, Paul the apostle invokes the image of virtuous, rhetorical nudity when he says, in the climactic argument from pathos in the letter to the Galatians: "From now on, let no one make trouble for me; for I carry the marks of Jesus branded on my body" (Gal 6:17). In this case, "the marks of Jesus"—most probably referring to Paul's battle scars acquired in preaching

---

35. Balch, *Roman Domestic Art*, 209 alludes to this variety of functions, noting "heroic nudity" of (209, CD #205a) and the naked blessedness of Endymion is a *topos* in Greco-Roman authors, e.g. Cicero (*Tusculan Disputations* 1.38.92; *Amicitia* 1.13.42–44). Propertius II.15.15–16 (c. 54 BCE) emphasizes his nudity in ekphrastic comments.

36. See the various beautiful color representations in relation to the experience of the Roman *domus* in Bergman, "Roman House as Memory Theater," 225–56.

37. Hallett, *Roman Nude*, 3, refers to the prevailing attitude of seeing Roman nude portraiture as "aesthetic catastrophe."

the gospel—are an effective argument to recapture the loyalty of the Galatians as well an exemplary replacement for circumcision.[38]

Thus, the understated reference to his nude body exposes Paul's theological point of view that the wounds of the cross are a sufficient and necessary substitute, at least for non-Jews, for circumcision.[39] Indeed, since it is because of faith in the power of the cross of Jesus that "the world has been crucified to [Paul], and [he] to the world" (Gal 6:15), for Paul, the cross was "the true circumcision" (Rom 2:28; Phil 3:1-3). The conclusion resulting from this reflection is that "neither circumcision nor uncircumcision is anything; but a new creation is everything" (v. 16). Barbarian, Jew and Greek, male and female might appropriate such "circumcision" as equals.[40] This ideological separation from "the world" was a replacement for physical circumcision.

Thus, the use of the term "circumcision" to refer to identification with Christ and de-identification with "the world" would have a deeper significance. It implies that a similar opprobrium attaches to identification with Christ. In effect, an uncircumcised Greco-Roman male who experienced conversion as a "circumcision" of his excluded "old identity" (τὸν παλαιὸν ἄνθρωπον Col 3:9) became a barbarian to his former self. At the same time, it becomes appropriate to describe the new life as ἡ ζωὴ ὑμῶν κέκρυπται σὺν τῷ Χριστῷ ἐν τῷ θεῷ "your life is hidden with Christ in God." Reading Col 3:2 in the light of Col 2:11 and Romans 2 and 6, suggests that "hidden" has the sense

---

38. See Betz, *Galatians*, 323-24, who does not, however, link τὰ στίγματα τοῦ Ἰησοῦ to the argument on *circumcision*, but to the deliberate case for accepting a stance that will result in the audience's persecution, even as it did for Paul (Cf. Gal 1:23; 4:29; 5:11; 6:12.). Quintillian (6.1.21) notes Cicero's effective use of reframing devices (περιστάσις) such as this to alter the perception of an issue (ὑποστάσις). Bringing up matters such as "worth, his manly pursuits, the scars from wounds received in battle" were a way of shifting focus as a means of recommendation to the judge.

39. Paul approaches conversion and faith in a similar manner in Rom 2:28 (NRSV), arguing "a person is not a Jew who is one outwardly, nor is true circumcision something external and physical." By implication dying with Christ and becoming "obedient from the heart to the form (τύπος) of teaching to which you were entrusted" (Rom 6:17) are already likely seen, in the case of non-Jews at the least, as a *substitution* for physical circumcision early in the development of the theology of the Pauline circle. On Rom 6:17b as an expression of later reflection on Paul's letter, see Jewett, *Romans*, 417. Against this view, see Gagnon, "Heart of Wax and a Teaching," 667-87.

40. One imagines that even ancient women were at an advantage over Westerners in appropriating this image.

Paul gave it in Rom 2:28, ἀλλ ὁ ἐν τῷ κρυπτῷ Ἰουδαῖος, "the Jew who is a Jew in the hidden [sense]."

A third literary portrayal of nudity demonstrates the dishonor attached to circumcision. Though Hellenistic and Roman societies practiced public nakedness in certain times and places (i.e. the *gymnasion*, "the place of nakedness,"), they abhorred exposing the glans, the tip of the penis. Exposing the glans was considered vulgarly humorous, indecent or both. Together these attitudes represented a devastating exclusion for Jews.[41] Artistic representations of male nudes feature an ideal and artistically emphasized πόσθη or prepuce.[42] Artistic representations of the circumcised prepuce that exposes the glans show that it was considered "shameless and dishonorable, something we see only in depictions of slaves and barbarians."[43] Hodges extends this interpretation of Greek attitudes, adding that literary mentions of the *psolos* (ψόλος) include the artistic representations of glans-revealing men: "ugly, decrepit old men, barbarian slaves, lecherous old satyrs," and comically lewd characters.[44] Suetonius, *Domitian* 12, depicts this attitude in describing the shameful fate of a man suspected of avoiding paying the tax levied upon Jews and Christians.[45] He recalled "being present in [his] youth when the person of a man ninety years old was examined before the procurator and a very crowded court, to see whether he was circumcised."[46]

The Crux Interpretum of Colossians 2:11

The key to understanding Col 2:11 is to relate circumcision to the vision of Christ on the cross as preached in the Christian gospel.[47] The

---

41. Hall, "Epispasm," 52.

42. Hodges, "Ideal Prepuce" conveniently gathers several striking images.

43. Zanker, *Mask of Socrates*, 28 n.25.

44. Hodges, "Ideal Prepuce," 393, suggests that in certain contexts the bawdy epithet ψόλος may at times refer to uncircumcised males, e.g. Aristophanes, *Birds* 502–9.

45. Feldman, *Jew and Gentile*, 100, argued that the success of Christian (and Jewish) proselytism led to the harsh prosecution of this tax.

46. Carew, ed. *Suetonius*, 367.

47. Balch, *Roman Domestic Art*, 80–81 used abundant images of the suffering of Isis/Io found on the walls of Roman houses in Pompeii and Herculaneum not to explain Paul's text, but how his auditors and spectators might have heard his proclamation. Here I go a step further and suggest that the author of Colossians starts with the

meanings and precise referents of every phrase are the topics of interminable dispute. [48]

Ἐν ᾧ καὶ περιετμήθητε
περιτομῇ ἀχειροποιήτῳ
ἐν τῇ ἀπεκδύσει τοῦ σώματος τῆς σαρκός,
ἐν τῇ περιτομῇ τοῦ Χριστοῦ

Here I give my own fairly literal translation:

A   *"In him also you were circumcised*
A1 *with a circumcision not [performed] by [human] hands,*
B   *in the denuding [or stripping] of the body of the flesh*
A2 *in the circumcision of Christ . . ."*

The function of these words in the flow of thought seems clear enough: they serve to articulate, through symbolic relations, the means by which believers enjoy the completeness of blessing (καὶ ἐστὲ ἐν αὐτῷ πεπληρωμένοι) that v. 10 asserts they have received "in Christ" as members of Christ's imperial household.[49] The meaning is "circumcision, circumcision, circumcision" (A, A1, A2). Though it might seem odd to bring up circumcision at this point in the letter, 2:20 and 3:3 plainly develop the parallel theme of death in a way that shows circumcision is a symbol for death that occurs through the identification with Christ through faith. In Col 1:12 this identification is described as transferring believers from one reign to another.

The symbol of circumcision is apt as a marker of this transference from one world, one kingdom, to another. Jewish notions of circumcision point to entry into an exclusive covenant relationship with God, like the sign that bound the descendants of Abraham to God (Gen 17).[50] Nevertheless, such aptness does not fully explain its appearance here nor its displacement of dying with Christ in this text. To fully explain the appearance of circumcision is to give an account of the in-

---

known, a common image of naked crucifixion, to vividly portray in laconic fashion the indecency of the cross. Colossae has never been excavated, but the likelihood is extremely high that homes were decorated with scenes similar to those found in Pompeii, Herculaneum, Ephesus and elsewhere.

48. See Harris, *Colossians & Philemon*, 97–116, for discussion of the pericope. A more complete summary of exegetical possibilities is given in King, *Exegetical Summary of Colossians*.

49. Sumney, *Colossians*, 135.

50. Ibid., 136.

vention of the metaphor as well as the most relevant ways the implied Colossian audience might have heard it. Furthermore, if *burial* is itself a symbol for baptism (2:12),[51] then it seems circumcision cannot be strictly equated with baptism, but rather with a previous identification with Christ through conversion of the heart and faith.[52] Jewett's comment on Rom 6:2 is appropriate here. "For a first-generation audience of converts, this moment is usually assumed to be each individual's conversion event associated with baptism. It is significant, however, that Paul refers here not to baptism but to death."[53]

In the case of Col 2:11 circumcision also equals death. Indeed, one expects the author to base the full blessedness of believers on participation in the death, burial and resurrection of Christ, as in Romans 6. But in grounding the fullness of blessing in *circumcision*, co-burial (συνταφέντες) in baptism and co-resurrection (συνηγέρθητε) by faith in God's power the argument takes a distinctive and significant turn. The oddness of the statement logically provokes the question: what makes the equation of circumcision with death relevant? And, is the circumcision in some sense a co-circumcision with Christ? The image of Christ as the one who performs the circumcision on believers would be out of place entirely. Since the letter contains no sustained polemic against circumcision, only this passing reference, the purpose of the reference is not polemical. Rather, though the author may be innovative in his language, the substance of his thought seems to be part of the common ground of belief and practice the writer can confidently assume his readers share with him.

Rather than take Christ as performer of this circumcision or see this representing Christ's circumcision as a little child,[54] it is best to see the "circumcision of Christ" as referring to a visual image of Christ's circumcision revealed in his nude body on the cross.[55] As such, it is a metaphor for the believer's death with Christ as a symbol of the initiatory experience of beholding by faith the εἰκών of God

---

51. The connection may seem obvious and inevitable, Cannon, *Use of Traditional Materials*, 41–43. However, the passage does not equate circumcision with baptism. Rather, baptism is equated with burial, as in Rom 6. Pace, MacDonald, *Colossians and Ephesians*, 99.

52. Jewett, *Romans*, 395.

53. Ibid.

54. For a discussion of the history, see Daniélou, *Bible and the Liturgy*, 63–69.

55. Lincoln, "Colossians," 623.

(ὅς ἐστιν εἰκὼν τοῦ θεοῦ τοῦ ἀοράτου, 1:15). The believer sees the εἰκών of God in a crucified Jewish teacher and rabble-rouser. With the preaching of the gospel the unsavory image becomes transformed into the glorious image of God. The experience is based in the concretely imagined physical body of the crucified and subsequently resurrected one (ἀποκατήλλαξεν ἐν τῷ σώματι τῆς σαρκὸς αὐτοῦ διὰ τοῦ θανάτου 1:22).[56] Such beholding works transformation by appropriation of Christ's circumcision revealed in the image of his nude crucified body.

Theologically, one may say that the Spirit works this appropriation through renewing the beholder "according to the image of his Creator" κατ᾽ εἰκόνα τοῦ κτίσαντος αὐτόν (Col 3:10), that is, Christ, perhaps thought of as the new Adam.[57] A similar thought can be discerned in the authentic Pauline letters. Just as artistic representations of Narcissus are transformative, catching a vision of God in the cross of Christ is similarly transformative. 2 Cor 3:18 is a profound example of this theology. In Galatians the miscarriage of the gospel is the failure of those who beheld Christ graphically portrayed before their eyes as crucified (κατ᾽ ὀφθαλμοὺς Ἰησοῦς Χριστὸς προεγράφη ἐσταυρωμένος) to be fully transformed by the Spirit that is at work among them (Gal 3:1, 3). To Paul's chagrin, instead of standing in their status as sons and daughters of God (3:26), the Galatians were falling under the spell of slavery to the law (4:1, 7, 22, 30, 31; 5:13).[58]

To properly understand the progression of believers' death as "circumcision," burial, and resurrection, it is necessary to return to the source of the metaphor, the vision of the glorified One who is also the crucified Christ, to which the author alludes in 1:22. Salient features of that death that could not be missed by a Greco-Roman audience are an ignominious crucifixion including the exposure of bodily nakedness, and especially, the fact that Jesus was a circumcised Jew. That a circumcised, crucified barbarian should be elevated to divine status as the very image of God was ludicrous to Greco-Roman sensibilities.

---

56. Paul refers to this transformation in his own life in saying, "we regard no one from a human point of view; even though we once knew Christ from a human point of view, we know him no longer in that way" (2 Cor 5:16, NRSV).

57. See Wiessenrieder, "Der Blick in Den Spiegel," 313 for a description of ancient perspectives in which beholding is transformation.

58. Balch, *Roman Domestic Art*, 57–108.

A Vivid Ambiguity

In 2:11 the first two lines A and A1, then, are a shocking application of the death of Christ to the life and identity of the readers.

> A *In him also you were circumcised*
> A1 *with a circumcision not [performed] by [human] hands*

However, the phrase ἐν τῇ ἀπεκδύσει τοῦ σώματος τῆς σαρκός seems deliberately and vividly ambiguous and can be understood as (1) a reference to shameful nudity, violently imposed upon the victim, (2) a way of speaking of violent physical death, understood graphically as the stripping off of Christ's fleshly body on the cross to reveal his deity as in 1:15–22 or (3) it can be understood as a metaphor for the death of the sinful nature of the believer. English translations vary but usually attempt to limit the reader's choices: the taking away "*selfish desires*" (CEV) or the "cutting away/stripping away/putting off" of "*the sinful nature*" (NLT/NIV/REB) or "the stripping away of *the old nature*" (REB). These translation strategies are designed to ease the reader's processing load so that the reader will at least find some meaning. The NET Bible attempts to lose nothing in translation and gives the rather literal and enigmatic "the removal of *the fleshly body*" itself (NET), which might cause the reader to ponder, "Whose body?" The reader has no apparent way to answer the question decisively one way or the other. In Greek the phrase ἐν τῇ ἀπεκδύσει τοῦ σώματος τῆς σαρκός generates a series of poetic effects in which various senses and resonances of the phrase are more or less weakly signaled.[59]

On the other hand, the deliberate, vivid ambiguity invites the reader to see Christ's experience of shame, nakedness and death as his or her own and to experience a cathartic transformation analogous to Christ's death, burial, and resurrection in their lives. It is an experience, to borrow a phrase from Miroslav Volf, of exclusion and embrace.[60] It is designed to evoke in the non-Jewish audience the worst

---

59. For the notion of poetic effects and more or less weakly signaled meanings, see Sperber and Wilson, *Relevance*, 217–24.

60. Volf, *Exclusion and Embrace*, 29: "The practice of 'embrace,' with its concomitant struggle against deception, injustice, and violence, is intelligible only against the backdrop of a powerful, contagious, and destructive evil I call 'exclusion . . . and is for Christians possible only, if in the name of God's crucified Messiah, we distance ourselves from ourselves and our cultures in order to create a space for the other."

responses of exclusion and bigotry, so that the best in the reader may stand up and admit to its evil. Accordingly, the phrase "the circumcision of Christ" is also a deliberately vivid metaphor, another delicious synecdoche for the entire crucifixion. The gospel as preached by the writer of Colossians in his prayer (1:11–23) fixes the imagination on the Divine One who reconciled all things through a shameful death on a Roman cross.

Similarly the writer invites the readers to contemplate the Divine One (2:9) whose utterly shameful death and vindication is the source of their blessing. That spiritual gaze created rhetorically by the author is a transformative gaze in which Christ's own death, which left him naked and exposed, becomes their own. His exposed circumcision becomes a way of speaking of their embrace of the rejection experienced by Christ. It is simultaneously Christ's circumcision and a circumcision experienced by those who see the glory of the crucified Christ. It is an exclusion of an old life and an embrace of reconciliation with the Father of Jesus Christ in a new life in the community of Christ made possible by the forgiveness of sins. It stands in this case in the place of co-crucifixion and both of these images are thereby related in 2:12 to baptism/burial and resurrection/faith in God's power. Hanging in the air, however, is the question: just how did Nympha (4:15), a female leader in the church in Colossae, read and appropriate the circumcision of Christ?

Conclusion

A comparison of English translations of Col 2:11 reveals the most diverse ways of relating the clauses and filling in the gaps left by the author's vivid, emphatic speech. Translators usually do not have the luxury of sitting on the fence in exegesis. They must often choose the meaning to present to their audience and neglect those that remain implicit in the original text. The *Good News Translation* gives a clear, but I believe mistaken, understanding: "In union with Christ you were circumcised, not with the circumcision that is made by human beings, but with the circumcision made by Christ, which consists of being freed from the power of this sinful self."[61] It reverses the order of the last two phrases and ultimately divorces "circumcision" from the idea

---

61. American Bible Society, *Good News Bible: With Deuterocanonicals/Apocrypha.*

of death, introducing the notion of freedom. My suggestion would be to retain both the connection of "circumcision" and death and keep the order of the phrases that helps express the double entendre of the last two phrases: "In union with Christ you were circumcised. No human being performed it. Rather, it happened by the fleshly body being stripped naked, when you contemplated the circumcision of Christ."

It is likely that Col 2:11 was vivid and allusive in the primary context. It is a mysterious saying, like that of Eph 5:30–33. The mystery (Col 1:26, 27; 2:2; 4:3) is the transformative experience of seeing the face of God in a naked Jewish man hanging on a cross. It shares with its context, where mystery religions abounded, the dynamic of personal transformation in the contemplation of suffering. That context was greatly enhanced by the richness of communication in the surrounding visual culture. Words like "circumcision" bristled with power and provoked visceral reactions. The use of ancient art to enhance our ability to catch the visual allusions greatly enhances our ability to use imagination critically as we read Scripture. We owe a debt of gratitude to David Balch for opening our eyes to the possibilities.

Bibliography

American Bible Society, *Good News Bible: With Deuterocanonicals/Apocrypha*. New York: American Bible Society, 1979.
Auguet, Roland. *Cruelty and Civilization: Roman Games*. London: Routledge, 1994.
Aune, David E. *The Westminster Dictionary of New Testament and Early Christian Literature and Rhetoric*. Louisville: Westminster John Knox, 2003.
Balch, David L. "Acculturation in 1 Peter." In *Perspectives on First Peter*, edited by Charles H. Talbert, 79–101. Eugene, OR: Wipf & Stock, 2010.
———. *Let Wives Be Submissive: The Domestic Code in I Peter*. SBLMS 26. Chico, CA: Scholars, 1981.
———. *Roman Domestic Art and Early House Churches*. WUNT 228. Tübingen: Mohr/Siebeck, 2008.
Balch, David L., and Carolyn Osiek. *Families in the New Testament World: Households and House Churches*. The Family, Religion, and Culture. Louisville: Westminster John Knox, 1997.
Banks, Marcus. "Visual Anthropology: Image, Object, and Interpretation." In *Image-Based Research: A Sourcebook for Qualitative Researchers*, edited by Jon Prosser, 9–23. London: Falmer, 1998.
Benediktson, D. Thomas. *Literature and the Visual Arts in Ancient Greece and Rome*. Oklahoma Series in Classical Culture. Norman: University of Oklahoma Press, 2000.
Bergman, Bettina. "The Roman House as Memory Theater: The House of the Tragic Poet in Pompeii." *The Art Bulletin* 76 (1994) 225–56.
Betz, Hans Dieter. *Galatians: A Commentary on Paul's Letter to the Churches in Galatia*. Hermeneia. Philadelphia: Fortress, 1979.
Cannon, George E. *The Use of Traditional Materials in Colossians*. Macon, GA: Mercer University Press, 1983.
Carew, John Rolfe, editor. *Suetonius: The Twelve Caesars, and Extracts from the Lives of Illustrious Men*. LCL. London: Macmillan, 1914.
Cicero, Marcus Tullius and J. E King. *Tusculan Disputations*. LCL 141. London: Heinemann, 1971.
Collins, Adela Yarbro. *Mark: A Commentary*. Hermeneia. Minneapolis: Fortress, 2007.
Collins, Raymond F. *The Power of Images in Paul*. Collegeville, MN: Liturgical, 2008.
Daniélou, Jean. *The Bible and the Liturgy*. University of Notre Dame Liturgical Studies 3. Notre Dame: University of Notre Dame Press, 1956.
Denzey, Nicola. *The Bone Gatherers: The Lost Worlds of Early Christian Women*. Boston: Beacon, 2008.
Dunbar, Nan, editor. *Aristophanes: Birds*. Oxford: Clarendon, 1995.
Feldman, Louis H. *Jew and Gentile in the Ancient World: Attitudes and Interactions from Alexander to Justinian*. Princeton: Princeton University Press, 1993.
Gagnon, Robert A. J. "Heart of Wax and a Teaching That Stamps: τύπος διδαχῆς (Rom 6:17b) Once More." *JBL* 112 (1993) 667–87.
Gutt, Ernst-August. *Translation and Relevance: Cognition and Context*. Manchester, UK: St. Jerome, 2000.
Guy, Laurie. "Naked Baptism in the Early Church: The Rhetoric and the Reality." *JRH* 27 (2003) 133–43.

Hall, Robert G. "Epispasm: Circumcision in Reverse." *BRev* 8.4 (1992) 52–57.
Hallett, Christopher H. *The Roman Nude: Heroic Portrait Statuary 200 BC—AD 300.* Oxford Studies in Ancient Culture and Representation. Oxford: Oxford University Press, 2011.
Harper, Douglas. "An Argument for Visual Sociology." In *Image-Based Research: A Sourcebook for Qualitative Researchers,* edited by Jon Prosser, 24–41. London: Falmer, 1998.
Harris, Murray J. *Colossians & Philemon.* Exegetical Guide to the Greek New Testament. Grand Rapids: Eerdmans, 1991.
Henderson, Jeffrey. *Aristophanes: Acharnians, Knights.* LCL. Cambridge: Harvard University Press, 1998.
———. *The Maculate Muse: Obscene Language in Attic Comedy.* Oxford: Oxford University Press, 1991.
Hodges, Frederick M. "The Ideal Prepuce in Ancient Greece and Rome: Male Genital Aesthetics and Their Relation to *Lipodermos,* Circumcision, Foreskin Restoration and the *Kynodesme.*" *Bulletin of the History of Medicine* 75 (2001) 375–405.
Hurwit, Jeffrey M. "The Problem with Dexileos: Heroic and Other Nudities in Greek Art." *AJA* 111 (2007) 35–60.
Jewett, Robert. *Romans: A Commentary.* Hermeneia. Minneapolis: Fortress, 2007.
Josephus, Flavius, and H. St. J. Thackeray. *The Jewish War.* LCL. Cambridge: Harvard University Press, 1997.
Justinian, *Digest.* Edited by Theodor Mommsen, Paul Krueger and Alan Watson. Philadelphia: University of Pennsylvania Press, 2009.
King, Martha. *An Exegetical Summary of Colossians.* Exegetical Summaries. 2nd ed. Dallas, TX: Summer Institute of Linguistics International, 2008.
Liddell, Henry G., and Robert Scott. *A Greek-English Lexicon: With a Revised Supplement.* London: Clarendon, 1996.
Lincoln, Andrew T. "Colossians." In *NIB* 11:553–665. Nashville: Abingdon, 2000.
MacDonald, Margaret Y. *Colossians and Ephesians.* SP 17. Collegeville: Liturgical, 2008.
Maximus, Valerius. *Memorable Sayings and Doings.* LCL. Edited and translated by Bailey Shackleton. Cambridge: Harvard University Press, 2000.
Meyer, Marvin W. "Making Mary Male: the Categories 'Male' and 'Female' in the Gospel of Thomas." *NTS* 31 (1985) 554–70.
Pack, Roger A., editor and translator. *Artemidorus Daldianus. Artemidori Daldiani onirocriticon libri.* Edited by R. A. Pack. Leipzig: Tuebner, 1963.
Perler, Othmar, editor. *Meliton de Sardes: Sur la Pâque et fragments.* SC 123. Paris: Cerf, 1966.
Quintilian. *The Orator's Education.* LCL. Translated by Donald Russell. Cambridge: Harvard University Press, 2001.
Snyder, Graydon F. *Ante Pacem: Archaeological Evidence of Church Life before Constantine.* Macon: Mercer University Press, 2003.
Solin, Heikki, and Marja Itkonen-Kaila, editors. *Graffiti del Palatino, raccolti ed editi sotto la direzione di Veikko Väänäne.* Acta Instituti Romani Finlandiae 3. Helsinki: Akateeminen Kirjakauppa, 1966.

Sperber, Dan, and Deirdre Wilson. *Relevance: Communication and Cognition.* 2nd ed. Malden: Blackwell, 1995.
Spier, Jeffrey. *Picturing the Bible: the Earliest Christian Art.* New Haven: Yale University Press, 2007.
Stevens, Wallace. "Adagia (1934–1940?)." In *Opus Posthumous: Poems, Plays, Prose,* edited by Milton J. Bates, 184–204. Rev., enl., and corr. ed. New York: Knopf, 1989.
Sumney, Jerry L. *Colossians: A Commentary.* NTL. Louisville: Westminster John Knox, 2008.
Usher, Stephen, editor. *Dionysius of Halicarnassus. The Critical Essays.* LCL. Cambridge: Harvard University Press, 1974.
Volf, Miroslav. *Exclusion and Embrace: A Theological Exploration of Identity, Otherness, and Reconciliation: Theological Exploration of Identity, Otherness and Reconciliation.* Nashville: Abingdon, 1996.
Webb, Ruth. *Ekphrasis, Imagination and Persuasion in Ancient Rhetorical Theory and Practice.* Farnham, UK: Ashgate, 2009.
Wiessenrieder, Annette. "Der Blick in den Spiegel. II Kor 3,18 vor dem Hintergrund antiker Spiegeltheorien un ikonographischer Abbildungen." In *Picturing the New Testament,* edited by Petra von Gemünden et al., 313–43. WUNT 193. Tübingen: Mohr/Siebeck, 2005.
Zanker, Graham. "Enargeia in the Ancient Criticism of Poetry." *Rheinisches Museum für Philologie* 124 (1981) 297–311.
Zanker, Paul. *The Mask of Socrates: The Image of the Intellectual in Antiquity.* Sather Classical Lectures 59. Berkley: University of California Press, 1996.
———. *The Power of Images in the Age of Augustus.* Thomas Spencer Jerome Lectures, 16th ser. Ann Arbor: University of Michigan Press, 1990.

20

Jonah in Early Christian Art
Death, Resurrection, and Immortality

EVERETT FERGUSON

DAVID BALCH HAS RECENTLY TAKEN A SERIOUS INTEREST IN ROMAN art of the first century, especially its relevance for early house churches and its possible influence on early Christian art. He wrote "From Endymion in Roman *domus* to Jonah in Christian Catacombs: From Houses of the Living to Houses for the Dead. Iconography and Religion in Transition."[1] I want to add my thoughts on the iconography of Jonah.

Jonah is far and away the most popular story from the Old Testament in pre-Constantinian Christian art.[2] The basic pattern is three scenes: Jonah swallowed by the sea monster, Jonah disgorged by the sea monster, and Jonah at rest under a pergola. This sequence is represented in perhaps the earliest depiction of Jonah in Cubiculum A6 in the Catacomb of Callistus. The sequence is notably from right to left: Jonah thrown overboard to the waiting sea monster (*kētos* in Greek), Jonah disgorged by the sea monster, and the naked Jonah reclining under a pergola.[3] A significant marble sarcophagus from the

---

1. In Brink and Green, *Commemorating the Dead*, 273–301; reprinted in Balch, *Roman Domestic Art*, 168–94.

2. Leclercq, "Jonas," 2572–2631; Dassmann, *Sündenvergebung durch Taufe*, 222–32, 385–97; Mazzoleni, "Jonah, II. Iconography," 1.450–51; Engemann, "Jonas," 689–99; Snyder, *Ante-Pacem*, 90–95. For paintings in the catacombs, see Nestori, *Repertorio topografico*. For sarcophagi, Deichmann et al., *Repertorium der christlich-antiken* with Lange, *Ikonographisches Register*.

3. Often reproduced, but see Spier, *Picturing the Bible*, Plate 3B. The right-to-left arrangement probably does not indicate that it was based on a Jewish model, the existence of which is speculative. Jonah was most often shown nude, but there are a significant number of scenes where he is clothed (see Bonansea, 199–202).

late third century in the British Museum (purchased 1957,10-11,l) depicts Jonah having been thrown to the sea monster, the monster spewing him out, and above the latter and larger Jonah resting under the gourd vine; on the curved ends of the sarcophagus are a sea monster and a peacock.[4] More often reproduced is the late third-century marble sarcophagus in the Vatican Museums (31448) with Jonah being thrown to the sea monster, the monster disgorging him, and Jonah at rest under a vine.[5]

A plaque from Velletri (Museo Civico, 171) dated about 300–310 shows Jonah thrown from the ship, the *kētos* casting him ashore, and Jonah resting under the gourd vine, shown larger as was typical.[6] Although most of the Jonah scenes are in the obviously funerary setting of catacomb frescoes and sarcophagi sculpture, they are not confined to that setting.[7] The floor mosaic of the early fourth-century church in Aquileia has the three Jonah pictures among fishing scenes, reflecting the popularity of nautical scenes.[8] A domestic setting, probably the fountain in a courtyard of the house of a well-to-do person, is likely the provenance of the statuettes from the late third century and probably from Asia Minor now known as the Cleveland marbles.[9] They have graphic portrayals of the three scenes, notable in that Jonah under the vine is clothed, in contrast to him in the two scenes with the sea monster and to his usual depiction.

The ivory box known as the Brescia lipsanotheca, from the fourth century, would have had domestic use. On the front Jonah is thrown from the ship into the mouth of the sea monster and then in a matching scene he emerges from the mouth of the sea monster. On the back of the casket he is reclining under a gourd vine.[10] An engraved glass

---

4. Weitzmann, *Age of Spirituality*, 398, fig. 52.

5. Spier, *Picturing the Bible*, plate 39.

6. Ibid., 413, #371.

7. Engemann, "Jonas," 695, says this use in other spheres calls in question a relation of the scene to the afterlife, but that seems unnecessarily reductionist. Afterlife scenes abound in pagan domestic art.

8. Ibid., 694; Duval, "Jonas à Aquilée."

9. Wixom, "Early Christian Sculptures ," 67–89; Kitzinger, "Cleveland Marbles," 653–75; reprinted in Finney, *Art, Archaeology*, 117–39; Wischmeyer, "vorkonstantinische christliche Kunst, " 253–77.

10. The cover and four sides reproduced in Grabar, *Christian Iconography*, #333–337.

plate from the fourth century, found at Podgoritza (in Montenegro) and now in the State Hermitage Museum in St. Petersburg, has a ship in which three sailors are in the posture of prayer, the sea monster swallowing Jonah, another depiction of the sea monster and Jonah on a rock under the vine.[11] The disgorging of Jonah and Jonah at rest have been collapsed into one scene. A gold glass bowl in Cologne (Römisch-Germanisches Museum, 991) has a small medallion at the bottom showing Jonah thrown overboard and up one side a larger medallion of the *kētos* expelling Jonah and Jonah at rest.[12]

An engraved carnelian gem dated late third or early fourth century from Asia Minor or Syria, now set in a modern ring in Boston's Museum of Fine Arts (03.1008), has a standing figure that may add a fourth scene of Jonah preaching or praying, a ship from which Jonah is cast to the waiting sea monster, Jonah expelled, and then Jonah unusually shown seated under a tree.[13] As the last item perhaps indicates, a fourth scene could be added to the Jonah cycle. A figure identical to the representations of Jonah among the Cleveland marbles is shown in the posture of prayer. If it belongs to the grouping, as seems likely, then we have a fourth scene, Jonah praying (Jonah 2). A broken glass bowl with gold glass medallions embedded includes four scenes related to Jonah: a ship with four persons and a sea monster swimming beside it, the sea monster swallowing Jonah head first, the sea monster disgorging him head first, and Jonah reclining under a gourd vine. The fragment is in the British Museum (MME 1881.06-24.1) and dates to the second half of the fourth century (Spier pl. 13A).[14]

A fourth scene is created for the sake of symmetry in a vault painting in the Catacombs of SS. Peter and Marcellinus. In addition to Jonah thrown to the fish and coming out of his mouth in the posture of prayer, he is seated under the pergola either pouting, suffering from the sun, or watching the city of Nineveh and in a separate scene is reclining at rest under the pergola.[15]

---

11. Spier, *Picturing the Bible*, fig. 4.
12. Weitzmann, *Age of Spirituality*, 421, #377.
13. Spier, *Picturing the Bible*, pl. 18.
14. Ibid., pl. 13A.
15. Reproduced in Grabar, *Christian Iconography*, #2; Spier, *Picturing the Bible*, plate 10C. Leclercq, "Jonas," 2572; Engemann, "Jonas," 691.

An unusual grouping and unusual sequence of five scenes occurs on a red earthenware bowl from North Africa, second half of the fourth century (Mainz, Römisch-Germanisches Zentralmuseum, 0.39677): Jonah thrown overboard, swallowed, sitting on rocks in a pensive gesture, disgorged, and awake under a vine to which he points.[16] Sometimes there are only two scenes, namely the central pair of Jonah swallowed and then disgorged. A marble statuette said to have been found at Tarsus in 1876 is unusual in showing Jonah lowered feet first into the open jaws of the sea monster and adjacent to this scene Jonah emerging head-first and in the posture of prayer from its mouth.[17] This depiction interestingly has the right-to-left sequence.[18]

Another two-scene presentation, focusing on his deliverance, is Jonah spewed out and then resting under a gourd vine, flanking a Good Shepherd, on a lamp found in a sepulture in Rome.[19] The Murano diptych (Ravenna, Museo Nazionale) at its bottom right shows Jonah thrown to the waiting monster and on the left the monster but with Jonah under the gourd vine.[20] A late combination of the beginning and end of the story is the sixth-century ivory pyxis in the Hermitage, St. Petersburg, with Jonah thrown overboard to the waiting *kētos* and then unusually resting on its back under the vine.[21] The late third-century sarcophagus in Santa Maria Antiqua, Rome, refers to the earlier part of the story by showing a ship and the sea monster, but its main representation is Jonah reclining under the vine.[22] Sometimes only one scene is depicted. A gold glass medallion from the fourth century in the Louvre has only Jonah being thrown into the mouth of the sea monster from a ship in which three men are seated.[23] An allusion to the rest of the story may be contained in the inscription "ZESIS," Greek for "May you live!" but written in Latin characters. In the Vatican necropolis, tomb N1, a mosaic depicts Jonah cast into the sea with two sailors in prayer, but other scenes from the sequence are lost.

16. Weitzmann, *Age of Spirituality*, 426, #384
17. Metropolitan Museum of Art, New York, 1876 (77.7).
18. Spier, *Picturing the Bible*, plate 15.
19. Finney, *Invisible God*, 119, fig. 5.6; Spier, pl. 2.
20. Weitzmann, *The Age of Spirituality*, 403, # 59.
21. Ibid., 427, #385.
22. Spier, *Picturing the Bible*, fig. 76.
23. Ibid., pl. 14.

The Catacomb of Priscilla has two frecoes of Jonah emerging from the mouth of the sea monster.[24] Rare is the single depiction of Jonah in contemplation shown on a red bowl from North Africa, fourth century, now in Mainz.[25] By counting the number of occurrences of each of the Jonah scenes, it is evident that the most popular was Jonah under the pergola. The bucolic setting was evidently taken as pointing to paradise, and the round gourd was a symbol of health. Where only one scene is shown, this is often the one selected. Cubiculum A5 in the Catatomb of Callixtus contains a single scene of Jonah under a pergola with a vine.[26] Although the proportion of Jonah scenes in relation to other biblical scenes declines in the post-Constantinian period, this is in part due to the larger repertoire as time went on, for Jonah continued to be present, and I have deliberately included a number of later representations in order to emphasize this. A linen textile, dated fifth century from Egypt, now in the Cleveland Museum of Art (51.400), has Jonah named and in a sitting posture of repose with the right arm behind his head.[27] A floor mosaic in a Byzantine church in Israel has the single scene of Jonah under the vine in an octagon in the north aisle.[28]

Space is not the reason for the scene chosen to represent Jonah in these examples, nor is it for the earlier ceiling fresco in the Coemeterium Maius, Rome, Cubiculum II.[29] In the center of the fresco is the Good Shepherd; on the four sides are an orant, Adam and Eve, Moses striking the rock, and the naked Jonah reclining. As this ceiling illustrates, Jonah in catacomb art and on sarcophagi is often in the company of other biblical scenes. Most frequent are Noah in the ark, Daniel in the lions' den, three young men in the furnace, Susannah, Moses striking the rock, Abraham sacrificing Isaac, and from the New Testament the raising of Lazarus. The theme uniting these scenes appears to be deliverance or salvation, appropriate for a funerary setting

---

24. Ibid., pl. 6 = fig. 52.
25. Weitzmann, *The Age of Spirituality*, 521, #405.
26. Spier, *Picturing the Bible*, pl. 3A.
27. Weitzmann, *The Age of Spirituality*, 433, #390.
28. Ovadiah, "Jonah in a Mosaic," 214–15, who thinks there may be shown the worm ready to attack the plant (if so, unique); Foerster, "Story of Jonah," 289–94.
29. Spier, *Picturing the Bible*, pl. 8.

but also central to Christian faith.[30] These are the stories recalled in prayers on behalf of the deceased, both Jewish and Christian. Fitting for the theme of deliverance is the occasional association of Jonah with baptism. The Jonah sequence in Cubiculum A3 of the Callixtus Catacomb also includes a baptism of Jesus flanked by a fisherman and the paralytic carrying his bed.[31] The baptism of Jesus and the Jonah story are the flanking scenes on the sarcophagus at Sta. Maria Antiqua (above). The description of baptism as a death and resurrection in Rom 6:1–4 facilitated the association of Jonah with baptism.

Graydon Snyder identified five major interpretations of the Jonah cycle:[32] (1) Narrative art telling the story of the book of Jonah.[33] The Jonah scenes are obviously based on the biblical story. Nevertheless, as Erich Dinkler observes concerning short scenes, including the Jonah scenes, "although the abbreviated representation is always rooted in a biblical episode, its symbolic allusions transcend that text."[34] Moreover, much that is central to the biblical story is not represented in the art: there is no call of God; Jonah's preaching is uncertainly represented if at all; there is no allusion to the repentance of the Ninevites; the plant that shaded Jonah is not cut down, and indeed the main thrust of the art is the peaceful repose of Jonah without acknowledgement of the close of the book of Jonah. A variation of this interpretation appeals to apocryphal and extra biblical versions of the story.[35] Clear instances of this are in the art following the Greek translation of the Bible, where the Greek has *kētos* (sea monster) for the Hebrew "big fish" (followed in the Vulgate) and *kolokunthē* (gourd) for the Hebrew "castor-oil plant" (Vulgate has "ivy"). But how far will this take us in interpreting all the scenes and their sequence?

(2) An interpretation of Jonah according to the words of Jesus (Matt 12:38–41) and patristic interpretation.[36] The theme of death and resurrection does seem evident, especially in a funerary context. The

30. Discussed by Provoost, "caractere et l'evolution," 79–101.
31. Spier, *Picuring the Bible*, pl. 3C.
32. Snyder, *Ante-Pacem*, 90–95.
33. Styger, *altchristliche Grabeskunst*, saw the biblical scenes as historical representations.
34. Dinkler, "Abbreviated Representations," 402.
35. Stommel, "Problem der frühchristlichen," 112–15.
36. Narkiss, "Sign of Jonah," 63–76.

art, however, more often presents the sea monster as the connection between the boat and Jonah under the vine, and the latter is the most prominent scene.

The use of Jonah in early Christian literature is quite varied and does not correspond very closely to the scenes in art. Balch has classified the principal references in the earliest writings.[37] Their applications of the story are the three days in the tomb and the repentance of Nineveh,[38] the resurrection of Jesus,[39] repentance only (the most common use),[40] prayer,[41] believers' resurrection,[42] allusion to monsters in Roman art,[43] warning against fleeing from the Lord,[44] and the only reference to souls in Paradise with the polemical thrust that this is not around the moon.[45] To these are to be added the lesson of God's mercy,[46] the conversion of pagans,[47] and from a later writer the need for obedience.[48] The most common use of the story, to teach moral and spiritual lessons, is different from the art.

(3) The soul of the deceased at rest.[49] This interpretation focuses on the scene that is most prominent in the art and appeals to the portrayal of a nude Jonah in a setting of pastoral serenity. Death as a restful sleep would fit the funerary context of the earliest Christian art. This narrow interpretation, however, does not do justice to the other scenes in the cycle, and it ill accords with the theme of deliver-

---

37. Balch, *Roman Domestic Art*, 192–93, whom I follow in this paragraph; more comprehensively Duval, *Livre de Jonas*; also Allenbach, " Figure de Jonas, " who views Jonah under the vine as typical of the Christianizing of pagan motifs in art, in this case a Christianized form of Endymion as used by Stoics.

38. Justin, *Dial.* 107–108; Tertullian, *Pud.* 10.

39. Origen, *Comm. Mt.* 12.3; *Acts of Paul* 8.29–31.

40. *1 Clem.* 7.5–7; Clement of Alexandria, *Strom.* 1.21; Origen, *Hom. Num.* 16.4; *Hom. Jer.* 1.1; Tertullian, *Marc.* 2.17 and 24; 4.10; 5.11.

41. Origen, *Or.* 13.2.

42. Irenaeus, *Haer.* 3.20; 5.5.2; Tertullian, *Res. carn.* 58.

43. Origen, *Or.* 13.4; Tertullian, *Carn.* 32.

44. Tertullian, *Fug.* 10.

45. Tertullian, *An.* 55.

46. Tertullian, *Marc.* 2.24.

47. Clement of Alexandria, *Protr.* 10.99.4. Testini suggests that the popularity of the Jonah cycle was a polemic on behalf of the universality of the gospel-*Atti del IX Congresso*, 484–485.

48. John Chrysostom, *Stat.* 5.15–17.

49. Stuiber, *Refrigerium interim*; review by de Bruyne, "Refrigerium interim," 112–14.

ance evident in associated biblical scenes. In a Christian context, the idea of resurrection could not be far away, especially in the light of Jesus's words. Robin Jensen sees the figure of Jonah as referring both to the "expected resurrection" of believers and the "interim wait for that resurrection, in a state of blissful repose."[50] From another standpoint, if there is any validity to a narrative sequence in the Jonah cycle, the intermediate rest of the soul is misplaced and is given a prominence above the resurrection.

(4) Jonah identified with the popular pagan sepulchral figure Endymion.[51] In frequent scenes on non-Christian sarcophagi, Endymion, reclining and nearly nude, is put to sleep by Night and attended by the moon goddess Selene. The popularity of Jonah is explained in part because profane art furnished elements of the composition (e.g. conjunction of marine and pastoral setting) and the artist's confusion of the biblical prophet with Endymion and secular shepherds.[52] The posture of Jonah resembles depictions of Endymion in perpetual sleep. But we should remember that Endymion as an iconographical model is quite another thing from seeing Jonah as a Christianized Endymion. As is true for interpretation (3) this view leaves the rest of the cycle inadequately explained. Other than the pose of Jonah and the bucolic setting, nothing in the Christian scenes evokes the mythological setting of Endymion. There are other possible pagan antecedents. A Campanian terracotta shows a naked Dionysus under a grape vine (Paris, Louvre) almost identical in pose to Jonah.[53] The reclining Jonah in the Cleveland marbles resembles pagan depictions of a river god (n. 7).

(5) The liturgical interpretation. The prominence of Jonah at rest is a factor in proposing the liturgical explanation. Prayers for the

---

50. Jensen, *Understanding Early Christian*, 72; further on pp. 172–73.

51. Lawrence, "Three Pagan Themes," 323–34, for Jonah as the Christian parallel for Endymion. He observes that the rams and goat on the Santa Maria Antiqua sarcophagus come from the representation of Endymion, whom Theocritus made a shepherd, not a hunter; he reads the sarcophagus right to left as initiation (baptism of Christ), ministry of Christ (Good Shepherd), and resurrection (Jonah); Lawrence, "Ships, Monster and Jonah," 289–96.

52. Simon, "Symbolisme et Tradition, " 307–19 on the fisher, the ship, and the story of Jonah.

53. Weitzmann, *The Age of Spirituality*, 402, fig. 58. Also, Stommel, "Zum Problem," 115. Grabar, *Christian Iconography*, 32, suggests other figures similar to the recumbent Jonah.

dead (*Ordo commendationis animae*) invoke the same examples of rescue in dangerous situations that are common in early Christian art.⁵⁴ Although the written texts are not earlier than the ninth century, the prayers are likely earlier. Yet the *Ordo* lacks Jonah, and one may question how early were the specific prayers? A closer liturgical parallel is the list of Bible readings used in Rome in the seventh century for the period from before Lent to after Easter, suggesting a possible correlation between catechetical instruction connected with baptism and the scenes in early Christian art.⁵⁵ The biblical scenes of salvation appear from the beginning of Christian art before the prayers for deliverance and the cycle of readings are likely to have been fixed. Furthermore, although many of the biblical scenes evoke or show the history of salvation, other biblical scenes appear with a significant frequency.⁵⁶ There is the further question, why are the scenes recalled in the liturgical texts for the most part represented in the art by a single scene, while Jonah appears in a cycle?

I would propose an interpretation that draws on the strengths of these interpretations but avoids their shortcomings. I anticipated it in my entry on "Jonah" for the *Encyclopedia of Early Christianity*: "[A] plausible meaning for the sequence is death, resurrection, and eternal bliss."⁵⁷ This simple understanding has several things in its favor. (1) It keeps Jesus's use of the biblical story but applied to individual believers. (2) It fits the theme of deliverance but adds a greater eschatological significance. (3) It maintains the biblical sequence in the order of the scenes and avoids the difficulty of putting the interim repose of the soul after the resurrection, yet accounts for the Paradise setting of Jonah under the pergola. (4) It explains the greater prominence given to the last scene as the final state of heavenly bliss. Jonah in early Christian art connects with various iconographical parallels

---

54. Ferrua, "Paralipomeni di Giona," 7–69 (68–69); Dinkler, "Abbreviated Representations," 397, who refers to prayers for salvation. The archetype of these prayers may be Cyprian of Antioch, *Oratio* 2 (fourth century?).

55. Martimort, "L'iconographie des catacombs," 105–14, who explains the importance of Jonah not only as a type of the resurrection but also as a witness to the calling of the Gentiles and the mercy of God to penitents.

56. Provoost, "caractère et l'évolution," 96, 99; he also indicates that the biblical scenes occur in contexts of the rich and cultivated Christians and not on objects pertaining to the less fortunate (p. 98).

57. Ferguson, "Jonah," 628.

and theological themes. His story was an important way Christians expressed and affirmed their faith in their cultural environment. The popularity of images of Jonah attest that this "Minor Prophet" had major impact.

Bibliography

Allenbach, Jean. "La figure de Jonas dans les textes préconstantiniens ou l'histoire de l'exégèau secours de l'iconographie." In *La Bible et les Pères: Colloque de Strasbourg, October 1969*, edited by A. Benoit et al., 97–112. Paris: Université de France, 1971.

Balch, David L. *Roman Domestic Art and Early House Churches*. WUNT 228. Tübingen: Mohr/Siebeck, 2008.

Bonansea, N. "La variante di Giona vestito nell'iconographia paleochristiana tra III e VI secolo." *VChr* 46 (2009) 199–202.

Brink, Laurie, and Deborah Green, editors. *Commemorating the Dead: Texts and Artifacts in Context*. Berlin: de Gruyter, 2008.

Dassmann, Ernst. *Sündenvergebung durch Taufe, Busse und Märtyrerfürbitte in den Zeugnissen frühchristlicher Frömmigkeit und Kunst*. Münsterische Beiträge zur Theologie 36. Münster: Aschendorff, 1973.

Deichmann, Friedrich Wilhelm, et al., editors. *Repertorium der christlich-antiken Sarkophage*. 3 vols. Wiesbaden: Steiner, 1967, 1998. Mainz: Zabern, 2003.

Dinkler, Erich. "Abbreviated Representations." In *Age of Spirituality: Late Antique and Early Christian Art, Third to Seventh Century: Catalogue of the Exhibition at the Metropolitan Museum of Art, November 19, 1977, through February 12, 1978*, edited by Kurt Weitzmann, 396–402. New York: Metropolitan Museum of Art, 1979.

Duval, Yves-Marie. "Jonas à Aquilée. de la mosaïque de la Basilique de Théodore aux textes de Jérôme, Rufin et Chromace." In *Aquileia romana fra II e V secolo*, edited by Gino Bandelli, 273–96. Trieste: Editreg SRL, 2000.

———. *Le Livre de Jonas dans la littérature chrétienne grecque et latine: Sources et influence du Commentaire sur Jonas de saint Jérôme*. Paris: Études Augustiniennes, 1973.

Engemann, J. "Jonas, V. Kunst." *RivAC* 18 (1998) 689–99.

Ferguson, Everett. "Jonah." *EEC* (1997) 628.

Ferrua, Antonio. "Paralipomeni di Giona." *RivAC* 38 (1962) 7–69.

Finney, Paul Corby. *The Invisible God: The Earliest Christians on Art*. New York: Oxford University Press, 1994.

———, editor. *Art, Archaeology, and Architecture of Early Christianity*. Studies in Early Christianity 18. New York: Garland, 1993.

Foerster, Gideon. "The Story of Jonah on the Mosaic Pavement of a Church at Beth Govrin (Israel)." *Atti del IX Congresso Internazionale di Archeologia Cristiana. Roma 1975*. 2:289–34. SAC 32. Vatican City: Pontificio Istituto di Archeologia Cristiana, 1978.

Grabar, André. *Christian Iconography: A Study of Its Origins*. Bollingen Series 35.10. Princeton: Princeton University Press, 1968.

Jensen, Robin Margaret. *Understanding Early Christian Art*. London: Routledge, 2000.

Kitzinger, Ernst. "The Cleveland Marbles." In *Atti del IX Congresso Internazionale di Archeologia Cristiana. Roma 1975*, 1:653–75. Vatican City: Pontificio Istituto di Archeologia Cristiana, 1978.

Lange, Ulrike. *Ikonographisches Register für das Repertorium der christlich-antiken Sarkophage*. Christliche Archäologie 2. Dettelbach: Röll, 1996.

Lawrence, Marion. "Three Pagan Themes in Christian Art." In *De Artibus Opuscula XL: Essays in Honor of Erwin Panofsky*, edited by Millard Meiss, 1:323–34. 2 vols. New York: New York University, 1961.
———. "Ships, Monster and Jonah." *AJA* 66 (1962) 289–96.
Leclercq, H. "Jonas." In *DACL* 7.2 (1926) 2572–631.
Martimort, A.-G. "L'iconographie des catacombes et la catéchèse antique." *RivAC* 25 (1949) 105–14.
Mazzoleni, D. "Jonah, II. Iconography." *Encyclopedia of the Early Church*, edited by Angelo DiBerardino. 1:449–51. 2 vols. New York: Oxford University Press, 1992.
Narkiss, Bezalel. "The Sign of Jonah." *Gesta* 18 (1979) 63–76.
Nestori, Aldo. *Repertorio topografico delle pitture delle catacombe Romane* . Rev. ed. Roma sotterranea cristiana Vatican City: Pontificio istituto di archeologia cristiana, 1993.
Ovadiah, Ruth. "Jonah in a Mosaic Pavement at Beth Guvrin." *IEJ* 24 (1974) 214–15.
Provoost, A. "Le caractere et l'evolution des images bibliques dans l'art chrétien primitive." In *The Impact of Scripture in Early Christianity*, edited by J. den Boeft and M. L. van Poll-van de Lisdonk, 79–101. Supplements to Vigiliae Christianae 44. Leiden: Brill, 1999.
Simon, M. "Symbolisme et Tradition d'atelier dans la première sculpture chrétienne." In *Actes du Ve congres international d'archéologie chrétienne*, 307–19. Paris: Città del Vaticano, 1957.
Snyder, Graydon F. *Ante-Pacem: Archaeological Evidence of Church Life before Constantine*. Macon: Mercer University Press, 2003.
Spier, Jeffrey, editor. *Picturing the Bible: The Earliest Christian Art*. New Haven: Yale University Press in Association with the Kimbell Art Museum, Fort Worth, 2007.
Stommel, Eduard. "Zum Problem der frühchristlichen Jonasdarstellungen." *JAC* 1 (1958) 112–15.
Stuiber, A. Review of *Refrigerium interim: Die Vorstellungen vom Zwischenzustand und die frühchristliche Kunst*, Theophaneia 11, Bonn: Hanstein, 1957, by L. de Bruyne, "Refrigerium interim." *RivAC* 34 (1958) 112–14.
Styger, Paul. *Die altchristliche Grabeskunst*. Munich: Kösel & Pustet, 1927.
Testini, P. Untitled. In *Atti del IX Congresso Internazionale di Archeologia Cristiana. Roma 1975*, 484–85. Vatican City: Pontificio Istituto di Acheologia Cristiana, 1978.
Weitzmann, Kurt, editor. *Age of Spirituality: Late Antique and Early Christian Art, Third to Seventh Century: Catalogue of the Exhibition at the Metropolitan Museum of Art, November 19, 1977, through February 12, 1978*. New York: Metropolitan Museum of Art, 1979.
Wischmeyer, Wolfgang. "Die vorkonstantinische christliche Kunst in Neuem Lichte: Die Cleveland-Statuetten." *VC* 35 (1981) 253–87.
Wixom, W. D. "Early Christian Sculptures at Cleveland." *BCMA* 54:3 (1967) 67–89.

21

"Created in the Image of God"
Graeco-Roman Jewish Art—
New Perspectives from Archaeology

RICHARD FREUND

Figure 21.1: Iron Age figurines from Bethsaida, Courtesy Bethsaida Excavations Project.

> God has taken his place in the divine council; in the midst of the gods he holds judgment.
>
> —Ps 82:1 (NRSV)

The Problem of Ancient Jewish Art

The first chapter of the book of Genesis includes "God created Adam in the image of God." The image of God was from the very beginning of the Bible a problem for artists. What would be a permitted way to depict the image of God? Jews, Christians, and later Muslims would alternatively find their own answers to this question. The question of the existence of an ancient Jewish representational art tradition is complicated by centuries of interpretations (by differing Jewish and Rabbinic sources) that lived in different countries with a variety of views about whether Jews were or were not permitted to produce and use representational art of any kind in any period. The question this chapter attempts to answer is whether or not there was an ancient tradition of representational art done by Jews, for use by Jews (or earlier done by Israelites for use by Israelites).

I have begun to understand the question in many different ways after looking at the corpus of material culture available in different time periods from the Iron Age through the Byzantine period in the historic "Land of Israel" and in the Diaspora. Was representational art an indigenous endeavor of the Israelites and later the Jews or was it simply a forbidden act that was later accepted by the Jews through their contact with Christianity in the Byzantine period (or even later)? It was almost a "given" for art historians in the modern period that the Bible and Judaism all but prohibited every form of representational art used by the ancient Egyptians, Mesopotamians, Phoenicians, Greeks, Romans and Christians. The traditional answer to the question of whether or not there was an ancient Jewish representational art tradition was simply: *No*. From the biblical period onward, Israelites and Judeans and later Rabbinic Jews had no representational art tradition. Some of the confusion about this question is based upon a selective reading and interpretation of the Second Commandment of the Ten Commandments in the Bible, but it is also based upon a cultural stereotype that emerged not out of a systematic understanding of antiquity but in a much later time period.

The Ten Commandments and Jewish Art

The Second Commandment of the Ten Commandments (Exodus 20.8) reads: "You shall not make for yourself a carved image, any likeness of what is in the heavens above, or on the earth below, or in the waters below the earth. **You shall not bow down to them or serve them** for I am the Lord your God." For some, this is an absolute prohibition of any art by anyone professing to follow the God of ancient Israel. For some biblical, Jewish and Rabbinic sources, this was understood as an absolute prohibition against any form of representational art that includes anything that is "on the earth or in the heavens." This might include virtually all representational art in and of anything that appears in the world. For others, this is a very pointed prohibition against creating artistic renderings that are used as objects of religious worship. In fact, over the past seventy years of systematic archaeology at Israelite and Judean sites in the historical "Land of Israel" reveals that there is enormous evidence of a representational art tradition used both a private and public Israelite sites from the Iron Age onward.

I start with the parameters of the time periods investigated and what constitutes biblical and Jewish art in this chapter. While this short survey of the question is not comprehensive, it is clear that biblical and Jewish art can be defined by artistic renderings of any kind created by ancient Israelites/Judeans (or found in public or private Israelite/Judean settings) from the Iron Age the Byzantine period. The themes of the art may or may not be Jewish or biblical in nature. This art may be used to venerate the God of ancient Israel or it may represent a surrogate or "lesser power" or a part of nature (associated by the faithful with the God of ancient Israel) and it may be displayed in a public (read: cult site) or private context (home).

Most scholars have assigned enormous importance to the Second Commandment in daily Israelite and Jewish life. These scholars accept that the Jews did use scenes of nature (flora and fauna), geometric and universal symbols of an abstract nature and even some fantastic mythological figures that do not appear "in the heavens above or on the earth beneath." There are some scholars that continue to say that *all* Israelite and Jewish groups in *all* periods forbade *all* representational images of *anything* from the heavens above or the earth beneath. In this view, ancient Judaism and even biblical Jews were "aniconic" or "iconophobic/idol-ophobic" and so the only possible art that was permitted to the artists was "fantasy" characters such as the medieval

Jewish so-called "Bird's Head Passover Haggadah" (Southern Germany, circa 1300 in which all of the people in the illuminated manuscript have a bird's head with a human body) or abstract/line renderings like an inverted meander. Today most art historians hold that the Israelites, Judeans and the early Rabbinic Jews were aniconic or iconophobic until the Jewish tradition changed suddenly in the Byzantine period.[1] Some scholars thought that a major change in Jewish thinking about art had started earlier, in the Greek period. So, for example, historians, Salo Baron and Erwin Goodenough both addressed this issue (in their multi-volume, *Jewish Symbols in the Greco-Roman Period* from the 1950s) Goodenough wrote about Baron's conclusions:[2] "Is it true, as he [the famous Jewish historian Salo Baron] says, that 'Greek art impressed itself upon the mind of the Jew more than Greek philosophy'? Although Baron gives us in a note in one of the best bibliographies of Jewish art for the period [*A Social and Religious History of the Jews* (multi-volume set, 1952, Columbia University Press)], he nowhere seriously examines its evidence. If we cannot go into the problem of the attitude of the Rabbis to images, let me beg the question for the moment and say that the art seems to me definitely a part of Judaism, but to have no real place in Rabbinic Judaism."

The Iron Age (thirteenth century BCE—fourth century BCE): From the Hebrew Bible to the Graeco-Roman Period

Although this chapter is devoted mainly to the Graeco-Roman period, part of my argument is that there was a long and well-known trail of material culture that indeed does demonstrate an Israelite and Judean representational art tradition that antedates the Graeco-Roman period. Archaeology has provided material culture of the Israelites during the biblical periods from the Patriarchs and Matriarchs in the Bronze through the Iron Age. Many small figurines with a variety of different images have been found in Israelite and Judean public and private settings in the Iron Age. Most of these figures (see figure 21.1)

---

1. The standard presentation is found in Hachili, *Ancient Jewish Art*, 237: "Figurative art is an extensive and essential part of Jewish art in Late Antiquity. A major, conceptual change in Jewish art occurs at the end of the second and particularly during the third century when representational art begins to flourish."

2. Goodenough, *Jewish Symbols*, 1:23.

cannot be explained away by assigning them all to non-Israelites and Judeans, especially in the classical Iron Age IIa. Stamp-seals and seal impressions (bullae) show beautiful depictions of animals, plants, and various other god-like images. Hundreds of thousands of different types of representational art are depicted on storage jar handle seals and seal impressions. Clay figurines of horses and naked women, among others, were quite popular, particularly in Jerusalem in what was clearly the time of the temple of Solomon between the tenth and the sixth centuries BCE. In Samaria, the capital of the northern kingdom of Israel, archaeologists found one of the largest and most lavish collections of ivory engravings of representational art ever found in the ancient near east.

Pottery vessels found at Kuntillet 'Ajrud in the eastern Sinai are covered with graffiti, which may include a depiction of a hand of the God of Israel. At Arad, a cultic site in the Negev desert, archaeologists have excavated the only relatively intact Israelite temple from biblical times, in which decorated cult pillars were found in the "the Holy of Holies." Othmar Keel and Christoph Uehlinger in their book, *Gods, Goddesses and Images of God in Ancient Israel*[3] demonstrate that in the period before Iron Age IIb (from the ninth and eighth centuries BCE) images of all kinds, sun-disks, Egyptian symbols of all kinds, were found on Judean seals and bullae, but he argues, after the reform instituted by the Judean King Josiah, (in the late seventh century BCE) a difference can be noted in the archaeological finds. According to Keel and Uehlinger, after Iron Age IIb, the images become purely ornamental design, and by the fifth century CE, they note that figurines seem to disappear as well. This is an important distinction because it shows that there was a time when the Israelites used these images and another time when they did not. The entire situation changes with the destruction of the Judean state and cult in the sixth century BCE and the exile of the Judeans to Babylonia. When Jewish history picks up in the period the new Judeans are very limited in their use of images but the beginnings of Judean coinage in this period immediately adds the images of Persia to the Judean pantheon of "permitted" images in the public and private spheres. So one can say that the ancient non-Israelite images appear, disappear and then new ones reappear in the short period of time which leads us into the Graeco-Roman period (see figure 21.2).

3. Keel and Uehlinger, *Gods, Goddesses*, 389.

Figure 21.2: A door lintel from Bethsaida (Courtesy of Bethsaida Excavation Project).

Decorative Art and Its Graeco-Roman Meaning

Unfortunately, most researchers look for Graeco-Roman gods and goddesses (figurines and statues) as the determining barometer of decorative art and the Jews. I begin with the inverted meander and the small rosettes that are placed inside of the meander that was found at our excavations at Bethsaida, a site on the northeast shore of the Sea of Galilee and according to the literary traditions of the New Testament and early Christianity was home to almost half of the apostles and the site of many of the miracles that Jesus performed. The same inverted meander was found on a stone from the excavations of the Temple Mount in Jerusalem and the design is most notably found on the Peace Altar in Rome. It is, no doubt, one of the iconic symbols of Rome, the Imperial Cult and all it represents and would have been as recognizable to a Roman citizen as any of the statues that one finds there. No one questions that this is an artistic rendering done by and for Jews that just happens to correspond to Roman art of the same period. It is certainly not the only rendering. At Bethsaida from the same time period we have oil lamps that tell us much more about the population. The influence of the Greeks and the Romans was enormous following the fourth century and into the third century BCE.

Eros was a popular figure in Graeco-Roman mythology, figurines and oil lamps in Rome and the appearance on small artifacts allowed for the deities to be reflected in the home as well as in temples. Starting in the third century BCE, areas all over northern Israel were affected by the Eros cult thanks to the influence of the Seleucid Greeks. The appearance of Eros on oil lamps used by Jews and non-Jews and in areas that were populated by Jews is important. Eros was, of course, the Greek and later Roman god of love. The image resembles what would later become a hallmark in all Hellenistic Jewish literature, angels and cherubic beings that inhabited the world between the world of the Jewish God and the world of humans, both in their homes and in ritual settings. By the Hellenistic period angels had become a literary device in apocryphal books such as Tobit, *Testament of Solomon,* and *1 Enoch* as surrogates for the all-mighty God of Israel. These books used angels as creations of God which were either created before or concurrently with the creation of the material world but were sufficiently separated from God that they were apparently not problematic (see figure 21.3).

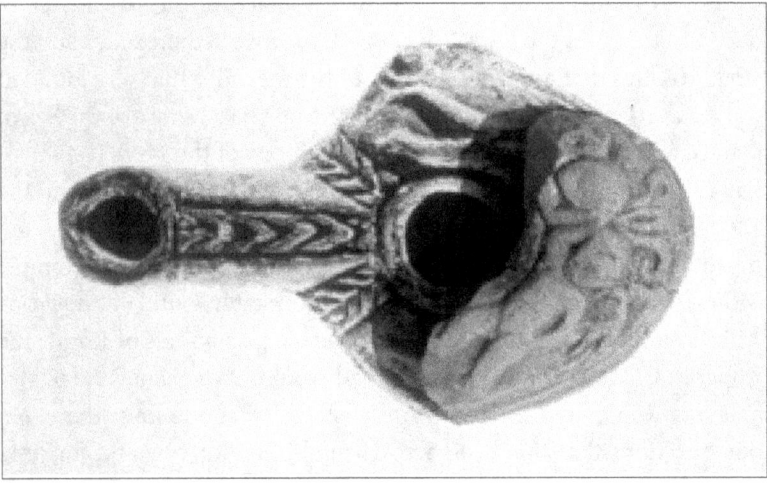

Figure 21.3: Graeco-Roman Period Eros oil lamp (Courtesy Bethsaida Excavations Project).

Graeco-Roman Gods and Goddesses in Jewish Contexts

The original Arch of Titus, built at the curved end of the Circus Maximus in Rome after the victories of Vespasian and Titus, no longer exists. The current "Arch of Titus," found at the end of the Via Sacra between the Roman Forum and the Colosseum, was completed in the period of Domitian, Vespasian's second son. It was rendered in the mid-80s CE either as a tribute to Domitian's father's victory in Jerusalem or in memory of his brother (perhaps to deflect criticism circulating in Rome that he had poisoned his brother). The Arch of Titus is built of imported white marble around a concrete core and has panels showing Titus carrying away the treasures of the Temple of Jerusalem. The artifacts shown on the Arch were probably kept in the Forum of Vespasian, built to identify the new dynasty with the blessings of peace after the period of strife within both the western and eastern empires. This is confirmed by the statements of Josephus in the *Jewish Wars* 7.5.5–7. The Menorah is depicted on the Arch of Titus. One of the main questions about the Menorah is its base, upon which is found the mythological figures (including Thetis). Unlike other scholarly understandings of the base as a foreign ornamentation or a Roman stabilizing device, I maintain that the base is original and known to the Jews from the Roman period until the rabbis. The base of the Menorah in the Arch of Titus is one smaller octagonal block stacked on a larger octagonal block, which resemble steps that are approximately nine inches thick when the height of the Menorah is compared with the height of the individuals carrying it on the Arch of Titus. Many scholars have noted that the base of the menorah on the Arch of Titus is decorated by Graeco-Roman mythological characters. There are various explanations of why these mythological characters are on the Menorah, but generally during the 1950s and 1960s, the prevailing view was that these characters on the steps could not have been done by a Jewish artist. One modern Rabbinic and even art historian explained that that the original base of the Menorah was probably broken when the Romans destroyed the Temple, so the Romans had to replace and stabilize the Menorah to transport it to Rome. According to this explanation, the Romans must have employed a Roman artist who decided to embellish the stabilizing steps with these mythological figures! When I first read this I was astonished. It is so improbable that the Romans, after destroying the Temple, the priesthood and exiling the Jews from Jerusalem in the year 70 CE they would suddenly take the time and expense to refurbish the item (see figure 21.4).

Figure 21.4: Drawing of the Menorah on the Arch of Titus, courtesy of the Cave of Letters Excavations Project.

Philo, Josephus, and the Roman Eagle

Against this background are the writings of Philo and Josephus that are used as the most reliable views of Jews from the Diaspora and Jews in Israel in the first century CE and which seem to reject any image in Jewish life. Philo, living in Alexandria, Egypt writes in *On the Giants*, 13.59: "Moses banished painting and sculpture, with all their high repute and artistry, because their craft belies the nature of truth and works deception and illusion through the eyes to souls that are ready to be seduced."

According to these much quoted sources, Roman representational art presented a radical conflict with Jewish values. Josephus Flavius asserts in *Against Apion* that: "No materials, however costly, are fit to make an image of Him; no art has skill to conceive and represent it; the like of Him we have never seen, we do not imagine, and it is impious to conjecture . . . [that God] *forbade the making of images, alike of any living creature, and much more of God.'"* (*C. Ap.* 2.75). This argument would strike a cord not only with Jewish readers but also strangely enough to his more philosophically oriented (non-Jewish/Roman) readers. Josephus relates the story of the eagle crisis: in *Antiquities* 17.6.2 (149–63) and *Jewish War* (1.648–54). People point to the famous incident that occurred near the end of Herod's life at the Temple, which seems to be critical to the story. Herod had added a golden eagle on the great gate dedicated to the Temple (Josephus makes it seem as if it is a new innovation, but it may in fact have been there for a while) and although Josephus had earlier mentioned that images were not forbidden if they were not worshipped (*Ant.* 8.7.5), in *Ant.* 15.272 he raises the issue of the images on the trophies of armor in Herod's theater in Jerusalem. The question is whether this and other incidents were a part of a protest movement precisely at the end of Herod's life. The main characters in Josephus's story are Judah, the son of Saripheus (Sepphoris?—the place where the First Revolt broke out in 66 CE) who was from a place where revolutionaries came from) and Mattiyahu, the son of Margaliot. They mentioned the second commandment and said: "that the law forbids that anyone proposing to live according to the law not erect images or representations of any living creature."

The question is whether this placement of the eagle was in fact a new innovation or simply a unique revolutionary/rebellious reaction or act that was consistent with the period but not necessarily indicative of the general rule? Josephus, in particular, may not be a disinterested observer of this phenomenon. He appears to be "icono-phobic" since he leaves out the Golden Calf account in his re-telling of the book of Exodus and even later chastises King Solomon (*Antiquities* 8.194–195) for using images in the first Temple of Jerusalem. Josephus mentions (*Life* 12) that he had been sent by the Jerusalem Sanhedrin to Herod Antipas's palace in Tiberias in 66 CE to remove the forbidden "imagery" of animals despite the fact that animals seem to have been exempt from the interpretation of the Second Commandment. So we have in the early Rabbinic Tosefta Tractate Avodah Zarah (5.2): "Rabbi Eleazar bar Tzadok, says: All sorts of images were in Jerusalem, except for the face of a human being." Were the views of Philo and Josephus a reflection of the greater population, emblematic of the problems of the first century CE or were they towing the "official" line of the Judaism in this period? It is hard to know given the wealth of artifacts that indeed did bear the forbidden images.

The Rabbis in the Byzantine Period

"In the days of Rabbi Yohanan (third century CE) they began to make images (*tziurim*) on the walls, and he [Rabbi Yohanan] did not stop them. In the days of Rabbi Abun (fourth century CE) they began to make images on mosaics, and he did not stop them."[4]

The idea that Rabbinic Judaism followed slavishly the prima facie understandings of biblical texts has been shown to be problematic. In fact the Rabbis followed a series of different local practices and location was important. The Diaspora of the Jews that had begun in the Babylonian Exile in the sixth century BCE continued to grow even as the restoration of Judea began in the Persian period. The Rabbis themselves were a diverse group, incorporating some who seem to have understood even in the first century CE that Judea was a Roman province and that the influences of Roman culture and especially art were profound. So we have the first century CE Rabban Gamliel in the early Rabbinic Mishnah of Tractate *Avodah Zarah* 4.3 who can see that bathing in Roman bathhouse dedicated and decorated with Aphrodite statues in Akko is not only permissible but can be a part of Jewish life in the first century CE in a place like Akko.[5] He understood the second part of the Second Commandment as the operative line when he stated: "If a [statue] is treated as a god, then it is forbidden, but if it is not treated as a god, then one [a Jew] is permitted [to be in its presence]."

What is clear from the material culture of the fourth century CE and onward is that indeed the Jews created representational art both on and for the "new" synagogue type that emerged in this period. In

---

4. Yerushalmi Talmud, Genizah fragment first quoted by Epstein in *Tarbiz*, 1931 from Tractate *Avodah Zarah* 42d. The ruling is not found in the Babylonian Talmud, and I note that this is not found in any of the main manuscripts of the Yerushalmi Talmud or in the later printed editions. It is possible that this points to how controversial the ruling was. It may indicate that although the ruling is accepted as authoritative in its time period, it was not universally understood or acknowledged by post-Talmudic rabbis.

5. In reaction to the writings of Goodenough and others, a professor of Talmud, Ephraim Urbach of the Hebrew University in Jerusalem, wrote in his seminal article, "The Rabbinical Laws," 150ff, that the Jews may have been using pagan symbols in the second and third centuries of the Common Era, but even then they did so without really attaching any pagan religious meanings to them. So even professor Urbach had solved the ancient Jewish art issue without positing a "direct conflict" between the people's "folk" religion and the rabbis' "official" religion.

addition to synagogue decoration we also have burial sites that are decorated with images from the Roman pantheon. At Beth Shearim in the Rabbinic burial caves we find that Zeus and many other images are accompanying the dead in a more than symbolic way by appearing on the sarcophagus (see figure 21.5).

Figure 21.5: Sarcophagus from Bet Shearim- Courtesy, Bethsaida Excavations Project).

The Zodiac with all of the mythological figures translated with Hebrew names are found in the central mosaic of these synagogues. They all date from the fourth to the sixth century CE and the best examples include seven in total from Hammat Tiberias, Yafia, Beit Alpha, Huseifa, Susiya, Naaran, and Sepphoris from the Galilee. Although these images may seem problematic, they are explained away by the fact that they emerge in a later time period; after the Rabbis have sanctioned them. In fact, it appears that the Rabbis were just accepting what had been a long tradition of Jewish art produced for the populous and created by the populous which they no longer felt they could ignore.

In summary, the ancient Israelites and Jews seem to have developed a two tiered system of ancient art in the Hebrew Bible through the Hellenistic Jewish tradition. One that officially banned the worship of artistic renderings of the God of ancient Israel but that allowed for differing images to be made and used for a variety of popular uses. While "official" Jewish teaching did not fully sanction art as a means to elevate the worshipper to greater spirituality as did Christian art, some parts of the Rabbinic tradition did come to accept that art could provide the Jewish masses with a way of integrating images into the official religious life of the Jews (as witnessed in the mosaic in figure 21.6).

Figure 21.6: Bet Alpha Synagogue Zodiac (Bethsaida Excavations Project).

Bibliography

Fine, Steven. *Art and Judaism in the Greco-Roman World: Toward a New Jewish Archaeology*. Cambridge: Cambridge University Press, 2005.

———, editor. *Sacred Realm: The Emergence of the Synagogue in the Ancient World*. New York: Oxford University Press, 1996.

Freund, Richard A. *Digging through the Bible: Understanding Biblical People, Places, and Controversy through Archaeology*. Lanham, MD: Rowman & Littlefield, 2009.

Goodenough, Erwin Ramsdell. *Jewish Symbols in the Greco-Roman Period*. 13 vols. Bollingen Series 37.12. New York: Pantheon, 1953–1965.

Hachili, Rachel. *Ancient Jewish Art and Archaeology in the Diaspora*. Handbuch der Orientalistik 35. Leiden: Brill, 1998.

Keel, Othmar, and Christoph Uehlinger. *Gods, Goddesses, and Images of God: In Ancient Israel*. Translated by Thomas H. Trapp. Minneapolis: Fortress, 1998.

Josephus. *Jewish Antiquities*. Translated by H. St. J. Thackeray et al. 9 vols. Loeb Classical Library. Cambridge: Harvard University Press, 1930–1965.

———. *The Jewish War*. Edited by G. P. Goold. Translated by H. St. Thackeray. 3 vols. Loeb Classical Library. Cambridge: Harvard University Press, 1927–1928.

———. *The Life. Against Apion*. Edited by G. P. Goold. Translated by H. St. J. Thackeray. Loeb Classical Library. Cambridge: Harvard University Press, 1926.

Philo. *Philo of Alexandria. Works*. Translated by F. H. Colson and G. H. Whitaker. 10 vols. LCL. Cambridge: Harvard University Press, 1929–1942.

———. *Questions and Answers on Exodus*. Vol. 2. Edited by G. P. Goold. Translated by Ralph Marcus. LCL. Cambridge: Harvard University Press, 1953.

Urbach, Ephraim. "The Rabbinical Laws of Idolatry in the Second and Third Centuries in the Light of Archaeological and Historical Facts." *Israel Exploration Journal* 9 (1959) 49–165, 229–45.

Ancient Document Index

Old Testament/ Hebrew Bible

Genesis
	58, 61, 232, 297, 355
1:28	152
2:24	58–60, 68
9:1	152
13:6	171
13:11–12	171
17	333
17:10–27	174
34:21	171
41:20	171

Exodus
	227, 363
20:8	356
32	227

Leviticus
11–15	174
19:18	59, 147

Numbers
21:24	152
32:22	152
32:29	152

Deuteronomy
21:22–23	161

Joshua
8:29	161

10:26–27	161

1 Samuel
13:17	79

2 Samuel
4:12	161
21:8–9	161

Ezra
10:3	174

Esther
2:23	161
5:14	161
7:9	161
9:25	161

Psalms
9:26 LXX	152
9:31 LXX	152
10:5–10	152
21:16 LXX	325
71:8 LXX	153
72	153
72:8	153
72:9–11	153
82:1	355
109:1 LXX	152
110:2	152
118:133 LXX	153
119:133	153

Proverbs
23:5	79

Ecclesiastes
3:2	310

Isaiah
35:1	171
35:7	171

Jeremiah
3:14	152
20:7	164

Ezekiel
37:1–10	316

Daniel
5:21 LXX	246
6	314
6:17	315
6:22	314
9:7	164
10:15–19	315
12:2–3	315
12:12	315

Amos
6:10	79

~

Apocrypha

Add Esth
4:17 LXX	174

Bel and the Dragon
33–39	317

Judith
10:5	174
12:2	174
12:17–19	174

1 Maccabees
1:62–63	174
7:16	161
16:17	164

2 Maccabees
2:21	174
4:13	174
7:1	174
7:36–37	174
8:1	174
15:10	164

Sirach
13:15–16	59
17:4	152

Tobit
	360
1:10–11	174

Wisdom of Solomon
	xxxvii, 183, 186, 191
1:1–15	190
1:1	192
1:4	192
1:6–9	189
1:6	191
1:7–11	192
1:12–15	188
1:13–14	192
1:15	192
1:16—2:24	190
10:1—11:1	185, 188, 190, 194
10:14	192
10:15—11:14	192
11:2—19:22	188, 190
11:2–4	188
11:5	188
11:6—19:22	188
11:6–14	188
11:15—16:14	188
11:15—12:2	192, 195

Ancient Document Index   371

Wisdom of Solomon
(cont.)
12:1–11	190
12:3–18	195
12:3–11	193
12:12	189
12:13–27	190
13:1—15:19	188
13:1–9	190
13:10–19	190
16:1–4	194
16:5–14	194
16:5	190
16:15–29	189, 194
16:15–19	189
17:1—19:21	190
17:1—18:4	189, 194
17:18–19	193
18:5—19:21	189
18:5–25	194
19:1–12	194
19:2	195
19:22	189–90, 192, 196

Old Testament Pseudepigrapha

1 Enoch
	360

Jubilees
22:16	174

Letter of Aristeas
	174

Testament of Solomon
	360

New Testament

Matthew
	xxxvi, 145–47, 310
1:1–3	149
1:5	149
1:11–12	149, 153
1:20	154
1:22	154
1:24	154
2:1–12	149
2:12	189
2:15	153
2:19–20	154
2:21–24	195
2:21–22	190
3:1–13	190
3:1–9	195
3:1–7	188
3:4	192
3:8	188
3:10–13	192
3:10	188
3:13	194
3:14	194
4:1	194
4:3–5	193
4:7–19	192
4:8–9	153
4:15	149
4:16	189
4:17	153
4:20—5:14	192
4:20	189
4:23–25	153
5:1–2	189
5:9–14	194
5:9–12	193
5:13	193
5:15–23	189, 192
5:18–23	192
5:43–44	147

Matthew (*cont.*)

5:47	149
6:1–6	146
6:7	149
6:12–16	194
6:12	194
6:28–29	318
6:32	149
7–9	191, 193, 195
7:1–22	194
7:9–10	193
7:15–22	192
7:21–22	154
7:22b—8:1	194
7:29	154
8:2—9:18	194
8:2	155
8:6	155
8:8c	193
8:12	192, 193
8:25	155
9:6	155
9:8	155
10:18	149
10:24–25	155
10:24	156
10:36	148
10:37	148
11:25	154
12:8	154
12:18	149
12:21	149
12:38–41	347
13:24–30	148
13:25	148
13:28	148
13:36–43	148
13:38–39	148
13:39	148
14:13–21	153
14:28	155
15:4	146
15:7	146
15:22	155
17:24–27	154
18:15–19	146
18:28–30	156
18:34	156
19–20	156
20:1–16	108
20:19	149, 153
20:20–28	150
20:24–27	145, 150
20:25b–28a	150
20:25–27	157
20:25	145, 150–53
20:26–27	155
20:26	155
21:35	156
21:43	149
22:1–14	156
22:15–22	154
22:44	148
23	146
23:8–10	146
23:16	146
23:17	146
23:19	146
23:24	146
23:26	146
24:7	149
24:9	149
24:14	149
24:29–34	154
24:50–51	156
25:26	156
25:30	156
25:32	149
26–27	154
26:14–25	149
26:31–35	149
26:36–46	149
26:47–55	149
26:51	156
26:56	149
26:69–75	149
27:20–23	146
27:25	325
27:28	325
27:35–38	161

Matthew (cont.)

27:35	325
28:18	155
28:19	146, 149

Mark

4:24	324
6:26	164
10	156
10:43	156
15:23	124
15:24–27	161
15:25	325

Luke

	133, 137
5:27–39	134
6:20–26	135
6:22	134
6:27–36	135
7:36–50	136
9:1–17	136
9:1–6	137
10:1–16	136
10:5	174
10:17	138
10:30	325
11:37–54	134–35
12:41–48	136
12:42	79
14:1–24	134
15:1–32	134
16:1–13	136
16:1–8	116
16:1	79
16:8	79
16:19–31	136
18:15–30	135
19:1–10	135
19:9	174
21:1–4	135
21:12–19	134
22:24–30	136
23:33	161

John

18:18	161
19:23	325
21:7	325

Acts

	xxxvi, 4, 6, 12–13, 89–92, 98, 138
2	90
2:36	161
2:46	174
4	90
4:10	161
5:42	90
7:48	90
8:3	90, 174
9:1	174
9:3–20	174
9:3–6	174
9:16	174
9:17–18	174
9:17	174
9:20	174
9:31	174
11:14	174
12:12–17	40
15:3	174
15:41	174
16:10–13	220
16:14–15	40
16:15	174
16:31	174
16:40	40
17:24	40, 90
18:8	174
20:20	90, 174
20:28	174
22:6	174
26:13	174
28	90

Romans

	7, 28
1:8	27

Romans (cont.)

2	331–32
2:8	172
2:28	331
6	311, 331, 334
6:2	334
6:4–5	310
6:17	331
6:17b	331
10:3	174
12:8	79
14:1—15:7	16
16	3
16:1–2	79
16:3–5	3
16:4	27–28
16:23	27–28

1 Corinthians

	10, 39, 64, 133
1:14	27
1:23	161
1:26	7, 25
5–7	43
5–6	60
6	59
6:9	247
6:12–20	59–61
6:15–18	60
7	xxxv, 38–45, 48–50, 60
7:1–7	43
7:1	45, 60
7:2–7	44
7:2–5	42
7:9	43
7:10–11	41
7:11–13	60
7:12–16	41–42, 44
7:14	44, 46–48
7:14c	42
7:21	44
7:25	38, 48
7:28	38, 48
7:29	60
7:31	42
7:32	60
7:33–34	40
7:34	38, 48
7:35	60
7:36–38	38, 42, 44, 48
7:36	42, 45
7:39–40	40
8–10	133
8:1—9:20	174
8	133
8:10	30
9:5	42
10:25–27	174
10:32	27
11–14	29, 49
11	57, 65
11:2–16	133
11:2–3	46
11:3	57
11:17—14:40	16
11:17–33	65
11:17–34	12, 22–24
11:18	24
11:22	28–29, 35, 49
11:34–35	64
11:34	28–29, 35
14:16	12
14:23	6, 11–12, 23, 28, 30, 33
14:30	11, 34
14:32–34	49
14:34–35	29, 35, 63–64
14:35	29
15:9b	174
15:20–26	310
16:5–12	15
16:19	3

2 Corinthians

3:18	335
5:16	335
11:2–3	46
13:4	161

Galatians

1:1–9	175
1:11–15	174
1:13–16	174
1:13–14	174
1:13	27
1:15–16	174
1:15	174
1:16	174
1:23	174, 331
2:4	175
2:6	28
2:7–9	174
2:11–14	16, 174
2:15	174
2:21	164
3:1–2	175
3:1	xxxvii, 132, 160–61, 239, 324, 335
3:3	335
3:4	175
3:10–13	175
3:15	164
3:26–29	174–75
3:26–27	175
3:26	335
3:27–28	17, 321
3:28	40
3:28a	175
4:1–31	174
4:1	335
4:7	335
4:13–14	15
4:22	335
4:29	331
4:30	335
4:31	335
5:11	331
5:13	335
5:19–20	172
5:21	174
6:11–17	322
6:12	331
6:15	331
6:16	331
6:17	330

Ephesians

	17, 54, 68, 138, 322
1:9–10	54
4:31	172
5	57
5:21—6:9	55
5:21–33	59
5:21	55
5:22 — 6:9	53, 55
5:22–33	55–56, 61
5:22–24	56
5:25–27	46
5:25	57
5:28	57
5:29	58
5:30–33	338
5:30	58
5:31	58
5:32b	58
5:33	59

Philippians

3:1–3	331
3:2–10	174
3:10–11	311
3:20	42

Colossians

1:11–23	337
1:12	333
1:15–22	329, 336
1:15	335
1:20	328
1:22	328, 335
1:26	338
1:27	338
2:2	338
2:9–15	329
2:9	337
2:10	333
2:11–12	321
2:11	320, 324, 326, 328–29, 331–32, 334, 336–38
2:12	334, 337

Colossians (cont.)

2:16–21	10
2:20	333
3:2	331
3:3	333
3:9	331
3:10–11	322, 335
3:10	335
3:18 — 4:1	53, 55, 320
4:3	338
4:5	3
4:15	40, 337

1 Thessalonians

4:8	164
5:12	79

1 Timothy

	xxxvi, 86
1:1	75
1:2	75
1:3–4	75
1:3–7	75
1:4	82
1:10	75
1:13	75
1:16	81
2	63, 66
2:1–7	63
2:(1)8–15	53
2:1	63
2:8–15	81
2:8	63
2:9	77
2:11	66
3	85
3:1–13	64
3:1–7	67, 82–83
3:1–2	74
3:2–7	xxxvi, 72–73, 75, 80
3:2–4	84
3:2–3	73, 78
3:2	73, 76, 83–84
3:3	333
3:4–5	76, 78–79, 81–82
3:4	76, 78, 80, 82, 84
3:5	64, 80, 82
3:6	76
3:7	76, 81, 83–84
3:14–15	75
3:15	66, 75, 82
4:3	84
4:11–16	81
4:12	81
5:1–16	81
5:3–16	40
5:5–10	76
5:7	76
5:10	77
5:13	83
5:17–23	81
5:17	77, 84
6	63
6:1–2	44, 53, 81
6:3–20	81

2 Timothy

1:5	48
2:23–25	78
3:15	48

Titus

1	85–86
1:5–9	82
1:5	75
1:6–9	xxxvi, 72–73
1:6–9a	83
1:6	83
1:7	73
1:9	77–78, 83–84
1:9b	83
1:10–16	67
1:11	83
1:13	83
2:1–10	53, 66
2:1ff.	62
2:1	83
2:2	76

Titus (*cont.*)	
2:3–5	48
2:6	83
2:7	81
2:9	81
2:15	83
3:12	82
3:13	82

Philemon

2	3
22	15

1 Peter

	17, 72, 119
2:(11)13–17	63
2:13—3:7	53
2:18–19	44
4:17	66
5:2	75
5:13	119

2 Peter

3:15	321
3:16	321

Revelation

12:7	232

New Testament Apocrypha

Acts of Paul

8.29–31	348

Nag Hammadi Codices

Apocryphon of John

	241

Gospel of Thomas

	318

Apostolic Fathers

1 Clement

1:3	53
7.5–7	348
21:6–9	53

Index of Ancient Sources

Achilles Tatius

1.3.5–6	110
1.3.6	109
1.4.1	109
1.4.9	109
1.15.1	110
1.18.3	109
2.1.1–3	110
2.26.1	109
5.7.3–10	113
5.17.2–10	111
5.25.1	109
6.2.2	109
6.3.3	109, 113
6.9.6	109
7.7.3	109, 113
8.14.5	109

Aelian

Historical Miscellany

2.20	155

Alcimus of Sicily

History of Italy

(FGH 560 F 2)	120, 122

Ambrose

De officiis ministrorum

1.18.79	301

Ambrosiaster

Commentarius in epistulam ad Romanos

6.1–6	311

Ampelius

Liber Memorialis

8.14	168

Apostolic Constitutions and Canons

1.3.9	301
5.7	310

Appian

Bella civilia

1:120	325

Aristotle

Magna Moralia

1.1194b.5–28	320

Politica

1.2.1	75
I 1253b 1–14	53

Rhetorica

I.4121b	146
2.1389a13–14	76
III.1425b–1427b	146

Artemidorus Daldianus

Onirocritica

2.39	269

Athenaeus

Deipnosophistae

4.151e–152b	165
10.441a–b	120
10.440e–f	122

Aulus Gellius

Noctes atticae

10.23.1	122
10.23.2	124
10.23.3	125
10.23.4	126
10.23.5	126

Basil of Caesarea

De Spiritu Sancto

15.35	311

Prot. bapt.

2	311

Celsus

The True Doctrine

2.68	250
6.30	249
6.34	250
7.14	250
7.40	250
7.68	251

Chariton

1.1.5	109
1.1.14	110
1.1.15	109
1.3.1	108
1.3.7	114
1.4.9	110
1.6.2–5	109
1.11.2	108
1.12.7	109
1.12.8	110, 114
1.12.9	114
1.13.1	108, 114
1.13.2	114
1.14.1	109
2.1.1	109, 114–15
2.1.2	108, 114
2.1.5	114
2.1.6	114
2.1.9	114
2.2.2	108
2.2.7	108
2.3.1–5	111
2.3.1–4	109
2.3.1	114
2.3.2	109
2.3.3	109
2.3.4	114
2.3.6	114
2.3.10	108
2.4.6	115
2.6.1	114
2.6.2	115
2.10.4	109
2.11.1	108
2.12.2	110
3.1.2	108
3.1.4–2.5	115
3.2.11	108
3.6.2–5	115
3.7	114
3.7.1–3	116
3.7.1	115
3.7.2	116
3.9.4–11	116
3.9.12	116
3.10.1	116
4.2.1–3	108
4.2.5	109
4.2.7	109
4.2.8	109
4.5.1	109
4.15.4	108
5.1	109
6.3.3	110
8.2–9	110
8.4.6	109
14.2–5	110
14.5	114

Chrysostom

Catecheses ad illuminandos

2.24	313

Index of Ancient Sources

Chrysostom (*cont.*)

Ad Innocentium papam epistula I
    313

Ad Innocentium papam epistula II
    313

Homiliae in epistulam ad Titum
Hom. 4 (PG 62.681–82)   76

Ad populum Antiochenum de statuis
5.15–17   348

Cicero

De amicitia
1.13.42–44   330

Brutus or De claris oratoribus
288   127

De divinatione
2.41.85–87   271

De officiis
1.126–29   300

De Oratore
2.43–46   146

In Pisonem
67   127

Pro Rabiro
16   161

De Republica
2.26   121
4.6   123
5.6   123

De senectute
1, 33   76
7   76
10   76
37–38   77
65   77

Tusculanae disputationes
1.38.92   330
4.70   299

In Verrem
2.5.162   161

Clement of Alexandria

Paedagogus
3.5   301
3.9–10   301

Protrepticus
4   305
10.99.4   348

Stromata
1.21   348

Clement of Rome

The First Epistle of Clement to the Corinthians
45.6   313

Columella

Agriculture
I.8.5   45

Cyprian

Epistulae
61.2.1   314
67.8.2   314

Ad Fortinatum
2.11   314

De habitu virginum
19   301

De lapsis
19, 31   314

Cyril of Jerusalem

Catechesis
5.4   314

Cyril of Jerusalem

Mystagogica Catechesis
2.1	310
2.2	313
2.4–5	311

Demetrius

Style
287	324

Dio Cassius

50.28	322

Roman History
58.2.4	299

Dio Chrysostom

Oration
69.2	79

Diodorus

5.26.3	165
18.32.4	164
31.45.1	164

Diogenes Laertius

6.43	74

Dionysius of Halicarnassus

Antiquitates romanae
1.31.1–58.2	168
1.72.1	168
1.77.1–2	168
2.24.1	126
2.25.6	125
2.25.7	126

De Lysia
7	323

Epictetus

Diatribai (Dissertationes)
1.24.3–10	74
3.22	74
3.24.3–10	74
24–25	74

Epistles of Paul and Seneca

6	313

Eustathius

Comm. Il.
19.160	123

Fabius Pictor

Annals 125

Gospel of Thomas

21–22	321

Gregory of Nazianzus

Oratio in laudem Basilii
48.74	314

Hippolytus

Commentarium in Danielem
10.16	315

Traditio apostolica
21.3, 5, 11	312–13

Homer

Ilias
2.545	168
2.547–48	163

Horace

Carmina
3.5.1	168

Ignatius

To Polycarp
4:1–3	54

To the Smyrnaeans
13.1	40
13.2	41

Irenaeus

Adversus haereses
3.20	348
5.5.2	310, 348

Isocrates

Panathanasius (Or. 12)
12.124	163

De Pace (Or. 8)
8.49	163

Jerome

Epistulae
107.11	301

Josephus

Jewish Antiquities
2.236	79
8.7.5	363
12.145	136
12.396	161
13.380	161
15.272	363
18.63–64c	161

Contra Apionem
2.75	363
2.79–80	248
2.80	248
2.112–14	248
2.145–95	145

Jewish War
1.10.2	330
1.97, 113	161
5.11.1	325

Julius Caesar

Gallic War
7.29	165

Justin

Dialogus cum Tryphone
107–108	348

Epitome of the Philippic History of Pompeius Trogus
24.4.1–4	165

Second Apology
2	41

Justinian

Digest
48.4.11	326

Juvenal

Satirae
14.269–270	124

Livy

Histories
1.3.10–4.3	168
1.57.9	124
3.28.11–29.1	299
39.6–7	100

Longus

1.1.2	108
1.2.1	110
1.4.3	110
2.1.1–3	112
2.1–3	110
2.1.3	110
2.12.2	109
2.19–20	111
3.29.1	110
3.29.2	110
3.31.4	111
4.1	110
4.1.1	109, 111
4.1.2–3	112
4.4.1–2	110
4.4.2–4	112
4.5.1	112

Longus

4.5.2	112
4.7.2–4	112
4.9.2	112
4.9.3	112
4.10.1–3	112
4.10.1	109
4.11.1	113
4.13.1–2	113
4.13.1	108
4.13.2	108
4.13.3–4	113
4.13.3	113
4.13.4	109, 113
4.14.2–3	113
4.15.1–3	113
4.16.3	109
4.25.2	113
4.26.2	110
4.32.2	109
4.33.2	110, 113
4.33.4	109
4.34.3	109
24.1	108

Lucian

De Saltatione

81	73

Martial

Epigrams

13.106	124

Maximus of Tyre

15.9c–d	74

Melito of Sardis

On the Passover

740–43	326

Minucius Felix

Octavius

1.2	245
9.3	245

Origen

Commentarium in evangelium Matthaei

12.3	348

Homiliae in Jeremiam

1.1	348

Homiliae in Numeros

16.4	348

De oratione

13.2	348
13.4	348

Ovid

Ars Amatoria

1.220–25	102

Fasti

1.315–17, 587–616	170
3.31–40	168
570–80	124

Passion of Saints Perpetua and Felicitas

Act I.V.3	206
Act I.V.6	206
10.7	203
20	299
20.7	202

Persius

Satirae

2.70	48

Philo

De agricultura

64	80

De congressu eruditionis gratia

74–76	184

De vita contemplativa

68	41
84–85	41

Philo

In Flaccum
65–72   187

De gigantibus (On Giants)
13.59   362

De Iosepho
37   80
38–39   80

Legum allegoriae
127–131   187
149–51   170

De vita Mosis
1.4   184
2.216   184

De opificio mundi
128   185

De posteritate Caini
181   78–79

On the Preliminary Studies
74–76   184

De providentia
2.44–46   184

Quod omnis probus liber sit
45   78
57   79

De specialibus legibus
1.16   80
1.314   184
2.62   184
2.63–64   185
2.230   184

De virtutibus
58   78, 80
63   80

Philodemus

Oeconomicus
A 3   77
A 22–25   80
1.6–10   75

1.16–17   78
3a.6–16   78
3   85
6   85
10.33, 39   77
11.1   77
14.9–15   79
18.23   80
19.34, 47   80
20.20   78, 80
20.39   78
21.37–44   79
23.40—24.47   78
24.38   80

Plato

Epinomis
987e   164

Gorgias
520A   78

Leges
5.747d   169
8.845b   123

Menexenus
237–239a   163
237b–240c   163
245d   164

Respublica
329D   76

Pliny the Elder

Naturalis historia
2.189–90   169
3.5.39–42   169
3.5.39–40   169
12.2.5   165
14.87–88, 91   123
14.89   122–23, 125, 127–28
14.91   126
15.92   124
33.153   300
34.18   303
34.84   167–68

Pliny the Younger

Epistulae (Epistles/Letters)
2.6.6	81
7.1.7	81
10.96	8

Plutarch

Advice to the Bride and Groom
142F–43A	44

Cato Major
20.6	300

Comparatio Aristidis et Catonis
3.2	79, 85

Comparatio Lycurgi et Numae
3.5	121
3.7	121

Consolatio ad uxorem
609E	77

De Iside et Osiride
358D	232
382E–383E	233

Moralia
7	195

Praecepta gerendae rei publicae
800A	73

Ad principem ineruditum
781CD	73

Quaestiones romanae et graecae
265b	120
265d	120
268d–e	129

Romulus
19.6	121
20:3	298

Polybius

The Histories
2.17.9–10	164
2.19.4	165
2.32.8	164–65
2.35.3	165
3.3.5	164
3.49.3	165
3.78.2	164
6.11a.1–10	122
6.11a.4	122, 124
12.4.2–3	165
18.17.9–12	164
18.41.7	164
21.38.2	173
24.14.7	164–65
35.3	172
70.4	165
78.2	165

To the Philippians
4:2–3	54

Ps.–Aristotle

Oec.
1.5.1344a27–29	80
1.6.1344b26–27	77

Pseudo-Dionysius

Ecclesiastical Hierarchy
2.2.7	313

Ps.-Plutarch

Educ.
4B	76

Quintilian

Institutio oratoria
5.9.14	300
9.2.65	325
9.2.66	325
11.1.15–28	195

Training of the Orator
6.2.34–36	323
6.32	323
8.3.61	323
8.3.64–65	323
12.10.6	323

Res Gestae Divi Augusti
21–22	170
24–27	170
34–35	170

Seneca
Epistulae Morales
6.5–6	81
52.8	81
94.40	81

Servius
Comm. Aen.
1.737	124, 127

Shepherd of Hermas
Vision
1.1	299
2.4.3	40–41

Stobaeus
Eclogae
2.7a.11d	79
2.67	74
2.114	74

Florilegium
4.22a24	79
4.504	79
4.505	77
4.510	85

Strabo
Geographica
12.5.1	165, 173

Suetonius
Divus Augustus
65	123

Domitianus
12	332

Tiberius
63	272

Tacitus
Annales
IV	137
6.29	326

Talmud
GenRab
65.22	161

m. Sanhedrin
6.4	161

Tertullian
Ad nations
1.14	245–47

De anima
55	348

Apologeticus
6.4	125, 127–28
6.5	122
6.6	126
16	246, 250
16.1–3	245

De carne Christi
32	348

De fuga in persecutione
10	348

De idololatria
15.10	313

Adversus Marcionem
2.17	348
2.24	348

Adversus Marcionem
4.10	348
5.11	348

De monogamia
V	61

De pudicitia
10	348

De resurrectione carnis
58	310, 348

Scorpiace
8.7	313

De spectaculis
18	302
21	302

Theodore of Mopsuestia

Baptismal Homilies
3.8	313

Valerius Maximus

Memorable Sayings and Doings
2.1.5b	123
2.7.12	325
6.3.9	127

Varro

Agriculture
I.17.5	45

Virgil

Aeneid
1.231–6.278–83	170
1.259	168
1.278–282	170
1.278	168
7.135–60	168
6.791–807, 851–53	170
8.370–453	168

Vitruvius
6.7.2–4	16

Xenophon of Ephesus
1.2.2–3	109
1.5.1	109
1.14.4	109
2.1.2	111
2.3.1–4	109
2.3–5	110
2.3.3	109
2.6.2–5	110
2.7.1	109
2.9.2	109
2.10.4	113
3.4.3	109
3.12.2	110
5.1.1	108
5.5.4	109
11.1	111

Xenophon

Oeconomicus
1.1–2	75
1.2	78, 110–11
1.5	78
2.1	110
2.1.2	111
2.4–12	85
2.10	110
3.15	110
5.1	110
6.4	110
7.5	79
7.8	110
7.36	110
7.41	80
11.1	111
11.12	110
12.4	80, 85
20.21	110
21.9	110

Zeno of Verona
Invitation to the Baptismal Font
6 313

Index of Modern Authors

Abrams, Dominic, 159
Adams, Edward, vii, xiii, xxxv, 22
Ådna, Jostein, 70
Aldrete, Gregory S., 245, 253
Alikin, Valeriy A., 225, 236
Allen, Willoughby C., 150, 158
Allenbach, Jean, 348, 352
Allison, Dale, 151, 158
Allison, Penelope M., 4-5, 12, 19
Althaus-Reid, Marcella, 205, 209-11, 216-17
Amat, Jacqueline, 200-201, 204, 216
Arterbury, Andrew E., 15, 19
Ascough, Richard S., 17, 19, 30, 36
Auguet, Roland, 326, 339
Aune, David E., xvii, xxiii, 70, 324, 339

Bagnall, Roger S., 237
Baird, J. A., 244, 253
Balch, David Lee, ii-iv, vii, xi-xii, xv-xxv, xxxv-xxxvi, xxxviii, 3, 10-13, 15, 19-23, 30, 33-36, 38-39, 51-53, 70, 72, 80, 87, 89, 104, 106, 108, 116-19, 130, 132-40, 145, 158, 160-61, 165-67, 169, 171, 174-75, 177, 179, 181, 218, 220, 225, 235-37, 239, 243, 251, 253, 294, 308, 319-22, 324, 326-27, 330, 332, 335, 338-39, 342, 348, 352
Baldassare, Ida, 238
Balz, H., 179
Bandelli, Gino, 352

Banks, Marcus, 324, 339
Banks, Robert, 23, 36
Barclay, John M. G., 29, 36, 184, 197
Barnard, Mary, 217
Baron, Solo, 357
Barrett, C. K., 59, 70
Barth, Markus, 57, 70
Barton, Stephen C., xix
Bauer, Walter, xxx, 179
Baum, Robert M., 172, 175-77, 179, 182
Baumgarten, G. Schneider, 179
Beard, Mary, 99, 104
Beavis, Mary Ann, 116, 118
Belayche, Nicole, 226, 236
Benediktson, D. Thomas, 323, 339
Benoit, A., 352
Berger, Catherine, 237
Bergman, Bettina, 330, 339
Berve, Helmut, 262, 264, 278
Beslier, G. G., 171-72, 179
Bettini, Maurizio, 129-30
Betz, Hans Dieter, xx, 173, 179, 195, 197, 331, 339
Beyer, H. W., 140
Bhabha, Homi, 68, 162, 179
Bianchi, Robert S., 228, 236
Billerbeck, Margarethe, 74, 87
Bizzeti, Paolo, 198
Blaiklock, Edward M., xv
Blanc, Nicole, 219, 236
Bloomer, W. Martin, 128, 130
Bonansea, N., 342, 352
Bonfante, Larissa, 298, 319
Bonnet, Corrine, 236-37
Bookidis, Nancy, 133, 140

Booth, Joan, 146, 158
Boswell, John, 201, 206, 208, 216
Bowden, John, 253
Boys-Stones, G. R., 180
Bradley, Keith R., 47, 51
Brant, Jo-Ann, 118
Braun, W., 134, 140
Brenk, Frederick E., viii, xiii, xxxvii, 218, 221, 225, 229, 236
Bricault, Laurent, 220, 232, 236–38
Brink, Laurie, xxiv, 319, 342, 352
Bromiley, Geoffrey W., xxxiv
Brooten, Bernadette J., 203, 206–8, 216
Brouwer, H. H. J., 129–30
Brown, Colin, 179
Brown, Frank E., 9, 19
Brown, Raymond E., xvi
Brown, Rupert, 147, 159
Burger, Thomas, 104
Burgess, Theodore C., 195, 197
Burnford, F., xix
Buttolph, Philip, 70, 87

Cabrol, F., xxxi
Cairns, Douglas L., 121, 130
Cancik, Hubert, xx
Cannon, George E., 334, 339
Cantilena, Renata, 219, 236
Capes, D. B., 130
Capriotti Vittozzi, Giuseppina, 218, 223, 228, 231–32, 236
Caragounis, C. C., 33–36
Carew, John Rolfe, 332, 339
Carter, Warren, viii, xiii, xix, xxxvi, 145, 149, 153–54, 156, 158, 170, 179
Casadio, Giovanni, 236
Castelli, Elizabeth, 118, 202, 205, 216
Cavanaugh, William T., 215–16
Cesare Cassio, Albio, 120, 130
Chadwick, Henry, 249–53
Champion, Craige, 168, 179
Chapman, David W., 251, 253

Charlesworth, James H., 140
Ciampa, Roy E., 45, 51
Clark, Kenneth Willis, 151, 153, 155, 158
Clarke, John R., viii, xiii, xxxvii, 4, 9–10, 14, 19, 98, 104, 257, 274, 278, 309, 319
Clarysse, Willy, 234, 237
Clinton, Kevin, 262, 278
Cobb, L. Stephanie, 202, 204, 216
Cobb, Michael, 210–11, 216
Cokayne, Karen, 76, 87
Cole, Thomas, 185–86, 197
Coleman, K. M., 253
Collins, Adela Yarbro, 326, 339
Collins, John J., 195, 197
Collins, Raymond F., 74, 87, 323, 339
Colson, F. H., 80, 367
Colwell, E. C., 244, 253
Comstock, Gary David, 211, 216
Conway, Colleen M., 251, 253
Conzelmann, Hans, 59, 63, 67, 70, 73, 80, 87
Coote, Robert B., xxiv
Corley, Kathleen E., 16, 19
Cornman, Robert, 198
Corso, Antonio, 221, 237
Cribiore, Rafaella, 185, 193, 197
Crossan, John Dominic, 171, 177, 179, 282, 288, 290, 295
Crossley, Nick, 93, 104
Cushman, Henry Wyles, 171, 179
Cushman, Robert, 171, 179

D'Alessio, Maria Teresa, 219, 237
D'Angelo, Mary Rose, 202, 206–7, 215–16
Daniélou, Jean, 334, 339
Danker, Frederick William, xxx, 179
Dassmann, Ernst, 342, 352
Davies, W. D., 151, 158
Davis, Basil S., 173, 180
De Brauw, Michael, 188, 197

Index of Modern Authors   393

De Bruyne, Lucien, 312, 319, 348, 353
De Caro, Stephano, 236, 238
De Fidio, Pia, 237
de Grummond, Nancy T., 181
De Vos, Craig S., 29–30, 34, 36
De Vos, Mariette, 221, 237
Deichmann, Friedrich Wilhelm, 342, 352
Delorme, Jean, 184, 197
Deming, Will, 45, 51, 60, 70
den Boeft, J., 353
Denzey, Nicola, 321, 339
Des Bouvrie, Synnøve, 53, 70
Diatta, Nazaire Ukëyëng, 177, 180
Dibelius, Martin, 63, 67, 70, 72–73, 80, 87
Dietler, Michael, 171, 180
Dillon, Matthew, 125, 127, 130
Dillon, Sheila, 105
Dinkler, Erich, 347, 350, 352
Dittenburger, W., xxxiii
Dix, Dom Gregory, 10, 19
Dixon, Suzanne, 46–48, 51, 53, 55, 70
Dobbins, John J., 19
Donaldson, James, xxx
Donelson, Lewis, xvii
Doran, Robert, 184, 197
Dougherty, Carol, 164, 180
Drerup, Heinrich, 274, 278
Dunbabin, Katherine M. D., 5, 13, 19, 30, 33, 36
Dunbar, Nan, 339
Dunn, James D. G., xxii, 27, 33, 36, 140
Duval, Yves-Marie, 343, 348, 352

Eck, Diana L., 257, 278
Eckstein, Arthur M., 123, 130
Elsner, Jaś, 258, 269, 278–79
Engberg-Pedersen, Troel, 88, 130
Engemann, J., 342–44, 352
Epstein, Julia, 216
Erim, Kenan T., 280, 284, 295

Esposito, Domenico, 219, 237

Fagan, Garrett G., 299–300, 319
Falconer, W. A., 77
Farina, William, 202, 205, 216
Farmer, William R., xxi
Fatum, Lone, 67, 70
Faubion, J. D., 104
Feder, Ernst, 111, 118
Feldman, Louis H., 332, 339
Ferguson, Everett, viii, xiii, xvii–xviii, xx, xxiii, xxxi, xxxviii, 342, 350, 352
Ferris, Iain M., 165, 168, 180, 253
Ferrua, Antonio, 308, 319, 350, 352
Filson, Floyd V., 91–92, 104
Fine, Steven, 367
Finney, M., 28, 35–36, 250, 252
Finney, Paul Corby, 251, 253, 343, 345, 352
Fitzgerald, John T., vii, xiii, xx, xxii, xxxvi, 78, 87, 119, 121, 130, 179
Foerster, Gideon, 346, 352
Fontenrose, Joseph, 266, 278
Foss, Pedar W., 19
Fotopoulos, John, xxiii
Fraser, Nancy, 95, 104
Frazer, J. G., 261, 278
Freeman, Charles, 204, 209, 216
Frerichs, Ernest, 158
Freund, Richard, viii, xiii, 354, 367
Freyne, Sean, 146–47, 158
Friedrich, Gerhard, xxxiv, 133, 140
Friesen, Steven J., 7, 19, 21, 37, 140
Froelicher, Capitaine, 171, 180
Fröhlich, Thomas, 276, 278

Gagnon, Robert A., 331, 339
Galeano, Eduardo, 200
Galinsky, Karl, 169–70, 180, 295
Gammie, John G., 186, 197–98
Garland, David E., 150, 155, 158
Garland, Lynda, 125, 127, 130

Garnaud, J.-P., 106, 118
Gasparini, Valentino, 219–20, 237
Gehring, R. W., 26, 36
Georgi, Dieter, xxiii
Gianakaris, C. J., 120, 130
Gielen, Marleis, xix
Gilbert, Maurice, 194, 197
Gillihan, Yonder Moynihan, 47, 51
Girard, Jean, 180
Glad, C. E., 81, 87
Glancy, Jennifer A., 45, 51, 299, 319
Glare, P. G. W., xxxii
Gnilka, Joachim, 150, 158
Golden, Renny, 200, 216
Goldhill, Simon, 181
Golvin, J.-C., 220, 237
Goodenough, Erwin Ramsdell, 186, 197, 357, 364, 367
Goold, G. P., 367
Grabar, André, 343–44, 349, 352
Graf, Fritz, 269, 278
Gray, P., 88
Green, Deborah A., xxiv, 319, 342, 352
Griffiths, J. Gwyn, 221, 224, 232, 237
Gruben, Gottfried, 262, 264, 278
Gruen, Erich S., 168, 170, 180, 187, 197, 238
Guest, Deryn, 208, 216
Gundry, Robert H., 150, 158
Gutt, Ernst-August, 339
Guy, Laurie, 329, 339

Haase, W., xxx
Habermas, Jürgen, 93, 104
Habicht, C., 122
Hachili, Rachel, 357, 367
Hagner, Donald, 150, 155, 158
Hales, Shelley, 4, 19, 98–99, 104, 274, 278
Hall, Robert G., 332, 340
Hallett, Christopher H., 298–302, 305, 319, 328, 330, 340

Hallett, Judith, 159
Hamilton, Mark W., 87–88, 130
Hanotaux, Gabriel, 171, 180
Hanson, K. C., ii, 140
Hardt, Michael, 95, 104
Harland, Philip A., 17–19, 29, 36
Harmon, A. M., 73
Harper, Douglas, 324, 340
Harrill, J. Albert, 156, 158
Harris, Murray J., 333, 340
Harrisville, Roy A., 104
Hartswick, Kim J., 165, 168, 180
Harvey, David, 29
Hays, Richard B., 34, 36
Heidegger, Martin, 94, 104
Hellholm, David, 70
Henderson, Jeffery, 181, 329, 340
Hengel, Martin, 161, 180, 251, 253
Herbert-Brown, G., 130
Herek, Gregory M., 212, 216
Herzer, Jens, 72, 75, 80, 87
Highet, Gilbert, 244, 253
Hill, David, 150–51, 155, 159
Hinkle, Steve, 147, 159
Hirschfeld, Yizhar, 4, 5, 13, 20
Hock, Ronald F., vii, xiii, xxxvi, 106, 108, 111–12, 115, 118
Hodges, Frederick M., 329, 332, 340
Hodske, Jürgen, 227, 237
Hogg, Michael A., 159
Holland, Glen S., xxii
Hornblower, Simon, xxxii, 198
Hornsey, Matthew, 147, 159
Horrell, David G., xxxv, 6–7, 20, 22–26, 30, 36, 49, 51, 133, 140
Horsely, Richard A., 158, 179, 181
Houtman, A., 87
Hurwit, Jeffrey M., 328, 340

Isaac, Benjamin, 163–64, 180
Itkonen-Kaila, Marja, 242, 254, 327, 340

Index of Modern Authors 395

Jacoby, F., xxxi
Jameson, Michael, 16, 20
Jensen, C., 75, 87
Jensen, Robin Margaret, viii, xiii,
    xxxvii, 251, 253, 296, 308,
    319, 349, 352
Jewett, Robert, 28, 36, 331, 334,
    340
Johnson, Luke Timothy, xxv, 73,
    75, 81, 87, 146, 159
Johnson, Marshall D., 20
Johnston, Patricia A., 236
Jones, C. P., 120, 130

Kah, D., 184, 197
Kahl, Brigitte, 168, 180, 286, 295
Kähler, Heinz, 271, 278
Kartzow, Marianne Bjelland, 64,
    67, 70
Kaschnitz-Weinberg, Guido von,
    261, 278
Käsemann, Ernst, xi, 89, 104
Kearns, E., 163
Keck, Leander E., xxxii
Keegan, Peter Mark, 124, 130
Keel, Othmar, 358, 367
Keener, Craig S., 151, 155, 159,
    316, 319
Keetley, Dawn, 217
Kennedy, George A., 185, 193, 197
Kent, Susan, 20
King, J. E., 339
King, Martha, 333, 340
Kittel, Gerhard, xxxiv
Kitzinger, Ernst, 343, 352
Kleinberg, Aviad, 202–3, 216
Klinghardt, Matthias, 15, 20
Koenig, John, 15, 20
Koester, Helmut, xxiv, 21
Kolarcik, Michael, 183, 197
Konstan, David, 79, 88
Koortbojian, Michael, 308, 319
Korostelina, Korina, 147, 159
Kraus, Wolfgang, 104
Krueger, Paul, 326, 340

Kuttner, Ann L., 284, 295
Kyle, Donald G., 207, 217

La Fosse, Mona Tokarek, 77, 84, 87
Laes, Christian, 45, 51
Laks, A., 88
Lamb, George, 198
Lamoreaux, Jason T., ii, xxiv
Lampe, Peter, 3, 15, 20, 23, 36
Landau, Rudolf, 104
Lange, Ulrike, 342, 352
Larcher, Chrysostome, 186, 193,
    197
Lawrence, Frederick, 104
Lawrence, Marion, 308, 319, 349,
    353
Leclercq, H., 313, 342, 344, 353
Lee, Thomas R., 185, 197
Lehmeier, Karen, 72, 87
Leitch, James W., 70
Leith, Mary Joan Winn, 251, 254
Lesourd, Paul, 163, 172, 180
Levine, Amy-Jill, 295
Liddell, Henry George, xxxii, 180,
    340
Lincoln, Andrew T., 334, 340
Ling, Roger, 135, 137, 140
Liverani, Paolo, 230, 237
Lohfink, Gerhard, xvii
Long Westfall, Cynthia, 158
Lopez, Davina C., vii, xiii, xxxvi,
    89, 100, 102, 104, 168, 180,
    282–83, 288–92, 295
Lührmann, Dieter, 72, 87, 320

Maass, Michael, 269, 278
MacDonald, Dennis Ronald, 40,
    51
MacDonald, Margaret Y., vii, xiv,
    xviii, xxxv, 3, 16–17, 20,
    38–41, 43–47, 49, 51–52, 62,
    64, 68, 70, 334, 340
MacDonald, William L., 242, 253
Mack, Burton L., 118, 185, 198
Maderna, Caterina, 305, 319

Madge, Clare, 176, 181
Maier, Harry O., 290, 295
Malherbe, Abraham J., vii, xiv–xviii, xx, xxii, xxxvi, 72, 76–77, 79–81, 84, 87, 179
Malina, Bruce J., 169, 181
Mantilla, Karla, 199, 212, 217
Marcus, Ralph, 367
Marinatos, Nanno, 257, 278
Mark, Peter, 177, 181
Marrou, H. I., 184, 198
Marshall, I. Howard, 75, 88
Marszal, John R., 168, 181
Martimort, A.-G., 350, 353
Martin, Dale, 44, 51,59, 70
Martinez, Florentíno García, 181
Martyn, J. Louis, 181
Matson, David L., xx
Mathews, Thomas F., 251, 253
May, Alistair Scott, 39, 43, 51
Mazzoleni, D., 342, 353
McNeile, Alan Hugh, 151, 159
Meeks, Wayne A., xvi–xix, 20, 66, 70, 92, 104
Meggitt, Justin J., 24–25, 36
Meier, John P., xvi
Meiss, Millard, 319, 353
Mendelson, Alan, 184, 198
Merz, Jörg Martin, 270, 273, 278
Metz, Johann Baptist, 200, 211, 217
Meyboom, Paul G. P., 221, 229–30, 237
Meyer, Marvin W., 321, 340
Meyers, Eric M., 17, 20
Michelet, Jules, 172, 181
Migne, J.-P., xxxii
Miller, C., xix
Miller, Stephen G., 184, 198
Mitchell, Stephen, 181, 295
Modrzejewski, Joseph, 187, 195, 198
Moessner, David P., xxi
Mommsen, Theodor, 326, 340
Moormann, Eric M., 218, 230, 237

Morley, Neville, 155–56, 159
Morrill, Bruce T., 200, 217
Moxnes, Halvor, xviii, 39, 52
Münzer, Friedrich, 126, 128, 130
Murphy O-Connor, Jerome, xxxv, 6–7, 11–13, 20, 22–26, 33, 36, 46, 49, 52, 133, 140
Murray, Oswyn, 130

Naerebout, F. G., 220, 237
Nanos, Mark D., 4, 20,
Narkiss, Bezalel, 347, 353
Nasrallah, Laura Salah, 282, 295
Natali, C., 79, 88
Negri, Antonio, 95, 104
Nemo, Geneviéve Lecuir, 171, 181
Nestori, Aldo, 342, 353
Neusner, Jacob, 158, 184, 198
Nevett, Lisa C., 4, 20
Neyrey, Jerome, 91, 104, 181
Niang, Aliou Cissé, iii–iv, viii, xiv, xxxvi, xxxviii, 89, 160, 177, 181
Nielsen, Hanne Sigismund, 21
Nielsen, Inge, 21
Nilsson, Martin P., 184, 198
Norden, Eduard, 74, 88

O'Day, Gail R., 88
Oakes, Peter, vii, xiv, xxxvi, 7–8, 13, 20, 132–33, 135–36, 140
Oberlinner, Lorenz, 73–74, 81–82, 88
Obbink, Dirk, xxii
Oesterheld, Christian, 266, 278
Økland, Jorunn, 10, 20, 28–29, 36, 49, 52, 65, 70, 136, 140
Olbricht, Thomas H., xxii
Olson, S. D., 122, 130
Orr, David, 276, 278
Osiek, Carolyn, ii–iv, vii, xx, xxii, xxiv, xxxv–xxxvi, 3, 11–13, 16–17, 19–23, 33–34, 36, 38–39, 41, 43, 46, 49, 51–52, 62, 64, 70, 89, 106, 108,

Index of Modern Authors   397

116–18, 134–35, 140, 160, 179, 181, 201–3, 206, 217, 220, 237, 239, 253, 321–22, 339
Östenberg, Ida, 99, 104
O'Sullivan, James N., 106, 118
Ovadiah, Ruth, 346, 353

Pack, Roger A., 326, 340
Pagulatos, Gerasimos, 98, 104
Parkinson, R. B., 225, 237
Paton, W. R. , 122, 131, 165, 181
Patterson, Orlando, 155, 159
Pauly, A. F., xxxiii
Pearce, Sarah J. K., 225, 236–7
Pélékidis, Chrysis, 184, 198
Penna, R., 130
Penner, Todd, vii, xiv, xxi, xxiii, xxxvi, 89, 102, 104, 179
Perdue, Leo G., viii, xiv, xx, xxxvii, 183, 197–8
Perler, Othmar, 326, 340
Perrin, B., 85
Pervo, Richard I., 4, 20
Petsalis-Diomidis, Alexia, 267, 269, 278
Pleket, H. W., 169, 181
Pőhlmann, Wolfgang, xix
Pokorny, Petr, xxi
Pollitt, J. J., 165, 168, 181
Pomeroy, Sarah, 42, 52, 78, 85, 88
Porter, Stanley E., 158, 197
Powell, J. G. F., 76, 88
Preston, Rebecca, 168, 181
Price, S. R. F., 164, 169–70, 181
Prosser, Jon, 339–40
Provoost, A., 347, 350, 353

Quasten, Johannes, 246, 253

Ramelli, Ilaria, 79, 88
Rawson, Beryl, 48–52, 70, 98, 104
Reardon, Bryan P., 106, 118
Rebillard, Eric, 226, 236

Reed, Jonathan L., 171, 177, 179, 282, 290, 295
Reese, James M., 194, 198
Reeve, Michael D., 106, 118
Reynolds, Joyce, 291, 295
Rich, Adrienne, 206–7, 215, 217
Richlin, Amy, 244, 253
Ridgway, Brunilde S., 181
Riemann, Hans, 239, 245, 253
Roberts, Alexander, xxx
Roberts, John Michael, 93, 104
Robinson, H. S., 32, 36
Roccati, Alessandro, 236
Roche, Christian, 172–3, 181
Rogerson, John W., xxii, 140
Roloff, Jürgen, 73, 81–82, 88
Romanelli, Pietro, 272–73, 279
Rosivach, Victor, 163, 181
Rudd, Niall, 244, 253
Russell, Brigette Ford, 124–25, 129, 131
Russell, Donald A., 190, 194, 198, 340
Rutherford, Ian, 258, 278–79

Salazar, Christine F., xxii
Salisbury, Joyce E., 201–2, 204–6, 208–9, 217
Salmeri, Giovanni, 151, 159
Sampaolo, Valeria, 218–26, 230–35, 238
Sampley, J. Paul, xxii, 19, 58, 70, 198
Sand, Alexander, 150, 159
Sande, Siri, 64, 70
Schäfer, Peter, 248, 253
Schmeling, Gareth, 107, 118
Schneider, Deborah Lucas, 140
Schneider, H., xx
Schofield, M., 88
Scholz, P., 184, 197
Schowalter, Daniel N., 7, 20, 26, 37, 140
Schwarz, Roland, 73, 88
Scott, Robert, xxxii, 180, 340

Scully, Vincent J., 258–59, 274, 279
Seeley, David, 155, 159
Seim, Turid Karlsen, vii, xiv, xxxvi, 53, 70
Sfameni Gasparro, Giulia, 226, 238
Shackleton, Bailey, 340
Shanin, Teodor, 118
Shanzer, Danuta, 257, 278
Shaw, Brent D., 202, 205, 217
Sheckler, Allyson Everingham, 251, 254
Sherk, Robert K., 173, 181
Siker, Judy Yates, 146–47, 159
Silk, Michael S., 194, 198
Simon, M., 349, 353
Skinner, Marilyn, 159
Slane, Kathleen Warner, 32–33, 37
Smith, Dennis E., vii, xiv, xxxv, 3, 5, 9, 15–18, 21, 23, 30, 34, 37
Smith, Jonathan Z., 65, 312, 319
Smith, Lacey Baldwin, 203, 217
Smith, Martin S., 14, 21
Smith, Roland R., 154, 159, 280, 282, 284, 287, 290–92, 295
Smith, Yancy W., vii, xiv, xxxviii, 320
Snyder, Graydon F., 308, 319, 327, 340, 342, 347, 353
Soble, Alan, xxiii
Solin, Heikki, 239, 242–43, 245, 254, 327, 340
Soyoz, Ufuk, 265, 268, 279
Spawforth, Antony, xxxii, 198
Sperber, Dan, 336, 341
Spicq, Ceslas, 79–80, 88
Spier, Jeffrey, 239, 254, 327–28, 341–47, 353
Spinola, Giandomenico, 230
Sprinkle, Stephen V., viii, xiv, xxx-vii, 199, 210–11, 215, 217
Stählin, Gustav, 15, 21
Stambaugh, Joan, 104
Stambaugh, John E., xvi
Starr, J., 88

Steinhauser, Michael, 20
Sterling, Gregory E., 197
Stevens, Wallace, 323, 341
Stewart, Peter, 98, 105
Stommel, Eduard, 308, 319, 347, 349, 353
Stone, Ken, 200, 217
Stone, Michael E., 197
Stowers, Stanley K., 195, 198
Straub, Kristina, 216
Strecker, Christian, 174, 182
Streete, Gail P. C., 201, 204
Stuart, Elizabeth, 210, 217
Stuiber, Alfred, 308, 319, 348, 353
Styger, Paul, 347, 353
Sumney, Jerry L., 333, 341
Swain, Simon, 151, 159
Swetnam-Burland, Molly, 218–19, 222, 231, 238
Swift, Emerson, 313, 319

Tajfel, Henri, 147, 159
Takács, Sarolta A., 220, 238
Talbert, Charles H., xvi, 155, 159, 339
Taussig, Hal, viii, xiv, xxxvii, 9–10, 15–17, 21, 118, 225, 238, 280–81, 285, 289, 291–93
Taylor, Clair, 244, 253
Taylor, Joan E., 41, 52
Tecusan, Manuela, 130
Temporini, Hildgard, xxx, 181–82
Testini, P., 348, 353
Thackeray, H. St. J., 340, 367
Theissen, Gerd, 57, 71
Thiselton, Anthony C., 28, 37, 133, 140
Thom, John C., xix
Thomas, Louis-Vincent, 172–73, 182
Thurén, Jukka, 75, 88
Todd, Jane Marie, 216
Towner, Philip H., 73–76, 81, 88
Trapp, Thomas H., 367
Treggiari, Susan, 76, 88, 128, 131

Troeltsch, Ernst, 57, 71,
Trümper, Monika, 4, 12, 21
Tsouna, V., 78, 88
Tulloch, Janet H., 3, 16–17, 20, 52, 62, 70
Turner, John C., 147, 159
Tyson, Joseph B., xvii

Uehlinger, Christoph, 358, 367
Urbach, Ephraim, 364, 367
Usher, Stephen, 323, 341

Vaage, Leif, 43–44, 47, 51
van Poll-van de Lisdonk, M. L., 353
Vander Stichele, Caroline, xxxi, 179
Verner, David C., 54, 63, 71
Volf, Miroslav, 336, 341
von Arnim, Hans Friedrich August, xxxiv
von Franz, Marie-Louise, 202, 217
von Gemünden, Petra, xxiii, 341
von Lips, H., 80, 82, 87

Wacht, M., xix
Walbank, F. W., 122, 126, 131
Walbank, M. E. H., 33, 37
Waldman, Marilyn Robinson, 177, 182
Wallace-Hadrill, Andrew, 4, 16, 21, 98, 105
Walters, Jonathan, 154, 159
Waterhouse, Richard, 278
Watson, Alan, 326, 340
Watson, Duane F., 195, 198
Watson, Wilfred G. E., 181
Webb, Ruth, 323, 341
Weissenrieder, Annette, xxiv–xxv, 295
Weitzmann, Kurt, 313, 319, 343–46, 349, 352–53
Welch, Katherine, 100–101, 105
Wendt, Frederike, xxiii

Whitaker, G. H., 367
White, L. Michael, xix, xxii, 5, 10, 12–15, 21
Whitelam, Keith, 104
Wilken, Robert L., 250–51, 254
Williams II, Charles K., 25–26, 37, 133, 140
Wilson, Deirdre, 336, 341
Wilson, N. G., 194, 198
Wilson, Walter T., 174, 182
Wimbush, Vincent, 42, 52
Winkes, Rolf, 169, 182
Winston, David, 194–95, 198
Winter, Bruce W., 40, 42, 52
Wire, Antoinette Clark, 39, 52, 64, 71
Wischmeyer, Wolfgang, 343, 353
Witherington III, Ben, 29, 33, 37
Wixom, W. D., 343, 352
Wolfson, Harry Austryn, 186, 198
Wolter, Michael, 79, 82, 88
Woodcock, Diana H., 139–40
Woodward, Kathryn, 147, 159
Woolf, Greg, 168–71, 182
Worthington, Ian, 197
Wright, K. S., 32–33, 37
Wulf-Rheidt, Ulrike, 4, 21

Yadin, Yigael, 139–40
Yarbro Collins, Adela, 70, 87, 339
Yarbrough, Oliver Larry, viii, xiv, xix, xxxvii, 239
Yardley, J. C., 180
Yasin, Anne Marie, 218, 238
Yegül, Fikret, 299, 319
Yeoman, Barry, 212, 217
Young, Robin Darling, 204, 217

Zahn, Theodor, 82, 88
Zanker, Graham, 323, 341
Zanker, Paul, 137, 140, 168, 170, 182, 323, 328, 332, 341
Zervos, O. H., 25, 37
Zetzel, James E. G., 123, 131

www.ingramcontent.com/pod-product-compliance
Lightning Source LLC
Chambersburg PA
CBHW071226290426
44108CB00013B/1302